LAW FOR THE LAYPERSON
Life, Work & Death

LAW FOR THE LAYPERSON
Life, Work & Death

Paula Scollan
LL.B, LL.M, Solicitor

Published by
Clarus Press Ltd,
Griffith Campus,
South Circular Road,
Dublin 8.
www.claruspress.ie

Typeset by
Deanta Global Publishing Services Limited

Printed by
SprintPrint Ltd,
Dublin

ISBN
978-1-911611-10-3

A catalogue record of this book is available from the British Library

All rights reserved.

No part of this publication may be reproduced, or transmitted in any form or by any means, including recording and photocopying, without the written permission of the copyright holder, application for which should be addressed to the publisher. Written permission should also be obtained before any part of the publication is stored in a retrieval system of any nature.

Disclaimer

Whilst every effort has been made to ensure that the contents of this book are accurate, neither the publisher or author can accept responsibility for any errors or omissions or loss occasioned to any person acting or refraining from acting as result of any material in this publication. This book is designed as a guide and should not but be substituted for legal advice for which you are encouraged to seek the same from a qualified lawyer

2020 © Paula Scollan

*This book is dedicated to
Padraig, Setanta, Solomon and Senan*

Preface

This book is for the busy person who needs a quick reference guide on the legal essentials of life, such as renting or buying a property, consumer rights, personal injuries, bullying issues, agricultural law, family or employment law queries or making a will.

No book can purport to deal with every point of law over such a wide range of legal topics: the purpose of this book is to allow one to access a synopsis of the law in one place. When a legal matter arises oftentimes a person is confronted by a bewildering array of legal concepts, procedures or complex jargon and are at a loss to understand what is going on. The purpose of this book is to simplify such complexities and multi-layered rules and provide quick solutions to various queries that may arise.

The approach I have taken is to provide an everyday query formulated much like a question one might find in legal column in a newspaper. An answer follows, highlighting the general issues that the reader should be aware of and what steps they might take next.

While it has been necessary to reflect on some of the large number of legislative changes and judicial decisions which have had an impact on law and practice, the advice in this book must be followed by an appointment with a solicitor as every case differs on its facts and outcome.

I must pay tribute to my publishers Clarus Press in Dublin and special thanks must go to David McCartney who co-ordinated this production in a splendid fashion.

Finally, I am grateful to my husband Padraig Gleeson, solicitor and philosopher, for his invaluable contributions to the project when other calls on his time have been most pressing.

In recording my thanks to the above, I must emphasise that none of them should be held in any way responsible for the text of the book.

Every effort has been made to state the law according to material available up to December 2019. I hope readers will find the book of some use.

Paula Scollan
January 2020

Short Table of Content

Preface vii

Detailed Table of Content xi

1. Buying or Selling a House, and Property Law Queries 1
2. Renting and Renters: The Law Involved in
   Renting a Property 45
3. Family Law 59
4. Employment Law 77
5. Defamation, Bullying and Harassment 143
6. Farming and Agricultural Law 187
7. Consumer Rights 201
8. Personal Injuries, Accidents and Negligence 221
9. Last Will and Testament, Probate Law, Trusts,
   Enduring Power of Attorney 249

Index 281

Detailed Table of Content

Preface vii

Short Table of Content ix

1. **Buying or Selling a House, and Property Law Queries** 1
    House Purchase – The Process Involved 1
    When was My House Built? 10
    Purchasing Property at Public Auction 11
    Rights of Way 12
    Rights of Way — Holiday Homes 13
    Partition and Sale of Co-Owned Land by Mortgagee 14
    Falling Behind in Mortgage Payments 15
    Legal Issues Affecting Repossessions 16
    Buying a Property from the Mortgagee in Possession
       (that is, the lender) or a Receiver 18
    Adverse Possession 19
    What is a 'Judgment Mortgage'? 21
    The Difference Between Buying a House and
       an Apartment 21
    The Difference Between Buying New and
       Second-Hand Property 22
    Sale of the Family Home – The Rights of Married Couples and
       Civil Partners 24
    Help-to-Buy Scheme 25
    Pyrite Damage in Residential Property 26
    Local Property Tax 29
    Selling a Property 30
    Septic Tanks and Holiday Homes 32
    Family Home in Negative Equity – Tracker Mortgage 32
    Allocation of Council Housing in Private
       Housing Estates 33
    Compulsory Purchase Order 34
    Ground Rent on Residential Property 34
    Planning Permission for an Extension 35

xi

Planning Permission – Can I Self-Build a House
without Planning Permission? 37
Grant for Repairing Vacant Properties 38
Converting an Attic... 38
Derelict and Vacant Sites.. 39
Changes in Zoning Law Rendering Field Unsaleable 40
Post-storm Insurance Claims 41
Buying a Home - Lending for Non-First Time
Buyers of a Primary Dwelling Home or
a Non-Primary Dwelling Home... 42
Business rates.. 43

2. **Renting and Renters: The Law Involved in Renting a Property 45**
Tenancy Agreements: Joint Tenancy v
Tenancy In Common 45
Rental Contracts – Paying the Deposit 47
Rent a Room Relief Scheme... 48
Security of Tenure for Private Tenants... 49
Commercial Leases: Receiver Sale, not Consenting
to Assignment (*Café en Seine* Case) 51
Commercial Leases: Breach of Planning and Fire Safety
(*Camiveo v Dunnes Stores* [2017] 3 JIC 0209) 52
Commercial Leases: Notice of Termination
(The *Carraig Donn* Case, 2015) 54
Specific Performance: *The Globe Bar & Rí Rá
Nightclub, George's Street* 55

3. **Family Law 59**
Judicial Separation.. 59
Spouse's Consent to Sale of the Family Home 59
Divorce: Dissolving the Contract of Marriage in Ireland............... 60
Divorce – Proper Provision for Spouses and
Dependent Children 62
Collaborative Law – What is Collaborative Law? 62
Maintenance for Children 63
Legislation for IVF Financial AID 64
Maintenance for Civil Partners and Spouses................................ 64

Detailed Table of Content

Maintenance Applications in the District Court 65
Maintenance, Father's Name on Birth Certificate,
   One-Parent Family Payments 66
Case Progression in a Family Law Matter 66
Guardianship and Step-Children 67
Guardianship Rights for Unmarried Fathers 67
Bringing My Child on Holiday Without
   Her Father's Consent 68
Domestic Violence and Court Orders 68
Home-Schooling and the Irish Constitution 70
Paid Leave for New Fathers (The Paternity
   Leave and Benefit Act 2016) 71
Proposed New Legislation on Adoption 73
Mediation Agreement 74
Rights of Cohabitants 74
The Rights of a Cohabitant After the Death of a Partner 75
Polygamous Marriages 75
Care Orders 76

4. Employment Law 77
Who Cares for Our Children? 77
Maternity Leave (Maternity Protection Act 1994, as Amended) 78
Unfair Dismissal 81
Unfair Dismissal – Employer Acting Impulsively 86
Constructive Dismissal 91
The Right to Fair Procedures – Disciplinary
   Proceedings in the Workplace 94
Transfer of an Undertaking or Business 96
Parental Leave 97
Redundancy 98
Statutory Remedies for Breach of Employment Law 101
The Workplace Relations Commission, Updated Guidelines 102
The Workplace Relations Commission (WRC) 103
Implied terms in a contract of employment 104
Terms of Employment (Information) Act 1994 106

Rest Breaks at Work (Terms of Employment (Additional Information) Order, 1998 and Annual (Statutory) Leave 107
Minimum Notice on Termination of Employment 108
National Minimum Wage Rates 109
Rules in Relation to the Employment of Young People (Under 18 Years) 110
Whistleblowing (The Protected Disclosures Act 2014) 112
The Probationary Period 117
Diplomatic Immunity 118
Apprentices 118
Absent From Work Due to Illness 119
Retirement 122
How to Dismiss an Employee 125
Direct and Indirect Discrimination 125
The Difference Between an Independent Contractor and an employee 130
Employers' Liability in Negligence 134
Insolvency Payment Scheme 138
Mediation 139
Redress Forums 140

5. **Defamation, Bullying and Harassment 143**
What is Defamation? 143
How much Compensation Can I Expect to Get in a Defamation Case? 144
Libel — Freedom of Expression v Online Defamation 146
False and Defamatory Google Reviews 147
Mistaken Identity Report Dealt with Under The Defamation Act 2009 149
Bullying in the Workplace and Non-Physical Personal Injuries Claims 149
Bullying and Stress in the Workplace as a Health and Safety Issue — Statutory and Common Law Duties 153
Employers' Liability in Negligence for Work-Related Bullying and Stress Claims 157
Bullying in School 158

Detailed Table of Content

	Bullying in School – When the Teacher is the Bully	164
	Bullying Versus Mean and Unkind Behaviour	168
	Liability of Parents for Students who Bully	169
	Elder Abuse	169
	Cyberbullying	170
	Free Speech v Hate Speech	175
	Legal Responsibility of those Controlling Websites	176
	Liability of Parents/Guardians for Defamatory Comments Made by their Children Online	177
	Liability of Schools for Their Pupils' Defamatory Comments Posted During School Hours	177
	How to Have an Offensive Image Removed from Google, Facebook or Snapchat	177
	Garda Juvenile Diversion Programme	179
	Threatening, Abusive or Insulting Behaviour	180
	Non-Fatal Offences (Amendment) Bill 2017	181
	The Role Played by the Irish Constitution in Bullying	181
	A School's Duty of Care Towards its Students (Outside School, Outside School Hours)	182
	Play therapy	183
	Children with ADHD or Special needs in the Classroom	184
6.	**Farming and Agricultural Law**	**187**
	Turbary Rights – An Important Role in Modern Rural Life	187
	Mediation – Farm Disputes	188
	Health and Safety Legislation	188
	Single Farm Payments – The Tipperary Farmer Case	189
	Agricultural Relief – Land and Tax Matters	190
	Agricultural Relief – Cash Inheritance	191
	Marriage Breakdown in the Farming Community	192
	Pre-nuptial Agreements, Wills and The Family Farm	192
	Agricultural Lease	193
	Stamp Duty and Other Taxes on Agricultural Land	194
	Controlled Burning and Cutting of Land, Vegetation and Household Waste	194
	Cutting Trees on My Land	195

    Liability for Fallen and Overhanging Trees 197
    Dogs and Livestock: The Animals Act 1985.................................. 197
    Employment Contracts for Farm Workers 198
    Creation of a Trust to Preserve Assets.. 199
    Damage to Public Roads by Landowners 200
    Conservation Work on Old Farm Buildings 200

7. **Consumer Rights...201**
    The Sale of Goods and Supply of Services Act 1980 201
    What is a Contract?.. 201
    Consumer Rights – Faulty Clothing 202
    Consumer Rights in Ireland 203
    Consumer Rights – Defective Products and Guarantees 204
    Consumer Rights – Changing Your Mind
        about a Purchase 205
    Consumer Rights in the EU 206
    Mistakes in Pricing and General Pricing Rules 206
    Flight Cancellations 207
    The Consumer Protection Act 2007 The Competition
        and Consumer Protection Act 2014 EU Unfair
        Commercial Practices Directive (Directive
        2005/28/EC of 11 May 2005) The Sale of Goods
        and Supply of Services Act 1980... 208
    Business Goes Into Liquidation 209
    Travel Claim Fraud.. 210
    Tracker Mortgage Scandal... 211
    Importing a Car into Ireland 212
    Online Purchases 213
    The Small Claims Court 214
    The Competition and Consumer Protection
        Commission in Ireland (CCPC) 215
    Paying a Deposit to a Shop to Hold a Product 216
    Unfair Terms in Consumer Contracts.. 217
    The Right to Make a Complaint 218
    Chargebacks... 218
    Customer Rights and Responsibilities in a Taxi 219

8. Personal Injuries, Accidents and Negligence 221
    Car Crash 221
    Personal Injuries on Holiday 222
    Personal Injuries on a Bouncy Castle 223
    Personal Injuries and Minors 224
    Personal Injuries: Scar Tissue 225
    How Much Should I Expect to get in Damages
        in a Minor Personal Injuries Case? 226
    What Factors Does the Judge Take into Account
        When Assessing Damages? 230
    Higher Financial Awards for Serious Injuries 231
    €5 Million Awarded in Hospital Negligence Case 231
    €500,000 Awarded in Road Traffic Accident 232
    Physical and Psychological Injuries 233
    Dublin Bus Cases 234
    Opportunistic Plaintiff 235
    The Duty of Owners and Occupiers of Land
        in Personal Injuries Cases 236
    Personal Injuries Claim Dismissed 237
    The Jogger who Tripped on a Hole in the Footpath 239
    PIAB – Personal Injuries Assessment Board 239
    Contributory Negligence 240
    The Duty of Care Owed by a Defendant to an Injured Party Under
        The Occupiers' Liability Act 1995 241
    Medical Negligence 242
    Medical Negligence Claims After Death 243
    Negligence Claims Against Prison Officers 244
    Consent to Violence Against the Person 245
    Vicious Dog Attack and Post-Traumatic Stress Disorder 246
    Personal Injury on a Package Holiday 247

9. Last Will and Testament, Probate Law, Trusts, Enduring Power of Attorney 249
    The 'Hands-On Guy' Drafting His Own Will 249
    Should I Make a Will? 251
    Duties of an Executor 253

Executor's Role in Preserving an Inheritance 254
Enduring Power of Attorney 255
Making a Will Pre-and-Post Marriage 255
Living Grandchildren and s 98 of the Succession
    Act 1965 (My Son's Children) 256
Inheritance Tax 257
Young Children 257
Trusts and Trustees 258
Creation of a Trust to Preserve Assets 260
Creation of a Trust to Prevent the Sale of Land 261
Testamentary Capacity 261
Conditional Bequests 263
Various Types of Legacy 263
My Wishes may not be Properly Carried Out 265
Deceased Leaves an Insolvent Estate 265
Ademption 266
Treating All One's Children Fairly 266
Intestacy — What Happens if I don't Make a Will? 267
Pre-Nuptial Agreements, Wills and the Family Farm 268
Protection for Surviving Spouses of Deceased Persons 269
Unmarried Testators with Non-Marital Children 271
Tax Exemption for Dwelling House 272
Nursing Home Support Scheme (Known as the
    Fair Deal Scheme) 272
Extracting a Grant of Probate 273
Ward of Court 274
My Social Media Account After My Death 275
Undue Influence 275
Best Will in the World Week 277
The Right of a Cohabitant to be Provided for
    Out of Deceased's Estate 277
The Rights of a Cohabitant After the Death of a Partner 278
Missing Beneficiary – Benjamin Order 278
Property Abroad 279

Index 281

Chapter 1

Buying or Selling a House, and Property Law Queries

House Purchase – The Process Involved

I am hoping to purchase a house soon. I would like to know the process involved from start to finish, that is, from the time I go to view the property to the moment I am presented with the keys to the property and the transaction is legally completed.

Purchasing a property may seem like a daunting task. However, it is relatively straightforward if you are familiar with the process involved. I would first advise you to look around and study the market. Find a property that you like and can afford. Speak with the seller directly or his auctioneer/estate agent if he has one. Negotiate the price. Most sellers do not expect to get their initial asking price. Depending on market conditions relating to the supply of housing in the area, the asking price may be either an ambitious target by the vendor which one should discount from or it may be a starting point for a bidding war between eager purchasers.

The budget

Arrange a meeting with the bank or you may decide to go through a mortgage broker. If you are going through a mortgage broker, you should ascertain whether they are a tied agent (that is, tied to one bank or particular banks) or whether they have access to the whole market. Some of our young clients have taken out mortgages with terms of 35 years and this is obviously a big commitment. It is advisable to get mortgage approval in principle before you look at the property. This will let you know how much you have to spend. Check the interest rates. Compare different banks or mortgage providers to get the best rate possible and any special offers they may have. Some banks have special offers but be careful with these to see if they offer long-term value. In any event you must have written loan approval before signing contracts.

Get a valuation of the property or talk to people living in the neighbourhood to see what they paid for similar property in the same area. Better still check the Residential Property Price Register to see what others paid for similar property. The register contains information on the price of residential property bought in Ireland since 1 January, 2010. It is an interesting way of keeping updated on property prices.

Take into account extra costs such as the surveyors' fee, stamp duty (1% on residential up to one million euro and 2% on the balance thereafter) and Property Registration Authority charges/Land Registry charges (budget at least €600 to

€1,000 for a standard house). Try to have these costs saved as you will need to show the lender that you can pay these costs. You will probably max your credit card just purchasing the basic furniture to move in! Factor in renovation costs if necessary. Most people underestimate the cost of renovating a house. Do you know what stone masons charge? Then there is the plumber, tiler, carpenter and electrician. The big one is the septic tank. Does the system comply with the new regulations? Is the heating system functioning? If buying a second-hand house get a structural survey done and that may answer some of these queries. Also look at the BER report. It will give you an outline of what is needed to improve the property's energy efficiency.

We have a lot of cash buyers also in this country; as many as five in every ten purchases in the residential market is by a cash buyer. Before the property crash, cash buyers appeared to be in scarce supply. Back in 2000 there were about 28,000 cash sales out of a total of 102,000. But as transaction levels plummeted, the proportion of cash buyers soared, reaching a peak of about 63% in 2013. Investors are some of the main drivers of cash sales because of the absence of buy-to-let mortgages or because it can be cheaper and they have access to the funds. A lot of buyers at auctions are cash buyers. Some parents are buying properties outright for their children to live in when they start college. We also have a lot of cash-rich returning emigrants. Downsizers are another key cohort of those buying in cash as, having sold their own house, they then have the cash to pay for their next purchase. Sellers tend to favour cash buyers as there is less of a chance of the transaction falling through. If you are fortunate enough to be a cash buyer, you may try and bargain a little harder.

Property chain

Make enquiries before you sign contracts or as soon as possible after viewing the property as to whether or not the transaction is going to be part of a property chain, as this could cause significant delays in completing the purchase. A property chain situation arises where the sellers of the property are themselves trying to buy a property and their sale to you depends on them being successful in their purchase. There could be several parties involved in a chain, for example, the parties selling to the sellers could also depend on securing a property.

Independent survey

Get a structural assessment done and get the geothermal system checked out. We always recommend that our clients instruct an independent chartered surveyor or engineer to survey the property before they buy it to check for any structural defects or to check if further investigation needs to be carried out. Check that the engineer or surveyor has professional indemnity insurance. When you sign the contracts, it will be deemed in law that you are aware of any problems before signing. One doesn't need any nasty surprises on moving in, such as a leaking roof, asbestos, pyrite or discovering that rats have eaten all the wiring. A seller is under no legal obligation to disclose defects in a property and you cannot legally rely on any

1. Buying or Selling a House, and Property Law Queries

representations made by an auctioneer prior to the issue of the contract. You may also check for radon if you wish. The Environmental Protection Agency's website has a map showing the areas predicted to be at particular risk from radon, referred to as high radon areas, although a high radon level can be found in any home in any part of the country. Building regulations require that all new homes in high radon areas are installed with a radon barrier.

Look at the BER report, that is the National Building Energy Rating certificate. Check if there is any right of way over the property. The survey would highlight any alteration to the property, such as an extension or planning implications. The seller's solicitor will have to provide planning documentation for any such alterations with the title deeds. Check that the property on the ground corresponds with the map of the property with the title deeds or on the Land Registry folio, that is, ensure you are buying what you think you are buying. Your solicitor should also look for a declaration of identity, that is, a declaration that all the services for the property are located within the boundaries of the property, including the septic tank or water well if there is one.

Planning permission and building control regulations

Planning permission is required for all development of land carried out since 1 October 1964 which is not exempted development. Your solicitor should go through all conditions imposed in any planning permission and must ensure that any financial conditions are complied with. If a particular development is exempt from planning permission, a certificate or opinion from an architect should still be obtained, as every exemption has limitations placed on it. A certificate or opinion of compliance with building regulations from an architect or engineer should also be obtained and your solicitor will check to ensure there are no exceptions noted in this. From June 1992, the building regulations apply in relation to works carried out, such as an extension or alterations to a property. The Building Control Regulations 1997 to 2013 provide for the need for a fire safety certificate to be obtained before work commences on certain types of development, to show that building designs comply with fire safety requirements. You may be familiar with a number of apartments in Dublin where the fire safety regulations were not complied with, causing untold hardship for the owners. General Condition 36 of the standard Law Society contract of sale requires the production of a certificate or an opinion on compliance with planning and building regulations from an architect or engineer.

Appointing/instructing a solicitor

Conveyancing is the term used to describe property transactions and the transfer of legal ownership of immovable property. Normally, in residential conveyancing, there are two solicitors acting in the transaction, one for the vendor and one for the purchaser. If your purchase includes an element of commercial property (for example, a shop, office, restaurant, pub) or is associated with agricultural land, then, when you are getting finance, if finance is required, there will be a third solicitor involved. You are free to choose any solicitor you want. Most solicitors deal with property. It does not have to be the solicitor the estate agent recommends. You should ask your solicitor for a written quotation of his or her fees and the costs of the transaction and your solicitor should hand or mail you a section 68 letter so you know exactly how much everything costs up front. A solicitor cannot act for both the purchaser and the seller (SI 375/2012 Solicitors (Professional Practice, Conduct and Discipline, Conveyancing Conflict of Interest) Regulation 2012). Solicitors will require a copy of your identification (that is photographic identification and an up-to-date utility bill) and your PPS number, and most solicitors try to conduct as much of the conveyance as possible by telephone and email. The conveyancing process will involve a number of different stages including pre-contract, contract, post-contract, pre-closing, closing/completion and post-closing/completion. Your solicitor will scan in copies of the documents and correspondence and forward these to you on request. Your solicitor will meet you to sign the contract for sale and deed of conveyance and some solicitors will arrange after-hours appointments in various locations, if necessary. In summary, the purchaser's solicitor will check the title documents and the contract and any special conditions in the contract, make pre-contract queries, draft any necessary clauses regarding loan approval or structural survey for inclusion in the contract, advise the purchaser in regard to the loan conditions, advise on stamp duty and any tax reliefs available, advise the purchaser to have a structural survey carried out, give the purchaser a 's 68 letter', raise requisitions and objections on title, set out the closing documents required and ensure the purchaser has loan approval, check the lending institution's requirements and furnish these, draft the deed of transfer to transfer the interest in the property to the purchaser, carry out searches and ensure stamp duty is ready to be paid. When buying second hand property, the principle of *caveat emptor* (that is buyer beware) applies to the physical description of the property, that is, the purchaser must be aware of the boundaries and condition of the property. When investigating title, your solicitor will look at the chain of title, events on title and the capacity of the vendor. For example, a life tenant has the power of sale but he or she cannot receive the proceeds of sale, which goes to the trustees, or some investigation may be necessary to ensure a mortgagee in possession properly obtained possession.

Pay booking deposit

When you have organised finance and have a solicitor on board, the next step is to pay the booking deposit. This is paid to the estate agent/auctioneer, and not to the seller directly. Check the auctioneer is on the public register and get a receipt confirming that the amount you paid is just a booking deposit. If you decide for any reason at all not to purchase the property, the estate agent must return the full booking deposit to you immediately.

1. Buying or Selling a House, and Property Law Queries

Contract for sale

Contracts will be forwarded to your chosen solicitor's office along with copy title documentation to see if everything is ok. Your solicitors may raise queries after having checked the documentation. Please be really sure you want to buy the property before you sign the contract. Check the property and the area thoroughly before you sign. Check if the area floods. If you are unfamiliar with the locality, check on social media or by 'Googling' the area to obtain more information. Request your solicitor to do a planning search to check if any planning applications have gone in for social housing or commercial units in the area which you might like to know about. A contract for sale of land must be in writing, or a note of the agreement must exist, and the contract must include the buyer's and seller's names, the price, address of the property and the particulars (Land and Conveyancing Law Reform Act 2009, s 51). Your solicitor will check your title deeds and contract for sale before you sign. This investigation of title is very important because, if a document is missing or incorrect, you may have difficulty selling on the property in the future. The contract for sale binds the parties to the completion of the sale, subject to the terms and conditions contained in the contract. Your solicitor may insert a special condition making the purchase subject to loan approval to cover circumstances where you have a loan offer but are unable to comply with some of the conditions of the loan offer. When signing contracts, you generally pay a contract deposit of 10% of the purchase price, less the booking deposit already paid. Contracts are issued in duplicate. When the vendor signs and sends back one of the contracts to your solicitor, the contracts are known as 'exchanged'. When they are exchanged, a binding agreement is in place. Do not sign any contract until you get formal mortgage approval because, if you sign a contract for sale and subsequently don't get mortgage approval, you will lose your contract deposit (remember the contract deposit is different to the booking deposit) and you may not get out of the contract. Once the seller has signed the contracts and returns one part to your solicitor, there is a binding contract in place. At this point, you will not get your deposit back if you change your mind. A seller can actually sue you for the balance of the purchase price and compel you to complete the sale (unless the contract was subject to finance).

Objections and requisitions on title

Your solicitor will raise queries about the property and the vendor's title with the seller's solicitor called 'objections and requisitions on title'. A solicitor may furnish you with a copy of the objections and requisitions on title and replies thereto if requested.

Mortgage/loan offer

If you are getting a mortgage, a loan pack is issued to your solicitor who will discuss the terms of the loan with you and give the bank a solicitor's undertaking, a copy of their professional indemnity insurance and, at the conclusion of the transaction, a certificate of title. On exchange of contracts, your solicitor will return loan acceptance to the bank. The solicitor's undertaking obliges the solicitor acting for the purchaser to ensure that the purchaser is acquiring good marketable title to the property and that the mortgage ranks as a first legal charge on the property, that the mortgage documents are signed by the purchaser and that all relevant documents are stamped and registered in the Registry of Deeds or the Land Registry. The bank will only release the loan cheque to allow completion of the sale when it has received the solicitor's undertaking duly completed. In some cases, the solicitor may have to qualify his or her undertaking because, for example, of a lack of proper planning permission. The bank may or may not agree to this. If they don't agree, they will withdraw the loan offer.

A 'certificate of title' is an approved form of certificate which is accepted by lending institutions arising from prudent standards of conveyancing in Ireland. It allows the lender to permit the solicitor for the purchaser to investigate title and gives responsibility to the solicitor for having the mortgage registered in the bank's favour and secured on the property.

A lot of mortgages nowadays have an 'all sums due' clause. This means that the borrower is pledging their property, not just for the property in question, but for all debts due to the lending institution now or in the future. That would include any car loan or credit card or any other loans you might have. Therefore the bank can use your house as security for all borrowings you may have. If self-building, funds are usually released by your lender at various stages of the build and this is known as stage payment mortgages. Once your solicitor is in receipt of a stage payment certificate, he or she will make a request to the bank for drawdown of the sum highlighted by the engineer required to facilitate the next stage of the building.

Life/home insurance

You must have mortgage protection insurance, life and home insurance unless you get an exemption due to inability to get life insurance, for example, if you have an illness that a life assurance company will not quote you for.

Check around for the best rates. Insure the property after you have paid the deposit on signing the contract to buy because, at this stage, you are legally committed to completing the purchase. Should the house go on fire in the meantime, you could suffer a huge financial loss. It is advisable to look into mortgage protection/ life assurance policies early, since the life assurance company may require either a medical or letter from your doctor confirming matters if you have certain medical conditions or illnesses.

1. Buying or Selling a House, and Property Law Queries

BER certificate and Advisory Report

All properties are now required to have a BER certificate and advisory report. These will tell you how energy-efficient the property is and suggest how it can be improved. BER certificates can be ordered from your selling agent or online companies. They have to go out to the property and assess it.

Management company

A management company is generally a company set up to run a development where there are common areas. The owners of the company are the unit owners. They usually employ a management agent to organise prepare and file annual accounts and collect the management fees from the owner of each unit. Your solicitor will obtain evidence to show that management fees are paid to date.

Service charges and the Multi-Unit Developments Act 2011 (MUD Act)

This applies to multi-unit developments with shared facilities and to housing estates which have an ownership management company overseeing common areas in the development, such as lighting, waste management, landscaping, insurance and grass cutting. The Act provides regulations for *inter alia* service charges. The 2011 Act provides rules on how a managed development should be run. When purchasing a property, your solicitor will make enquiries to ensure that the management company is in compliance with the Act.

Extensions

If there is an extension on the house, we may require a declaration of exemption from planning by an engineer or architect, or declaration of compliance with planning and building regulations and a copy of the planning permission. Your solicitor will request this from the seller's solicitor. If there is not an extension on the house but you might possibly want one in the future, consider other potential difficulties – would a two-storey extension cause problems for neighbours? What size of garden would you be left with?

Property tax receipts

Your solicitor will get receipts from the seller's solicitor proving that all household charges, local property taxes are paid to date of closing. If the house is serviced by a water scheme, your solicitor will get a receipt showing that the fee is paid and get a consent to enter the scheme. Your solicitor will also make enquiries with the vendor's solicitor to ensure the non-principal private residence tax is paid or that the property is exempt.

Septic tank

If the house is serviced by a septic tank, your solicitor will check if the house is registered by means of a certificate of registration. One should also be aware of the fact that, if the septic tank is old, it may fail a test and need improvement/replacement. Your surveyor should be able to confirm the cost. There is currently a process where councils are obliged to inspect septic tanks. Eventually all septic tanks will be inspected. If the tank was recently inspected, the question arises as to whether any improvements were ordered.

Converting attic space

Ask yourself if the attic is easy to convert. Some roofs may not be suitable. Check whether the existing insulation is on top of the ceiling (a cold roof) or the inner face of the roof (a warm roof). Some houses have a mixture of both. The latter makes the attic space more easily usable and convertible.

Car parking

Is there space for two cars to park? If not, could you change the front garden to allow for this? Is there on-street parking for guests? In the case of narrow townhouses, is there enough space on the street between gates for a car to park?

Snag list

With a new build, a purchaser will need to compile a snag list, usually after the sale is agreed but before possession. It is worth getting an architect or building surveyor to compile this. They will address things that might not occur to you.

Aspect

Consider the light in the property you are buying. Think about how you might like to use the property, for example, if you intend to have a breakfast room. Consider whether it will get the morning light. What aspect has your garden? Will your garden get sunshine all day long or only for a certain period, or will you be permanently in the shade?

Stamp duty

Stamp duty is a tax on documents and the purchaser is liable for stamp duty. Stamp duty on an instrument which witnesses residential property transactions under one million euro is calculated at 1% of the purchase price. Each year the government in the Finance Act may change the rate of duty. Your solicitor will request stamp duty from you before the closing of the sale. The stamp duty is paid to the Revenue Commissioners within a strict timeframe and they place a stamp on the deed (Stamp Duties Consolidation Act, 1999). Without this stamp, the deeds cannot be registered. The deeds name the owner of the property. Stamp duty reliefs apply in some cases. There is an online stamping service (e-stamping) provided by the Revenue Commissioners.

Deed of conveyance/transfer

Your solicitor will provide a draft deed to the vendor's solicitor for approval, along with a list of closing requirements. If your solicitor is satisfied with replies to the objections and requisitions on title, he or she will contact your bank to request/order the loan cheque. Requisitions are post contract, pre-closing enquiries, a kind of solicitor's checklist to confirm everything is in order.

Searches

Searches are carried out against the property, the sellers and the purchasers to ensure there are no outstanding judgments or claims on the property. Your solicitor will order bankruptcy judgment folio searches to ensure there are no judgments against the parties and also ensure there is no mortgage attaching to the property. Search agents generally charge between €50 and €150 for this service. A planning search can be requested before signing contracts. This would generally attract an additional charge and generally requires advance notice. Check your local planning office for any change in planning, change of use, intensification of use, fire certificates and building regulations, the zoning of adjoining lands, and any plans for the area, such as road widening or compulsory purchase orders.

Documents required when purchasing a property in the course of construction

When purchasing a property in the course of construction, your solicitor will request *inter alia* the building agreement, contract for sale, Home-bond or premier guarantee, booklet of title showing the seller's legal title, replies to objections and requisitions on title, an indemnity in respect of roads and services, a declaration of identity to showing that all services and easements are within the boundaries of the seller's folio, family law declarations, the deed of assurance of the site or lease and a s 72 declaration.

Closing the sale/completion date/ready to get the keys at last

This is the formal completion of the purchase. As the old saying goes, 'The day you buy is the day you sell' and therefore it is most important that you obtain good marketable title. There will be a closing date for completion in the contract and, once you sign, you are committed to completing on time, which can leave you open to a liability for daily interest on the full purchase price. If you are unable to complete the purchase, the seller can serve a completion notice on you and the seller can rescind the contract and pursue you for damages. The grounds for this are usually set out in the general conditions of sale and are subject to strict time limits. You should consult your solicitor in regard to this.

Just before completion, the purchaser should have carried out a final inspection to ensure the house is left in the agreed condition and the garden and garage (or sheds if there are any), are not full of rubbish which should have been disposed of by the sellers. Check the inventory of items included in the sale. Your solicitor checks the vendor's title and then, if all is in order, he or she accepts good marketable title with fully signed documents and hands over the balance of the purchase money. Keys are given to your solicitor or left with the estate agent for collection. You can move in to your new home.

Registration of ownership after the sale is completed (you have your keys now)

Your deeds showing the new ownership details and mortgage details will be registered with either the Land Registry and Registry of Deeds or the Land Registry only. This can take some time, due to the conversion of a lot of title from an older system called Registry of Deeds to the Land Registry, but you can still sell your property on again, even if the registration is not complete using a dealing number. There are two systems of registration of property in Ireland, namely the Registry of Deeds and the Land Registry. The Registry of Deeds deals with the registration of documents, and Registry of Deeds properties are usually (but not always) in urban areas, such as Dublin. The Land Registry deals with registration of title, and all counties are now compulsorily registrable. The Land Registry operates under the Property Registration Authority and the most important document here is the folio which gives details of the property and a map, details of the registered owner and class of title, and lists any burdens, such as a mortgage on the property. Ownership of Land Registry property is transferred by a deed of transfer and title passes when the transfer is registered in the Land Registry.

After registration, your solicitor returns your title deeds to the bank, and the bank keeps them until you have your mortgage paid off in full.

In conclusion, I would advise you to keep in regular contact with your solicitor and always request a meeting with him or her if you feel you require further clarification on any issues that arise. Good luck with the property search - and don't forget to redirect your post if you are successful.

WHEN WAS MY HOUSE BUILT?

I inherited a beautiful old house and I am curious about the history of this unique building. How do I find out when this house was built?

It is always nice to know the history of any property you purchase or, in your case, were lucky enough to inherit. The title deeds for the property may be available

1. Buying or Selling a House, and Property Law Queries

from your solicitor, and I would advise you to make enquiries there first. If that search is not successful, then I would check the Registry of Deeds next. The Registry of Deeds in the King's Inns building, Dublin 1 may have a record of the deeds pertaining to your property. It has books of records called memorials which are effectively summaries of deeds. Alternatively, the Land Registry may hold the answer to your query. There is available online at https://www.landregistryireland.com/ a search facility where you can order a folio which is the equivalent of a car registration book in regard to your property. The folio may list the previous owners of the property. The registration of the first owner may show a number alongside it. This refers to a set of documents held in the Land Registry which is called an instrument. If you are an owner of the property, you can get a copy of the instrument showing the original deed of transfer. Basically, the deeds can offer information on when the site was originally sold or leased, previous owners and site dimensions.

A map search can provide some immediate information in a cartographic format. Between 1829 and 1842, Ordinance Survey Ireland completed the first-ever large-scale survey of the entire country. This 6-inch survey is available to view online at www.osi.ie, as well as the more detailed, later 25-inch 1897-1913 survey. Other available maps include the Rocque's 1756 map of Dublin, and the Glucksman Map Library in Trinity College retains a comprehensive range of historic maps for the country and can be viewed for free or copied for a small fee. The map search will reveal if the building existed at the time of survey, but not necessarily the date of construction.

You could also arrange for an architect to view the property, as a qualified architect can often determine the date of construction of a property by assessing its physical features. Certain features pertain to certain periods.

Local libraries and archives may have written histories of the area your house was built in. Thom's directory, first published in 1844, is a street directory for Dublin and other towns in Ireland and lists the occupants and valuations of properties each year. The National Archives have an online record of the censuses of 1901 and 1911. You could also consult www.iarc.ie and www.ria.ie/research-projects/irish-historic-towns-atlas.

Finally, I would suggest meeting other people living in the area. They may have a lot of information on the history of the house and some may have carried out similar searches themselves regarding similar property in the area. Local knowledge is always a great help.

PURCHASING PROPERTY AT PUBLIC AUCTION

I recently saw a property I am interested in purchasing. The property is for sale by auction in the coming weeks. My family and I have never purchased a property at auction before. Is there anything different I should look out for?

Buying a home is probably one of the biggest financial transactions you'll ever make. If you decide to purchase a property by way of public auction, you should contact your solicitor immediately so that he or she will make the necessary precautionary enquiries and he or she will also attend the auction with you if required. It is essential that you notify your solicitor well in advance of the auction so that he has an opportunity to review the legal title. The rule of auction is buyer beware, and you buy the property warts and all. So, along with the review of legal title, you should also have a surveyor or a suitably qualified professional examine the property. You should review his or her report before going to the auction. Title in relation to property means the documents that show one's ownership of the property. There are two types of title in Ireland, known as Land Registry title and Registry of Deeds title. A numbered folio in the Land Registry records the name and address of the owner, together with a description and a map of the property. This folio number is necessary in order to sell the property. Registry of Deeds documents would include deeds of conveyance used to conduct a transfer. You must have your financial arrangements in place before you attend the auction. This is imperative because, if your bid is successful, you are obliged to pay a deposit of 10% of the value of the property immediately. The balance price of the property is then due within the month. When purchasing a property, remember also that there are hidden government and third-party costs to include stamp duty. Check the up-to-date rates of stamp duty, as they often increase or change in the budget. There are also surveyor's fees, search fees, registration fees and insurance costs. Be sure to calculate all the outlay before you attend the auction. Good luck! I hope it all goes well for you.

RIGHTS OF WAY

I am a farmer working and living in County Leitrim. My father and I have enjoyed the use of a right of way over our neighbours land. When I was looking at the maps in relation to our farm, I noticed there was nothing recorded regarding this right of way. This concerns me and therefore I would like at this stage to register our right with the Property Registration Authority.

Generally speaking, a right of way is a type of property right called an easement. It arises where a person has a right to pass over another person's land.

Regrettably, rights of way can be sources of controversy and disputes between neighbours. You may remember the controversy over the Lissadell estate where a dispute arose between the land owners and Sligo County Council that was fought over the best part of a decade and ended up in the Supreme Court, resulting in a victory for the land owners and astronomical legal costs (*Walsh and Another v The County Council for the County of Sligo* [2013] IESC 48). While this case can be distinguished from your own in that it related to public rights of way, it does show how things can spiral out of control when the matter goes before the courts.

1. Buying or Selling a House, and Property Law Queries

Currently, there are three ways one can obtain and register a right of way. The first is by a grant – basically a legal document signed by the landowner giving or granting the right of way. This grant is then registered with the Land Registry. The second is by making an application directly to the Land Registry. The Land Registry will notify the landowner and, if he does not object, they will grant the right of way and have it registered as a benefit to your land and burden on the landowner's land. The third method is that you apply to the courts for an order confirming the existence of the right of way. This order is then registered with the Land Registry.

The first method is normally used where a new right of way is being granted. The grant will set out the terms and conditions in regard to the use of the right of way agreed between the parties. The second method is used where a right of way has existed for a period of time (over 12 years) and it is basically a confirmation that it does exist. It is done on the consent of both the right of way owner and the land owner. The third method is to have the court decide whether a right of way exists. This method is normally only used where a dispute has arisen between the landowner and the right of way user.

There is some urgency for you or any other owner to have their existing right of way registered. Land law is preparing to move to a digital age and all rights in regard to the land will be required to be registered in the Land Registry for this to happen. To this end, the Land and Conveyancing Law Reform Act, 2009 provided for a deadline of the 30 November 2012 to register all rights of way. The Civil Law (Miscellaneous Provisions) Act 2011 extended the deadline for registration until 30 November 2021. It is essential to note that the owners of rights of way must act in good time to have their rights registered or they may lose or have great difficulty registering them.

RIGHTS OF WAY — HOLIDAY HOMES

I am in the process of purchasing a holiday cottage up a small country roadway. My friend advised me to check if there are any issues around rights of way.

As the cottage is up a small country roadway, you should first find out if it is a public road maintained by the local authority or if it is private land owned by someone else. If it is private land, make sure you have a right of way to cross that roadway, so that you can access your property. You could face expensive court action to establish a right of way. Your solicitor may have to register the right of way with the Property Registration Authority and this could be difficult if the person who owns the property or land which you require the right of way over does not want to register the right of way. Prai.ie is the website of the Property Registration Authority with whom your solicitor can register a right of way to a property. A document entitled 'Easements and Profits à Prendre acquired by Prescription under section 49A' outlines the PRA's practice in relation to rights of way which are acquired by prescription, that is after the continuous use of the land as a right of way for a certain amount of time. Essential services — such as water for a rural property

— can sometimes come through a neighbour's home, so consider this before you purchase your retreat. You don't want a financial headache if rights of way are not clearly established. Rights of way are an extremely important issue to clarify before you sign a contract to purchase a property.

PARTITION AND SALE OF CO-OWNED LAND BY MORTGAGEE

My husband took out a large loan with the credit union. I did not know anything about the loan at the time. I did not sign any documentation. My husband defaulted on the repayments. I am worried that we will have to sell our family home to pay back the credit union.

I am sorry to hear about your predicament. This must be a very stressful time for you. However, you mention that it is your family home you are worried about losing and therefore there may be some light at the end of the tunnel. The courts, where possible, usually try to protect an innocent spouse. I have come across a relatively recent case that addressed a situation like you describe that may be of some interest to you and which may somewhat clarify your position.

Muintir Skibbereen Credit Union v Crowley (2016) IECA 213 related to unsecured lending by a credit union. A judgment mortgage was obtained and the credit union sought well charging orders against the debtors' shares in their family homes. The debtors' wives were not parties to the lending. In the High Court, White J found that, as the defendants were in serious debt, "50% of the net proceeds any sale of the family home due to the spouse would not provide the family with sufficient resources to purchase another family home". In the Court of Appeal, Hogan J commented that:

> "where appropriate, the Court must endeavour to balance and respect competing constitutional rights, including the property rights of the judgement mortgagee and those of the spouse. The second factor was that the lending by the credit union was unsecured and personal to the judgement debtor. The spouse was not consulted regarded the taking out of the loan and she was not required to sign or execute any documentation. It is true that the rights of the judgement mortgagee are liable to be defeated if the family home is not sold. But the Credit Union's entitlements cannot prevail as against the rights of the innocent spouse."

The Court of Appeal upheld the ruling of White J in the High Court, with Hogan J concluding that

> "I reach this conclusion principally because the effect of any such order would be to direct the sale of the family home over the wishes of the innocent spouse who was not a party to the loan transaction which gave rise to the judgement mortgage in the first instance and who had never formally consented to same".

The effect of this case is that it is likely to be quite difficult for creditors to enforce judgment mortgages against co-owned property which constitutes a family home and where only one of the owners is a judgment debtor.

1. Buying or Selling a House, and Property Law Queries

FALLING BEHIND IN MORTGAGE PAYMENTS

We are finding it very difficult to pay our mortgage at the end of the month. My wife was working when we bought the house but she cannot work now due to illness after the birth of our last child. Will the bank take our house?

You are most definitely not alone in the situation you find yourself in. A lot of couples fell behind in mortgage repayments during the recession and indeed, with the high cost of child care, it is often not economically feasible for both parents to work outside the home.

You could start by trying to negotiate a better deal with the bank. For example, if you are on a variable mortgage, you could arrange a meeting with the bank and ask them to consider putting you on an interest-only payment plan for a specified period of time. They may or may not agree to this. Several organisations, including the Money Advice and Budgeting Service (MABS) offer advice and support to people who are facing repossession. MABS is involved in the Abháile scheme for people who are in serious mortgage arrears and at risk of losing their home. This scheme provides a range of services to help you to deal with your situation, including advice on financial, legal and insolvency matters. If you have to go to court, MABS will explain the type of questions you can expect from the judge and the documentation you need for your case, such as a statement of income and expenditure. The MABS helpline 0761 07 2000 is open from 9am to 8pm, Monday to Friday. You can also contact a Free Legal Advice Centre (FLAC) to get some advice on legal issues. New Beginnings is a not-for-profit organisation which aims to represent people in this situation.

There are a number of options open to the bank when a borrower defaults on his loan payments. The most common is a court order for possession of the property and then sale of the property. The bank can sell the property in accordance with the terms of the mortgage without going to court. If you do not vacate the property to allow the sale, the bank will go to court to obtain an order for possession. Foreclosure involves the bank taking court proceedings' to allow the bank become owner of the property. The bank could also try taking legal action to obtain the amount outstanding.

There are also options under the Personal Insolvency Act 2012, including a debt relief notice, a debt settlement plan and a personal insolvency arrangement. The principal private residence is recognised in s 69 of the Act: s 104 of the Act looks at the principal private residence under the personal insolvency arrangement. The personal insolvency arrangement allows you to restructure your debts over six to seven years and includes mortgage debt. It is for debtors with debts between €20,000 and €3,000,000. The personal insolvency practitioner will formulate a proposal that will not require the debtor to dispose of an interest in, or cease to occupy, the property and must consider any appropriate alternatives (s 104(1)). They will refer to the costs likely to be incurred by the debtor by remaining in occupation of his or her principal private residence including mortgage loan repayments, the reasonable living accommodation needs of the debtor and his or her dependants, and have regard to the cost of alternative accommodation. Where the debtor confirms in writing to the personal insolvency practitioner that the debtor does not wish to remain in occupation of his or her principal private residence, or the personal insolvency practitioner, having discussed the issue with the debtor, forms the opinion that the costs of continuing to reside in the property are disproportionately large, then the personal insolvency arrangement shall not contain terms providing for the disposal of the property unless the debtor has obtained independent legal advice in relation to such disposal.

If you have exhausted all the options open to you, the lender can repossess your home in order to recover the amount you owe. If your home is repossessed, you will need to find somewhere else to live. You can apply to your local authority to be housed and there are also a number of voluntary housing associations which provide social housing and that have been approved under the Housing (Miscellaneous Provisions) Act 1992 for the purpose of assessing assistance from local authorities for housing provision.

I am sorry to hear about your wife's illness. I hope she recovers to full health.

LEGAL ISSUES AFFECTING REPOSSESSIONS

It's not looking good. I think the bank is going to repossess my home. Is there anything I can do to fight this?

There have been a number of developments in mortgage enforcement and possession proceedings in Ireland in the past years. A lot of mortgages created during the economic boom (and especially those created between 2002 and 2007) were created over registered land, and one of the impacts of the economic downturn was the widespread default in repayments of loans by homeowners and investors. The slow economic recovery has contributed to significant increases in the amount of mortgages in arrears.

In *Start v Gunn* (2011) IEHC 275, the High Court established that there were legal difficulties with getting orders for possession of certain properties. The same decision was made in a number of cases where mortgage providers were applying to repossess mortgaged property. These decisions meant that, in the case of a mortgage created before 1 December 2009, it was very difficult for a mortgage provider to get an order for possession unless the court proceedings were started before that date.

This situation arose because the law was changed on 1 December 2009. An existing law governing repossessions was repealed by the Land and Conveyancing Law Reform Act 2009 which provided for repossessions but applied only to mortgages created after it came into effect. The Act contained a provision in s 8 whereby s 62(7) of the Registration of Title Act 1964 was repealed. This basically removed the right of a charge holder to apply to the court for an order for possession of registered land where they held a first legal charge on foot of a mortgage created prior to 1 December 2009.

As a result of pressure exerted by the troika, the government introduced the Land and Conveyancing Law Reform Act 2013 to remedy the legal difficulties described above. The effect of s 1 of the 2013 Act was that the right to apply to the court for an order for possession remained as if it had not been repealed. It also provides for a court to adjourn repossession proceedings for up to two months in certain situations, to allow the possibility of a personal insolvency arrangement to be explored as an alternative to repossession (s 2). The Circuit Court has sole jurisdiction in mortgage cases where the property is the principal private residence of the defendant (s 3).

If you are in a situation where the bank or lending institution is pursuing you for possession of your home, you have a number of options open to you. You can consent to have your home repossessed. You may agree terms with your lender for the sale of the house if you are unable to pay your mortgage. The lending institution must get a court order to repossess or sell your house unless you consent in writing seven days before the repossession or sale. If the issue has to go to court and you lose, then you are generally liable for the costs of the court action.

If you don't agree to have your home repossessed or you haven't agreed a realistic repayment plan with the lender, the lender may take you to court to repossess your home and it may start the proceedings for repossession in the Circuit Court. The Circuit Court process starts when the mortgage provider issues you with a civil bill accompanied by an affidavit setting out the claim that is being made against you. The civil bill has a return date and must be served on you at least 21 days before the return date (that is the date on which the matter will come before the County Registrar). If you intend to fight the action, you must enter an appearance within 10 days of being served with the civil bill. You must then file an affidavit replying to the mortgage provider's claim and serve that on the mortgage provider at least four days before the return date. I would advise you to get a solicitor to help you with this, or make an appointment with the Free Legal Advice Clinic in your area for some guidance. When you case come before the County Registrar, it will be decided on the basis of what is in the affidavits. The County Registrar has the power to make a number of orders, including adjournments, notice to third parties and more time to file affidavits. The County Registrar may make an order for possession and/or a well-charging order (this is a court order which allows for the sale of the property) if you have not entered an appearance. The Registrar can also make an order for possession if you have entered an appearance and filed a replying affidavit, but the affidavit does not show an obvious defence. If you have an obvious defence, the case must be sent by the Registrar for hearing by a judge. The judge may grant or refuse the order requested.

If the County Registrar makes an order for possession, an unhappy party can appeal the decision to the Circuit Court judge. A further appeal lies from a decision of a Circuit Court judge to the High Court (*Smith v Considine* [2017] IEHC 22).

It is the practice of the courts to allow you some time to make arrangements to repay the money owed before making any final orders. If the final order is made and you do not hand over possession, the order may be enforced by the County Sheriff or the Registrar.

You might also note that as a result of s 1 of the Courts Act 2016, where market value is the basis upon which jurisdiction is claimed in the Circuit Court as not exceeding €3 million, there will be a presumption in favour of this plea. A valuation from an estate agent will not be a necessary proof unless the party challenging jurisdiction shows evidence of the property having a market value exceeding that figure.

Buying a Property from the Mortgagee in Possession (that is, the lender) or a Receiver

I viewed a property I am interested in purchasing from the mortgagee in possession. The property is exceptionally cheap. Are there any additional factors I should consider before I purchase this property? What is a receiver?

When purchasing a property in a situation such as this, the lender may have limited information about the services to the property, identity, planning issues or whether any notices were received by the legal owner. The contract for sale by way of insertion of a special condition will reflect this limited knowledge and it will be clear that you are purchasing in full knowledge that no warranties are being made and you will have to make your own enquiries about any concerns you may have. It's very much a case of buyer beware, this is it, take it or leave it. Your solicitors will usually get very sparse or extremely limited replies to standard objections and requisition on title, and generally no further queries will be replied to or entertained. Any requests for additional information than that which is in the possession of the bank's solicitors is usually refused.

In law, a receiver will act as agent for the legal owner of the property and is appointed by the lender by deed of appointment on foot of the mortgage document. We know this is a legal fiction, since it is the lender who is in control, not the original owner. The powers of the receiver are set out in the Land and Conveyancing Law Reform Act 2009. The receiver does not have the power to sell the property free of all interests, rights and estates in respect of which the mortgage has priority because, in law, he is acting as if he was the owner. If any charges, judgments or mortgages are registered after the registration of the mortgage and charge, the receiver may give possession of the property to the mortgagee in possession to complete the sale, thereby wiping out those burdens by overreaching, and sells the property free of the burdens. In conclusion, you may be obtaining the property at a much cheaper price than usual but I would advise you to investigate thoroughly what exactly you are getting for your money before you sign on the dotted line.

1. Buying or Selling a House, and Property Law Queries

ADVERSE POSSESSION

I have used a few fields for the last 20 years to graze cattle on without anyone saying anything to me about my use of them. Can I claim ownership of the land by virtue of squatter's rights?

A client once told me that this country was full of unpossessed land. I am not sure where he got this statistic from, but I know that same client's application for adverse possession was not as simple as he thought it would be.

You have given me sparse details in your letter. To establish a claim to ownership by adverse possession, you must have exclusive possession of a property for a set period. In the case of a claim against a landowner (not being the state), the period is 30 years. In the case of a claim against an individual, it is generally 12 years and, on land being foreshore, the period is generally 60 years. In this period you must perform acts of ownership sufficient to claim ownership and the period must be unbroken.

In the case of *Dunne v Irish Rail* [2016] IESC 47, the Supreme Court contemplated these issues. In this case, Dennis Dunne claimed to have been in possession of a plot of land beside Clondalkin railway station from 1977 to 2007. He claimed to have used the land for grazing and training horses and to have built stables and sheds. He claimed adverse possession as the period of his possession was well in excess of the 30 years required by statute. However, CIE also claimed ownership of the land and asserted that there had been no possession by Dennis Dunne which was adverse to their rights. The evidence at the trial showed that a number of informal paths through the lands were used by local people to access the train station and Dunne could do nothing to prevent this access, so Dunne was not in exclusive control of the lands. Fencing was put up by Dunne but not before 1993 when CIE entered the land and used it for 18 months between 1993 and 1995 while the railway station was being renovated. In 2001, CIE employees went into the field to repair fencing following complaints that horses had been let onto the lands.

In the Supreme Court it was held on the evidence that

> "Dennis Dunne did not make sufficient use of the field belonging to CIE over an uninterrupted period so as to be able to establish adverse possession. For the first 16 years, his use of the land was sporadic and lacking in exclusivity. What was missing was occupation through sufficient acts of possession to unequivocally indicate that he was taking possession of the land. Where the owner asserts rights to property through, as in this case CIE did, repairing fencing in 2001 and earlier in 1993 removing a wall, culling portions of the land and establishing modern fencing to protect a railway, time thereby has ceased to run in favour of the person attempting to establish adverse possession and the clock must be started again.
>
> Exclusive possession amounting to occupation of this land was never established on the evidence. The title of CIE to the land is, on the other hand, clear".

Coincidentally, I applied for adverse possession on behalf of another client recently. It was a case similar to your own. It was rejected, that is, the application would or could not be registered until several issues were remedied or clarified. The client had to assist with this. The Property Registration Authority queried whether the registered owners of the folio were still alive and if they were alive we were to provide an address for them for the purpose of service of notices. If they were deceased, we had to confirm whether they died testate (that is, they left a valid Will) or intestate (that is, they did not leave a valid Will). They queried whether a grant extracted to their estates and we were requested to lodge evidence of their deaths, if applicable. We were further required to supply the names and addresses of those entitled to their estates under the Statutes of Distribution or under the Succession Act (entitlement under the Status of Children Act 1988 and Adoption Acts must be considered) and whether or not there was any issue of a predeceased child. Any grant or unproved will must be lodged, together with the original state death certificates in respect of all deaths on the title.

Next, we were advised to lodge a Land Registry-compliant map at a requisite scale of the part of the property being claimed, with the area for registration clearly defined with a thin red line and to lodge a certificate by the Revenue Commissioners pursuant to s 62(2) of the Capital Acquisitions Tax Consolidation Act 2003.

I am referring to the above details so you understand that an application for the adverse possession of land takes some investigation and time, and is not as straightforward as some clients appear to think it is.

In your application for adverse possession, you will be required to provide full details and give the full circumstances of the original entry into occupation of the property by you and show that your possession was adverse (or became adverse). You must not have occupied the property by permission, by agreement as a caretaker, as a tenant or on any understanding with the registered owner.

Is the property securely bounded or fenced off from all adjoining property? What is the age, nature and condition of such boundaries?

You will be required to lodge photographs of the property, together with an account of where the photographs are and where they are taken from and also lodge photographs of all boundaries of the property, accounting for where they correspond with the boundaries on the map.

Has the property been acquired by you for use in conjunction with other property in your possession? If so, you will be required to provide the folio number of such property or, if unregistered title, the location of such property and describe your title thereto.

In conclusion, I would need more details before coming to a decision in regard to your case but grazing animals without other acts of ownership would, in my opinion, be insufficient to establish ownership of the land.

1. Buying or Selling a House, and Property Law Queries

You might also like to refer to the videos and checklists on the Property Registration Authority website, that is, prai.ie or www.landdirect.ie

The Land Registry is located at Chancery Street, Dublin 7, telephone 01 804 8028 or 051 303 000. Good luck with your application.

What is a 'Judgment Mortgage'?

I am in debt and the creditor has threatened to create a judgment mortgage on my home. Can the creditor do this?

If you owe money and the creditor has tried unsuccessfully to get repayment from you, one of the options open to the creditor is to create a judgment mortgage on property you legally own. It is much the same as a conventional mortgage and can be enforced by way of a mortgage suit. The creditor must first go to either the District, Circuit or High Court to get a judgment order. The court they go to depends on the amount you owe them. If the court establishes that you owe the creditor the money, it will make a judgment order against you, the judgment debtor. The creditor will usually have 12 years in which to enforce the judgment order. The creditor then has to get an execution order which allows him or her to enforce the judgment. The execution order will usually remain in force for one year.

The Difference Between Buying a House and an Apartment

I am currently viewing property and I am undecided between a small townhouse and a two-bedroom apartment. Is there any difference to the purchasing process from a legal point of view?

There are a few differences that you may like to familiarise yourself with. The first is that an apartment will be part of a shared building and will have common areas. A management company will most likely manage those common areas. What I mean by common areas are, for example, the entrance which would be shared by all entrants to that block, a stairway, a car parking area, shrubs at the entrance to the apartments or a green area. There are two types of property ownership in Ireland, leasehold and freehold. The legal title to an apartment is virtually always leasehold and there would usually be three parties to such a lease, that is, the builder or developer known as the lessor, the apartment owner known as the lessee and finally the management company. The apartment owner is liable to pay a nominal rent to keep the lease operating. A lease allows mutual conditions or covenants by the apartment owners and the management company. The Land and Conveyancing Law Reform Act 2009 provides for the enforcement of these conditions against future owners or purchasers of the apartment. Such conditions would include an obligation on the apartment owner to pay the service charge. The management company in turn would have an obligation to maintain the apartment building and common areas and also to insure the building and take out public liability insurance. Apartment owners become members of the management company when they purchase an apartment.

If you decide to purchase a second hand apartment, we would recommend that you have a surveyor check the entire building first to see if there are any major or expensive repairs needed in the near future. Have your solicitor check that the service charge of the previous owner and other owners in the apartment block was collected, a sinking fund is in place to cover major repairs, the management company owns the freehold title to the property, the rules relating to the voting rights in the management company and whether the block insurance is up to date and adequate.

When a purchaser leases an apartment, they get a set amount of space which includes the walls, ceilings and floors, but not the structural parts.

A lot of apartments have a patio area or a small balcony and an exclusive licence to use this space is usually granted to the purchaser. The same would usually apply to a car parking space and the management company would be responsible for the maintenance and the repair of these areas.

Therefore, to summarise, owning a leasehold interest in an apartment means that you just own the internal walls and roof and floor area of the apartment. You do not own the land it is on, except in common with others as a member of the management company. You have rights to use certain areas in common with fellow apartment owners. Your ownership is for a fixed number of years but this is not really relevant because the terms are usually 500 to 999 years!

In contrast, the legal title to a house would be freehold (or the freehold would be attainable through a small additional payment). Owning the freehold interest in a property means that you own the land and buildings. There is no period of years attached to ownership.

In historic times, freehold meant you had virtually unfettered control from earth to sky. Regulations have altered such unfettered freedom, for example, planning laws which provide that you cannot just build or do whatever you want regardless of these regulations on your own land. But in the main freehold ownership allows you much more leeway in doing what you want with your own property.

THE DIFFERENCE BETWEEN BUYING NEW AND SECOND-HAND PROPERTY

We viewed two properties that we like. The first property we viewed is a new build in the course of construction and the second one is an old house in need of renovation. Are there any differences or advantages from a legal viewpoint in buying a new build?

1. Buying or Selling a House, and Property Law Queries

Yes, there are significant differences in both process and practicalities when buying new or second-hand property. A building agreement is drawn up when buying a new apartment or new house. This is a contractual agreement setting out the rights and obligations of both the contractor (the seller) and the employer (the buyer). Builders are prohibited from using certain onerous conditions in the building agreement, but some builders do not comply with this.

There will also be a contract for sale for the transfer of the site on which the new build is built and it details the legal title to the site and boundaries. It will contain, *inter alia*, special and general conditions, the price and the closing date.

The building agreement will contain general conditions, such as the materials to be used, insolvency of the contractor, liability for defects, estate services, completion date, insurance, planning permissions and building regulations and that the property is fit for human habitation.

When purchasing a property in the course of construction, payments are sometimes made in stages if it is a single house. This depends on when the builder requires money to allow the next step in the building process to proceed. Stage payments do not apply to large developments. The purchaser is obliged to provide the lender with an interim stage payment certificate before the lender will release any funds in this way for a one-off house.

We would advise our clients to instruct an engineer or surveyor to ensure that the property is built in accordance with the plans and specifications contained in the building agreement, that is, to ensure that the property is built correctly. Ensure the surveyor or engineer has professional indemnity insurance and instruct them to issue a certificate providing that the property has been built in accordance with planning and building regulations and in compliance with plans and specifications in the building agreement.

Closing dates can sometimes be an issue when buying off the plans because the builder cannot be exactly sure when the property will be ready. It is a general guideline only, unlike a second-hand property purchase where the purchaser can have an accurate closing date. When buying a second-hand property, the purchaser should always have a surveyor check the property, as the principal of 'buyer beware' applies — unlike the new property, which must comply with the standards set out in the building agreement.

In contrast, in buying a second-hand property: (a) the property is already built, meaning that there is no opportunity until you buy to see beyond the surface; (b) the property may have been be built before 1 October 1964, meaning that it was built before planning came into existence; (c) building regulations or building bye-laws did not apply to many of the properties built in the past (for instance, an old cottage in the countryside would normally have been built from rubble stone without much of a foundation); and (d) generally one would buy the property as it is with defects and all, as vendors are usually unwilling to spend money on property they are selling to remedy defects.

In light of the above, it is imperative when purchasing a second-hand property that a competent person carries out a full structural survey.

When speaking with your solicitor regarding purchasing a second hand property, one should make him or her aware of any porches to the front of the property, extensions to the rear, attic conversions and any other alterations to the property, since these may require certificates from architects confirming either that the additions were in compliance with planning or are exempt.

When purchasing a new property, your neighbours will generally be in or around the same stage of life as you are. For example, their children may be the same age as your children and can grow up together. In regard to second-hand property, this may not be the case in that you are buying in to a settled community, which may be older.

In purchasing a second-hand property, there is of course the advantage of knowing what is built around you in that, generally in a city or town, there is little room for further development around second-hand residential properties. In contrast, when purchasing a new property in a new estate one does not know and the builder does not guarantee that the estate would be completed. This was a problem during the recession where people were stranded in half-built estates.

Associated with the above point is that, in purchasing a second-hand property in an established area, all the facilities are usually already in place, such as schools, public transport, shops, pharmacies, doctors and general services, while in new build, these facilities have yet to be established (which may or may not happen, depending on the economic climate).

Finally, there is a slight advantage in terms of stamp duty in regard to buying a new property in that, for calculation of stamp duty purposes, the VAT element of the price can be deducted. For example, if you buy a new property for €113,500, the VAT on building costs is 13.5%. You will then pay stamp duty on €100,000.

Ultimately it is a matter of personal taste which type of property you prefer and decide to purchase but hopefully the above is of some assistance from a legal point of view.

Sale of the Family Home – The Rights of Married Couples and Civil Partners

Our family home is in my husband's name only. It was never put jointly into both our names. Regrettably, after 20 years of marriage, we are not on friendly terms at present and I am worried my husband might sell the family home without my consent. Can he do this?

1. Buying or Selling a House, and Property Law Queries

The family home is protected by the Family Home Protection Act 1976. The Family Home Protection Act prevents one spouse or civil partner from selling, mortgaging, leasing or transferring the family home without the prior written consent of the other spouse or civil partner. Therefore if consent is given, it must be in writing. This requirement for the consent in writing of the other spouse or civil partner applies regardless of whether the home is owned jointly by the married couple or civil partners or whether the home is owned by just one party. Therefore you are worrying unnecessarily because your husband may not legally sell the family home without your consent in writing first. If your husband does manage to sell your home without your consent or knowledge, the transaction is voidable at your discretion. If such an occurrence happens, you should act immediately.

There is no differentiation between husband and wife (s 3(1) Family Home Protection Act 1976). Section 54 of the Family Law Act 1995 imposes a six-year time limit within which proceedings must be taken by the non-owning spouse to have a conveyance declared void. There are four exceptions to this, and those are arrangements made in contemplation of marriage, a conveyance to a bona fide purchaser for full value, conveyance of an interest by a person or body other than the spouse, such as a bank, and finally where the court orders the sale of the home in a judicial separation or divorce.

A family home is a dwelling in which a married couple ordinarily resides and would include a former residence of a couple who are separated (s 2, Family Home Protection Act 1976). It also includes a dwelling in which a spouse is residing having been forced to leave the family home by the other spouse.

HELP-TO-BUY SCHEME

We are newly engaged and in the process of buying our first home. We are only interested in new houses and hope to purchase a nice house under €350,000. We are both first time buyers. Do we qualify for the 'Help-to-Buy' scheme?

The Help-to-Buy scheme only applies to properties costing €500,000 or less and the first-time buyer must build his own new home or buy a new house or apartment. Both of you must be first-time buyers and you must live in this property as your home or occupy the property for at least five years. Cash buyers do not qualify. In fact, you must take out a mortgage of at least 70% of the purchase price. The idea behind the Help-to-Buy scheme is to assist first-time buyers raise the deposit required to purchase their first home. The scheme provides for a refund of income tax and Deposit Interest Retention Tax (DIRT) paid over the previous four years. The relief is restricted to key dates, that is, you must either buy or self-build a new residential property between 19 July 2016 and 31 December 2019. If you signed a contract to buy a property or drew down the first instalment of the mortgage for a self-build prior to 19 July 2016, you will not qualify.

PYRITE DAMAGE IN RESIDENTIAL PROPERTY

I own a house in an estate in the north side of Dublin. It's a beautiful home, plenty of space, nice garden and friendly neighbours. However, recently I noticed cracks in the plasterboard and the windows are not opening properly. The doors have started catching on floors. There are cracks in the tiles. The cracking is both internal and external. There is talk of pyrite damage due to defective infill. Is there anything I can do to have my house repaired? Who is legally responsible for this? Will I be compensated? Am I eligible for the pyrite remediation scheme?

Pyrite is a common mineral that occurs in rocks. It is sometimes referred to as fool's gold and I have often seen little sample jars of it in tourist shops as a symbol of good luck. It's silver in colour. In some circumstances, a chemical reaction which creates expanding crystals within the material can occur which causes the pyrite to swell causing the construction material in which the pyrite is present to expand, heave, crack and eventually crumble. When buying a house, have a structural survey carried out and your engineer should be able to advise you whether further investigation is necessary to ascertain the position in relation to pyrite. You may have to take samples from the floor of the house and have them tested in a laboratory in the UK. Meath, Offaly, Kildare and North Dublin were the areas most affected by pyrite because the builders used stone from quarries in this area which contained pyrite.

In modern houses with a concrete floor, there is gravel underneath that floor, that is, infill. In some properties, that gravel contained a material that expanded when it got wet called pyrite. The expansion pushed the concrete floors up and that in turn pushed the stud walls up and led to cracking. In some houses the pyrite was in the blocks and in some the pyrite was in the material used to build the structural walls.

A number of years ago, we were involved in a settlement with a builder involving one of the first known cases of pyrite in Ireland. We had to act fast and get the infill replaced with new infill that didn't have this expanding material in it.

We pursued the developers on our client's instructions that they wanted their properties repaired and we were very successful. The developers paid for everything and repaired all the properties. To the date of writing, we have not received any complaints. The repair work involved sending in mini-diggers to dig out the old infill and replace it with new infill. All interiors from a cosmetic view point were fully replaced to the same standard as before. This was all done at no expense to the homeowners, who were given nice local alternative properties to stay in while the repair work was carried out.

We had all legal documentation and certification proving the properties were fully repaired forwarded to our offices and we lodged them with our clients' title deeds. Our clients were very happy with the results. Our legal fees and engineers' fees were discharged by the developers, so the homeowners were not out of pocket in any way.

1. Buying or Selling a House, and Property Law Queries

Remember, when buying a property in a development that different developers often build in the same development. Different developers often use different quarries and therefore, just because you heard there was pyrite in an estate you're interested in, doesn't necessarily mean there is pyrite in all the estate. Do your research first. Find out who the developer is and what quarry he used.

It is important to note that the above is based only on our experience with the owners of properties our practice represented. We are not obviously in a position to comment on all properties affected by pyrite. We cannot comment on the standard of repair work carried out in developments we are not familiar with. Please organise an appointment with your own solicitors and engineers before deciding on any course of action.

We may not have had in our opinion this problem 40 years ago when houses had suspension floors. Builders started using concrete because it was seen as more energy efficient.

You might note also that, in some developments in County Mayo, pyrite got into the actual blocks, that is, blocks that were mixed with gravel and the gravel had pyrite in it. That's a whole different ball game. We're not engineers but those houses will probably have to be completely reconstructed.

Home-bond, Premier Guarantee, negligence, breach of contract

Generally, if any structural or physical defects become apparent after purchasing a new home, the main options open to the homeowner would be a claim to the National House Building Guarantee Company or the Home-bond guarantee scheme. However, the High Court in the Ballymun Community Centre case deemed pyrite a product defect, that is, not a structural defect and therefore not part of the Home-bond scheme, which covers structural defects.

Premier Guarantee is another option in some cases. Premier Guarantee in contrast to Home-bond has accepted pyrite damage is covered under their insurance policy. If you suspect pyrite damage in your property, it is important to check with your solicitor which scheme your home is covered under. There are strict time limits, generally 10 years from the date of insurance of the property, so it is important, if you suspect pyrite damage, to act fast.

The homeowner might consider taking legal action against the builder for negligence. Legal action against the builder for breach of contract might also be considered on the basis that the builder failed to comply with specific terms in the building agreement.

Possibility of claims under contract or the Liability for Defective Products Act 1991

You might note also that, if a builder supplied construction services only (and supplied the pyrite-affected material) but did not supply the land, then the Liability for Defective Products Act 1991 (as amended) may apply to the supply of the pyrite-affected material. Otherwise, being an immovable, the building is not covered by the Liability for Defective Products Act 1991. Where a claim can be made in contract, only the builder is answerable to the consumer. Where the claim can be made under the Liability for Defective Products Act 1991, the consumer may also sue the suppliers of the pyrite-affected material.

In all these cases, there would have been a contract between the consumer and the builder. In each contract is incorporated either expressly or implied under statute a term that the goods supplied under the contract would be of merchantable quality. Material such as pyrite that deforms the structure of the building is not of merchantable quality.

Time period for issuing proceedings

The Statute of Limitations (s 11(1) Statute of Limitations, 1957) sets out the period for issuing proceedings as six years for breach of contract (irrespective of knowledge) and under the Liability for Defective Products Act 1991 (s 7(1) of the Defective Product Act 1991) at three years

> "from the date on which the cause of action accrued or the date, if later, on which the plaintiff became aware, or should reasonable have come aware, of the damage, the defect and the identity of the producer".

This is subject to a maximum time limit of 10 years from the date the producer put the product into circulation in the European union (s 7(2) (a) of the Liability for Defective Products Act 1991).

Consider the possibility of the builder going into liquidation

Another important point to consider is that legal proceedings can be time consuming and costly. If a builder has gone into liquidation that may extinguish the possibility of any successful litigation.

Insurance policy

In Ireland, a consumer cannot claim directly on the insurance policy of a defunct company or person. This is the case even where all the premiums were paid as they fell due and the insurance company is at no disadvantage in settling the claim.

Pyrite remediation scheme

As pyrite is widespread, a remediation scheme was later put in place to address it.

The aim of the pyrite remediation scheme is to procure the remediation of certain dwellings with damage caused due to pyrite. The relevant legislation is the Pyrite Resolution Act 2013. To be eligible for the pyrite remediation scheme, dwellings must be located within the administrative areas of Dun Laoghaire-Rathdown, Fingal, Kildare, Meath, Offaly or South Dublin County Councils or Dublin City Council. Dwellings must have been constructed and completed between 1 January 1997 and

1. Buying or Selling a House, and Property Law Queries

12 December 2013. Dwellings must have been assessed, tested and certified as having a damage condition rating of two and it must be verified that damage is attributable to pyrite heave. An application can only be made in respect of one dwelling and the dwelling must have been purchased before 12 December 2013. The applicant must be able to show to the satisfaction of the PRB, that he or she does not have available to them any practicable option, other than under the scheme or the use or his or her own resources, to remedy or secure the remediation of the dwelling. The scheme covers the sampling, testing and damage verification, the preparation of the specification of remediation works in accordance with IS398-2: 2013. The scheme also covers the management of the tender process and implementation of the remediation works, the remediation of the dwelling as per specification and schedule to the required standard and the monitoring and inspection of works, snagging and final certification. Certain costs may also be recovered by the applicant under the scheme, such as the costs of alternative accommodation, removal and storage of furniture and the vouched cost of procuring the initial Building Condition Assessment from a competent person.

So, to get on the scheme, the property owner makes an online application to the Pyrite Resolution Board. The Housing Agency will assess whether the damage recorded in the building condition assessment is attributable to pyrite and notify the applicant accordingly. This decision may be appealed. A guide for scheme participants is issued which explains what is involved in the remediation process. The housing agency assigns a project manager and engineer to each project. On completion, the works will be certified in accordance with IS398-2:2013 and you can move back into your property.

We were also instructed by clients who used the remediation scheme and they were happy with the results. Their homes were fully repaired and certified. Please make an appointment with your solicitors to get advice on the best option for you.

LOCAL PROPERTY TAX

I refuse to pay my local property tax. I live in the city and the amount I am taxed is very high. Must I pay local property tax? Would revenue notice if I didn't pay it or if I paid a lower amount?

Local Property Tax was introduced in 2013 and is based on the market value of the home. The Revenue Commissioners are particularly strict when it comes to payment of property tax. It must be paid or you will receive a summons to go to court, that is, legal proceedings will be issued and if you don't pay, the Revenue will seize your goods. The tax has been criticised especially by people with property in the city where prices are higher. Homes are due to be revalued in 2019 which will result in further hikes.

The Revenue Commissioners are now using Google Maps to track non-payers. Using satellite images of streets and townlands, properties where the tax has been paid are highlighted, allowing officials to target those where no payment has been made. If a property owner is paying a lower amount than their neighbours, revenue will investigate this. In conclusion and to answer your question, I would advise you to pay the local property tax to avoid getting in trouble with the Revenue Commissioners and to avoid a court summons.

SELLING A PROPERTY

I am putting my house up for sale through my local auctioneer. I understand I need to get in contact with my solicitor but should I wait until a buyer is found? Is there anything else I should be doing?

We would advise that you should contact your solicitor immediately. Your solicitor may have to take up your title deeds from a bank/lending institution if you have a mortgage and this may take time. Furthermore, your solicitor is required to draft contracts and order an up-to-date folio from the Land Registry. It would be better, in my opinion, when you do find a buyer to have the contracts ready to issue to them, rather than have any further delay.

With reference to what you are required to do legally, we would recommend you address the following issues;

1. All properties for sale are now required by law to have a BER rating. You will need to commission someone to issue a BER certificate and report. You may speak with your estate agent in regard to this;
2. If you are aware that title to your house is Registry of Deeds title, rather than Land Registry title, you will need an engineer/architect to provide a Land Registry-compliant map for first registration of the title in the Land Registry (under the compulsory registration rules). Your solicitor after reviewing the title will tell you whether you need this or not. A good rule of thumb is that most agricultural land is Land Registry, while older houses in towns may be Registry of Deeds. Your solicitor will also want to check if there is anything wrong with the title to the property and consideration should be given as to how to deal with it, such as providing an insurance bond by way of an indemnity to the purchaser in respect of the missing documents;
3. You will need to gather receipts of payment of the Local Property Tax and its precursor the Household Charge and, if the house was rented, discharge of Non Principal Private Residents' Tax. Even if you did not rent the house, many purchasers' solicitors are now insisting on being provided with a certificate of discharge of NPPR because of the putative nature of that tax. You may apply to the council for this. If any other outgoings apply, pay them and have the receipts to hand;
4. If you are serviced by a water scheme, you will need to get a receipt that the fees are paid to date;
5. If your house is serviced by a septic tank, you will be required to show the tank is registered by means of a certificate of registration;
6. If you have put on an extension to the house since it was built, you should - depending on the size of it - have a declaration of exemption from planning by an engineer or architect or a declaration of compliance with planning and building regulations and a copy of the planning permission;

1. Buying or Selling a House, and Property Law Queries

7. If you have required planning permission, you should also have receipts that the financial levies have been paid and confirmation that the commencement notice was issued. If there is any doubt in respect of the planning aspect, it may be necessary to insert special conditions in the contract for sale;
8. Inform your solicitor if you received any notices which affect the property such as a compulsory purchase order;
9. Consider whether you have to pay capital gains tax. Is a probate tax certificate of discharge applicable? If so, have it ready;
10. Request a section 68 letter outlining legal fees and government outlay;
11. Provide your solicitor with an up-to-date mortgage statement (with your account details if applicable);
12. Is the property held in sole ownership or is the written consent of a spouse necessary in order to sell it? Your solicitor could have the family law declaration drafted and ready. Inform your solicitor of any family law proceedings, such as separation. Have a copy of your state marriage certificate to hand as your solicitor will want to be satisfied that no difficulties will arise under family law legislation;
13. Provide your solicitor with information regarding any boundary issues and furnish maps if you have them;
14. What are the outgoings on the property such as a service charge, local authority charges, water charges, ground rent or insurance? Have up-to-date receipts ready for electricity, telephone, gas or other outgoings to vouch their payment on closing. Make a note of the alarm code;
15. Provide your PPS number(s).
16. Are there any contents included in the selling price? Make a list of same for inclusion in the special conditions of the contract;
17. Consider any easements, rights of way, forestry, fishing or sporting rights.
18. Are there any tenants in the property?
19. Other costs to factor in are your solicitor's professional fee, a fee to your lending institution to take up your deeds, a fee to the local authority for a letter confirming whether the roads and services are in charge and a fee to the management agency for replies to standard pre-contract questions if your house or apartment is in an estate with a management company;
20. There may be penalties for breaking a fixed mortgage. Enquire with the lending institution as to what the penalties or fee may be. If, for example, there are only a few months left to run on the mortgage, it might be worth your while to hold off from selling until the mortgage runs its course to avoid paying penalties, and then sell.

If you address the above issues now, it will mean that, when you do find a buyer, you are ready to act immediately and there are no delays while you await any of the above receipts or certificates.

Note that the use of the term 'subject to contract' in correspondence will, except in rare and exceptional cases, establish the non-existence of a previously concluded oral contract. The issue of a contract by the sellers' solicitor under the protection of the term 'subject to contract' is an 'invitation to treat' only, and not an offer to sell. The return of this contract signed by the purchaser is an offer to purchase and is not an acceptance of an offer from the seller. The return of this contract duly signed by the seller to the purchaser or his or her solicitor is an acceptance of the offer to purchase by the purchaser (Law Society of Ireland, conveyancing manual volume 1, second edition, oxford university press, page 60, contract for sale).

Best of luck with your sale.

Septic Tanks and Holiday Homes

I am in the process of purchasing a holiday home in a remote rural location. The property has its own septic tank. Should I have an expert examine the septic tank before I sign the contract for sale?

Many rural properties have their own septic tanks, but a septic tank servicing a holiday home could possibly be on a neighbour's property. I would advise you to make sure there will be no legal issues or you could find it hard to enjoy the property or to sell it in the future. Before buying a house with a septic tank, have it inspected by a qualified person. The seller should furnish you with installation and maintenance records for the system. Get a copy of its certificate of registration and make sure it has met planning rules. All septic tanks must be registered with the local authority for the area and can be inspected. Should an inspection find that the septic tank for your holiday home is faulty, you will either have to upgrade the tank or carry out whatever remediation works are deemed necessary by your local authority. This can be very expensive. You may also need to put in a percolation area and you must have a suitable site for this. This will cost several thousand euro. So don't rush into purchasing a holiday home and ask the vendor first whether the local authority has inspected the septic tank or not. If they have not inspected it, ask whether they have indicated or served notice providing that they want to inspect it. If the local authority has inspected the tank, ask the vendor whether any recommendations have been made for improvement and get proof of same. You want to be really sure you will not have any difficulty with the septic tank during the quiet enjoyment of your holidays and in the future if selling on the property.

Family Home in Negative Equity – Tracker Mortgage

We live with our children in a relatively small house. We would like to sell this house and move to a four-bed with a garden. However, we are in negative equity and therefore concerned the banks might not give us a bigger mortgage. We would also like to keep the tracker rate we are on. Is this possible?

1. Buying or Selling a House, and Property Law Queries

In order to keep the tracker rate, you will have to stay with the same bank. If you switch banks, you will lose your tracker mortgage as trackers are no longer being sold. Of course, that will make a big difference in repayments. Some banks are offering loans to those in negative equity but they are very selective. Have you both got good, stable jobs? Have you a good credit rating and good payment history? Can you comfortably afford a bigger mortgage? Get your financials down on paper and approach your own bank first. You might note that those banks offering portable trackers, like Ulster Bank, have arrangements whereby you can move your tracker with you, not at the same rate you're currently paying but with a 2-2.5% margin, and effect any extra loan requirements via a regular variable rate mortgage.

I used to refer to it as property porn during the boom where I would spend hours on all the property web sites looking at prices and design. But perhaps speak with your broker or lending institution first and then let the fun begin. (note: A Tracker Mortgage is a type of home loan where the interest rate charged on the loan tracks that of another publicly available rate, typically the interest rate set by the European Central Bank. Refer to www.centralbank.ie for further details).

ALLOCATION OF COUNCIL HOUSING IN PRIVATE HOUSING ESTATES

I'm in a bit of a pickle. The county council purchased houses in the housing estate I live in. It is a private estate and I paid quite a lot of money for my house. I have young children and I am curious as to the social mix of the estate.

First I would like to say that, just because someone is on a housing list, does not make them anti-social or a bad person. Since the property crash, we all know how precarious life can be. Many of the residents already living in your estate who purchased their houses may be on a form of income support or getting help with their mortgage. You might like to start by enquiring with the county council as to whether they plan on dividing up the houses into apartments for emergency accommodation. If they do, and if you feel you would be uncomfortable with this, you can object to planning permission. Generally, councils have policies in relation to mixed developments where they limit the amount of housing stock they have in a particular area. You could query the council's policy in regard to this and ask them what special strategies they have. Perhaps you should organise a meeting with the council and request a copy of their guidelines. Every estate has to take council houses, but there is a limit on how many council houses an estate gets, so ask them that question and ask what amount of the allocated quota is already filled.

While developers must offer councils 10% of all newly-built units at a discount, there is no requirement for the properties to be spread throughout a development to ensure a social mix. A review of part V of the Planning and Development Act 2000, commissioned by the Housing Agency in 2012, identified locating social housing in single blocks, rather than peppered around a scheme, as a drawback of the system. It noted that, in many cases, the blocks set aside by developers for social housing were in "least favoured ends of developments". Houses or apartments for social housing would not have any lesser specification than those for sale privately.

Recently, Dublin city council struck a deal with Cairn Homes to buy 19 units for social housing in the Marianella development in Rathgar for €4.75 million, an average of €250,000 per unit. The council paid €480,000 for a large two-bed in the development which is a luxury scheme of apartments with its own gym and concièrge, playground, private cinema and a residents' club with a wellness suite.

Compulsory Purchase Order

I have just received a formal notice providing that my land is going to be compulsorily acquired by the local council. Can they do this? Is it possible for me to object?

Yes, they can take it and, yes, it is possible for you to raise objections, but you must act quickly as strict time limits apply for lodging same and for any court actions which may be required to challenge the compulsory purchase order. You have the right to object, make representations, negotiate, refer to property arbitrators and have your objections heard. The local council can take land without the consent of the owner by means of a compulsory purchase order and it's usually done to facilitate a public project for the common good. CPOs are most often used for road improvement schemes and urban development schemes, such as the Luas project in Dublin. You will be eligible for compensation, and such compensation should as far as possible restore you to the same financial position you were in before your land was acquired, that is, based on the market value of your land. The compensation should reflect both the value of the land acquired and also the reduction in value of your remaining land as a result of the compulsory purchase order.

You should get the professional advice of a chartered surveyor as soon as you are served with a notice relating to a compulsory purchase order. The fees charged by the chartered surveyor are part of a normal claim for compensation.

A local authority can buy dangerous land in its area by compulsory purchase and they must advertise the details of any such purchase in the local newspaper and send a notice to the owner or occupier giving information about how and where to object to the proposed purchase. The same applies to derelict sites.

Appeals are made to An Bord Pleanála (the Planning Board). If an objection is made, the local authority cannot buy the land without the consent of An Bord Pleanála. If the Bord approves the compulsory purchase, the local authority can buy the land using a vesting order.

Ground Rent on Residential Property

My solicitors informed me that the property I am purchasing is leasehold and that I must pay ground rent to the ground landlord. Alternatively I could try buying out the ground rent once the purchase of the property is concluded. What does this involve?

1. Buying or Selling a House, and Property Law Queries

There are two major types of property ownership in Ireland, that is, leasehold and freehold. Owning the leasehold interest in property mean that you own just the building and not the land it is on and that your ownership is for a fixed number of years. If you own a leasehold property, you must pay a ground rent to the person who owns the ground it is built on (the ground landlord) which is, in some cases, the local authority. The amount of ground rent varies. If you own the freehold interest in the property, that means you own the land and buildings and there is no ground rent. When you are buying or selling a property, any ground rent will be recorded on the lease.

A person who is buying a property may be able to buy out the ground rent privately once the purchase of the property has been concluded, or through the Property Registration Authority's (PRA's) ground rents purchase scheme. This allows leasehold owners to buy out their ground rents and become outright owners of their property, unless there is a specific clause in the lease preventing it or if it is not in the public interest.

Residential property is covered by the Ground Rents Acts of the 1970s. The legislation obliges the landlord to sell the freehold interest in the property. There is a ban on further ground rents being created. The Landlord and Tenant (Ground Rents) Act 1978 (number 1 Act of 1978) is entitled "an Act to prevent the creation of new leases reserving ground rents on dwellings and to provide for related matters". Section 2 of the Act of 1978 provides that a lease of land made after 16 May 1978 is void if the lessee would, apart from this section, have the right to enlarge his interest into a fee simple and the permanent buildings are constructed for use wholly or principally as a dwelling. This does not apply to apartments. Apartments and multi-unit developments are not covered by the legislation. If the landlord cannot be found, money can be paid into court or the Land Registry to be held for the benefit of the landlord (if he or she ever turns up). There is a specific way of calculating the amount owing to a landlord. It uses a multiplier of the rent and the amount of years left on the lease.

Virtually every residential property house purchaser has the right to buy out the ground rent.

The amount to be paid when buying out the ground rent can be agreed between the purchaser and the ground landlord or obtained through an arbitration procedure. It is more expensive if an arbitrator is involved. If you buy out your ground rent, whether from a private or a local authority, the PRA will issue a vesting certificate. This is a new title deed to your property and should be registered with the Land Registry or Registry of Deeds to record the fact that the ownership of your property has changed from leasehold to freehold.

PLANNING PERMISSION FOR AN EXTENSION

We live in a beautiful home outside Carrick-on-Shannon and, now that we have a new baby, we are considering building an extension. Will we need to apply for planning permission? We do not have any previous extensions.

First, I would like to congratulate you on the birth of your new baby. How exciting! With regard to your query, I am pleased to advise that some extensions do not require planning permission provided they are under a particular size. New regulations announced for domestic extensions will make life easier and less costly for individuals and families planning to extend their own home. An information note and associated forms for home owners will be available from the planning departments' website and the local building control authority. I will give you some basic guidelines, but please also speak with your architect and engineer regarding your specific extension requirements prior to commencing works. Generally, a small domestic extension will not require planning permission if it does not exceed 40 square meters in size. For semi-detached or terraced houses, the floor area of any extension above ground level may not exceed 12 square meters. The extension must not reduce the area of private open space to less than 25 square meters and it must not exceed the height of the house. If the rear wall of your house has a gable, the walls of the extension must not be higher than the side walls of your house; if the rear wall does not include a gable, the height of the walls of the extension must not exceed the height of the rear wall of your house. If you are putting in new windows, please consult your architect as there are rules relating to size and design here also. If you decide on a flat-roofed extension the height of the highest part of the roof may not exceed the height of the eaves or parapet. In other cases, no part of the roof may exceed the highest part of the roof of the house.

Generally, you will not need planning permission for capped walls made of brick, stone or block. Wooden fences - but not security fences - can be erected as long as they do not exceed 1.2 meters in height or two meters at the side or rear. Gates may be built, provided they do not exceed two meters in height. Planning permission is always required if you wish to widen or create new access to the public road. A central heating system chimney, boiler house or oil storage tank (up to 3,500 liters capacity) does not require planning permission. A satellite dish (up to one meter in diameter, and no higher than the top of the roof) at the back or side of the house is allowed. However, planning permission is needed for a satellite dish on the front of the house. Only one dish may be erected on a house.

While we are discussing planning issues, you might note proposed changes to the Planning Act would see developments by Irish Water related to the provision of water services or maintenance-type works exempted. The change of use relating to the conversion of vacant commercial premises to residential use would also be exempt, as would the undertaking of work to support the rollout of the National Broadband Plan and extend mobile phone coverage.

Good luck with your project.

1. Buying or Selling a House, and Property Law Queries

Planning Permission – Can I Self-Build a House without Planning Permission?

I bought some land off an elderly farmer and I am going to build a house on it. The land is in a beautiful location overlooking a lake. I am a good tradesman and I want to get started on the building as soon as possible. I have not applied for planning permission because it would take forever to get it and, besides, it is such a quiet part of the countryside, I don't think anyone would notice or complain. Do you think I should proceed without the planning permission?

The law requires that you need planning permission for virtually every significant development. Therefore in a nutshell I would say no! It is important to be aware from the start, that if you fail to obtain planning permission where it is required, you may run the risk of penalties which can carry heavy fines and even imprisonment. I would never advise anyone to build a house without planning permission. I could list numerous cases where people have done so and regretted it. In a recent Supreme Court case, a plumber and his wife built a 588sqm home on lands near Navan, despite being told not to. Meath County Council brought a case against them and they were given one year to demolish the house built without permission "in flagrant breach of the planning laws". Giving the Supreme Court's decision Mr Justice William McKechnie said the court was mindful of the hardship its decision would cause to the family involved, but it could not lose sight of the fact they had been living for over a decade in an unauthorised development. The Murrays were fully aware of the need to obtain planning permission and the Supreme Court agreed that what they did was particularly flagrant and completely unjustified (*Meath County Council v Murray and Another* [2010] IEHC 254, *The County Council of Meath v Murray and Another* [2017] IESC 25.

The overall plan for the area where you wish to build your home is called the development plan. This plan is drawn up by your local authority and sets out your local authority's objectives for the use of particular areas where you live. You should look at the development plan before you make an application for planning permission. If you need to clear a site first, you will need planning permission if you are proposing to make or widen an access onto a public road or demolish a structure that was last used as a residence or demolish a building in a terrace, or a building that is attached to another building in separate ownership. You must give the public notice of your proposals before making an application for planning permission. This is done by placing a notice in your local circulating newspaper and putting up a site notice on or before the day you make the application which can be clearly read and it must stay there for five weeks afterwards. Sometimes planning permission is granted subject to conditions which may require changes to your proposals. Planning permission normally lasts for five years.

If the local authority refuses your application, they will give you reasons for this and you have one month to appeal this decision in writing to An Bord Pleanála.

An Bord Pleanála's decision is final and can only be challenged by judicial review in the High Court. This process will judge whether the board followed due process in reaching its decision and will not include an examination of the planning merits.

Part III of the Local Government (Planning and Development) Act 2000 sets out the procedure for applying for planning permission and gives the planning authority the power to impose conditions when granting planning permission. Any financial conditions imposed must be complied with. Part VIII of the Act provides for enforcement mechanisms, including criminal prosecution, an enforcement notice under s154/5 of the Act or a planning injunction under s 160 of the Local Government (Planning and Development) Act 1963.

GRANT FOR REPAIRING VACANT PROPERTIES

I have an old farmhouse on my land. It's not in use and is semi-derelict for years. I would like to renovate it and possibly lease it out. Are there any grants available to help finance this sort of thing?

There is a Repair and Lease scheme which was developed under Building Ireland to help property owners prepare their vacant homes for the rental market. The nationwide scheme provides funding of up to €40,000 including VAT to bring a property up to a liveable state. The Repair and Lease scheme will pay for the repairs upfront in return for the property being leased to a local authority or approved housing body to be used as social housing for a period of at least 10 years. The cost of the repairs will be repaid by offsetting it against the rent due to the owner of the property over the period of the lease agreement. There must be a demand for social housing in the area. Funding covers items such as new flooring, kitchen, plumbing, furniture, heating, insulation and windows. I would advise you to contact your local authority to see if you can avail of the scheme.

There was some criticism of the scheme in rural communities as most of the applications received were in rural locations where the council has no social housing demand or where the allocated budget would not return the properties to a useable state, due to their poor condition. The scheme may possibly work best in large urban areas where there is a higher demand for social housing. The reconstruction grant would perhaps be a better option, but that grant is not in operation at the moment. Please contact Building Ireland or your local county council regarding any new grants that may be available.

CONVERTING AN ATTIC

I would like to convert the attic of our semi-detached house into a bedroom. What are the rules relating to conversions?

1. Buying or Selling a House, and Property Law Queries

It is important to talk to your architect first but, in summary, for an attic conversion to comply with building regulations, it is recommended that 50% of the space should be a minimum height of 2.4m when measured at 1.5m from the floor below. Please refer to part K in the building regulations (ventilation). If you can satisfy the structural and space requirements, it's mandatory to meet the latest fire safety requirements, especially the escape provisions. A lot of conversions have difficulty meeting the location and size of roof lights and windows for escape purposes, but these are a must. There are others in relation to fire separation and doors that must be complied with. Your architect will advise you. You must also meet the latest regulations on smoke detectors (one in every bedroom and on all landings) which need to be linked to the power supply. In installing compliant roof-lights, work to a protected structure will not normally be exempt. Roof-lights to the rear are considered exempted development under planning, but not those to the front or side. All other work must comply with the building regulations. If you don't meet the building regulations, then you might consider converting the attic for storage only or as a laundry room, but be sure to comply with fire safety measures.

You may, in fact, use the converted space as a bedroom but be aware that if you go on to sell the property in the future, it cannot be marketed as a bedroom because this will create difficulties which may lead to the purchaser's solicitors qualifying legal title to the purchaser's bank. That may in turn result in the purchaser's bank withdrawing finance. This, of course, may then result in the purchaser being forced to withdraw from the sale.

Derelict and Vacant Sites

I am the owner of a site with a derelict structure on it and I received a statutory notice from my local authority informing me that my property has been added to the Derelict Sites Register and that the authority wants me to clean up the site or they may decide to purchase the site compulsorily. Can I object to this?

Under the Derelict Sites Act 1990, local authorities can force owners to clean up derelict sites in its area. The Act defines a derelict site as any land that detracts, or is likely to detract to a material degree, from the amenity, character or appearance of land in the neighbourhood of the land in question because of structures which are ruinous, derelict or in a dangerous condition or the neglected, unsightly or objectionable condition of the land or the structures on it or the presence, deposit or collection of litter, rubbish, debris or waste.

The Act allows local authorities to prosecute owners who do not comply with notices served, to purchase land compulsorily and to carry out necessary work themselves and charge the owners for the costs. If you are the owner or occupier of a derelict site, you will receive a statutory notice from your local authority informing you that your property has been added to the Derelict Sites Register and that the authority wants you to clean up the site. The authority may decide to purchase the derelict site compulsorily, which is something you can object to. If an objection is made, the local authority cannot buy the land without the consent of An Bord Pleanála. If An Bord Pleanála approves the compulsory purchase and the local authority has dealt with any objections received, the local authority can buy the land, using a vesting order.

Under the Urban Regeneration and Housing Act 2015, each local authority is required to compile a vacant sites register, starting from January 2017. This is a register of lands in the local authority's area that are suitable for housing but are not coming forward for development. From January 2019 onwards, a vacant site levy will be charged on such sites.

If you are the owner of urban land that has been put on the Derelict Sites Register, you must pay an annual levy to the local authority. If you do not pay the derelict sites levy within two months of receiving the demand, interest will be charged on the full amount at a rate of 1.25% a month. The local authority can take you to court to recover the amount. Any change in the valuation of the land means that the amount of the derelict sites levy on that land will also change. If the local authority is satisfied that you have plans to develop the property, and planning permission has been granted for this development, you can enter into a bond, instead of paying the derelict sites levy.

Under the Derelict Sites Act 1990, it is an offence to remove, damage or deface a notice posted by the local authority regarding a derelict site or to fail to carry out the measures required by the local authority to prevent a property from being classed as derelict within an allocated time. You must notify the authority of any transfer of land.

On conviction or indictment for failing to carry out the measures required by the local authority to prevent a property from being classed as derelict within an allocated time, you can be fined or imprisoned for a term not exceeding two years, or both.

CHANGES IN ZONING LAW RENDERING FIELD UNSALEABLE

I have a field in the south of Ireland that my mother bought freehold when we were children. After a few years, the zoning law changed and my mother was given a year to get her house built, which she was unable to do. As a family, we have had to accept that. We applied periodically for permission to build, but to no avail. Recently I had a chance to sell the field to legitimate motorhome holiday people. I checked with the council to see if it was still OK to do this and discovered they had changed the zoning law yet again in 2016, rendering the field unsaleable and unusable. The council say they have no legal responsibility to pay any compensation. Do I have any legal redress in this matter?

1. Buying or Selling a House, and Property Law Queries

In principle, the council's primary responsibility is to the county. They normally create a development plan and part of the development plan is the zoning of certain areas for particular uses - for example, residential. There may only be legal redress in a situation such as yours if the council has made a decision that is prejudicial to your field only, other than the whole area. Even if this was the case, you would have to prove that the council had acted in such a manner that their actions were unreasonable and prejudicial to you in particular over everyone else in the same area. The alternative avenue of redress is to look at whether the council has complied with all the procedural/statutory duties it needs to in reaching such a decision. Finally, you would have to look at time limits in regard to any legal challenge to the council's actions. There are strict time limits in regard to judicial review actions.

POST-STORM INSURANCE CLAIMS

A tree fell on the roof of our house and damaged the roof during hurricane Ophelia. Some slates from the roof then fell onto our neighbour's car and damaged it. The gates at the entrance to our house were also damaged. My garage door won't open. I am hoping our home insurance policy covers the cost of the repairs. Furthermore, our mobile home in Wexford and our children's school was damaged. Will my household policy extend to my mobile home?

It will all depend on the type of insurance cover you signed up for, and the terms and conditions of same. An insurance policy is personal to you. It's a legally binding contract between the contracting parties who are bound to comply with the terms agreed. Contact your broker or insurance company and, in the meantime, watch out for any electric wires. A storm is seen as an Act of God and that is the legal term often used as a defence. There is usually a strict time limit within which to claim and 30 days is standard in the industry.

Some people prefer to engage a broker when organising insurance cover as opposed to purchasing straight from the internet. The broker may get commission from the insurance company. Get independent legal advice if you are unsure. If you are even one day out of cover, then that's that. The insurance company will not cover you if you are outside the date at which cover expires.

If you have a claim and you are unhappy with your insurance company's response or the advice they are giving you, then it may be worth your while engaging a claims handling company.

As slates have fallen onto your neighbour's car, then your neighbour can claim under his own motor policy. It will depend on whether he has fully comprehensive insurance or third party insurance. Fully comprehensive will usually cover damage to a car if a tree falls on it and breaks the windscreen. This may also be covered by your household insurance policy as it is your fault. Again, it would depend on the terms and conditions of your policy. Gates are generally excluded from household policies. Garage doors on the other hand are generally included. If you have a shed beside your house or even a short drive from your house, tell the insurance company at the time of entering into the agreement for cover in order to have your policy extended to cover domestic outbuildings.

If your household policy is extended to cover mobile homes, then you are covered. You must inform your insurance company at the time of signing the contract that you want the mobile home included on the policy. So whether you are covered for the mobile home or not depends on the terms you agreed at the time.

If you have a claim, your insurance may well creep up in price next year.

Your school should contact the Department of Education regarding damage to schools after a hurricane or severe storm.

Tree removal after a storm depends on the policy. If something is broken, most people may want to try and fix it or have it fixed as soon as possible, possibly even before the insurers come out to assess it. Take photographs first, keep receipts and video recordings before you clean up as evidence for the insurance company.

As a general rule, a land owner or occupier is responsible for ensuring that trees are safe from falling branches and they are generally liable for any loss or damage resulting from falling trees. However, tree damage caused during stormy weather is usually considered a natural event and the land owner or occupier may not be considered liable. In terms of damage to property or injuries caused as a result of trees or branches falling in non-stormy weather liability of the land owner or occupier will depend on the condition of the tree before it fell.

For further information, I would recommend contacting the Citizens' Information Centre and your insurance providers.

BUYING A HOME — LENDING FOR NON-FIRST TIME BUYERS OF A PRIMARY DWELLING HOME OR A NON-PRIMARY DWELLING HOME

I recently moved back to Ireland after spending many years in Dubai working as a teacher. I owned my own home in Dubai which I sold before I left and bought another in Dubai. Thankfully, I have secured a permanent job as a teacher in a local school here and I am now in a position to purchase a house again. I am contemplating whether or not to be the owner-occupier of the house or whether I should just keep it as a holiday home or rent it out and live with my parents. I have saved a 10 % deposit. Will I qualify as a first-time buyer in Ireland as I have not bought a property here before? I am single and therefore I will be making a single mortgage application.

There was good news recently for first-time buyers, as the Central Bank agreed to reduce deposits from 20% to 10%, regardless of the price of the property. Therefore,

1. Buying or Selling a House, and Property Law Queries

first-time buyers will now be able to borrow up to 90% of the price of their new home. This took effect from 1 January 2017. Regrettably, due to the fact that you bought a property in Dubai, you will not be considered as a first-time buyer when you purchase a property in Ireland. A first-time buyer is defined as a buyer who has never purchased a property in Ireland or abroad. The can be exemptions in regard to this, for instance in certain family law proceedings the revenue may take a person as a first time buyer.

There are different limits for different categories of buyers. For non-first time buyers of primary dwelling homes, a limit of 80% loan-to-value applies on new mortgage lending, that is, banks are only allowed to lend up to 80% of the value of the property to owner-occupiers. Therefore you may need a 20% deposit for a house, as you do not qualify as a first-time buyer. Some banks may allow part of the 20% deposit requirement to be provided by a gift, but this will vary and you should check this with your bank first. You did not mention the price of the house but, if it is under €220,000, some banks may lend you up to 90%. You mention that you are single, so please note that loans may be limited to 3.5 times your income. Confirm this with your lending institution. Lending for non-primary dwelling home purchase can be considered more risky for the lender. Central Bank research shows that buy–to-let mortgages are more likely to be in arrears. Therefore a limit of 70% LTV applies. The LTV limits do not apply to borrowers in negative equity applying for a mortgage for a new property. However, lenders may still opt to apply stricter lending standards, based on their assessment of each case. It is imperative that you make an appointment with your lending institution before making any decision.

BUSINESS RATES

What are business rates?

Business rates are a tax on businesses that occupy commercial premises and are payable to the local authority. The charge you pay depends on the rateable value of your property, which is assessed by the valuation office. The Valuation Act 2001 introduced a national programme to revalue all commercial property in Ireland. The Act was amended by the Valuation (Amendment) Act 2015 which further refines the revaluation and appeals process. The revaluation is intended to bring more equity, fairness and transparency into the local authority rating system by creating a closer relationship between modern rental values and commercial rates payable.

It is important when you buy commercial premises to ensure you have them measured or assessed for rates at the time you purchase them to ensure you are not paying rates on a part of the property not being used for commercial purposes.

If rates are due and you don't pay same after several reminders from the council, they are open to issuing legal proceedings against you.

Chapter 2

Renting and Renters: The Law Involved in Renting a Property

Tenancy Agreements: Joint Tenancy v Tenancy In Common

My friend and I live in Roscommon town. We both have three children who are planning to go to college in Dublin in the next couple of years. We are therefore thinking of buying a house for them to use in Dublin as we both feel that this would be a better option for them than paying rent and it would also be nice to have an asset in the city that will increase in value. Is there anything specific that we should be looking at in terms of the legal side of things?

I presume that you have done your research into the market and you now have a preferred location with good public transport links to the colleges your children have chosen and that you either have the finances to fund the purchase or have secured mortgage approval for the purchase of a property. I am also presuming that you have investigated the various incentive schemes such as the Living City Initiative for investment regarding Special Regeneration Areas in Dublin, Cork, Limerick, Galway, Waterford and Kilkenny. I will therefore not be dealing with location, finance and incentive schemes in the short space I have here.

In Ireland, there are two ways of owning property together (if we are to leave aside any equitable/legal rights in regard to transfers, as set out in the Family Home Protection Act, 1976 and subsequent additions in regard to civil partners and some rights accrued by co-habitants under the Civil Partnership and Certain Rights and Obligations of Cohabitants Act, 2010). The first way is by 'joint tenancy' and the other way is by being a 'tenant in common'. Tenancy is used in these terms as a technical term designating ownership of property and should not be confused with a rental agreement. In joint tenancy, the owners own the property together in undivided shares and, if one dies, the remaining owners continue to own the property without the deceased. This pattern continues until the joint tenancy is severed (by agreement/court order to end the joint tenancy) or the remaining joint tenant gains the whole property by right of survivorship (that is, he is the last one alive). In a tenancy in common, the part owners own the property by specific shares, for example 50/50 or 30/70 or 40/30/10. The tenants can hold unequal shares whilst, in a joint tenancy, everyone is equal. In the event of the death of a part owner in a tenancy in common, the share which the deceased owner owned will form part of his or her estate. This estate is what remains of his or her assets which are distributed in accordance with his or her will (last will and testament). If the deceased owner has not made a will, that is he or she has died 'intestate', their assets will be distributed under the rules of intestacy as set out in the Succession Act 1965. We would always advise one to make a will, but it is not a requirement of owning property.

In your case, we would advise that the property is purchased as tenants in common. This will ensure that your share in the house will go to whoever you wish in your will. That is assuming you do not want your share to go to your friend on your death.

I also strongly advise you to enter into a co-ownership agreement with your friend. This is a comprehensive formal legal agreement setting out rules for how the property will be maintained, paid for and eventually sold. The logic of agreeing to this in advance of entering into any such arrangement is that there is full clarity as to what happens in specific circumstances as previously mentioned, and you can also include what happens on the death of one of the co-owners.

While I appreciate that your main focus is to avoid the 'dead money' of rent, you should be made aware that, when you go to sell the property, whatever gain (in terms of capital appreciation, that is a rise in the value of the asset) you have made will be subject to Capital Gains Tax since it will not be your principal private residence (Capital Gains Tax being a tax on the increase in value of the property). Normally this tax is not charged on the house you live in, which is called your principal private residence. You should keep records of all costs involved in the purchase and improvement of the property so that they may be offset against the eventual sale of the property. These costs could include your legal costs in buying and selling the property, and your selling agent's fees. Improvements to the property not considered general maintenance can also be offset.

Finally, you should look at whether it is in your best interests to buy the properties in your own names. This is a concept that would not occur to most people. It may be better to buy using a company structure. Companies may be purchased from an agent who specialises in the registration of companies, or may be done through your solicitors or, if you are very brave/foolhardy, with the Companies Registration Office. At present there are tax benefits regarding rental income for companies, in that Corporation Tax is currently lower than Income Tax, and a company can offset income in more tax-efficient ways than an individual. If you buy the property in your own names, the law may look on the arrangement as two persons carrying out a business together, meaning a partnership in accordance with the Partnership Act 1890. A partnership agreement should be considered. You may wish to consult your solicitors about setting up a partnership agreement. Also the type of partnership structure should be considered. The partnership/co-ownership agreement should provide details of what happens in all circumstances, including if something were to go wrong.

2. Renting and Renters: The Law Involved in Renting a Property

RENTAL CONTRACTS – PAYING THE DEPOSIT

I am 18 years old. I am starting college in Galway in September. I am very excited and getting everything organised at the moment. My main concern is accommodation because I understand there is a shortage of rental properties. I was looking online and found a beautiful house available for rent beside the college at a price I can afford. I emailed the landlord and he said he was happy to rent the property to me as soon as I transfer my deposit and first month's rent to him. He lives abroad and said I can simply use a money-wiring service to transfer the money and then he would send the keys on to me. I was delighted and told my dad, who said it sounds a bit like a scam. What should I do?

I agree with your dad. I would never transfer money to a stranger via a money-wiring service. You cannot trace the payment and have no comeback if it's a scam. Scammers are aware of the shortage of student accommodation and it's a perfect opportunity for them to try taking money from vulnerable students. First, go to Galway and view the property. Does it even exist and, if it does, who owns it? Find out if it is, indeed, available for rent, because some scammers put up fake profiles of houses online. Arrange a viewing and inspect the property. I would only pay a deposit when face-to-face with someone. While we are all familiar with the internet, as you are aware, there are a lot of scammers online and you should be extra-cautious when handing over money. The landlord can arrange for someone to meet you on his behalf. If possible, bring your dad with you or another adult you know well. Do not make any payments until you have been given the keys and have signed a rental contract. The rental contract is most important because it sets out all the terms and conditions of the tenancy. When both sides have signed and exchanged the rental contracts, you can then pay by cheque or bank draft, both of which are traceable if something goes wrong. If you are paying through an estate agent, it may have the facility to enable payment by credit card. Check the terms and conditions of your card. Some credit card agreements have a facility whereby the money may be refundable if it is a scam.

A rental contract is standard when renting most property (long-term or short-term) in Ireland, with the exception of digs/rent a room scheme because one is renting part of their home while the landlord is still in occupation. A standard contract must contain the address of the accommodation, the names and addresses of the landlord and/or the letting agent, the tenant's name, the length of the tenancy, the amount of rent due and when and how it is to be paid, details of any other charges that are not included in the rental fee, the deposit to be paid, the conditions under which the contract may be revoked, the basic rights of the tenant and the landlord and an inventory of items included with the accommodation. Tenants' rights are set out in the Residential Tenancies Act 2004, as amended. Under this Act, a tenant has the right to a property that is in good condition, that is, it must be structurally sound, have hot and cold water and adequate heating. The electricity and gas supply must be in good repair and all appliances must be working. The landlord can only enter the property with the tenant's permission, unless every attempt has been made to contact the tenant. The tenant must be told about any increase in rent and the tenant must be able to contact the landlord or an authorised agent at any reasonable time. The tenant must be paid back money from the landlord for any required repairs the tenant carried out on the property that he or she asked the landlord to fix but which the landlord did not carry out within a reasonable time. The tenant must be given a valid notice of termination before the end of the tenancy. The tenant may refer any disputes to the Residential Tenancies Board. The RTB has replaced the courts for landlord and tenant disputes and has a quasi-judicial role, with many of the powers of the courts. You do not need legal representation to make a complaint to the Residential Tenancies Board. The board remains strictly impartial and does not provide advice to either party in dispute, beyond general information. Since 1993, and the introduction of the Housing (Rent Books) Regulations, landlords must provide tenants with a written lease and rent book which records all of the above, and records all rental payments made. Ask your landlord for an emergency contact number for him or her, and establish when or if your landlord will have access to the premises while you are renting it. Confirm who is responsible for the cost of maintenance or repairs. As you are going to rent in Galway, there is a Threshold Advice Centre there (5 Prospect Hill, Galway H91 HC1H) or email advicegalway@threshold.ie. This organisation publishes information leaflets to help you find suitable accommodation. Rent is usually payable monthly in advance with an initial upfront deposit as security. Best wishes with your future studies.

RENT A ROOM RELIEF SCHEME

My daughter has moved to Australia. Her bedroom is vacant and I would like to rent it out to a private tenant, possibly a student. Can I rent a room in my house and receive tax-free rental income?

Under the Rent a Room Relief Scheme, which started in 2013, the rental income a home owner receives for renting a room in their home will be tax-free, provided the income from the rent does not exceed €14,000 in a tax year. Renting a room to a person is covered under this scheme. To avoid most of the obligations and responsibilities of landlord and tenant law, the rental accommodation you are providing must be a room in your house, rather than a self-contained unit/flat. Tenants living in your home are living under a "licence agreement" and are entitled to only reasonable notice if you decide to terminate the agreement. A licence agreement means that the arrangement can be terminated in accordance with the terms of a written contract/licence. I would advise you to set out some terms in writing to avoid confusion and make it clear from the outset to your tenant what you expect. The terms of the agreement should include the amount of rent payable and how often and by what means it is paid (that is, cash, cheque or monthly standing order to your account), notice periods should either party wish to end the tenancy, house rules and arrangements regarding the payment of utility bills or any other terms you might consider necessary or appropriate. If you are providing "digs" (the term "digs" usually refers to an arrangement where food is also provided with the accommodation), you can take into account the cost of food.

In order to qualify for rent-a-room relief, you must actually occupy the property as your sole residence during the year of assessment, but you do not have to own the property. You could be a tenant and sub-let to another person with your landlord's permission.

A self-contained unit, such as a basement flat or a converted garage attached to your home, can also qualify for this relief. However, renting out a self-contained unit is covered by landlord and tenant legislation. Under this legislation you are obliged to register the tenancy with the Residential Tenancies Board, provide a rent book to the tenant and ensure the accommodation meets reasonable standards. A reasonable standard of accommodation would include secure accommodation, and the unit should have its own bathroom and access to light and heat. In the event of a dispute, HSE health inspectors are normally employed through local county councils and they can inspect the property to see if it meets reasonable living standards. Tenants may qualify for Housing Assistance Payment or Rent Supplement in some circumstances and they may be entitled to claim tax relief on rent they pay to you. One can also refer any disputes that arise to the Small Claims Court which is, in effect, a small claims procedure service provided by the District Court. Any dispute in a landlord and tenant agreement goes to the Residential Tenancies Board.

The income you receive from the scheme is not liable to PRSI, the Universal Social Charge or Income Tax, but it must be included on your annual income tax return if you are self-employed. The scheme does not apply to renting a room to your son or daughter. It will not affect your widow's/widower's pension — that is the pension you get if your spouse dies — or the state pension, but it will be assessed as means if you are getting means-tested social assistance payments.

SECURITY OF TENURE FOR PRIVATE TENANTS

I own a few properties in Dublin which I have been renting to the same tenants since 2012. They are great tenants who always pay the rent on time and never give me any trouble. I have not increased the rent during this time and they have never mentioned leaving. Are there any new developments in tenancy law I should be aware of, should there ever be a need to terminate the tenancy?

I understand it can sometimes be difficult to get good tenants, and it appears from your query that you are happy with the tenants you have. You may be unaware that, in the intervening years, the government has brought in legislation that controls the amount of rent you can increase for your tenants, and rules regarding termination of tenancies.

Some would say this unfairly discriminates against good landlords who have not increased the rent for several years. As far as we are aware, the legislation has not been constitutionally tested and as such it is as set out below.

The Planning and Development (Housing) and Residential Tenancies Act 2016 applies to all tenancies created from 24 December 2016. It extended the period of a 'part 4 tenancy' from four years to six years. A part 4 tenancy gave tenants the right to stay in rented accommodation for up to four years following an initial six-month period (Residential Tenancies Act, 2004). The 2016 Act changed the rules on termination of an extended part 4 tenancy, with effect from 17 January 2017. Therefore, once a part 4 tenancy comes into existence, it can only be terminated if:

- there has been a failure to comply with obligations under the tenancy, such as payment of rent;
- the dwelling is no longer suitable to the needs of the occupying household. This would be on the facts of the case, for instance if a one-bedroom apartment was rented to a single person and the person is now living there with a spouse and a number of children, the accommodation may be deemed unsuitable. In the event of a dispute, this would be determined by the Residential Tenancies Board;
- the landlord intends to sell the dwelling within three months of the termination date, that is, three months from the date the notice is served;
- the landlord requires the dwelling for his own or family member occupation;
- vacant possession is required for substantial refurbishment of the dwelling; or
- the landlord intends to change the use of the dwelling.

As your tenants have been renting your property for over six months and you have not served them with a valid notice of termination or had any need to do so, they acquire 'security of tenure' and can stay in the property for a number of years. As the tenancy started on or before 24 December 2016, this period is four years. If the tenancy started after 24 December 2016, this period is six years. After the first six months, the tenancy became known as a 'part 4 tenancy' because it was brought in by part 4 of the Residential Tenancies Act 2004. If the tenants have a fixed-term lease and they wish to remain in the property, they have to claim the part 4 tenancy in writing between one and three months before the expiry of the fixed-term tenancy or lease agreement. If the tenant fails to do this, he or she does not lose the right to a part 4 tenancy, but may have to compensate the landlord for any financial loss incurred by the landlord due to the tenant's failure to inform him within the set time of the intention to remain in the property. A fixed-term lease agreement has a specific starting and ending date, which is decided by both the landlord and tenant. The head office of Threshold located at 21 Stoneybatter, Dublin 7, provides a template that tenants may use when claiming a part 4 tenancy in writing.

After the first cycle of the part 4 tenancy has ended, a new tenancy begins. A further part 4 tenancy can arises under the same circumstances as outlined above. The landlord could end this tenancy at any time in the first six months of the tenancy without having to give a reason but, with effect from 17 January 2017, the landlord can terminate the tenancy only in the limited circumstances outlined above.

COMMERCIAL LEASES: RECEIVER SALE, NOT CONSENTING TO ASSIGNMENT (CAFÉ EN SEINE CASE)

I have run a restaurant business successfully for a number of years. However, I now want to sell the lease. The landlord said he will buy it back from me for a pittance of what it is worth on the open market and that, if I don't take his offer, I will not be allowed to sell it to anyone else.

A recent high-profile case in the High Court dealt with a similar issue to your own, in that a landlord was deemed to be withholding his consent so that he might take back the leasehold interest. Let us look at this case in more detail and then we shall try to apply the reasoning of the High Court's decision to the facts of your own case.

The case of *Perfect Pies Ltd v Chupn Ltd* (2015) IEHC 692 concerned Café en Seine (a nightclub/public house) on Dawson Street in Dublin city centre and businessman Louis Fitzgerald, and addressed issues in relation to assignment of leases, that is, the transfer of the lease from one tenant to another. The first-named plaintiff (that is, the person initiating the court action), Perfect Pies, was a tenant and the second-named plaintiff was the receiver over its leasehold interest in Café en Seine (the receiver was appointed by a bank, due to a default in a loan the first-named plaintiff had with the bank). As you are perhaps aware, a commercial lease can be sold during its term for value and therefore a bank can take out a loan and can appoint a receiver on this type of asset. The defendant was a company controlled by the Fitzgerald group called Chupn Ltd, which controls a number of pubs and was the landlord of the Café en Seine premises.

The receiver wished to sell the leasehold interest in Café en Seine (as well as the leases to the George, Howl at the Moon and the Dragon, which are also well known pubs in Dublin) to recover money owed to Allied Irish Banks, and so the receiver lined up a buyer. The receiver and Perfect Pies sought the landlord's consent to the assignment of the lease - that is, there was a clause in the lease that allowed the tenant to transfer its interest to another tenant as long as the landlord agreed, but the landlords refused to give their consent to the transfer. However, the lease contained clauses providing that the landlord's consent could not be unreasonably withheld. Section 66(2) of the Landlord and Tenant (Amendment) Act 1980 also provides that the landlord's consent to assign the lease shall not be unreasonably withheld. The onus of proving that consent has been unreasonably withheld is on the tenant to show that no reasonable landlord would have refused consent in the circumstances. This is proved through evidence in court. The proofs would include that the tenant taking over the lease has a good record in running such an establishment, that the tenant is solvent and that the tenant's proposal for the use of the space is in accordance with the terms in the lease (if the lease specifies that a public house/night club should be run from the premises, then the new tenant should not be proposing to run a hardware shop from same).

Initially the reasons given by the landlord for the refusal to consent to the assignment were that the tenant was in breach of the covenant to repair, that is, the tenant in accordance with the terms of the lease had not up kept the premises as he should have. The landlord later contended that it had concerns about the reliability of the sureties being offered for the proposed assignee — in other words, the landlord was concerned as to whether the new tenant had the financial means to pay the rent and run the business. The High Court judge in this case was Mr Justice Haughton and he held that it would be unreasonable for a landlord to refuse consent on the basis of dilapidations, which the proposed assignee was agreeable to remedy (that is, the premises requiring repairs alone was not a sufficient ground to withhold consent to the transfer, especially under circumstances where the new tenant was agreeable to repair same). He further found that the defendant had refused to consider the request for consent to assignment of the lease because it had an ulterior motive, namely to acquire Café en Seine itself.

Haughton J granted a declaration that the landlord had acted unreasonably in refusing to consent to the assignment of the lease. However, he declined to dispense with the requirement for the defendant's consent to the assignment because "had the defendant given due and proper consideration to the application for consent to assignment, it would have been reasonable to refuse consent on a number of grounds related to shortcomings in the sureties offered and the financial references provided". In other words, there was uncertainty as to the financial means of the new tenant. In the absence of proof of that tenant's means, the judge stated it would be unreasonable for him to rule that the landlord had to give his consent. He ruled that the landlord should have the opportunity to review the financial means of the proposed tenant.

If we apply the facts of this case to your situation, and if you find a willing, solvent assignee of the lease, the landlord cannot withhold his consent simply because he wants to acquire the leasehold interest himself. This would not be seen as a reasonable ground for refusing an assignment.

COMMERCIAL LEASES: BREACH OF PLANNING AND FIRE SAFETY (CAMIVEO V DUNNES STORES [2017] 3 JIC 0209)

I am a commercial leaseholder. I have no trouble paying the rent. I want to build a store outside the back of the premises I am leasing. I have been told that the size of the store would need planning permission. However, the backs of all the other adjacent buildings have been extended and I don't think the planning authority would notice or care if I built out the back. I don't want to go to the expense of applying for planning permission. I know if I got caught, the authorities could make me take down the store or apply for retention permission, but I am willing to take this chance. Would I encounter, in your opinion, any difficulties with my landlord, in that I think there is a clause in the lease that I must comply with all laws of the country, including planning permission?

A recent decision of the High Court may be helpful in determining the trouble you may become involved in if you breach a term (usually referred to as a covenant) in the lease. You might well have a vigilant landlord who is determined to keep you to the terms of the lease.

The courts considered among other things commercial leases and a breach of the planning application in the case of *Camiveo v Dunnes Stores* [2017] IEHC 147. In May 2015, Camiveo Ltd obtained summary judgment (summary judgment is a procedural device used during civil litigation to dispose promptly of a case without a trial when there is no dispute as to the material facts of the case and a party is entitled to judgment as a matter of law) from the Supreme Court in respect of non-payment of rent by Dunnes Stores. In response to that, Dunnes Stores disabled the automatic opening mechanism for a set of doors into its store in the Eyre Square shopping centre in Galway. These doors were used by the public as a quick way of getting into the shopping centre by crossing through Dunnes Stores from Eyre Square. In fact, they were used so much that they became regarded as the main way of getting into the shopping centre from Eyre Square. In September 2015, the High Court granted the landlord of the shopping centre (Camiveo Ltd) an interlocutory injunction (that is, a court order by which an individual is required to perform, or is restrained from performing, a particular act) ordering Dunnes Stores to keep the doors open pending the trial.

A significant part of the judgment focused on the question of whether closing the doors was in breach of the applicable planning permission and the judge in this case, Barrett J, held that, by closing the doors, Dunnes Stores had breached the planning permission and had thereby breached a covenant in the lease to comply with all applicable planning permissions. The Court also concluded that closing the doors was a breach of the covenants in the lease relating to fire safety. The landlord also provided evidence that it had been advised by the insurer that, if a claim arose by reason of the doors being closed, the insurer would most likely refuse to meet the claim. On this basis, Barrett J held that Dunnes Stores was in breach of the covenant prohibiting it from doing anything which would lead to the insurance policy becoming void or voidable. The Court further concluded that closure of the doors constituted a breach of a clause in the lease requiring the tenant to obtain the landlord's prior written consent to any non-structural alterations to the premises.

The Court granted a permanent injunction restraining Dunnes Stores from disabling the doors during the opening hours of the shopping centre, as well as a series of other orders requiring Dunnes Stores to comply with specific covenants in the lease.

In the above case, the tenant, Dunnes Stores, did an act that was deemed in breach of planning permission. The landlord had the right to stop the tenant from breaching planning permission and had the right to make the tenant comply with planning permission. If we apply this logic to your own case (considering the terms of your lease would be similar to Dunnes), it may be deduced that, if you build the store, the landlord can make you take it down. If you refuse, the landlord can bring you to court and there is a recent decision of the High Court which other judges from the High Court down, to include District Court and Circuit Court, are obliged to follow. This means it would be highly unadvisable to proceed with your intentions without getting the consent of your landlord first and planning permission from the local authority.

COMMERCIAL LEASES: NOTICE OF TERMINATION (THE CARRAIG DONN CASE, 2015)

I own a mixed-use property in a small town in the midlands. Downstairs there is a hairdressers and upstairs there is an apartment. The hairdressers got into financial difficulty during the recession and I agreed to a temporary reduction in rent to help them out. We agreed that if I got someone else to take over the shop within a year of the reduction of rent commencing, I could serve a notice to quit and the hairdressers would give up the lease. I served the notice, but now the hairdressers are claiming that they are entitled to a new lease at a lower rent.

Interestingly enough, a very similar case to yours came before the Supreme Court in 2015. In *Stapleside Company v Carraig Donn Retail Ltd* (2015) IESC 60, the defendant leased a retail unit in the Crescent shopping centre in Limerick from the plaintiff under a 25-year lease, which commenced in 2001. In 2009, the defendant encountered some financial difficulties and negotiated a reduced rent. The parties agreed that the defendant would pay 33% less rent for one year, and that the plaintiff would have the option of taking a surrender of the lease, that is, the landlord could take back the lease on the unit and rent it out to someone else, on 90 days' notice. Later that year, the plaintiff served what purported to be a notice of termination on the defendant. The defendant regarded the lease as being at an end and invoked its right to seek a new tenancy under part 2 of the Landlord and Tenant (Amendment) Act 1980. This gives tenants a right to renew a lease when their old lease has expired. The plaintiff contended that the defendant had lost its right to a new tenancy by reason of the 2009 agreement. Section 17(1)(a)(iii) of the 1980 Act precludes a right to a new tenancy where the tenant has surrendered the lease.

One of the judges in this case, Clarke J in the Supreme Court, found that the plaintiff had no entitlement to terminate the lease and, furthermore, the defendant had not in fact surrendered its lease nor had it been ordered by the Court to do so.

2. Renting and Renters: The Law Involved in Renting a Property

Therefore, the lease continued to subsist, meaning that the original high rent was applicable to the property.

If we apply the facts of this Supreme Court judgment to your situation, it would seem that you would be allowed to raise the rent back to what it was. The Court found that there was no termination of the lease in the case and therefore a new lease did not come into existence. If the tenant does not pay the full rent, you would have a right under the terms of the lease to terminate the lease and take legal action against the tenant for recovery of rent owing to you.

When terminating the lease, you must adhere strictly to the terms contained in the lease. It is advisable to have legal advice from the start of the process, since the termination is quite technical and all conditions in the lease should be complied with in full. Even if everything is done right, the tenant may still over-hold, that is, stay in the property, which would require you to serve ejectment proceedings through the courts. If the matter did go to court, you would have to prove every step of the termination was done in accordance with the terms in the lease.

SPECIFIC PERFORMANCE: THE GLOBE BAR & RÍ RÁ NIGHTCLUB, GEORGE'S STREET

I was going to buy a property and I negotiated the transaction directly with the vendor himself. We took a note of our agreement, putting down the property he had agreed to sell to me, the price of the property we had agreed on and the timeframe within which the property would be purchased. We both signed the agreement. The seller's solicitor was to draft contracts, so the deal could be finalised. In the meantime, the property next door to the one I was buying came up on the market for half the price. I want to try and get out of the agreement since I have haven't signed anything with my solicitor. Will I be able to do so? The vendor had initially said he would get someone else to buy the property, but now he has come back to say that he wants me to buy it. We had agreed in our note that the matter would close within six weeks. It is now over two months, so surely, even if somebody was to take our note as a contract, the vendor is in breach of same in that he went off and offered the property to others and he did not close the sale in the agreed timeframe?

In a situation like you describe, the remedy of specific performance may be available to the vendor since you have signed an agreement. In simple terms, specific performance is the ability of either party to an agreement regarding property to force the other to purchase/sell it.

The law around specific performance was addressed by the courts in a number of recent cases.

Globe Entertainment Ltd v Pub Pool Ltd (2015) IEHC 115 addressed this issue where a case was brought by a prospective purchaser where the proposed sale fell through. The well-known Globe Bar and Rí Rá nightclub on South Great George's Street,

Dublin, were owned by Pub Pool Ltd, and the company had gone into receivership. The businessman and publican Sean Doyle wanted to buy the Globe Bar on South Great George's Street, Dublin. First, he had to settle or refinance a few debts with Bank of Scotland and Ulster Bank in the region of €73 million. Doyle had a series of meetings with Ulster Bank on a without prejudice basis, (that is, the meetings were only to discuss matters, until such time as a formal agreement was reached. None of the negotiations or representations made can be relied on or used in a court of law) and agreed in principle to offer to buy the Globe for €2.3 million, subject to acceptance by the receiver, proof of funds by Doyle and agreement as to a closing date.

In the meantime, a higher bid was made by the property developer Greg Kavanagh. The receiver, who had as yet had not received a signed contract from Doyle, accepted the higher bid. Doyle sued the bank and the receiver seeking specific performance.

In the High Court, the judge, Costello J, noted that it had been the receiver — and not the bank — who had been selling the premises, and that Sean Doyle was aware of this fact. He refused to grant specific performance. Doyle had made an agreement with the bank directly. The receiver was the person in control of the property. In the law of mortgages/loans, while the receiver is appointed by the bank, he is meant to be acting for the person who is in default of their loan. This is in reality a legal fiction in that the person in default has no control over the receiver and the receiver answers to the bank/lender. Doyle appealed the decision of the High Court to the Court of Appeal and the Court, which is made up of a panel of judges, upheld the refusal of the High Court to grant specific performance. Geoghegan J stated that, where a party was relying on a series of documents alleged to comprise a note, it was essential to prove that the negotiations between the parties had "ripened into the fullness of an entire contract". The judge basically stated that, for a contract to exist where no formal contract was signed, the written documentation had to unequivocally prove the parties had finished their negotiations and had an agreement to sell/purchase the property.

Others recent cases to note in terms of specific performance include *Wynn Clons Developments Ltd v Cooke* ((2016) IECA 317), where the Court of Appeal said that a vendor does not lose the right to sue for specific performance merely by exploring the possibility of reselling the property to a different purchaser. In this case, sale was agreed and a contract signed, but the purchasers later tried to pull out. The vendor then went ahead and sought alternative purchasers but, by doing this, the vendor did not lose the right to sue for specific performance against the initial purchaser. In *Mac A'Bhaird v Commissioners of Public Works* ((2016) IEHC 233), Baker J concluded that the purchaser did not have a right to rescind the contract by reason of the vendor's failure to complete within the 28-day period given. The vendor was now ready, willing and able to close, and no argument was made that the purchaser had not been afforded reasonable time to close. Consequently, the Court made an order for specific performance.

2. Renting and Renters: The Law Involved in Renting a Property

We can apply the facts of the above cases to your question in the following manner. The court will apply specific performance where there is a formal agreement in place, and it will not be swayed from applying this doctrine even in the case of delays and aborted sales to third parties. First, we note that you signed a piece of paper with the three P's on it, that is, the price, the parties and the property. Under Irish law, this is sufficient to bind parties to an agreement for the sale of property. This has been the case in Irish law since the Statute of Frauds was adopted into Irish law in 1695. This notion was renewed in the Conveyancing Act, 2009. Normally practitioners preface any note with such details with the heading 'Subject to contract/contract denied' and include a paragraph at the end of such a note specifically stating that the note is not a contract/agreement for sale of property. You have not provided any confirmation in your question that such phrases were used in your note and therefore, unless you can provide evidence to the contrary, we are taking the view that the note has the formal requirements to constitute a contract and be enforceable by specific performance.

The court will examine any such evidence that would contradict this conclusion but, on the facts given, it would be hard to conclude otherwise. As you can see from case law provided, the offering of the property to another does not stop the vendor from forcing you to purchase the property. In regard to the timeframe, this may provide a glimmer of hope if it could be proven the vendor was not ready and willing to close on time or within a reasonable length of time thereafter. This may breach a fundamental part of the contract and make it voidable but, again, we would need more detail from you.

Chapter 3

Family Law

Judicial Separation

My husband and I are separated. I moved out of the family home last year. However, we understand that we cannot get a divorce until after we are four years living apart. Are there any other legal options open to us? We have no interest in ever getting re-married. Although we are separating, we have remained friends and the separation will be amicable.

A judicial separation would suit you both best for now. You can get divorced later. One can get a judicial separation after living apart for 12 months. When both you and your spouse have filed all the necessary documents, you will be given a date for the court hearing.

A judicial separation does not entitle you to remarry. In order to get a judicial separation, you would first both be advised to instruct separate solicitors. Prepare a statement of all your assets and liabilities. Instruct your solicitor to serve court proceedings. Then instruct your solicitor to file the civil bill, affidavit of means and all other necessary papers. Your solicitor will apply for a hearing date. A judicial separation under Irish family law must be obtained in either the Circuit Court or High Court. An amicable agreement may be reached before court between the parties, in which case the settlement is presented to court for approval and a court order follows such approval. If a judicial separation cannot be reached amicably, then the matters in dispute in the judicial separation case must be heard before a judge, and the judge will decide.

Spouse's Consent to Sale of the Family Home

My husband and I are together over 20 years. He is an alcoholic, but I stayed with him for the sake of our five children. We do not have much money and our family home is in the name of my husband only. Now that the last of our children has moved out, my husband said we do not need the family home anymore and he is going to sell it. Can he do this? I really do not want to sell it as it is all we have.

The good news is that there is legislation in place to protect a spouse such as yourself in a situation like this. The Family Home Protection Act 1976 prevents one spouse from selling, mortgaging, leasing or transferring the family home without the consent of the other spouse. Therefore, your husband cannot legally sell your family home, lease, mortgage or transfer it without your prior consent in writing.

The requirement for your consent to sale in writing applies regardless of whether the home is owned jointly by you and your husband or, as in your case, the home is owned by/in the name of just your husband.

In conclusion, I would advise you to make it very clear to your husband that you do not wish to sell your family home, and furthermore that he cannot sell it without your written consent.

DIVORCE: DISSOLVING THE CONTRACT OF MARRIAGE IN IRELAND

I am separating from my husband. What are my legal options? What's the best way to legally separate?

While we hear of many cases in the media of Hollywood stars and multi-million dollar settlements, the reality for most couples when they separate is that they are both financially worse off. The reality is that it is more costly to run two households than one. When contemplating separating, it should be borne in mind that, the more the parties disagree in regard to the dissolution of the marriage, the greater the costs. An effort should be made at an early stage to resolve issues. Solicitors in Ireland are provided with strict rules in regard to providing information so that matters may be resolved as swiftly as possible.

The Irish legal system has adapted to marriage dissolution by providing three distinct methods of separating;

1. Decree of divorce
2. Judicial/legal separation
3. Separation agreement

A *decree of divorce* dissolves the contract of marriage and enables either party to re-marry. Divorce normally terminates certain rights such as succession and pension rights.

A separation agreement is, in effect, an agreement between the parties to vary the contract of marriage, allowing either party to go their separate way with provisions for assets of the marriage and dependants.

A *judicial/legal separation* is where the parties cannot agree and the matter is ruled upon by a judge of the Circuit Court or High Court, or where it is necessitated by the facts of the case that the matter is required to go before the courts (normally pension adjustment orders). It is obtainable after one year of living apart by agreement – it is in effect a divorce without the right to remarry.

Before commencing divorce proceedings, your solicitor must discuss the alternatives with you (a) such as the possibility of resolving the difficulties in your marriage,

3. Family Law

and furnish you with information in regard to accessing counselling. (b) If reconciliation is not a possibility, your solicitor should explain the possibility of consulting a qualified family mediator to negotiate in a non-adversarial manner the separation. (c) You can enter into a separation agreement, which is an agreement in writing between you and your spouse which may not require attendance at court (this can be done by a combination of mediation and your solicitor negotiating with your spouse's solicitor or by means of employing a third lawyer in a collaborative law negotiation) (d) judicial separation by way of court order (this is normal where the parties cannot come to an agreement, and what cannot be resolved will be decided on by the judge).

The Circuit or High Court can grant a decree of divorce if the judge is first satisfied that proper provision has been made for the spouses and dependent children and that there is no prospect of a reconciliation between the husband and wife. Proper provision depends on the circumstances of each individual case. The husband and wife must have lived apart for periods amounting to four of the previous five years. Divorce proceedings are commenced by issuing a family law civil bill and serving it on your spouse. This document must be accompanied by a sworn affidavit of means and (if there are dependent children) an affidavit of welfare. The affidavit of means lists all of your assets, debts and liabilities, income details, pension details and weekly/monthly expenditure. The affidavit must be supported with documentation such as bank statements, P60s and pay slips. The affidavit of welfare sets out all of the information in relation to dependent children, such as the living, care and access arrangements or any special needs. Try to have as much information as possible available for your solicitor to avoid delay. If the divorce is contested, then the respondent will file a defence and counterclaim. If an agreement is negotiated, then an application can be made to court for a date to have the consent divorce ruled. The court can make orders, known as ancillary reliefs, in relation to maintenance for the dependent spouse and children, custody and access to the dependent children, the right of residence/transfer/ownership or sale of the family home or any other property owned by the family, succession rights, life policies and pensions. The court will take into account the accommodation needs of the family, the contributions made, through work outside of or inside the home, to support the welfare of the family, the length of the marriage, the standard of living enjoyed by the family and the income, earning capacity and financial resources of the couple. If your spouse does not contest the application, it may take up to six months to secure a date to rule the consent divorce, depending on the court lists. If your spouse does contest the case, and once the defence and counterclaim is filed, a case progression hearing will be held by the County Registrar to determine what the outstanding issues are, and ascertain whether your case is ready to be allocated a trial date. After your case is dealt with in court, a divorce decree will be sent to you setting out the terms of your divorce. The decree declares legally that your marriage is dissolved.

Divorce – Proper Provision for Spouses and Dependent Children

I am a stay-at-home mother of four very young children. I am married to a wonderful man, a great father. Recently, I went on a parents' night out with other mothers from my children's school. One of the mothers said she had to speak with me and that was when I discovered for the first time that my husband had a mistress. I was shocked. I confronted him about it and he admitted everything. He's leaving me and our children to start a new life. I am worried for my own and my children's future financial security. My husband is quite well off financially.

I am very sorry to hear about this. How devastating it must be for you and your children. Before commencing divorce proceedings, your solicitor must consider the alternatives with you, such as the possibility of resolving the difficulties in your marriage. You will probably first want to discuss all your options with your husband. You might consider entering into a separation agreement, which is an agreement in writing between you and your husband which does not require attendance at court. Alternatively, there is the option of a judicial separation by way of court order. You might also consider negotiating the terms of your separation or divorce through traditional negotiation methods or collaborative law, which can be ruled in court by agreement.

I understand proper provision for you and your children is foremost on your mind. Proper provision is not defined and varies depending on the circumstances of each case. The court must take a number of factors into consideration to ensure the spouse and dependent children are properly provided for. The court can make orders, known as ancillary reliefs, in relation to custody of and access to the dependent children, maintenance for the dependent spouse and dependent children, the right of residence, ownership, transfer or sale of the family home, the ownership, transfer, sale of any other property owned by the couple, life policies and pensions and succession rights. The factors that the court will take into account include the income, earning capacity and financial resources of the couple, the standard of living enjoyed by the family, the ages of the spouses and length of the marriage, the contributions made, through work outside or within the home, to the welfare of the family, the conduct of either spouse and the accommodation needs of the family.

Therefore your work within the home caring for your children will be considered and the fact that your husband is well off financially. I hope it all works out well for you.

Collaborative Law – What is Collaborative Law?

I am separating from my husband. I hate the thoughts of going to court. Is there any other way around this? I don't have very much money.

Collaborative law is an alternative way of resolving family law matters, including separation and divorce. The general aim is for couples to try to resolve their difficulties in a civil and non-confrontational manner with the help of collaborative lawyers. It is a way of avoiding going to court. The parties will have to agree and be willing to be open and honest and disclose all information and assets. Meetings will be organised and the parties will be required to meet in a civil manner with a view to organising their relevant affairs, such as custody and access to children, maintenance and property rights. If the process is successful, then the parties have an agreement for which they both have responsibility. The agreement can be drawn into a deed of separation or used as a basis for a decree of divorce. If the collaborative process does not work out for you, then you can always go to court afterwards, but the collaborative lawyers you were dealing with will not represent you in court.

You mention that you are not well off financially. Therefore you may be eligible for legal aid and the Legal Aid Board can provide a lawyer trained in collaborative law for you.

MAINTENANCE FOR CHILDREN

I recently split up with my partner. He is now refusing to pay me maintenance towards the children of the relationship. He says that he has enough expenses now that he is living alone, and cannot afford to pay even though he is working full time. He also says that he provides for his children by bringing them out for meals and activities when he has access to them. We live in Leitrim.

While emotions are probably still raw after the breakdown of the relationship, if we can leave these to the side for the moment, there is clearly an immediate need for maintenance to be paid to you in regard to your children.

The District Court sitting in Carrick on Shannon or Manorhamilton is available to you to resolve this immediate pressing need if your partner is refusing to pay maintenance to you. Which court you attend will depend on where you are located in the county, and you should check with the court clerk in Carrick on Shannon or Sligo (or Manorhamilton) to see which court you are covered by. The court clerk can assist you in making an application for maintenance directly.

It is advisable that you are represented in court by a solicitor (although this is not a requirement and, if you so wish, you may represent yourself). If you do not have the means to employ a solicitor, you may apply to the Legal Aid Board for legal aid. Numerous solicitors in the county are on the private practitioners' panel which you can choose from. If you want to represent yourself, there are some support groups that may be of assistance to you and some will even attend court with you – enquiries should be made with the District Court clerk.

When you go to court, you will be required to show your income from all sources and your expenditure. An affidavit of means should be prepared by you. This is a sworn document (witnessed by a solicitor or court clerk normally) listing, on the one hand, your weekly income and, on the other, your weekly expenses. Both the income and expenditure should be proved by means of payslips and receipts of other payments for income and receipts for all outgoings. Bills that occur over the course of a month or a quarter should be apportioned down to a weekly level. The affidavit should be done in triplicate (one to keep, one for the judge and one for your partner or his solicitor).

On the day of court, your initials will be called out to see if your case is going on in what's call a "call over". Presuming that no agreement is reached, then your case will be called in turn. When your case is heard, there will be no one present in court except the judge and his official (called the registrar), yourself and your partner and the solicitors representing you and your partner. Journalists are not allowed in. The judge will simply ask for the facts of the case and he or she will listen to evidence from both parties, submissions made by the solicitors and then make a decision on the appropriate level of maintenance needed. You should note that, when giving evidence on the stand, your partner's solicitor or partner may ask you questions in regard to your income or expenditure. If you think that your husband will ignore the court order, you can ask that payments are made through the District Court office. After the case is heard by the judge and she or he has made a decision, the case may be adjourned for a number of months to check how the order is working out.

I hope the above is useful and you will have a suitable resolution of your case by whichever means you decide to proceed with.

Legislation for IVF Financial AID

We are struggling to afford IVF treatment. Is there any financial aid available for couples like us?

In October 2017, the Cabinet approved legislation to regulate assisted human reproduction, which should lead to financial aid for couples struggling to afford treatments, such as IVF. It is the first time regulation has been approved in the area of assisted reproduction.

Maintenance for Civil Partners and Spouses

Do I have a duty to support my civil partner financially?

Married couples and civil partners have a legal duty to help support one another financially. Whether maintenance is ordered from one party to another will often depend on the disparity and level of their respective incomes. Even if an agreement is reached without the need to make an application to the court, it is still important that any agreement is legally formalised. If not, there is a risk of financial claims being brought by either party at some later date, even after a divorce is finalised. If there is a change in your financial circumstances, you may seek to have any maintenance order or agreement varied. If there are any arrears in maintenance payments which are the subject of a court order, an application may be made to the District Court for the enforcement of the maintenance order. There are penalties for not complying with a maintenance order, including jail.

Maintenance Applications in the District Court

I do not live with the father of our child and I do not receive any maintenance from him. We were never married. I contacted him several times requesting financial support for our child, but he didn't respond positively. Is it possible for me to bring an application before the courts for maintenance? Will the application be heard in open court?

Both parents of a child have a legal obligation to maintain their child, regardless of whether they are married or unmarried, or whether they ever lived together or not. If both parents are unable to reach an agreement about maintenance, then an application may be brought before the District Court and the court will have to establish that the respondent failed to provide adequate maintenance, that is, money for the benefit of the dependent child. A dependent child is a child who is under 18 years of age (or under 23 years if in full-time education) or a child of any age who is dependent as a result of a disability. Maintenance applications are heard in private. The court will look at the child's requirements and the parent's means. This will include looking at the income of the parents, earning capacity, what property is held by either party, other financial resources including income or benefits to which either spouse or any children are entitled to under statute, the financial and other responsibilities of the spouses towards any dependent children of the family and the needs of dependent children, including their need for care and attention. The maximum maintenance that the court will order is €150 per child per week and €500 per week in the case of a spouse or civil partner. The court will also order how the payments are to be made, whether they are to be made on a weekly, fortnightly or monthly basis and whether the payments may be made through the court office or directly to the applicant. If maintenance payments fall into arrears, you can apply to the court for an enforcement order or an attachment of earnings order if the person paying the maintenance is employed. The penalty for not complying with a maintenance order can include a prison sentence.

Maintenance, Father's Name on Birth Certificate, One-Parent Family Payments

I have a three-year old daughter. I am not married to the father of my daughter and I do not live with him. However, I would like to receive financial assistance from my daughter's father. At the birth of my daughter, I did not put her father's name on the birth certificate and my daughter was registered in my name only. Does this mean I cannot get maintenance from him? Could I retrospectively apply to put his name on the birth certificate? I am in receipt of one-parent family payment. Would having my daughter's fathers name on her birth certificate prevent me from getting one-parent family payments? Will he have any rights over my daughter? I do not want him in my daughter's life on a regular basis.

A child has a right to be financially maintained by both parents and a right to inherit from both parents, once paternity of the child is established. This applies regardless of whether or not the father's name is on the child's birth certificate. If you put the father's name on the birth certificate, this will not stop you from getting one-parent family payments, and having the father's name on the birth certificate does not give the father any rights in respect of his child.

You may re-register the birth in order to have the father's details included. You will have to get the father's consent in order to do this. If he agrees, you may both go to the local registrar's office and register, or you can go by yourself, provided you have a statutory declaration with you, signed by the father and swearing he is the father.

Case Progression in a Family Law Matter

I am involved in a family law case. Recently I was summoned to attend a case progression hearing. What does this mean?

Case progression is the term given to the management of a case before it comes to trial to ensure that proceedings are prepared in a manner which is fair, efficient and likely to keep the costs as low as possible. In family law cases in Ireland, most case progression hearings take place in the Circuit Court. A hearing takes place before the County Registrar after court proceedings have issued. The solicitors for both parties and the parties themselves attend. Each party to the case must complete a detailed questionnaire which helps identify any issues the parties are disputing, and whether any further pleadings are needed.

The County Registrar oversees the preparation of the case for trial. The registrar establishes what steps need to be taken to prepare the case for trial and sets a timetable for the steps to be completed. It's basically a stepping stone to ensure the parties are prepared and organised for trial.

GUARDIANSHIP AND STEP-CHILDREN

I have a step-daughter. Can I become a legal guardian to my step-daughter?

Guardianship means the rights and duties of parents in respect of the upbringing of their children. Guardians have the right to make all major decisions affecting the child's upbringing, and they are responsible for the welfare of the child. The natural mother of a child is automatically the guardian of the child. In marriage, the husband is automatically the guardian of his natural child.

In certain circumstances, a step-parent, a civil partner or a person who has co-habited with a parent for not less than three years may apply to the court to become a guardian where they have co-parented the child for more than two years. A person who has provided for the child's day-to-day care for a continuous period of more than a year may apply for guardianship if the child has no parent or guardian who is willing or able to exercise the rights and responsibilities of guardianship. Most applications for guardianship are made through the District Court.

GUARDIANSHIP RIGHTS FOR UNMARRIED FATHERS

I have a three-year-old child and I would like to apply for guardianship rights. I am not married to my child's mother.

In Ireland, a mother of a child is an automatic guardian of that child. However, the same does not apply to a father of a child who is not married to the child's mother. In order for a father of a child to obtain guardianship rights, he must either:

a) Sign a statutory declaration for guardianship with the mother of the child. This declaration must be witnessed by a solicitor or commissioner for oaths. This declaration states the name of both parents, that they are unmarried and that they agree to the father being appointed as joint guardian. Then they become joint guardians of the child. The declaration also states that the parents have agreed arrangements regarding custody and access.

b) Seek a court order for guardianship. If the mother does not agree to the father becoming the child's guardian, then the father can apply to court to be appointed as a joint guardian. This is possible whether or not his name is on the child's birth certificate.

c) Under the Children and Family Relationships Act 2015, a father to a child will acquire guardianship rights if he lives with the mother of a child for a period of 12 consecutive months, three months of which are after the birth of the child. This Act commenced on 18 January 2016 and is not retrospective. If there is a disagreement as to whether or not the father has been cohabiting for the required length of time, an application for the necessary declaration can be made to the court.

Please note that the naming of the father of the child on the birth certificate does not give the father automatic guardianship rights.

Most applications for guardianship are made in the District Court. You can make the application yourself or instruct a solicitor to do so on your behalf. You may be entitled to free legal aid. There is no register of guardianship.

BRINGING MY CHILD ON HOLIDAY WITHOUT HER FATHER'S CONSENT

I am not married to the father of my daughter and I hope to take her on holidays soon. Do I need his permission to take her out of the country? He is named on my daughter's birth certificate.

The naming of the father of the child on the birth certificate does not give him automatic guardianship rights. If the father to your child does not have guardianship rights or if he has not initiated the guardianship process through the courts, then you may bring your child on holiday without his consent. Therefore, the answer to your question depends on whether or not your child's father is also her legal guardian. It is an offence to remove a child under 16 years from the State:

a) without the consent of each person who is a guardian to the child;
b) in defiance of a court order; or
c) where a summons has been served in respect of a court application by a father seeking guardianship.

In Ireland, a mother of a child is an automatic guardian of that child. A father who is married to the mother of his child also has automatic guardianship rights in relation to that child. This applies even if the couple married after the birth of the child.

In order for a father of a child to obtain guardianship rights, he must either: (a) seek a court order for guardianship, (b) sign a statutory declaration for guardianship with the mother of the child - his declaration must be witnessed by a solicitor or commissioner for oaths, (c) Under the Children and Family Relationships Act, 2015, a father to a child will acquire guardianship rights if he lives with the mother of the child for a consecutive period of 12 months, three months of which are after the birth of the child. This only applies where the parents live together for at least 12 months after 18 January 2016, which was the date the Act commenced.

DOMESTIC VIOLENCE AND COURT ORDERS

When I first met my husband, I thought he was the most kind, sensitive, caring and gentle person. Everyone loved him. He was very attentive towards me. Sadly, his behaviour changed shortly after we got married. He lost interest in me very quickly

3. Family Law

and slowly became physically and emotionally violent towards me. I don't know what to expect from him anymore and I am living in fear. I am considering getting a court order and separating from him but I do not have anyone to help me. I have one dependent child. I don't have very much money.

Domestic violence is the physical, emotional, sexual or mental abuse of one person by another within close, intimate or family relationships. There are over 21 domestic violence services in Ireland providing 24 hour emergency accommodation and advice, which is free and confidential. Women who are pursuing legal options through the courts, such as obtaining an order, breaches of orders and judicial or legal separations, can be provided with a court accompaniment to act as a support at a time when the woman may feel frightened or isolated.

If you don't have very much money then you may be entitled to legal aid.

There are various different orders you can apply for. A safety order prohibits the person against whom the order is made (the respondent) from engaging in violence or threats of violence. It does not oblige the person to leave the family home. If the person does not normally live in the family home, it prohibits them from watching or being in the vicinity of where the person applying for the order and dependent children live. A safety order can be made for up to five years. A barring order requires the respondent to leave the family home and stay away from the family home of the applicant. It may also include terms prohibiting the respondent from using or threatening to use violence. A barring order can be made for up to three years. A protection order is a temporary safety order. It gives protection to the applicant until the court decides on a safety or barring order application. It is intended to last until the case is heard and a decision made. It does not oblige the respondent to leave the family home. An interim barring order is a temporary barring order. It is intended to last until the barring order application is heard in court and a decision made. If you are applying for an interim barring order, there must be evidence of immediate risk of significant harm to you or your child if the court does not grant the order immediately. Under the Domestic Violence Act, 2002, a full court hearing must take place within eight working days of the granting of an interim barring order. The court must be of the opinion that there are reasonable grounds for believing there is an immediate risk of significant harm to the applicant or any dependent person if the order is not made immediately.

Application for an order under the domestic violence legislation are made in the District Court. You can engage a solicitor to make an application on your behalf or you can make the application yourself by contacting the District Court in the area where you live and lodging the relevant forms in the court office. The forms must be lodged in the District Court for service on the respondent. The respondent must attend in court on the day of hearing. Evidence is presented to the judge at the hearing. A witness such as a Garda if applicable will be called to give evidence. If an order is granted, the Garda Síochána will be informed.

Home-Schooling and the Irish Constitution

I met a lovely lady at the swimming pool recently while our children were taking swimming lessons and we were making small talk to pass the time. She informed me that she home-schooled her children. I thought this was a very interesting idea. However, I am unsure if this is legal.

Some people don't like the conformity of the school system. In Ireland, we live in a country where parental choice in education is recognised by law as both a right and a duty. As in Denmark and Finland, our Constitution provides that parents are entitled to provide education in their own homes, unlike Germany where laws introduced during the Nazi era continue to criminalise parents who home-school.

The State acknowledges that the primary and natural educator of the child is the family and guarantees to respect the inalienable right and duty of parents to provide, according to their means, for the religious and moral, intellectual, physical and social education of their children (Art 42.1 of the Constitution of Ireland). Parents shall be free to provide this education in their homes or in private schools or in schools recognised or established by the State (Art 42.2 of the Constitution of Ireland). The State shall not oblige parents in violation of their conscience and lawful preference to send their children to schools established by the State, or to any particular type of school designated by the State. The State shall, however, as guardian of the common good, require in view of actual conditions that the children receive a certain minimum moral, intellectual and social education. (Art 42.3 of the Constitution of Ireland).

In the United States, it is estimated that almost 1.8 million children are home-schooled. Many parents see the benefits of a more natural home setting offering more time together as a family. There are plenty of ways to educate a child and we must acknowledge that children have different abilities and talents, and learn differently. With home-schooling, parents can tailor-make a curriculum to the needs and talents of their children. Some children's needs may not be met in school and we're aware now that not all children learn in the same way. Children with special needs, such as mild conditions of autism, dyslexia, hearing or sight problems and other issues, often fall behind in school and teachers may not have the resources to help them. There is a shortage of special needs assistants in many schools. Some parents of particularly gifted children may want to focus in detail on those talents at home and indeed some parents may decide to home-school because their child is being bullied at school. Children who are very bright, independently minded, talented or perhaps musically-gifted, for example, are often bullied by school children of lesser abilities and it would be very wrong, in my opinion, to keep them in that environment.

There are a number of reasons why home-schooling may be best for some families and we are very lucky in this country to be legally allowed to home-school our children if we so wish.

3. Family Law

While the law allows parents to educate their children at home if they so wish, the State will insist that the child receives a certain minimum education under the Education (Welfare) Act 2000, as amended. The State will intervene in the case of an appeal from an expulsion or long suspension of a student from a recognised school or the refusal of such a school to enrol a student.

PAID LEAVE FOR NEW FATHERS (THE PATERNITY LEAVE AND BENEFIT ACT 2016)

Our first son was born shortly before Christmas during the Celtic Tiger era. My husband went back to work immediately after the birth. Back in 2007, paid leave was not available for Irish dads. Parental leave has been available to men and women in Ireland since 1998, but the uptake among men was low because it was unpaid. Has this changed at all? Can men now take paid paternity leave?

In 2016, the Cabinet finally met to discuss the terms of paternity leave in Ireland. The Paternity Leave and Benefit Act, 2016, provides for statutory paternity leave of two weeks. With effect from 1 September 2016, a new father is entitled to paternity leave from employment or self-employment following the birth or adoption of a child. You can start paternity leave at any time within the first six months following the birth or adoption placement. Your entitlement to pay and superannuation during paternity leave depends on the terms of your contract of employment. Employers are not obliged to pay employees who are on paternity leave. You may qualify for paternity benefit from the Department of Social Protection if you have sufficient PRSI contributions. However, an employee's contract could provide for additional rights to payment by the employer during the leave period, so that, for example, the employee could receive full pay less the amount of paternity benefit payable. Under the Act, a "relevant parent" for the purposes of paternity leave entitlement includes the father of the child, the spouse/civil partner or cohabitant of the mother of the child and the parent of a donor-conceived child. In the case of an adopted child, the relevant parent includes the nominated parent in the case of a married same-sex couple or the spouse, civil partner or cohabitant of the adopting mother or sole male adopter. The entitlement to two weeks' paternity leave from employment extends to all employees, including casual workers, regardless of how long you have been working for the organisation or the number of hours worked per week. You can choose to take paternity leave at any time in the 26 weeks following the birth or adoption. You must notify your employer in writing that you intend to take paternity leave and provide your intended dates no later than four weeks before you leave. You will be required to provide a certificate from your spouse or partner's doctor confirming when your baby is due, or confirmation of the baby's date of birth if you apply for leave after the birth has occurred. Under s 11 of the Act, if you are sick before your paternity leave starts, you may postpone the paternity leave until you recover (Paternity Leave and Benefit Act, 2016) (Citizens' Information, employment rights and conditions).

Other statutory leave available to employees includes parental leave, adoptive leave, *force majeure* leave and carers' leave. If you have a dispute with your employer about paternity leave or if you have been dismissed for claiming your rights under paternity leave legislation, you may make a complaint within six months of the dispute using the online complaint form available on www.workplacerelations.ie. You should apply for paternity benefit at least four weeks before the date you intend to start your paternity leave. If you are self-employed, you should apply 12 weeks before. You can apply for paternity benefit online at https://services.mywelfare.ie.If you are already on certain social welfare payments, then you may get half-rate paternity benefit.

From 13 March 2017, paternity benefit is €235 per week. The Department of Social Protection will pay €235 for the first two weeks of paternity leave, and it is based on the same PRSI requirements as maternity leave. This allows fathers to start a combined package of both paternity leave and paternity benefit at any time within the first six months following birth. After taking parental leave, workers have the right to return to the same job. If that is not possible, the employer must offer them an equivalent or similar job, consistent with their employment contract. Rights acquired or in the process of being acquired by the worker on the date on which parental leave starts shall be maintained as they stand until the end of the leave. Workers are protected against less favourable treatment or dismissal on the grounds of an application for, or the taking of, parental leave (s 23 of the Paternity Leave and Benefit Act 2016)

Great as this combined package is, it nonetheless still places us well behind our continental friends. In Germany, a mother and father can take up to 14 months' leave between them, but only if the father signs up for at least two of those months. When Quebec placed similar conditions on parental leave, the number of men signing up jumped by 250 %. Iceland offers new fathers up to 91 days' paid parental leave, Norway 70 days and Sweden 60 days. I felt tired and overwhelmed after the birth of all my children. I'm sure most mothers feel the same. In my opinion, surely the support of the father is in the best interests of the mother and child at this early stage. Numerous studies have also proved that the opportunity to bond with the baby at an early stage has not only been beneficial for the child, but also for the father. This step will contribute to better life-work balance for families.

In summary, the Paternity Leave and Benefit Act, 2016, provides for statutory paternity leave for two weeks. You can start paternity leave at any time within the first six months following the birth or adoption placement. You may qualify for paternity benefit from the Department of Social Protection if you have sufficient PRSI contributions. You can choose to take paternity leave at any time in the 26 weeks following the birth or adoption. You should apply for paternity benefit at least four weeks before the date you intend to start your paternity leave. The Department of Social Protection will pay €235 for the first two weeks of paternity leave, and it is based on the same PRSI requirements as maternity leave.

3. Family Law

PROPOSED NEW LEGISLATION ON ADOPTION

I am a 24-year old Irish woman. I was adopted when I was two years old by a wonderful Irish couple. Sadly my adoptive parents have now died and I am hoping to get some information on my birth mother. Should I contact the Adoption Authority regarding their voluntary contact register?

Proposals were unveiled to put the voluntary contact register on a statutory footing. It is part of proposed new legislation that will allow people over 18 years of age who were adopted to have access to their birth certificate and other information. Regrettably, the National Adoption Contact Preference Register had not yet been put on a statutory footing. I was speaking with a representative from the Adoption Rights Alliance recently and she informed me that the proposed legislation would abolish the existing register. Further details are available in their briefing note on the legislation, a link to which is available in the notes to editors on this PR: http://www.adoptionrightsalliance.com/ARA%20PR_21-03-17.pdf

The mission of the Adoption Rights Alliance is to advocate equal human and civil rights for those affected by Ireland's closed adoption system.

The Adoption Rights Alliance recommends that the Irish government introduce legislation to grant adopted people automatic access to their birth certificates (s 6.2, Legislative Proposals) and all files, records, documents, papers on their origins, family history, early care and medical records held within the Irish State, the UK and also the US (s 6.3, Legislative Proposals). Furthermore, it proposes that the Irish government introduce statutory based information and tracing services for all adopted people without a two-tier system (s 6.1, Legislative Proposals) and that the Irish government place the National Adoption Contact Preference Register on a statutory footing (s 4, Legislative Proposals).

Currently, the register has around 11,500 adopted adults and birth relatives on its books. One in 20 of these birth parents have indicated that they do not want to be reunited with their adopted son or daughter. The law will require those who were adopted before the legislation is enacted to sign a statutory declaration stating they will undertake to respect the privacy of their birth parent and not contact them before seeking assistance from Tusla. Your birth mother may indicate in the register that she does not want any contact with you at present.

Legislation will not be enacted for a year after being passed to allow for an information campaign. Children adopted after the law is in place will have an automatic right to their birth certificate, and birth parents will be informed of this provision during the adoption process. Children adopted from abroad will also be able to avail of the process.

You may also be familiar with the Philomena Project. This is a fund to provide finance to the Adoption Rights Alliance to help raise public awareness in Ireland, the United States and internationally on the issue of forced and illegal adoptions in

Ireland and denial of access to birth certificates for Irish adopted people, or efforts to reunite families with the advancement of open records legislation in Ireland.

You might like to refer to the Adoption Rights Alliance website (www.adoptionrightsalliance.com) for a summary of their proposals regarding adoption legislation submitted to the Minister for Children on 11 August, 2011. You will also find them on Twitter and Facebook.

MEDIATION AGREEMENT

I am separating from my wife and I was referred to the Family Mediation Service. Will I have to pay for this? If we reach an agreement, will it be legally binding?

The Family Mediation Service is provided free of charge by the Legal Aid Board. You may contact the Bar Council or Mediators' Institute Ireland or Friary Law and engage a private mediator if you wish. Any separating couple can avail of mediation, regardless of whether they are married or not, including same-sex couples.

The mediator does not give legal advice. Please ensure that you obtain legal and financial advice before and during the mediation process so that you make an informed decision. The purpose of mediation is not to help couples reconcile. The mediator is neutral and is only there to help couples work out mutually acceptable agreements that they can both stick to in relation to important issues, such as child custody or access, maintenance and property rights. It is not marriage counselling. If an agreement is reached, the mediator will draw up the terms of the agreement and this is signed by both parties. The agreement is generally stated not to be legally binding unless the parties arrange for a solicitor to draw up a legal separation agreement based on the mediated agreement.

RIGHTS OF COHABITANTS

Marie and I lived together as a couple for seven years. Marie worked full-time as a teacher and I depended on her financially. I did not work outside the home because I was caring for her two children. Sadly, Marie has now died and I was wondering if I will be provided for financially out of her estate.

Section 194 (1) of the Civil Partnership and Certain Rights and Obligations of Cohabitants Act 2010, entitles a person who claims to have been in an intimate cohabiting relationship with another to make application for financial provision to be made out of the estate of the deceased cohabitant. To succeed, the applicant must show that the parties have lived together as a couple for a period of two years or more where there are dependent children, or five years or more in any other case. The relationship must be between two persons, whether of the same or opposite sex, who have been living together as a couple in a committed relationship. Section 172 (2) obliged the court, in assessing cohabitation, to examine each of the following:(a) duration of the relationship, (b) the basis on which the couple lived together, (c) the degree of financial dependence of either adult on the other and any agreements in respect of their finances, (d) the degree and nature of any financial arrangements between the adults, including any joint purchase of an estate or interest in land or joint acquisition of personal property, (e) whether there are one or more dependent children, (f) whether one of the adults cares for and supports the children of the other and (g) the degree to which the adults present themselves to others as a couple.

The Rights of a Cohabitant After the Death of a Partner

I have lived with my partner for seven years. However, I do not wish my partner to have a claim over my estate when I die. It is my wish that all of my estate pass to my children. Am I legally bound to provide for my partner?

The Civil Partnership and Certain Rights and Obligations Act 2010, established a redress scheme for qualified cohabitants which may be activated on the death of one of the parties. The Act also allows cohabitants to opt out of the provisions of the Act and they may agree not to seek provision from the estate of the other in the event of the death of that partner.

I would advise you to discuss your intentions with your partner and draw up a written agreement or legal contract, which must be signed by both of you. You must both get independent legal advice prior to signing the agreement in order for the agreement to be valid. You or your partner may confirm in writing that you have waived your right to independent legal advice if you wish. However, a court can set aside such an agreement if the enforcement of the agreement would cause serious injustice.

Polygamous Marriages

Are polygamous marriages recognised in Irish law? My neighbour is an asylum seeker and he has two lovely wives. Lucky him.

In a recent ruling involving a Lebanese man with two wives, the Supreme Court ruled the second marriage was not valid while the first marriage subsisted, that is, the first marriage of a man living here with two wives whom he married in his native Lebanon is valid under Irish law. Recognition of an actually polygamous marriage would be contrary to a fundamental constitutional principle of equality and contrary to public policy, it ruled. In finding the second marriage not valid under Irish law, it said the institution of polygamy was not contemplated by the Constitution and was contrary to principles of various international instruments. Giving legal recognition to such a structure would 'give legal effect to discrimination and subordination where the principle of equality should hold sway'.

Ms Justice Iseult O'Malley stressed that her conclusions were subject to the rights of the Oireachtas to consider and legislate for issues of public policy, subject to and in conformity with the Constitution. This case has implications for family reunification of successful asylum seekers. Some Muslims living here would have been married under a law that permits polygamy, even if they are practising monogamy. While taking the view that the man's second marriage is not valid under Irish law while his first marriage subsists, that did not necessarily mean such a marriage "can never have legal consequences here". Public policy changes over time (*H v A* [2010] IEHC 497; *HAH v SAA & ors* [2017] IESC 40).

CARE ORDERS

My child is being put into the care of the HSE. I was on a methadone treatment plan but it didn't work. I am very upset about this. Does this mean I will never see my child again?

A care order places a child in the care of the Health Service Executive either temporarily or permanently. A care order can, in some circumstances, continue until the child is 18 years of age. The Health Service Executive may apply to the courts for a number of different orders when dealing with children who are at risk or who are in need of care. These orders give the courts a range of powers regarding the type of care necessary and access to the children for parents and other relatives.

Therefore, to answer your question, how soon you see your child again depends on the type of care order the Health Service Executive has applied to the court for. An emergency care order places a child in the care of the HSE for a period of not more than eight days. It is sometimes accompanied by a "search and find" warrant to enable the Garda or other people to remove a child to safety. The HSE can also apply for an interim care order pending the making of a full care order. The effect of this order is that the child is placed in the care of the HSE for a period not exceeding 28 days. This period may be extended by the District Court if both the HSE and any parent with custody of the child consent. A supervision order allows the HSE to monitor a child considered to be at risk. The child is not removed from his or her home environment. A supervision order will be for a fixed period of time not longer than 12 months initially.

Chapter 4

Employment Law

Please note that employment law is very legislative based and I always recommend that clients contact a solicitors firm that specialises in the area of employment law and taxation of employment law awards and settlements to discuss whether there are any recent changes in legislation before considering legal action. There are several such firms in Ireland such as Richard Grogan and Associates.

WHO CARES FOR OUR CHILDREN?

We pay our au pair €120 per week to care for our three children. She lives with us full-time and has the benefit of using our car. We read the recent ruling by the Workplace Relations Commission whereby they ruled in favour of a Spanish au pair who had been in receipt of €100 a week, a rate found to be in breach of the law. Should au pairs be treated like regular employees?

It is perfectly fine to pay €120 per week if your au pair is doing no more than 20 hours a week because, on to their wage, you add the cost of board and lodging which takes it above the minimum wage. The law permits a maximum deduction of €54.13 per week for room and board. The duties you ask your au pair to perform must be agreed in advance and au pairs are entitled to work in a safe and healthy working environment. They have the right to privacy and to pursue personal leisure activities. The issue arises when au pairs are expected to work a 35 hour week and are still only paid €100 per week. In making its ruling, the Workplace Relations Commission said domestic workers enjoyed the same protection under Irish employment legislation as other legally-employed workers. They are entitled to a written statement of their terms and conditions of employment, a payslip, to be paid at least to the national minimum wage, receive breaks of at least 15 minutes after a 4.5 hour work period, are entitled to annual leave and public holidays, to work no more than 48 hours per week, minimum notice before dismissal and to be registered as an employee with the Revenue (*Migrant Rights Centre Ireland (MRCI) v Workplace Relations Commission*, March 2016 WRC 227). If you don't comply with the legislation and a case is taken against you, you'll have to pay up anyway. A person performing a duty for another person in exchange for a payment would suggest the existence of a contractual relationship. The WRC case has actually brought about no change in the law, that is, the WRC decision does not constitute any change to existing employment law.

People working in other people's homes have broadly the same employment rights as other workers. Once the employee has taken up the job, they are protected by employment equality legislation. Domestic workers should pay tax and PRSI in the same way as other employees and it is the responsibility of the employer to deduct this from the worker's wages and also to pay the employer's PRSI contribution on their behalf. If you are employing someone to do domestic work, such as the care of children, and you are paying them €40 a week or more, you must register as an employer with the Revenue using their online service or TR1 form available from your local Revenue office.

Domestic workers from outside the European Economic Area require employment permits in order to work in Ireland (Employment Permits Acts 2003 – 2014).

MATERNITY LEAVE (MATERNITY PROTECTION ACT 1994, AS AMENDED)

Am I entitled to be paid during maternity leave? Can I take paid time off for antenatal care? What happens if I have to go on early maternity leave for health reasons? Can my employer terminate my contract of employment when I am on maternity leave?

Since 25 March 2019, a standard rate of €245 per week maternity benefit must be paid to all women on maternity leave. The Maternity Protection Act 1994 and the Maternity Protection (Amendment) Act 2004 operating in conjunction with the Safety, Health and Welfare at Work (Pregnant Employees) Regulations 1994, SI 446/1994 set out all your maternity leave entitlements. The minimum maternity leave entitlement for a pregnant employee is 26 consecutive weeks of leave (s 8 of the 1994 Act, as amended by the 2004 Act). Under s 9 of the Act, you must inform your employer in writing of your intention to take leave and you must have a medical certificate confirming your expected date. Section 10 of the Act provides that the maternity leave shall commence when the employee decides, but it must not be later than two weeks before the end of the expected week of confinement (that is, labour). Section 11 provides that maternity leave can commence at an earlier date if there are medical grounds. Section 12 of the Act provides for an extension of maternity leave if your baby is born later than expected. Additional leave of up to 16 weeks is a possibility but this is unpaid and must start immediately after the end of maternity leave (see ss 12 and 14). Section 13 refers to unexpected early commencement of maternity leave. If the baby is born four weeks or more before the due date, the employee is still entitled to 26 weeks, but the commencement date of the maternity leave will be the earlier of the two dates when she commenced maternity leave or the date of confinement (labour). Section 14(a) provides that, in the event of the sickness of the employee, the employee may request her employer to terminate her period of additional maternity leave. This absence from work will be treated in the same manner as any absence from work of the employee due to sickness. Section 14(b) provides that, in the event of the hospitalisation of the child (in respect of whom the maternity leave is taken), an employee may request her employer to postpone her maternity leave/additional maternity leave and allow her to return to work on an agreed date. Maternity leave can only be postponed in the case of an employee who has taken at least 14 weeks' maternity leave, four of which are after the end of the week of confinement. The employee shall be entitled to take the postponed maternity leave/additional maternity leave in one continuous block known as resumed leave, commencing not later than seven days after the discharge of the child from hospital. Under s 15 of the Act, you are entitled to paid time off for ante-natal and post-natal care. Pregnant women are entitled to be paid for time off for medical appointments, examinations and tests. Section 15(b) provides that an employee who is breastfeeding shall be entitled, without loss of pay, either to breastfeeding breaks, where facilities for breastfeeding are provided in the workplace or a reduction of working hours. The employer is not required to provide facilities for breastfeeding in the workplace if the provision of such facilities would give rise to more than a nominal cost. The employee is entitled without loss of pay to take one hour from her work each working day as a breastfeeding break (Maternity Protection (Protection of Mothers who are Breastfeeding) Regulations 2004, SI 654/2004). Maternity leave is protective leave, and any termination notice by an employer when the employee is on protective leave is void (s 21). You have a right to return to work to the position held before going on maternity leave (s 26). This does not necessarily mean going back to the original job, but suitable alternative work must be provided (s 27). You must notify your employer of your intention to return to work (s 28). Employers cannot apply the normal provisions of their sick pay schemes when dealing with pregnancy-related illness (*North Western Health Board v McKenna*, ECJ case C-191/03, European Court of Justice on 8 September 2005, reported at [2006] ICR 477 (also [2005] IRLR 895). An employer must move a pregnant employee to alternative work if a risk assessment shows unacceptable risks for the pregnant employee (s 18 of the Maternity Protection Act 1994). In *Flanagan v Byrne Ltd* (UD 542/2006), the EAT considered the termination of an employee's employment following her return to work from maternity leave. While she was on maternity leave, the company underwent re-organisation of its business. As a result, the employee was informed that she was being made redundant. The tribunal found that the employer had failed to establish that there were substantial grounds which would have justified the dismissal. The employer failed to provide the employee with alternative employment on her return from maternity leave and did not allow her to return to her previous role. These failures were deemed to be a dismissal and the EAT ordered that the employee be re-engaged by the employer.

Section 23 of the Maternity Protection Act 1994 provides that any purported termination, notice of termination or purported suspension of an employee's employment while absent on protective leave will be void. This includes while the employee is absent to attend ante-natal classes or any period of absence attributable to breastfeeding. Dismissals are automatically unfair if connected with pregnancy or giving birth (s 38(1) of the 1994 Act). This includes women made redundant during the maternity period and not offered suitable alternative employment if such is available. No qualifying period is necessary to bring a claim for unfair dismissal by reason of pregnancy or the taking of maternity leave.

Olga Seniv v Tamem Michael Bridal Ltd (2011) EAT (www.adarehrm.ie/employment-law/maternity-leave/d-cases) relates to a claim of discriminatory dismissal relating to pregnancy The Complainant submitted that she started working with the Respondent in November 2004, and in September 2006 went on maternity leave. When the Complainant contacted the Respondent on 17 May 2007 in anticipation of returning to work on 21 May 2007 she was informed that the Respondent was not sure whether there was work. When the Complainant contacted the Respondent again on 21 May 2007 she was told that the Respondent would not take her back because they had someone else. The Complainant further submitted that she was told the other person was very good and had no small children or words to that effect. The Respondent denied discriminating against the Complainant and pointed out that the Complainant's statutory maternity leave started on 8 September 2006 and ended on 8 March 2007. The Respondent submitted that in early March there was an attempt to contact the Complainant to no avail. In mid-April the Complainant and her husband contacted the Respondent, asking the Respondent to write a letter, a copy of which was attached to the Complainant's submission, which stated that the Complainant would be on maternity leave until 21 May 2007. The Respondent disputed that another person had been hired in lieu of the Complainant. The Equality Officer found that the Complainant established a prima facie case of discrimination. The Equality Officer did not accept that there was a resignation by the Complainant from her employment and was not convinced a genuine redundancy situation existed. The Equality Officer found that the Complainant was discriminatorily dismissed and ordered that the Respondent pay the Complainant €20,000. This case highlights to Organisations that there are few instances where an Organisation cannot permit a female Employee to return to work following maternity leave. Organisations need to be cognisant of the fact that Employees are very much shielded when on periods of maternity, adoptive, parental, or any other type of protective leave.

In *Dymnicka v Kylemore Foods Group Ltd* (UD 1033/2007), the EAT considered whether the employee was dismissed because of her pregnancy. The onus was on the employer to demonstrate that the decision to dismiss the employee was fair and that the employee's pregnancy was not relevant. The employer failed to satisfy the EAT that pregnancy was not a relevant factor, nor did it demonstrate that the dismissal was reasonable and fair. The EAT noted that it was significant that the employee had been an excellent and hard-working employee and also noted that the employer's decision to let the employee go, having then almost immediately taken on extra staff, flew in the face of any logic. The EAT held that the employee succeeded in her case and awarded her €10,000 under the Unfair Dismissals Acts.

The Safety, Health and Welfare at Work Act 2005 and the Safety, Health and Welfare at Work (General Application) Regulations 2007, SI 299/2007 require employers to carry out risk assessments in respect of their employees. The 2007 regulations require employers to carry out a specific risk assessment for pregnant employees, employees who are breastfeeding or post-natal employees. As soon as an employer is on notice of an employee's pregnancy or the fact that she has just given birth to a child or is breastfeeding, the employer must reassess the risk in the workplace for such employee without delay and take preventative and protective measures to

4. Employment Law

ensure she is not exposed to anything which will damage either her health or have any adverse effect on her pregnancy or breastfeeding. The employer must move the employee to alternative work if a risk assessment shows unacceptable risks or if the employee cannot be required to perform night work. If this is not possible, the employee is entitled to leave on health and safety grounds (s 18 of the 1994 Act). The employee is entitled to receive her normal weekly pay from her employer for the first 21 days (Maternity Protection (Health and Safety Leave Remuneration) Regulations, 1995). For any leave after the 21 days, the employee is entitled to social welfare benefits (Social Welfare (Consolidation) Act 2005). Any pregnancy-related disputes are dealt with by the Workplace Relations Commission, with appeals to the High Court on a point of law only.

You might note that the Cabinet has agreed plans to extend maternity leave and benefit in cases of premature births. Currently, maternity benefit is paid by the State for 26 weeks. The Minister for Employment and Social Protection brought a memo to Cabinet to extend this payment and leave from the time a baby is born prematurely. These will be added at the end of the 26 weeks. There are around 4,500 premature births in Ireland annually.

The Maternity Protection (Disputes and Appeals) Regulations 1995, SI 17/1995 set out the procedures to be followed and incidental matters, in relation to the hearing of disputes and appeals under the 1994 Act.

Unfair Dismissal

A few months back, I informed my employers that I was expecting a baby and would be taking maternity leave in October. My employers said that was OK and the meeting ended. Everything was fine in work until last week when I received a letter stating that my services were no longer required. I was totally shocked. Can my employers do this? Can they just suddenly dismiss me? My employers said the dismissal was not related to the fact that I was expecting a baby and required maternity leave. They said their decision was based on another incident I was involved in at work where misconduct was alleged.

I would recommend that you contact a specialist firm in the area of employment law and taxation of employment law awards and settlements for up to date advice in this area.

Unfair dismissal arises when the employer terminates the employee's employment (Unfair Dismissals Act 1977 and the Unfair Dismissals (Amendment) Act 1993).

In an unfair dismissal case, the burden of proof is on the employer. Under Irish employment law, a dismissal may be unfair if a fair reason for dismissal has not been established and if correct procedures have not been adopted leading up to and including the dismissal, or if the dismissal was for an automatically unfair reason, for example, because you wanted to take maternity leave.

Boyne and Moran v EAT (November 11, 2014 IEHC 154) involved an appeal to the Employment Appeals Tribunal of a Rights Commissioner decision who had decided the two men involved, Boyne and Moran, were fairly dismissed. The background to the case is the 2 men worked for Keelings Logistics Solutions who operated as a distribution company for the supply of goods to one customer. The 2 employees worked in the warehouse. The security manager saw the 2 men "acting suspiciously" beside an open cage and saw the cage being moved. He also said he saw the men eating something and putting their hands inside the cage and stated the men had no business standing together in front of a cage. The employer had a policy that no food would be consumed on the warehouse floor and installed vending machines on the shop floor to prevent staff tampering and/or eating stock. The Warehouse Manager was alerted and it became clear that a box containing jam tarts had been tampered with and two individual tarts were missing from a packet.

An investigation was carried out and after a CCTV footage reviewed many times. The men said they were sharing a Mars bar and denied eating the jam tarts. The employer carried out a disciplinary procedure and dismissed the men who appealed the decision but lost.

The EAT found that the men's evidence was not credible and on the balance of probability that they did tamper with the stock.

The Tribunal also found that there were no procedural defects which would render the dismissal unfair. The investigation, disciplinary meetings and appeal were thorough, fair and objective. What is interesting about this case is that the EAT found that the employers zero tolerance policy in relation to staff tampering with stock was "reasonable in the circumstances".

Many cases similar to this one has seen the EAT finding that the response of the employer was excessive and disproportionate. But the fact that Keelings Logistics Solutions had only one customer and there was naturally a very high degree of trust required between them and their customer seems to have been critical in the EAT finding that the zero tolerance policy was reasonable.

In *Gate Gourmet v Employment Appeals Tribunal (EAT 2014)* (Independent Newspaper, November 28, 2014 Gordon Deegan) a sacking sparked by a stale chicken wrap cost food firm Gate Gourmet more than €50,000. The Employment Appeals Tribunal ordered the airline catering firm to pay sacked supervisor Joe Smith €50,899 after ruling that he was unfairly dismissed. Gate Gourmet, based in Dublin Airport, sacked Mr Smith for gross misconduct following a probe sparked by the gone-off snack. Mr Smith had an unblemished 19-year service record. The investigation began after one of Gate Gourmet's customers complained in April 2012 that Gate Gourmet supplied it with a wrap that was out of date since February 2012. The probe found Mr Smith failed to follow standard operating procedures and Gate Gourmet's production manager fired him on the grounds that he did not take responsibility for his job as store supervisor; failed to address poor staff performance; the wrap incident; and out-of-date stock and stock control issues. Mr Smith's internal appeal failed, with Gate Gourmet saying its reputation had been put at risk.

The Employment Appeals Tribunal (EAT) found there was a failure of stock control standard operations procedures. However, it found "it was unfair and unreasonable to conclude that the claimant was solely and exclusively responsible for such failure. Termination of employment on the grounds of gross misconduct was a disproportionate sanction in all the circumstances." The EAT awarded Mr Smith €45,000 for the unfair dismissal and a further €5,889 in lieu of eight weeks' minimum notice.

In the case of *Mark Bentley v Tesco*, 2014 Employment Appeals Tribunal (EAT) 2014 (EAT UD818/2012) a Tesco worker who was dismissed after it came to light that he had received double payments was awarded €70,000 compensation by the Employment Appeals Tribunal. The worker had worked with Tesco in the UK since 2007 and progressed to a deputy manager role. He moved to Ireland to progress his career in January 2011 and he worked as a stock control manager at one of the largest stores in the country.

It emerged the UK hub store where the worker previously worked had continued to pay him. The tribunal heard that the store director met him on September 11, 2011. The worker was "shocked" when the issue was put to him. Later that month, the claimant was suspended on full pay. At a subsequent meeting in November, he was informed of his dismissal.

Mr Bentley began working in Ireland on January 25, 2011, so when a payment came through in February, his wife who was dealing with his accounts believed it was a payment due to her husband. In May, she accessed the online payslips and at that stage realised the payments were wage payments. She did not tell her husband. She admitted knowledge of the payments in September 2011. The EAT awarded €70,000 to Mr Bentley. It found he was unfairly dismissed.

In *Eleanor Preston v Dunnes Stores*, 2014 (Employment Appeals Tribunal EAT Cork) the EAT stated: "As this was the claimant's first offence, committed in a time of great personal difficulty which the respondent was aware of, the sanction of dismissal was disproportionate". The EAT awarded her €14,000 compensation and €2,630 or four weeks' notice.

In Julie O'Brien v O'Callaghan Hotels (O'Brien v Persian Properties trading as O'Callaghan Hotels Dec – E 2012-010) the former marketing director of a hotel group was awarded over €315,000 by the Equality Tribunal after it found that she was discriminatorily dismissed and victimised while pregnant.

A judgment published by the tribunal revealed that Ms O'Brien had become ill due to stress placed on her at work while pregnant. An attempt was made to convince her to take redundancy. Ms O'Brien first became pregnant in 2004 and worked until late Friday, January 14, 2005. A few hours after finishing work she went into labour and her son was stillborn the following day.

She alleged that she was put under pressure to work during her subsequent maternity leave and regularly received calls and emails and was couriered documents from the office. Ms O'Brien alleged that she was also put under pressure to work during a second maternity leave in 2008 after losing another baby. She was told by the managing director that he would prefer for her not to be on the staff of O'Callaghan Hotels if she had a third pregnancy, she claimed.

The tribunal was told that the business was hit by a sharp decline in business in 2008 followed by redundancies.

Ms O'Brien claimed that when she again became pregnant in 2009 she was "extremely anxious" about informing the managing director. She claimed to have told both the managing director and general manger that she previously lost two babies and did not want to work during her maternity leave. Prior to the start of her leave in November 2009, she claimed she was asked to take redundancy and she was shocked when she was presented with a letter to sign agreeing to receive her P45 after being paid for maternity leave and holidays up to November 2009. She refused to sign the letter and alleged that there were 11 meetings in which she was put under "intolerable pressure" to do so.

She was later certified by her doctor as unfit for work due to work-related stress. Despite the medical cert, she received a termination letter. The company directors denied Ms O'Brien's version of events and said that she wanted to resign. They agreed that she performed very well in a very senior role in the company.

The Employment Appeals Tribunal found that she was victimised and discriminated against. She was awarded her €220,500 (21 months' salary) for the harassment and discriminatory dismissal. She was further awarded €94,500 (nine months' salary) for the distress caused by victimisation.

Under Irish employment law, a dismissal may be deemed fair if an employer can show that it resulted from one or more of the following causes: a) the capability, competence or qualifications of the employee for the work he or she was employed to do; b) the employee's conduct; c) redundancy; d) the fact that continuation of the employment would contravene another statutory requirement; or e) that there were other substantial grounds for the dismissal.

Examples of automatically unfair dismissals would be if you were dismissed for taking parental leave, for taking time off for pregnancy and childbirth or for health and safety reasons, taking time off to act as a representative in certain situations, whistleblowing, victimisation, seeking flexible working hours, being summoned or absent from work for jury service or taking part in protected industrial action. If you believe your dismissal was related to any of these reasons, you could have a strong case to make an employment claim.

If you believe that your dismissal was due to the fact that you would be taking maternity leave, then I would advise you to contact your solicitor immediately.

4. Employment Law

A complaint must be submitted within the correct time limit. If you decide to bring a claim to the Workplace Relations Commission, you must do so within six months of the dismissal, unless you can show reasonable cause, in which case you may be allowed 12 months by the WRC.

A recent case with facts somewhat similar to your own involved an employee of Auralia which is a Dublin based cosmetic surgery and fertility clinic. The employee Dympna Boyce was awarded €32,000 at the Workplace Relations Commission for being sacked after telling her boss she was pregnant. Ms Boyce argued the attitude of her employer's chief executive was remarkably different after she notified him of her pregnancy. She had begun working at the company in February 2017 and became pregnant three months later. Ms Boyce said comments made by the chief executive about someone having 'an identity crisis' were directed at her and she felt distressed and humiliated as a result of these comments. Ms Boyce also felt stressed by other negative behaviour she felt was directed at her in the workplace. Employees of Auralia argued that Boyce had performance issues before her manager was informed of her pregnancy. The clinic argued that they had an exemplary track record in dealing with pregnancy matters. Valerie Murtagh, an adjudicating officer at the Workplace Relations Commission found the manner of the dismissal by Auralia 'was seriously flawed' and further that Boyce's dismissal was in relation to her pregnancy. Auralia have submitted an appeal regarding the decision (*Boyce v Ras Medical Limited Auralia* (November 2018 ADJ-0001105)). (see *The Sunday Times*, 16 December 2018 for a further discussion on this case).

Depending on what action you decide to pursue and noting that all decisions differ, the redress possible for you if you win your case can be reinstatement, re-engagement or financial compensation.

The maximum amount that can be awarded in an unfair dismissal case is two years' remuneration (s 7, Unfair Dismissals Act 1977).

In the case of *DHL Express (Ireland) Limited v Michael Coughlan* (Labour Court, July 2017) the employer appealed the decision of the Adjudication Officer in accordance with the Unfair Dismissals Act 1977 to 2015. A Labour Court hearing took place on 13 July 2017 and the Labour Court awarded Mr Coughlan (a van driver) €72,042.88 by way of compensation, being the equivalent of 104 weeks' remuneration, which it viewed was the employee's financial loss to date attributable to the dismissal.

Receipt of social welfare payments by the employee is disregarded in calculating financial loss. An employee who is on probation, or who has less than 12 months' employment, is excluded from the rights afforded by the unfair dismissals legislation but there are some limited exceptions, for example, a dismissal arising from a discriminatory ground. An employer must give an employee a written statement of the procedure to be used in dismissing him within 28 days of commencement of employment. An employee must be afforded fair procedures and natural justice prior to termination of employment, unless the matter is one of gross misconduct which can justify a summary dismissal. In a gross misconduct case, the suspension should be carried out as soon as possible *(Duffy v Hugh McAvoy T/A 'Talk To Me'* (UD 1948/2009) and the employee should be suspended with pay. If a suspension is merely to allow an investigation be carried out and it transpires that the employee is innocent, then he or she would be entitled to be paid in accordance with their contract of employment.

You also have the option of going to the civil courts with a common law claim of wrongful dismissal (breach of contract), but you cannot do both - that is, you must choose between the Workplace Relations Commission or the civil courts.

A female employee is entitled to 26 weeks' unpaid maternity leave and may qualify for maternity benefit and 16 weeks' additional maternity leave with no maternity benefit and reasonable time off for medical visits connected with pregnancy (the Maternity Leave Act 1994, and Maternity Protection (Amendment) Act 2004). The contract of employment may provide for pay during maternity leave, but there is no legal obligation on the employer.

Section 6(2)(f) of the 1977 Unfair Dismissals Act provides however that the dismissal of a pregnant employee will not be unfair if the employee was unable by reason of the pregnancy or matters connected therewith: (a) to do adequately the work for which she was employed; or (b) to continue to do such work without contravention by her or her employer of a provision of a statute (or instrument made under statute); and (c) there was not, at the time of the dismissal, any other employment with her employer that was suitable for her and in relation to which there was a vacancy, or she refused an offer by her employer of alternative employment on terms and conditions corresponding to those of the employment to which the dismissal related, being an offer made to enable her to be retained in the employment, notwithstanding her pregnancy.

An employer may therefore dismiss a pregnant employee who is incapable of doing her work provided the employer has sought a suitable alternative vacancy and there is not one, or she refuses a reasonable offer of one *(Hallissey v Pretty Polly (Killarney) Ltd* (UD 1984/362)) and *McCarthy v Sunbeam Ltd* (1991) ELR 38).

Regard must be had in all such cases to the provisions of the Maternity Protection Acts 1994 and 2004. Any purported termination of employment while the employee is on protective leave will automatically be void *(Reardon v Global Shares (Ireland) Limited* (UD 2009/611)).

Unfair Dismissal – Employer Acting Impulsively

One of my employees whom I had employed for over 12 months started showing up late, and sometimes not at all. She had little interest in her work and she was rude to clients. One busy weekend, she was due to work on the Saturday but she rang in sick. I lost my patience with her the following Monday and told her she could go and get a job somewhere else and to pick up her P45 in a few days. Shortly after

that, I received a letter from the Workplace Relations Commission informing me that an unfair dismissal claim had been filed against me and there were also claims for failure to give the required notice, failure to give proper rest breaks, failure to have a written contract and failure to pay the correct pay for annual leave and public holidays. What are my options? I am not taking her back.

Please contact your solicitors immediately. I would recommend seeking advice from a solicitors' practice that specialises in Employment law for advice in this situation. Before an employer commences any form of Disciplinary or corrective action against an employee he should consider whether this is in breach of the employee's rights and consequently whether it is likely to give rise to an Employment Law Claim. A careful employer will seriously consider taking legal advice at this point in time. A solicitor experienced in Employment Law will ensure that measures taken by the employer are appropriate. Consulting a solicitor experienced in employment law for advice on the predicament you find yourself in may well help you avoid high awards being made against you. An amicable resolution may even be reached between employer and employee with the help of a solicitor.

While one cannot prevent an Employment Law Claim being issued by an aggrieved employee a sensible employer will ensure to take timely advice to minimize cost.

You can expect to receive notice of a hearing date shortly with the Workplace Relations Commission. From your instructions it appears that you did not follow any procedure and therefore it might be in your best interest to settle the case. At least that would be one option to discuss with your solicitor.

Do you have any records recording rest breaks in accordance with the Organisation of Working Time Act regulations? Do you have a proper written contract of employment? Do you have a record of annual leave? You don't appear to have given the proper minimum notice of dismissal or followed fair procedures. In a case like this, your ex-employee could claim up to two years' salary. Always use good judgment when dismissing an employee, and follow fair and proper procedures and natural justice prior to termination of employment, unless the matter is one of gross misconduct which can justify summary dismissal. Always ensure you have a proper written contract of employment in place, and proper written records of all rest breaks and annual leave entitlements.

The employee you dismissed will be relying on, *inter alia*, provisions of the Unfair Dismissals Acts 1977 – 2007 and the Minimum Notice and Terms of Employment Act 1973 which provide remedies for dismissed employees and the minimum notice to be given by an employer to an employee when terminating a contract of employment. Employees who have one-year continuous service with the employer, and employees who have not yet reached the normal retirement age for the employment in question, are covered by the legislation. Civil servants, officers of health boards and VECs and persons employed in the defence forces or Gardaí are not covered by the legislation (*Central Bank of Ireland v Gildea* [1997] 1 IR 160 SC, *O'Callaghan v Cork Corporation* IR 354, *Murphy v Minister for Social Welfare* (1987) IR 295).

In *McNally v Tesco Ireland* (UD80/2015) the employment appeals tribunal awarded an employee €18,000 award after dismissal for theft. Mr McNally was a security guard for Tesco. The company operated an *Honesty Policy and Staff Purchase policy*. The security guard was dismissed after he had "*removed an item of stock from the respondent's premises without authorisation and without having paid for it.*" The EAT assessed the reasonableness of the dismissal and concluded that "*Given the claimant's level of seniority; given his role as security manager and the trust that that entails; and given that there was no culture of bringing unpaid-for goods home, the Tribunal is satisfied that the decision to dismiss was a reasonable one.*" However, even though the EAT felt that the decision to dismiss was reasonable, they still found the dismissal unfair due to "*significant procedural unfairness*", particularly the fact that there was a 7 month delay in arranging for the employee's appeal hearing. The employee was awarded €18,000.

The EAT in *Buckley v Dunnes Stores* (UD1064/2014) awarded an employee €8,000 after dismissal for telling workers to 'slow down'. The employer in this case decided to dismiss the employee after they became aware that she was telling a co-worker "*that he had to slow down and that this would create more work. She then had a text sent to him through MV again telling him to slow down. Extra hours would lead to extra pay for him and others. He would make more money if he 'dragged himself around'...*" Obviously, this type of behaviour would greatly upset an employer – after all, employees are employed to carry out their work to the best of their ability. If it were the case that an employee was not only deliberately working slowly, but also encouraging other employees to do the same - and the reason for this was to generate more paid work - then many employers would consider dismissal. However, the EAT found that this was an unfair dismissal and, in doing so, deemed certain aspects of the dismissal process to be particularly unfair. They noted in particular that "*the claimant had not had a witness or was unaccompanied during some meetings.*" In addition to not being allowed a representative, the EAT noted that the disciplinary hearing was held the same day that the investigation process was completed, and that the employee only received key evidence that same day. Ultimately, the EAT felt that an €8,000 award was just and equitable in the circumstances.

In *Last v Suir Pharma Ireland Ltd* (*UD343/2015*) an employee was awarded €5,400 and reinstated after dismissal for 'horseplay'. The employee here was struck in the groin with a towel by a colleague (it seems from the decision that this was more in jest than anything) and that the employee reacted in a way that could have been construed as dangerous, or a possible serious breach of health and safety rules. Where employees engage in dangerous behaviour or breach health and safety rules, this could possibly warrant dismissal. However, the EAT noted here that "a level of horseplay was tolerated in the workplace" and that the workplace could be described as "high spirits". The EAT ultimately concluded that the dismissal was unfair as a result. The basic point here is that you can't reasonably allow behaviour to occur by employees in general, and then dismiss an employee for engaging in that behaviour. If employees are treated inconsistently, then it's very likely that the dismissal will be deemed unfair. (www.peninsulagrouplimited.com publishes up to date cases on unfair dismissal).

4. Employment Law

In order to succeed with a claim under the legislation, the employee must be able to show that she was actually dismissed. A person who has voluntarily resigned his position, or whose contract has come to an end by reason of frustration, could not establish a dismissal and cannot proceed with an unfair dismissal claim *(Nolan v Brooks Thomas Ltd* (UD 179/1979)). Dismissal subject to an appeal will still be a dismissal *(Kenny (Michelle) v Warner Music (Ireland) Ltd* (1992) (UD 389/92) 263, 264). In order for a contract to terminate properly where notice is given, the notice must specify the date of termination, or be given in such a way that the date is ascertainable. A warning of dismissal at some time may not amount to a dismissal (*Morton Sundour Fabrics Ltd v Shaw* (1966) KIR 1, (1967) I TR 84 Article in Managerial Law 2(1):1-5, April 1967 with 63 Reads. DOI: 10.1108/eb021286). Issuing a P45 does not of itself terminate employment, as it is a separate statutory requirement governed by tax law and, while it is an action that commonly follows the termination of employment, it does not of itself constitute termination but, from an evidential perspective, may be indicative of an intention to terminate. (A P45 is a statement of your employee's pay and deductions for the year up to the date they leave your employment. The statement will cover any deductions for: Pay As You Earn (PAYE), Pay Related Social Insurance (PRSI) Local Property Tax (LPT), Universal Social Charge (USC).

You should complete a P45 when your employee leaves your employment, is granted a career break or dies while in your employment).

In *Ennis v Carroll, David Carroll and Scale Force Ltd* (1999) (UD 586/1999 360) the employee was offered and sought her P45, but this was held not to have been an indication of dismissal.

SI No 49/1998 – Terms of Employment (Additional Information) Order 1998, sets out the information which must be provided by employers regarding rest breaks. Section 3(1) refers to an employee who enters into a contract of employment after the commencement of this Order. The employee's employer shall, within two months after the employee's commencement of employment with the employer, give (or cause to be given) to the employee a statement in writing containing particulars of the times and duration of the rest periods and breaks referred to in ss 11, 12 and 13 of the Organisation of Working Time Act 1997 that are being allowed to the employee, and of any other terms and conditions relating to those periods and breaks. Section 2 refers to a contract of employment entered into before the commencement of this Order. An employee's employer shall, if requested by the employee to do so, give (or cause to be given) to the employee within two months of the request, a statement in writing containing particulars of the times and duration of the rest periods and breaks referred to in ss 11, 12 and 13 of the Organisation of Working Time Act 1997 that are being allowed to the employee, and of any other terms and conditions relating to those periods and breaks.

Therefore the order provides that where, under the Terms of Employment (Information) Act 1994, an employer is required to provide an employee with a written statement of certain particulars of his or her terms of employment, such statement shall, after 1 March 1998, include details of the times and duration of (and any other terms and conditions relating to) the rest periods and breaks referred to in ss 11, 12 and 13 of the Organisation of Working Time Act 1997 that are being allowed to an employee.

Annual statutory leave entitlements for full-time and part-time employees and public holiday entitlements are provided for in the Organisation of Working Time Act 1997.

Section 4(2) of the Minimum Notice and Terms of Employment Act 1973 provides that the minimum notice to be given by an employer to terminate the contract of employment of his employee: (a) if the employee has been in the continuous service of his employer for less than two years, shall be one week; (b) if the employee has been in the continuous employment of his employer for two years or more, but less than five years, two weeks; (c) if the employee has been in the continuous service of his employer for five years but less than ten years, four weeks; (d) if the employee has been in the continuous service of his employer for ten years or more, but less than 15 years, six weeks; (e) if the employee has been in the continuous service of his employer for 15 years or more, eight weeks.

The Terms of Employment (Information) Act 1994 sets out the basic terms of employment which the employer must provide to the employee in a written form within two months of starting the employment. Failure to do so will leave the employer open to a claim from the employee, pursuant to the terms of the Act. The maximum amount that can be awarded to the employee is four weeks' remuneration (s 7 of the Act). The employee can bring a claim to the Workplace Relations Commission. A written contract of employment should always be furnished to the employee within the timeframe.

Section 6(4) of the Unfair Dismissals Act 1977 provides that

> "the dismissal of an employee shall be deemed for the purposes of this Act not to be an unfair dismissal, if it results wholly or mainly from one or more of the following: (a) the capability, competence or qualifications of the employee for performing work of the kind which he was employed by the employer to do; (b) the conduct of the employee; (c) the redundancy of the employee; (d) the employee being unable to work or continue to work in the position which he held without contravention by him or of his employer of a duty or of a restriction imposed by or under any statute or instrument made under statute".

You must have substantial grounds justifying the dismissal (s 6(1) of the Unfair Dismissals Act 1977), and you must afford your employee fair procedures and natural justice.

You mention that your employee is not particularly competent. Before you could dismiss her on the grounds of lack of competence, you should have first pointed out her shortcomings to her and your required improvements, and given her a set period to make the improvements. Issue a warning regarding dismissal. Please contact your solicitors for advice in your particular situation.

4. Employment Law

CONSTRUCTIVE DISMISSAL

I had been working with the same company for many years and I recently resigned because of a significant deterioration in my working conditions. I was due a promotion and I didn't get it. I was disappointed, as a new employee was promoted above me, even though I am much better qualified than she is and I have much more experience. I did not receive a pay rise and my wages were reduced. My employer changed my job functions. I was sent to a new work location without any explanation. I felt I had no other option but to resign. Are there any employment law options open to me?

Again I would recommend that you contact a solicitors firm that specialises in the area of employment law and taxation of employment law awards and settlements for up to date advice in this area. There are several such firms in Ireland such as Richard Grogan and Associates. Under Irish employment law, constructive dismissal may occur when employees resign because their employer's behaviour has become so intolerable or made life so difficult that the employee has no choice but to resign. Since the resignation was not truly voluntary, it could possibly be in effect a termination. At least this would be an option to consider. When an employer makes life extremely difficult for an employee in an effort to have the employee resign, rather than outright firing the employee, this could be a constructive dismissal. In this case, an employee's legal rights are the same as if he or she had been unfairly dismissed (https://employmentrightsireland.com/). The conditions which give rise to constructive dismissal may include deliberate cuts in pay or status, persistent delayed wages, withdrawal of a car, refusal of a holiday, suspension with or without pay, dramatic changes to duties, hours or location of work, ignoring complaints, persistent unwanted amorous advances, harassment and bullying at work, verbal abuse, singling out for no pay rise, criticising in front of others, lack of support, being overworked, failure to notify a woman on maternity leave of a vacancy or revealing secret complaints in a reference. Under Irish employment law, both unfair dismissals and constructive dismissals are serious breaches of an employee's rights. Unfair dismissal refers to a situation where the employer dismissed the employee and the employee believes the dismissal to be unfair or illegal. Constructive dismissal refers to a situation where the employee believes that, because of the conduct of the employer towards him, he has no alternative but to resign. The employee may then bring a claim to the WRC claiming unfair dismissal by way of constructive dismissal. In an unfair dismissal case, the employer must prove to the WRC that the dismissal was fair. In a constructive dismissal case, it is the employee who must prove that they were constructively dismissed, that is, the burden shifts from the employer to the employee. The employee must prove that he or she left the employment due to the conduct of the employer, which he or she could no longer be expected to tolerate. Under Irish employment law claims for constructive dismissal must be submitted to the WRC within certain time limits. Even if an employee is to be dismissed, he or she should be afforded fair procedures and natural justice prior to termination. Please contact your solicitors as soon as possible.

With reference to resignation, some employers may try negotiating an exit settlement agreement with their employee on a "without prejudice" basis. "Without prejudice" negotiations are generally excluded from being introduced into evidence in subsequent legal proceedings. However, the High Court has held that "without prejudice" discussions can be admitted in evidence in the interest of justice. Both parties should seek independent legal advice first.

In *Liz Allen v Independent Newspapers (Ireland) Limited*, 2002 (UD 641/000) Ms Allen had been employed as a crime correspondent with Independent Newspapers for four years until she resigned her position. She alleged that she had been constructively dismissed in that the conduct, treatment and attitude of her employer towards her left her no choice but to terminate her employment. She maintained that she had been subjected to harassment and bullying, and that the conduct of her employer undermined her confidence and her health to such an extent that she was forced to resign. The Employment Appeals Tribunal held that Allen had been constructively dismissed. In relation to the issue of assessment, it was accepted that there was a period of time that Allen was unable to work attributable to her medical condition. The Employment Appeals Tribunal found that the employee's illness was caused by the factors which led to her constructive dismissal. The tribunal was satisfied that the employee's illness led to her financial loss and that the financial loss was therefore attributable to the conduct of her employer. In those circumstances, the employee was entitled to be compensated for that, notwithstanding the fact that she was unable to work due to her medical condition (Law Society of Ireland, employment law).

A unilateral reduction in pay, even for good reasons and to a relatively small extent, may be a material breach of a fundamental element in the contract of employment (*Industrial Rubber Products v Gillon* (1977) IRLR 389). The employer may however have a contractual right to vary the employee's income (*White v Reflecting Roadstuds Ltd* (1991) IRLR 331: (1991) ICR 733 EAT). A lack of a pay rise may not entitle an employee to claim constructive dismissal depending on the circumstances. In *Murco Petroleum Ltd v Forge* (1987) EAT (1987) ICR 282) the employer was found to have acted unreasonably but was not in significant breach going to the root of the contract where what they had done was not a 'capricious exercise' and was not an 'arbitrary decision'. The employee's claim of constructive dismissal failed. 'There is no general principle that an implied obligation to provide regular pay increases should be read into a contract of employment and that the industrial tribunal had erred in law in holding that there was such an implied term in the employee's contract; that further, even if there was an implied term that an employer would not treat an employee arbitrarily, capriciously or inequitably in matters of pay, the industrial tribunal had failed to consider whether the employers had in fact acted arbitrarily; and that if the industrial tribunal had considered the matter, they would have concluded that the employers had not acted capriciously and, accordingly, the employee had not been unfairly dismissed.'

4. Employment Law

In *Katherine Stephens v Archaeological Development Services* (EAT 2012) (*Irish Examiner*, Monday, 2 January 2012, Sean McCarthaigh) an executive with an archaeological firm was awarded €90,000 after the Employment Appeals Tribunal ruled that she had been constructively dismissed after the company tried to impose extra conditions on her return to work following a period of sick leave due to breast cancer. Katherina Stephens, a former head of operations of Archaeological Development Services, claimed that she was effectively sacked after obstacles were put in the way of her return to work after being ill for nine months. Ms Stephens, who worked with the firm since 1997, explained she had felt pressurised by a series of e-mails, texts and telephone calls sent by the firm's chief executive to her in early 2008 while she was on sick leave. She claimed she felt stressed by repeated requests for meetings to discuss her situation and felt they were affecting her recovery. Ms Stephens was deemed fit by her own doctor to return to work in October 2008 but was told in an e-mail by the company that her return was not as straightforward as simply picking up exactly where she had left off. Ms Stephens also found her desk and her belongings had been moved while on sick leave. She was informed that she would be located at a new desk beside the chief executive on her return and working with a defined set of clients. Ms Stephens said she felt she was being demoted and given a task where she was being set up to fail. She maintained she was then suspended without pay until she agreed to the new terms of her employment, and said she felt she was constructively dismissed in March 2009 after receiving no correspondence from the company over the previous six months. The EAT ruled that Ms Stephens had an entitlement to return to work as soon as she was deemed medically fit again. It also found that Ms Stephens was entitled to consider herself constructively dismissed from the date that her return to work was made contingent on factors other than being medically fit and awarded her €90,000 in compensation. The Tribunal said there was equivocation on the part of both sides in relation to Ms Stephens return to work but that such uncertainty had resulted from the actions of Archaeological development Services. The EAT made no finding as to whether the firm's actions had contributed to any personal injuries which she suffered.

In *Riddell v Mid-West Metals Ltd*, 1980/687 the employee's terms and conditions were changed in that he received a lesser bonus than he had been led to believe he would receive. The Employment Appeals Tribunal noted that the remuneration was reviewable under the terms of the contract and the employee did not seek to engage in negotiations on the issues causing him concern. He could not accept the proposal and terminated his employment. His claim failed.

A change in job function imposed by the employer may give rise to an entitlement to claim constructive dismissal (*Coleman v S. and W. Baldwin* (1977) IRLR 342 142. If, however, an employer for good commercial reason directs an employee to transfer to other suitable work on a purely temporary basis at no diminution in salary, and it is made clear that it is only a temporary arrangement, the employee may not be entitled to claim constructive dismissal. An imposed change of location, where the employee is not contractually obliged to work at a new location, may give rise to a constructive dismissal claim (*Bass Leisure Ltd v Thomas*, (1994) IRLR 104, EAT 561). Where an employer has the contractual right to alter hours of work and shift systems, doing so did not constitute a breach of contract and did not give rise to a constructive dismissal claim (*Dal v Orr* (1980) IRLR 413). In conclusion, I would advise you to contact your solicitors for a more detailed consultation.

The Right to Fair Procedures – Disciplinary Proceedings in the Workplace

I am an employee involved in a disciplinary procedure in the workplace. What are the rules applying to such procedures at both the investigatory stage and the ultimate disciplinary procedure where a sanction may be imposed against me?

In 2017 Mr Justice Eager in the High Court in *Lyons v Longford Westmeath Education and Training Board* ([2017] IEHC 272) held, *inter alia*, that "the proceedings adopted by the HR company who were engaged by the employer to investigate allegations of bullying on the part of a teacher were in breach of Art 40(3)(1) and (2) of the Constitution of Ireland by the refusal to allow legal representatives to appear on behalf of the applicant. The process adopted by the HR company failed to vindicate the good name of the applicant, in their refusal to hold an appropriate hearing, whereby the applicant through legal representation may have cross-examined the complainant. Equally the complainant should then be entitled to then cross examine the applicant. Mr Justice Eager went on to state that "the court is clear that in circumstances where a complaint is made which could result in an individual's dismissal, or where it impinges on the individual's right to a good name, the individual is entitled to fair procedures".

Therefore it is very important, as we saw in the above case, that an employer follow fair procedures when dismissing an employee. This is a reflection of the constitutional right to fair procedures. All employees are entitled to fair procedures if their job is at risk. The employer should follow the principles set out in statutory instrument, Industrial Relations Act 1990 (Code of Practice on Grievance and Disciplinary Procedures) (Declaration) Order 2000 (No 146/2000). When taking the path towards dismissal of an employee, the employer should first write to the employee inviting him or her to a formal disciplinary meeting. The letter should clearly set out why the meeting is being requested and that the outcome of the disciplinary meeting could be dismissal. Furthermore, the employee should be told that he or she has a right to representation at this meeting such as a trade union representative or a legal representative (*Lyons v Longford Westmeath Education and Training Board* [2017] IEHC 272) and the employee should be given the opportunity to respond fully to all allegations and have the responses fully considered before a decision is made to dismiss. The employee should be given a bias-free hearing with no predetermining of the outcome. Any penalty imposed must be a proportionate response to the alleged wrongdoing. If termination of an employee's employment is at stake,

4. Employment Law

then the employee should be given the right to appeal a decision to terminate the employment.

If the employer does not follow fair procedures along the lines outlined above, the employee may have a successful claim for unfair dismissal. Therefore, both employers and employees should familiarise themselves with the principles of fair procedures where such employment-related issues arise. The right to fair procedures is a fundamental one under natural and constitutional law.

The Unfair Dismissals Act 1993 enshrines procedural requirements in the legislation by providing at s 5(b) that, in determining fairness, the decision-maker shall have regard to: (a) the reasonableness or otherwise of the conduct (whether by act or omission) of the employer in relation to the dismissal; and (b) the extent (if any) of the compliance or failure to comply by the employer, in relation to the employee, with the procedure referred to in s 14(1) of the Unfair Dismissals Act 1977.

The WRC has traditionally taken the view that, if an employer acts in a manner that is procedurally unfair, the dismissal itself will be held to be unfair (*Caulfield v Verbatim Ltd*, 1993) (UD 938/1993, 374, 394)). In *Gearon v Dunnes Stores Ltd* 1988 (UD 367/1988) 375, the EAT held that fair procedures had not been followed and concluded that:

> "the right to defend herself and have her arguments and submissions listened to and evaluated by the respondent in relation to the threat to her employment is a right of the claimant and is not the gift of the respondent or this tribunal ... the right to fair procedures is a fundamental one under natural and constitutional justice, it is not open to this tribunal to forgive its breach".

The Workplace Relations Commission is very strict regarding the following of fair procedures. Even in cases where the employer was clearly right to dismiss the employee for poor conduct or performance, if the employer didn't follow fair procedure, the employee will win his or her case, that is, the WRC will usually find in favour of the employee. However, in such circumstances the WRC might reduce the compensation as much as 100% in some cases (*White v Cadbury (Ireland) Ltd* (1979) (UD 44/1979)). Even where there are serious findings made against an employee, it is incumbent on the employer to provide fair procedures to an employee in any disciplinary action taken against the employee (*Higgins v Irish Rail* (2006) UD 2006/480). Fair procedures are required even where the dismissal is on a lawful ground (*McGrath v Irish Distillers Ltd* (2006) UD 2006/417). Please contact your solicitors to discuss this matter further. (you might like to also refer to Ms Frances Meenans (Senior Counsel at the Law Society of Ireland/the Bar Council of Ireland) book *Employment Law* (1st edn, Round Hall 2014) for further information on this topic).

TRANSFER OF AN UNDERTAKING OR BUSINESS

What should I address in terms of pre-contract queries in the transfer of an undertaking or business?

The European Council directive on the approximation of the laws of the Member States relating to employees' rights in the event of transfers of undertakings, businesses or parts of undertakings or business was transposed into Irish law by the European Communities (Protection of Employees on Transfer of Undertakings) Regulations 2003 (SI No 131/2003). Regulation 3 provides that "these regulations shall apply to any transfer of an undertaking, business, or part of an undertaking or business from one employer to another employer as a result of a legal transfer (including the assignment or forfeiture of a lease) or merger". In these regulations, "transfer" means the transfer of an economic activity which retains its identity. "Economic entity" means an organised grouping of resources which has the objective of pursuing an economic activity, whether or not that activity is for profit or is central or ancillary to another economic or administrative entity. The regulations apply to public and private undertakings engaged in economic activities, whether or not they are operated for gain.

When considering the transfer of an undertaking, due diligence and pre-contract enquiries are of utmost importance. One should first obtain a list of all employees, details of their status, their date of birth and all entitlements, including VHI, pensions and notice entitlements. Check if there has been compliance with the Terms of Employment (Information) Act 1994 and ask for copies of all records under the Organisation of Working Time Act 1997 and the Protection of Young Persons Act 1977. Are any trade unions involved? Request copy contracts and statements of terms and conditions of employment under the Terms of Employment (Information) Act 1994.

Next, enquire whether the vendor complied with all employment and health and safety legislation. Has the vendor complied with all codes of practice made under employment legislation? Has the vendor been involved in any Workplace Relations Commission or Labour Court cases? If so, have all orders, determinations, decisions been implemented? Is there any employment litigation or personal injury litigation threatened or pending?

Enquire as to what the vendor's arrangements or commitments are in respect of holiday pay, sick pay, overtime payments, disturbance money, redundancy payments, company cars, compassionate leave and any other terms and conditions of employment. Has the vendor fully complied with all agreements in relation to the wages of the employees? Is the vendor paying at least the national minimum wage? Are all wages/salaries paid to date? Is all PAYE/PRSI/USC paid to date? Has there been compliance with the Payment of Wages Act 1991 regarding pay statements? Are these available? Are there any amounts due to directors?

Copies of all documentation should be produced, together with absenteeism records, pension arrangements, bonuses and commission. Check whether there have been any promises of *ex gratia* payments. Are there restrictive covenants in the contracts of employment? With reference to consultants and independent contractors, are there any agreements/contracts for the provision of services and if so, obtain copies and particulars. There has to be compliance with the Protection of Employment Act 1977.

What is one going to do after they buy the business? Will there be redundancies? Will the defence of economic, technical and organisational reasons apply? Have there been discussions with staff or their representatives as regards the proposed sale? Is there to be a reorganisation of the business prior to the sale or transfer? This above is a non-exhaustive list of pre-contract queries that was set out very well by Francis Meenan SC at a conference on employment law (October 2017, Gresham Hotel, Dublin).

Parental Leave

I have a child with a disability. He is going through a particularly hard time at the moment and I would like to take time off work to take care of him. He is 12 years old. Am I entitled to time off work to care for him?

The Parental Leave Acts 1998 to 2006 (as amended by the European Communities (Parental Leave) Regulations 2000, confer an entitlement to parental leave on employees with one year's continuous service with the employer from whose employment the leave is taken (s 6(3)). The natural parent, adoptive parent, adopting parent or a person acting *in loco parentis* of the child is entitled to 14 working weeks' parental leave to enable him or her to take care of the child (s 6(9)). An employee is entitled to parental leave in respect of each child of which he or she is the relevant parent (s 6(4)). A minimum of six weeks' notice in writing of intention to take parental leave must be given to the employer, specifying the date of commencement, the duration, the manner in which it is proposed to be taken, and the notice shall be signed by the employee (s 8(1)). The employer is entitled to call for evidence in relation to the date of birth or disability of the child.

The period of parental leave must end not later than the day on which the child reaches its eighth birthday. Where the child has a disability, the leave will come to an end on the day on which the child turns 16 years of age, or ceases to have a disability (s 6(2)).

Where the employee becomes sick and is unable to care for the child, the period of parental leave may be postponed or suspended until the employee is no longer sick (s 10(2)). Employers may postpone parental leave entitlement for no more than six months, by notice in writing, where the taking of parental leave would have a substantial adverse effect on the business by reason of seasonal variations in the volume of work or the unavailability of another person to carry out the duties of the employee. Where an employer has reasonable grounds for believing that an employee is not using his or her parental leave to look after their child, he can terminate the leave by given seven days' notice in writing, and the employee must then return to work.

Parental leave may be taken as a continuous period of 14 weeks or two separate blocks of not less than six weeks not exceeding a total of 14 weeks or any combination of days or hours, with the agreement of the employer (s 7) and this can only be done with the permission of the employer (*O'Neill v Dunnes Stores* (2000) ELR 306).

REDUNDANCY

I was called to a meeting in my employer's office. She informed me that the work for which I was employed would in the future be done in a different manner by another person who was better qualified and trained than I am. I was in effect made redundant. Is this legal?

For the purposes of answering this question, we will presume that the redundancy is a valid one. Of course, it should be noted that not all redundancies are valid. Again I would as always recommend that you contact a specialist firm in the area of employment law and taxation of employment law awards and settlements.

Redundancy occurs where you lose your job due to circumstances, such as the closure of a business or a reduction in the number of staff. The Redundancy Payment Acts 1967 to 2014 provide certain entitlements for employees. Your employer must follow fair procedures. Section 7 of the Redundancy Payment Act 1967 provides for a redundancy payment entitlement. You are entitled to two weeks' gross pay for every year of service, subject to a maximum of €600 per week and plus one bonus week, tax-free. On the date of the termination of employment, your employer should pay the redundancy lump sum due to you. If your employer does not pay your redundancy lump sum, you should apply to your employer for it, using form RP77. If your employer still does not pay it, you can apply to the Department of Social Protection for direct payment from the Social Insurance Fund. It is also common practice in Ireland for employees and trade unions to negotiate extra statutory redundancy payments, usually calculated as a set number of weeks' pay, with no ceiling on the amount of a week's pay, for each year of service.

Section 10 of the Protection of Employment Act 1977 provides that an employer must give certain information regarding the redundancy to your representative. Section 39 of the Redundancy Payment Act 1967 allows you to appeal a decision of the Workplace Relations Commission if you are unhappy with the amount of redundancy the deciding officer has decided on.

Under Irish employment law, a genuine redundancy situation arises if the employer has ceased or intends to cease carrying on the business for which the employee is employed or the requirements of the business have ceased or diminished or are expected to cease or diminish. A genuine redundancy also arises where the

4. Employment Law

employer has decided to carry on the business with fewer or no employees or, as in your case, the employer has decided that the work for which the employee has been employed will in future be done in a different manner, or done by a person who is also capable of doing the work for which the employee is not sufficiently qualified or trained. A dismissal by reason of redundancy will only be deemed unfair if the employer is not considered to have acted reasonably, for example, unfair selection of a particular employee for redundancy, failure to properly consider an alternative to redundancy, failure to pool comparable employees, re-hiring at lower salaries or not providing selected employees with a right of appeal. In *Byrne v Trackline Crane Hire Ltd*, 2003 EAT 314 (unreported, 2 May 2003), the employer was a crane hire business with cranes varying in size from 10 tonnes to 120 tonnes. It was the policy of the employer that, when a driver was employed, he was assigned to a particular crane. The claimant was employed to drive an 18-ton crane but the use of the crane became redundant because it was unprofitable. Evidence from the employer was that an excessively long time would be required to train the claimant in the use of another more profitable crane. The Employment Appeals Tribunal was satisfied from the evidence that a genuine redundancy existed at the company.

Employee v Employer (UD 1169) (EAT) (www.adarehrm.ie-employment-redundancy) relates to a complaint of unfair selection for redundancy. The Claimant was employed as a Development Officer with the Respondent. The Claimant was made aware that he was being made redundant, although he claimed that other Development Officers did not have the same level of experience and expertise as him. Twenty days after the Claimant was made redundancy the Respondent advertised a Development Officer position, the Claimant applied for this vacancy and others but was unsuccessful. The Respondent stated that there were 58 to 60 DVO's and 8 were made redundant. Out of these eight redundancies the company decided to restructure and make two new positions. The Tribunal found that the Respondent did not use fair procedures. They did not consider possible alternatives to redundancy and the Claimant was not offered an appeal of the decision to make him redundant. The Tribunal found that the Claimant was unfairly dismissed under the Unfair Dismissals Acts 1977–2007 and was awarded the sum of €27,500. This case highlights the importance of following fair procedure. An employer must consider alternative employment for an employee being made redundant and they should also be offered an appeal of the decision to make them redundant.

Intrium Justitia v Kerrie McGarvey (2011) ED AO95 (www.adarehrm.ie) relates to a complaint of unfair selection for redundancy on the grounds of gender and family status. The Equality Officer recommended an award of €30,000 in compensation to the Claimant, the Respondent appealed this decision to the Labour Court. Redundancies arose in this Organisation as a result of merging three production systems into one. There was a matrix system developed to select staff for redundancy. The Complainant was informed that she was selected for redundancy when she was seven months pregnant. The facts established were that the Complainant was pregnant and known to be so at the time of the selection for redundancy, previous remarks had been made about her family status and the basis for the matrix and the method of calculation was unclear to the Court. The findings of this case were that the Complainant was made redundant on the basis of being discriminated against on grounds of gender and family status the Labour Court reduced the compensation amount to €20,000. This case highlights the need for Organisations to take care when selecting Employees for redundancy and to ensure that any selection matrix used is clear. Furthermore, it highlights the additional care that should be taken when selecting pregnant Employees for redundancy.

You are entitled to bring a claim for unfair dismissal if you consider that you were unfairly selected for redundancy or if you consider that a genuine redundancy situation did not exist. If your employer makes you a reasonable offer of alternative employment and you refuse it, you may lose your entitlement to a redundancy payment. Alternatives which involve a loss of status or worsening of the terms and conditions of your employment would not be considered reasonable. You may be justified in refusing an offer that involves you travelling an unreasonable distance to work. The employment equality legislation also prohibits selection for redundancy that is based on gender, civil status, family status, age, disability, religious belief, race, sexual orientation or membership of the Traveller community. As with any dismissal, if you feel you were made redundant unfairly, you must make an appeal to the Workplace Relations Commission under Irish employment law and within the specific time allowed. All employers are obliged to pay statutory redundancy pay to workers who have at least two years' continuous service. This payment is tax-free.

You are entitled to a minimum of two weeks written notice of redundancy (Redundancy Payments Act, s 17). This notice period goes up depending on the period of service. If you have worked there between five and 10 years you are entitled to four weeks' notice and, if you have worked there over 15 years, you are entitled to eight weeks' notice. Long-standing employees will have longer notice entitlements under the Minimum Notice and Terms of Employment Acts 1973 to 2005. Contractual notice entitlements should also be borne in mind, as they must be complied with in order to avoid a wrongful dismissal claim. If you are made redundant and you are not required to work out your notice, you are entitled to payment in lieu of notice which is your normal pay for that notice period. If you are being made redundant, you are entitled to reasonable paid time off in order to look for a new job (Redundancy Payments Act 1979, s 7). You are entitled to any holidays that are outstanding, or payment in lieu of holidays. When you lose your job, you should register as unemployed by signing on with your local welfare office.

Redundancy payments are not available where an employee resigns from their employment (*Collins v Excel Property Services Limited*, 1998/RP 27). An employee who has been dismissed is not entitled to redundancy payment if his employer terminates the employment because of misconduct.

Just to note, the Department of Social Protection has provided a redundancy calculator online to help you with calculating your redundancy payments. To be entitled to a redundancy payment, you must have worked 104 weeks of continuous employment attained after the age of 16 years, and you must have been dismissed from your job. If you are given a new contract of employment or your old contract is renewed, you will not be entitled to redundancy. The renewal must be on the same terms as the old contract. Redundancy payment entitlements are calculated by reference to weeks per year of service and you generally get two weeks' pay for each year of continuous employment over the age of 16, and an additional one week's normal earnings. All earnings over €600 per week are disregarded in calculating statutory redundancy payments. An employee who is being made redundant is entitled to two weeks' notice and must be given a redundancy certificate by the employer. The employer is entitled to a rebate from the Irish government of 60% of the statutory element of each lump sum payment, provided he has given the requisite two weeks' notice. Please note also that an employee who has been laid off for four or more consecutive weeks can give written notice to his employer indicating his intention to claim redundancy.

STATUTORY REMEDIES FOR BREACH OF EMPLOYMENT LAW

I am starting a new job and I would like a little guidance about the various statutory laws in Ireland to protect my rights in the workplace.

At a very minimum employees must be furnished with a written statement of the terms and conditions of their employment within two months of starting a new job. Failure of the employer to provide them can be punished as set out in s 7 of the Terms of Employment (Information) Act 1994. The WRC adjudicator can order the employer to give the statement to the employee and can award up to four weeks' remuneration by way of compensation for failure to provide this information on time. Section 7 of the Redundancy Payment Act 1967 sets out an employee's right to a redundancy payment. If unhappy with the payment you can appeal the amount you have been awarded under s 39 of the Act. The Protection of Employment Act 1977 obliges an employer to inform and consult with employees in a collective redundancy situation. Section 7 of the Unfair Dismissals Act 1977 sets out reinstatement, reengagement and compensation of up to 104 weeks' remuneration in respect of the financial loss due to an unfair dismissal.

An employer must comply with the terms of s 27 of the Organisation of Working Time Act 1997 regarding rest breaks and working time. Failure of an employer to comply can result in employee compensation of up to two years' remuneration. Section 6 of the Payment of Wages Act 1991 provides for compensation of the net amount of wages which would have been paid the previous week prior to the reduction/non-payment, or twice the net amount of wages that would have been paid to the employee in the week immediately preceding the deduction. The National Minimum Wage Act 2000 protects employees in relation to minimum wage rates. An employer can be prosecuted in the District Court for breaches of the Minimum Wage Act.

Section 27 of the Safety Health and Welfare Act 2005 protects employees from penalisation or dismissal for making a complaint in respect of health and safety in the workplace. The Equal Status Act 2000 protects an employee in relation to discrimination in respect of goods or services. Discrimination and equality based claims are dealt with in the Employment Equality Act 1998. The Protection of Employees (Fixed Term Work) Act 2003 looks at the protections afforded to fixed-term workers and, if you are a part-time worker, please refer to the Protection of Employees (Part Time Work) Act 2001.

If you are an agency worker, refer to the Protection of Employees (Temporary Agency Work) Act 2012 which states, in schedule 2, that the Workplace Relations Commission can order rectification of whatever breach of the Act is proved, including reengagement, reinstatement and compensation. Compensation can also be awarded to an employee for any loss sustained by reason of the default of the employer (Minimum Notice and Terms of Employment Act 1973).

If an employer breaches the Adoptive Leave Act 1995, an employee can be granted compensation of up to 20 weeks' remuneration. Breach of employee entitlements under the Maternity Protection Act 1994 can lead to an award of compensation of up to 20 weeks' remuneration (irishstatutebook.ie)

THE WORKPLACE RELATIONS COMMISSION, UPDATED GUIDELINES

I understand the WRC has issued updated guidelines about the conduct of WRC hearings.

In summary, the WRC has issued a general guide for the structure and procedure of a WRC adjudication hearing as follows:

> "It is a matter for the Adjudication Officer to run the hearing/investigation as appropriate for the circumstances of the case and in accordance with fair procedures. At the start of the hearing the adjudicator will welcome the parties and introduce themselves as the person appointed by the Director General to investigate the claims being heard. The adjudicator will clarify the claims before them and verify appropriate data. The hearing is confidential and no recording of the hearing is permitted. Investigation into claims being made under the Industrial Relations Act are less formal and hearings will be conducted by the adjudicator as appropriate to the claim before them. All other claims will be conducted in accordance with listed guidelines as follows: The Adjudication Officer will ask if any preliminary issues need to be addressed. In the vast majority of cases the Adjudicator will take evidence in relation to preliminary points raised from both parties and then proceed to hear the substantive claims. Both parties will, in turn, be asked to give a concise outline of their position in relation to the claims made. Then the Adjudicator will take direct evidence from both parties and all other relevant witnesses. The other party or their representative will be given the opportunity to question the parties and other witnesses regarding the

evidence they have given. When all evidence has been taken both parties are given the opportunity to present a summing up of the case, firstly by the party on whom the burden of proof rests including submission of legal points and the introduction of relevant case law. The same applies to the other party. In exceptional circumstances only the Adjudicator may accede to a request for or decide that further information needs to be submitted after the hearing and the timelines for such submissions will be agreed at the hearing. These timelines must be strictly adhered to. A written decision stating their names will be issued to the parties. An anonymised version of the decision will be uploaded to the Workplace Relations website. The exception to this are claims taken under the Employment Equality Acts, Pensions Acts and Equal Status Acts and parties will be named on the version uploaded to the website unless the Adjudication Officer decides there is a reason to anonymise the parties. All parties and their representatives need to be respectful of both others at the hearing and the role of the Adjudication Officer". (Workplace Relations Commission guidelines).

THE WORKPLACE RELATIONS COMMISSION (WRC)

I have a complaint about an employment issue. Where should I go first?

The Workplace Relations Commission was established on 1 October 2015 under the Workplace Relations Act 2015. The Act looks at adjudicating employment complaints and disputes and makes provision as respects the resolution and mediation of disputes. The main functions of the WRC are to promote the improvement of workplace relations, promote compliance with the relevant laws, review workplace relations, advise the Minister for Business, Enterprise and Innovation in relation to the application of, and compliance with, relevant laws and provide information to the public in relation to employment laws.

If you have a complaint about an employment or equality issue, or have a grievance under industrial relations legislation, you should refer to the Workplace Relations Commission complaint form first. The complaint must be made in writing within six months of the claimed breach of your right, although the Workplace Relations Commission adjudicator can extend this time to 12 months where reasonable cause is decided by the adjudicator. If you wish to bring an employment rights claim, you may apply using the online complaint form available on workplacerelations.ie

The WRC has a mediation service which will be offered in some cases to try to resolve the issues but, if that does not work, the case will go ahead for adjudication. You can apply for mediation using the online mediation referral form available on workplacerelations.ie.

The complainant must submit a clear statement setting out the details of the complaint. In an employment equality case, the complainant must set out in detail the facts from which discrimination can be shown or inferred. In a constructive dismissal case or other unfair dismissal case, the complainant should set out as much detail as possible, including any disciplinary hearings, grievances raised, investigations carried out or appeals. If the respondent intents on relying on statutory records in his defence, these should be sent to the WRC prior to the hearing. Any other issues should be raised within 21 days of receipt of the complaint from the WRC. Both parties will be contacted with a date for the hearing. It is up to the parties to ensure that the WRC has all relevant documentation prior to the hearing. The adjudicator will question any party or witness and allow each party to question the other party and any witness. The hearing is in private. The written decision will issue within 28 days of the hearing. The decision can be appealed within 42 days to the Labour Court and the decision can be enforced through the District Court after 42 days if no appeal is lodged.

Information on rights and entitlements under employment legislation is provided by WRC information and customer service.

The WRC's advisory service provides advice on grievance procedures and has published codes of practice on grievance and disciplinary procedures and procedures for addressing bullying in the workplace.

IMPLIED TERMS IN A CONTRACT OF EMPLOYMENT

I understand that it would be impossible for my employer to provide for every eventuality in my contract of employment and, furthermore, that some blatantly obvious terms would be implied into the contract in order to make the work relationship possible. What are the most commonly implied terms in employment contracts?

There are four main categories of implied terms, namely, terms implied by statute, terms implied by custom or practice, collective agreements and terms implied by law.

Terms implied by statute would include the right not to be unfairly dismissed, the right to equality, safety from harassment or the right to redundancy.

There are implied contractual obligations for employees too in any contract of employment, including obligations such as an obligation to obey lawful and reasonable instructions, to provide personal service, that is, an employee must in the absence of a special contractual provision do her/his work for the employer personally, an obligation to exercise reasonable care and skill in carrying out duties and to take care of the employer's property or interests, to adapt to reasonable requirements to change methods of working and to protect an employers confidential information.

In *Janata Bank v Ahmed* [1981] IRLR 457, CA, a bank manager failed to use due care when vetting applications for overdrafts, causing the bank to suffer loss when debtors defaulted; he was successfully sued for breach of contract.

4. Employment Law

In *DP Refinery (Westernport) Pty Ltd v Shire Hastings* ((1978) 52 AJLR 43), the court set out the test that will normally be applied before a term may be implied into a contract as follows: (a) the term must be reasonable and equitable; (b) it must be necessary to give business efficacy to the contract, so no term will be implied if the contract is effective without it; (c) it must be so obvious that it goes without saying; (d) it must be capable of clear expression; and (e) it must not contradict any express term of the contract.

In unionised employment, employers usually copy written collective agreements to new employees advising them that such agreements form part of their terms and conditions of employment. If members do not want to be bound by collective agreements, then the trade union cannot force them to be bound (*Goulding Chemicals Ltd v Bolger* (1977) IR 211).

In another case in 1994, where a collective agreement had been concluded with a representative trade union which had the effect of changing the employees' terms and conditions of employment, the Supreme Court found the employees were bound by the change (*O'Cearbhall v Bord Telecom Éireann* (1994) ELR 54).

Terms will be implied where necessary to give commercial efficacy to a contract of employment on the basis of the presumed intention of the parties and as a matter of law, independently of the intention of the parties, as a necessary legal incident of a definable category of contract (*Sweeney v Duggan* (1997) 2 ILRM 211).

Implied terms would include the employer's duty of care to his employee and the employee's duty to take reasonable care in the performance of his work.

It would reasonably be expected by any employer that their employee would be loyal to them and not act against the best interests of the employer, that is, a duty of fidelity, trust and confidence (*Boston Deep Sea Fishing & Ice Co v Ansell* (1888) 39 Ch D 339).

If the employee had a work-related problem, it would be implied that the employer would deal with it in a professional and timely manner. Of course, an employer would have to be able to trust his employee (*Soros and Soros v Davison* (1994) IRLR 264). An employer would also have to be able to trust his employee when his employee is dealing with customers or clients or left in trust of cash or business assets, and this expectation would be simply implied. It would also be implied that the employee should be able to trust his employer. Most employees could reasonably expect to get a fair and accurate reference, and this could also be implied, even where there is no actual obligation on the employer to provide same. An obvious implied term would be the obligation on the employee to show up for work and to show up on time and in a presentable state. If there is no notice period expressly stated in the contract, it is implied that the statutory notice period will apply.

If the employer and employee acted in a particular way on a regular basis after the contract is made, then it could be implied that these everyday actions are part of the contract. It would be necessary in such a case to show an intention by the parties to include it as a term. To enable a business to operate, some obvious terms might be implied, for example, the obligation on a child care worker to know basic first aid or a taxi driver to have a licence. Some employers might have a long history of certain work extras or customs, such as hosting a Christmas party every year or paying an annual bonus, and this could also be regarded as an implied term in the contract of employment.

We looked above at some basic implied terms. If you wish to review the basic terms of employment which an employer must provide to the employee in a *written* form within two months of starting the employment, please refer to the Terms of Employment (Information) Act 1994 which sets out same.

TERMS OF EMPLOYMENT (INFORMATION) ACT 1994

I started a new job. My boss said he will provide me with written terms of employment. What can I expect from this?

The Terms of Employment (Information) Act 1994 sets out the basic terms of employment which the employer must provide to the employee in a written form within two months of starting the employment. Failure to do so will leave the employer open to a claim from the employee, pursuant to the terms of the Act. The maximum amount that can be awarded to the employee is four weeks' remuneration (s 7 of the Act). The employee can bring a claim to the Workplace Relations Commission. A written contract of employment should always be furnished to the employee within the timeframe specified. Section 2 provides that the Act shall not apply to employment in which the employee is normally expected to work for the employer for less than eight hours in a week. Section 3 of the Terms of Employment (Information) Act 1994 provides that

> "an employer shall, not later than two months after the commencement of an employee's employment with the employer, give or cause to be given to the employee a statement in writing containing (a) the full names of the employer and the employee (b) the address of the employer in the state or, the address of the principal place of the relevant business of the employer in the state or the registered office (c) the place of work or, where there is no fixed or main place of work, a statement specifying that the employee is required or permitted to work at various places (d) the title of the job or nature of the work for which the employee is employed (e) the date of commencement of the employees contract of employment (f) in the case of a temporary contract of employment, the expected duration thereof or, if the contract of employment is for a fixed term, the date on which the contract expires, (g) the rate or method of calculation of the employee's remuneration (h) the length of the intervals between the times at which remuneration is paid, whether a week, a month or any other interval, (i) any

terms or conditions relating to hours of work, including overtime, (j) any terms or conditions relating to paid leave (other than sick pay leave), (k) any terms or conditions relating to incapacity for work due to sickness or injury and sick pay leave and pensions and pension schemes, (l) the period of notice which the employee is required to give and entitled to receive to determine the employee's contract of employment or where this cannot be indicated when the information is given, the method for determining such periods of notice, (m) a reference to any collective agreements which directly affect the terms and conditions of the employee's employment including, where the employer is not a party to such agreements, particulars of the bodies or institutions by whom they were made".

Section 5 of the Act obliged the employer to notify the employee of changes to a term or condition within one month. Section 6 of the Act provides for employees who were in employment before the commencement of the Act. They can request a statement in accordance with s 3 and must be given it within two months of the request. Section 7 of the Act sets out how complaints will be dealt with. An employee will provide a staff handbook which will highlight the procedures that apply in the workplace regarding, for example, grievance procedures, discipline or dignity at work policies.

As you can see above, it is very important that your employer complies with the provisions of the 1994 Act.

Rest Breaks at Work (Terms of Employment (Additional Information) Order, 1998 and Annual (Statutory) Leave

Am I entitled to take rest breaks at work? How often am I allowed to take a rest break in my new job?

Apart from setting out the basic hours of work, an employer should make reference to breaks, shifts and overtime, particularly where an employee may be required to work beyond the normal hours on a regular basis.

Terms of Employment (Additional Information) Order 1998 (SI No 49/1998) sets out the information which must be provided by employers regarding rest breaks. Section 3(1) refers to an employee who enters into a contract of employment after the commencement of this Order. The employer shall, within two months after the employee's commencement with the employer, give or cause to be given to the employee a statement in writing containing particulars of the times and duration of the rest periods and breaks referred to in ss 11, 12 and 13 of the Organisation of Working Time Act 1997 that are being allowed to the employee, and of any other terms and conditions relating to those periods and breaks. Section 2 refers to a contract of employment entered into before the commencement of this Order. An employer shall, if requested by the employee to do so, give or cause to be given to the employee within two months of the request being made, a statement in writing containing particulars of the times and duration of the rest periods and breaks referred to in ss 11, 12 and 13 of the Organisation of Working Time Act 1997 that are being allowed to the employee, and of any other terms and conditions relating to those periods and breaks.

Therefore the order provides that where, under the Terms of Employment (Information) Act 1994, an employer is required to provide an employee with a written statement of certain particulars of his or her terms of employment, such statement shall after 1 March 1998, include details of the times and duration of (and any other terms and conditions relating to) the rest periods and breaks referred to in ss 11, 12 and 13 of the Organisation of Working Time Act 1997 that are being allowed to an employee.

Annual statutory leave entitlements for full-time and part-time employees and public holiday entitlements are provided for in the Organisation of Working Time Act 1997.

The Carer's Leave Act 2001 provides for carer's leave and the Parental Leave Act (as amended) provides for parental leave. *Force majeure* leave is paid leave.

MINIMUM NOTICE ON TERMINATION OF EMPLOYMENT

I started a new job and it's not going very well. I suspect my employer may not keep me on and, even if he does continue to employ me, I might leave because I find the work difficult. What is the minimum notice to be given by an employer to terminate the contract of employment, and what is the minimum notice I must give my employer if I decide to leave?

Section 4(2) of the Minimum Notice and Terms of Employment Act 1973 provides that the minimum notice to be given by an employer to terminate the contract of employment of his employee shall be: (a) if the employee has been in the continuous service of his employer for less than two years, one week; (b) if the employee has been in the continuous employment of his employer for two years or more, but less than five years, two weeks; (c) if the employee has been in the continuous service of his employer for five years or more, but less than 10 years, four weeks; (d) if the employee has been in the continuous service of his employer for 10 years or more, but less than 15 years, six weeks; and (e) if the employee has been in the continuous service of his employer for 15 years or more, eight weeks.

During the notice period, the employee has the right to be paid in accordance with his contract of employment, even if the employer gives him no hours or has no work for him.

Section 6 of the Act provides *inter alia* that an employer shall be entitled to not less than one week's notice from an employee who has been in his continuous employment for 13 weeks or more of that employee's intention to terminate his

4. Employment Law

contract of employment. However, under s 7 of the Act, both the employer and the employee have a right to waive the notice period, with the employee accepting pay in lieu of the notice period. Complaints by employees are dealt with by the Workplace Relations Commission and the Labour Court on appeal (s 11)

I would also advise you to look at your contract of employment. If the contract provides for a longer period of notice, then this must be complied with. The employer could take a breach of contract action against you if do not give the contractual period of notice. You might like to refer to the case of An Employee v An Employer (2011) UD 82644/2009 Employment Appeals Tribunal (EAT) with discusses the Minimum Notice and Terms of Employment Acts 1973–2005, Organisation of Working Time Act 1997, Unfair Dismissals Acts 1997–2007, Contracts of Employment, Pay and Conditions of Employment, Failure to consult with employees and seek their consent to change the terms and conditions of employment and constructive dismissal.

Carey v Independent Newspapers (Ireland) Ltd -P9237 2012 (www.adarehrm.ie) relates to a High Court Judgement. The Plaintiff in this case, Mairead Carey was approached by the Evening Herald Newspaper to enquire if she would be interested in taking up a position with the Organisation. The Plaintiff advised the Defendant that she would not be able to work early hours as it was not practical for her, with a child at home. A new Editor was appointed who did not agree with the working arrangements. As the role of political correspondent is a very specific role, with few jobs in the market, counsel for the Plaintiff submitted that one year's notice would have been reasonable. The Defendant and a number of witnesses submitted that one months' notice is reasonable. There was no termination procedure or notice period agreed between the parties. The High Court concluded that in all the circumstances of this case, including the factual background as to how the Plaintiff came to be employed by the Defendant, the importance which Mr Paul Drury attached to the Plaintiff's employment, her esteemed professional ability, the fact that she was moving from a job to take up this position and most importantly the difficulty that she would undoubtedly face as a Political Correspondent in achieving a similar position in the greater Dublin area lead me to the conclusion that a reasonable period of notice of termination of the Plaintiff's employment with the Defendant Group would be six months or alternatively six months' net loss of earnings in lieu of notice. This case highlights to Organisations the importance of considering custom and practice in an industry in relation to notice periods for certain roles.

Therefore, both you and your employer must comply with the above legislation and please read your contract of employment before you make a final decision.

NATIONAL MINIMUM WAGE RATES

What is the current minimum wage rate in Ireland?

Since 1 January 2019, the national minimum wage is €9.80 per hour, as set out in the National Minimum Wage Order 2018.

The National Minimum Wage Act 2000 provides for a minimum hourly rate of pay. It is a criminal offence to breach the terms of the Act and this applies to record keeping, failure to pay the minimum wage, failure to give a written statement of average hourly pay within four weeks of being requested by the employee or obstructing a national employment rights inspector. Breaches of the terms of the Act are punishable by the imposition of a fine or a prison sentence or both.

All employees, including full-time, part-time, casual and temporary are covered by the Act, with the exception of close relatives of the employer and certain apprentices. Every employer must choose a pay reference period for each employee, and this can be a week, a fortnight or a month (but not longer than a month). An employee is entitled to a written statement from an employer detailing his or her reckonable pay, working hours, average hourly rate of pay and statutory minimum hourly rate of pay entitlement under the Act, in a pay reference period or periods within the previous 12 months. If the employer is not able to pay, he or she may apply to the Labour Court for an exemption from paying the minimum hourly rate. In order to obtain it, he must show that he would probably terminate the employment of an employee or put the employee on lay-off. The employer must have the consent of the employee (or the majority of employees) to apply for such an exemption. If an employee is not being paid the minimum wage, he or she may refer a complaint to a Rights Commissioner or make a complaint to the National Employment Rights Authority. The onus is on the employer to prove that the law has been complied with.

Rules in Relation to the Employment of Young People (Under 18 Years)

I got a job in the local supermarket for the summer. I am almost 16 years old. I have also applied for a job in a local flower shop because I want to build up a few extra hours' pay and I feel I am well able to work two jobs.

The Protection of Young Persons (Employment) Act 1996 provides protection for young people at work. Sections 3(1) and 4(1) and 10(1) are most applicable to your query. There are rules in the legislation relating to a child over the age of 14 and over the age of 15 but not yet 16. Your employers would have to comply with these rules as you are not yet 16 years old and your employers could be held guilty of an offence if prosecuted for breaching the rules.

Section 3(1) of the 1996 Act prohibits an employer from employing a child to work. The Minister may, however, by regulations, authorise the employment of children over the age of 13 years in cultural, artistic, sports or advertising activities which are not harmful to the safety, health or development of children and are not likely to interfere with their attendance at school (s 3(3)).

4. Employment Law

An employer may employ a child who is over the age of 14 to do light work during any period outside the school term, provided that the hours of work do not exceed seven in any day or 35 in any week, the work is not harmful to the health, safety and development of the child and, during the summer holidays, the child does not do any work for a period of at least 21 days (s 3(4)).

An employer may employ a child who is over the age of 15 to do light work during school term time, provided that the hours of work do not exceed eight in any week (s 3(5)).

Section 4(1) of the 1996 Act provides that an employer shall not employ any child on any work between 8pm on any one day and 8pm on the following day. Section 4(2) provides that. subject to subs (3), an employer shall ensure that an employee who is a child receives a minimum rest period of 14 consecutive hours in each period of 24 hours. The minimum consecutive hours of rest specified in subs (2) may be interrupted by an employer in the case of a child employed in activities that do not exceed two hours in each day or are separated, exclusive of breaks, over the day, provided that, in each period of 24 hours, the child receives a minimum rest period of 14 hours (s 4(3)). An employer shall ensure that an employee who is a child receives, in any period of seven days, a minimum rest period of two days which shall as far as possible be consecutive (s 4(4)).

An employer shall not permit a child employee to do any work for any period exceeding four hours without a break of at least 30 consecutive minutes (s 4(8)), and a child is not entitled to be paid in respect of this break (Section 4(9)). An employer who contravenes subsections (1), (2), (4) or (8) shall be guilty of an offence.

Section 10(1) of the Act prevents two employers from allowing a child/young person's total work hours exceeding their limits. An employer shall not permit an employee to do any form of work on any day on which the employee has done any form of work for another employer, except where the aggregate of the periods for which the employee does work for such employers on that day does not exceed their limit allowed under the Act. It may be a defence for employers, if prosecuted, to prove that they could not reasonably have known the child was also working somewhere else (s 10(4)).

Every employer must display at the principal entrances to the premises where any employees work, in such a position that it might be easily read by employees, the prescribed abstract of this Act (Section 12(1)), and an employer who fails to comply with the provisions of this section shall be guilty of an offence (s 12(2)).

The employer must keep records in respect of the employment of children/young people in order to prove that the Act is being complied with (s 15)

Whistleblowing
(The Protected Disclosures Act 2014)

I work in a factory and I am concerned about a number of health and safety issues at my workplace. I am worried that, if I complain about my concerns to my employer, he might dismiss me. Are there any legal remedies available to me that would prevent my dismissal if I proceed with making a complaint?

Whistleblowing refers to raising the alarm in public about a wrong being committed in private (Vickers, *Freedom of Speech and Employment*, OUP, 2002).

Do not mix this up with a grievance. There must be a genuine wrongdoing on the part of the employer. If you have a grievance against your employer, that is an entirely different matter. You cannot make a protected disclosure purely for personal gain. A person cannot be penalised for making a protected disclosure.

Most of us would be familiar with the high profile case of Garda Sergeant Maurice McCabe who was recognised for being a whistleblower on corruption within An Garda Siochàna, Irelands national police force. The casualties of the scandal reached the highest levels of government. A new 'policing authority' was established to ensure that scandal within Garda Siochà na remained at a minimum and that the Government could have more involvement with the daily operations of the organisation (Tribunal of Inquiry into Protected Disclosures Made under the Protected Disclosures Act 2014 and Certain Other Matters (Ireland)).

The most topical piece of legislation in this area is the Protected Disclosures Act 2014 which is an almost prescriptive piece of legislation. A "protected disclosure" is a disclosure by a worker of "relevant information", defined as information that "(a) in the reasonable belief of the worker...tends to show one or more relevant wrongdoings, and (b) comes to the attention of the worker in connection with the worker's employment". It must be "information" of a wrongdoing, an allegation is not sufficient, it must show a "relevant wrongdoing", as defined in the Protected Disclosures Act 2014 and it must have come to the worker's attention in connection with his or her employment. The Protected Disclosures Act 2014 provides an exhaustive list and very broad definition of what is a "relevant wrongdoing" and it includes the commission of a criminal offence, the failure to comply with a legal obligation, the occurrence of a miscarriage of justice, the endangerment of the health and safety of an individual, damage to the environment, misuse of public funds, mismanagement by a public body and the concealment or destruction of information tending to show any of the above. The definition of wrongdoing includes: (a) that an offence has been, is being or is likely to be committed and (b) that a person has failed, is failing or is likely to fail to comply with any legal obligation, other that one arising under the worker's contract of employment or other contract whereby the worker undertakes to do or perform personally any work or services, (c) that a miscarriage of justice has occurred, is occurring or is likely to occur, (d) that the health or safety of any individual has been, is being or is likely to be endangered, (e) that the environment has been, is being or is likely to be endangered, (f) that an unlawful or otherwise improper use of funds or resources of a public body or other public money has occurred, is occurring or is likely to occur, (g) that an act or omission by or on behalf of a public body is oppressive, discriminatory or grossly negligent or constitutes gross mismanagement or (h) that information tending to show any matter falling within any of the preceding paragraphs has been, is being or is likely to be concealed or destroyed. This is so broad, one might, in my opinion, ask if this is a charter for interference.

In September 2016, the Labour Court awarded €17,500 to the employee, in *Monaghan v Aras Chois Fharriage*, which was the first award for penalisation under the Act.

The case related to a nursing home worker who complained about health and safety issues at work. The employer mistakenly believed that the complaints were grievances (as distinct from treating the complaints as protected disclosures) and suspended the employee on full pay in accordance with its grievance procedure. The employee brought a claim alleging that she had been penalised for making the disclosure.

The Labour Court found in favour of the employee and held that her complaints were protected disclosures. The Court was satisfied that the employee had satisfied the "but for" test as but for her protected disclosures, she would not have been suspended by her employer.

In relation, to the employee's suspension in this case, it was very clear that the employee would not have been suspended, if she had not made the protected disclosure. However, it is not this clear cut in all cases.

A matter is not a relevant wrongdoing if it is a matter which it is the function of the worker or the workers employer to detect, investigate or prosecute, and does not consist of or involve an act or omission on the part of the employer (*Donegal County Council v Carr*, June (2016) Labour Court, PDD161). In that case, a Fire Station Officer alleged that he had made six separate protected disclosures. Four of the complaints related to the alleged behaviour of fire-fighters in the station. One related to a work payments claim and the other related to the physical fitness of two fire-fighters in relation to their ability to carry out their jobs.

The employee alleged that as a result of these protected disclosures, he suffered penalisation in the form of being undermined in his position as Station Manager.

The Labour Court held that the allegations could not constitute protected disclosures, as it was part of his role as a Station Officer to detect and report such matters.

In *A Public Servant v A Government Department* (AdJ-00004925), the employee, as part of his job, provided training at an off-site location and observed a business, who he was overseeing, failing to comply with their legal obligations. He communicated this to his line manager.

Two months later, he was suspended for unrelated allegations, which an independent investigator concluded were well founded. The employee alleged that this suspension amounted to penalisation resulting from his protected disclosure.

The WRC held that his disclosure was not covered by the Act, as it was part of his job, to detect such matters. Furthermore, it did not constitute a wrongdoing by *his own employer*.

The motivation for making a disclosure is irrelevant to whether or not it is a protected disclosure. In proceedings involving an issue as to whether a disclosure is a protected disclosure, it shall be presumed, until the contrary is proven, that it is a protected disclosure.

The Protected Disclosures Act 2014 provides protection to all workers, including employees, contractors, agency workers and trainees. The Act also provides significant protection for whistleblowers against penalisation. That would include suspension, dismissal, demotion or loss of opportunity, transfer of duties, change of location of work, reduction in wages, unfair treatment, coercion, intimidation, discrimination, injury or threat of reprisal.

It also protects a worker making a protected disclosure from defamation claims and from any civil or criminal liability in respect of same. However, the immunity in relation to criminal liability is limited to circumstances where the whistle-blower reasonably believed that he was making a protected disclosure.

Section 11 of the Protected Disclosures Act 2014 provides for the protection of employees from dismissal for having made a protected disclosure. Section 11(2), schedule 1, contains provisions for interim relief in cases where a claim is brought for redress for a dismissal which is an unfair dismissal by virtue of s 6(2) (b) of the Unfair Dismissals Act 1977. The Unfair Dismissals Acts 1977 – 2007 have been amended to provide that, if an employee is dismissed for making a protected disclosure, then it is an unfair dismissal and there is no requirement for one year's service.

There is a severe penalty in s 11 for dismissal of an employee for making a protected disclosure of up to five years' (260 weeks) remuneration. However, in reality this would probably be appealed and, quite frankly, one might never get it. If investigation of a wrongdoing is not the main motivation for a protected disclosure, then there will be a reduction of 25% of the reward.

In *Philpott v Marymount University Hospital & Hospice Limited* (2015) IECC 1 Judge O'Donohoe stated that the Court only had to satisfy itself that the beliefs and disclosures were reasonable. The plaintiff did not satisfy that test, even though the sincerity of the plaintiff was accepted. It was in fact an application for an injunction. The application failed.

4. Employment Law

One can make a claim to the Workplace Relations Commission and get an award, but it is in my opinion better to claim in the Circuit Court. Under s 11, an employee can seek an order from the Circuit Court preventing dismissal prior to the determination of a claim for unfair dismissal.

Section 13(1) of the Act provides that, if a person causes detriment to another person because the other person or a third party made a protected disclosure, the person to whom the detriment is caused has a right of action in tort against the person by whom the detriment is caused. Detriment includes coercion, intimidation, harassment, discrimination, disadvantage, adverse treatment in relation to employment or prospective employment, injury, damage and threat of reprisal (s 13(3)).

In *Dougan and Clarke v Lifeline Ambulances*, Circuit Court (2016) two ambulance service workers were made redundant. They were granted an order in the Circuit Court directing the continued payment of their salaries pending the outcome of a claim for unfair dismissal. They had brought their claim to the Workplace Relations Commission on the basis that they were unfairly dismissed for making a protected disclosure to the Revenue Commissioners. The Court held that they had substantive grounds for claiming this, because they had met the burden of proof placed on them in the Protective Disclosures Act 2014. All they had to show was substantial grounds for claiming a connection between the dismissal and the protected disclosure. Judge Comerford provided that both men had been dismissed by reason of redundancy from having made two separate protected disclosures. On hearing the employees' application for interim relief, the Court considered the statutory test and concluded that "it is likely that there are substantial grounds for contending that dismissal results wholly or mainly from the employee having made a protected disclosure". The Court looked at the connection in time, animus and the fact that there was no genuine consultation over the redundancies. An order was made for the continued payment of both men's salaries until their unfair dismissal case was heard. Costs were awarded to the men.

The case illustrates that employers need to exercise particular caution if they are considering dismissing an employee who has previously made a complaint which could be considered a protected disclosure. If the employer cannot prove that the dismissal is not connected to the protected disclosure, it may be ordered by the Court in the interim to reinstate, re-engage or pay the former employee. Such an order allows the employee to accrue service and s/he would remain in place until the unfair dismissal claim is heard before the WRC.

In *Catherine Kelly v Alien Vault Ireland Limited and Alien Vault Inc* (2016) Cork Circuit Court, the claimant was granted interim relief under the Protected Disclosures Act 2014.

Ms Kelly, an office manager, made some complaints to her employer about health and safety issues in the office workplace. The employer dismissed her and claimed that the decision to dismiss her was made some days before her complaints.

It's important to understand that the employee's motive is irrelevant when it comes to determining whether it's a protected disclosure or not.

Cork Circuit Court found that the plaintiff had substantial grounds for claiming that her dismissal was linked to her protected disclosure and granted her an interim order preventing her dismissal and keeping her on full pay until her case was heard in full by the Workplace Relations Commission.

This case reiterates that employers need to tread carefully if they dismiss an employee who has made a protected disclosure. The threshold for bringing a claim for interim relief is relatively low – all the employee needs to show is that there are "substantial grounds" for contending their dismissal was linked to their protected disclosure. There is no requirement for the applicant to prove that the dismissal was, in fact, wholly or mainly due to whistleblowing.

This case also highlights the significant protections the Act affords and the increasing willingness of the courts to apply these protections. Such successes will likely encourage future whistle-blowers to seek protection under the Act where they perceive a connection between their dismissal and any disclosure made by them in the past.

In the Labour Court in *Monaghan v McGrath* (2016) PDD162, the employee was a care assistant with a nursing home and made a protected disclosure to HIQA of alleged abuse. The Court considered what the motives were which placed the employee on suspension with basic pay only, and was of the view that the suspension of the employee was influenced by the complaints made by her to the HIQA. Her employer ordered a provider-led investigation. The question to be asked is whether the employee would have been placed on suspension other than for the protected disclosure? What were the motives of the employer for placing the employee on suspension? There was undue haste in making the suspension without giving the employee an opportunity to comment on the report. This was a causal connection between the making of the complaint by the employee and her suspension.

The Court further concluded that the making of the protected disclosure was an operative reason for the suspension and was retaliation for the making of the disclosure of alleged abuse. The employee was awarded €17,500.

If you consider that you have a strong case, then an application should be made to the Circuit Court for interim relief on the basis that there are substantial grounds for contending that the dismissal was wholly or mainly due to the protected disclosure. This should be done within 21 days following the dismissal. If a dismissed employee can make a good argument to establish that the dismissal was wholly or mainly due to the protected disclosure, he or she may lodge a claim under the Unfair Dismissals Acts 1977 as amended seeking the increased five years' compensation.

This is an important piece of legislation in the protection of whistle-blowers from dismissal pending a further investigation of any claims made (Law Reform Commission, www.irishstatutebook.ie, *Protected Disclosure and Employment* by

4. Employment Law

Frances Meenan Senior Counsel at the Law Society of Ireland/the Bar Council of Ireland (employment law – 1st edition, Round Hall Press, 2014))

There is also a code of practice, but it is quite poor, in my opinion. S.I. No. 464/2015 - Industrial Relations Act 1990 (Code of Practice on Protected Disclosures Act 2014) (Declaration) Order 2015. The European Union (Protection of Trade Secrets) Regulations 2018 were implemented in Ireland on 9 June 2018.

From the point of view of employers protecting their businesses a decision of the WRC has highlighted the importance of having a whistleblowing policy in place, which prescribes how a disclosure should be made by an employee and how it will be dealt with upon receipt by the employer. Having a policy in place may bolster an employer's defence, if a claim is subsequently brought against it by the employee.

In an *Employee v Employee* (ADJ-00003371(2016)), the WRC criticised the employee for not using the comprehensive whistleblowing policy, which had been put in place by the employer. The WRC held that the employee had not made a protected disclosure until the letter of complaint from her solicitor was received, as her previous method of disclosure was not in line with the employer's policy.

THE PROBATIONARY PERIOD

I am a social worker. I started a new job recently and I was on probation for 12 months. While on probation, I noticed a few issues I was unhappy about in the workplace. I approached my employer about my concerns and he dismissed me. What are my rights during the probation period?

Unfair dismissal legislation provides that a probationary period cannot exceed one year. You do not have any statutory protection offered by the Unfair Dismissals Act 1977, as amended, or any unfair dismissal legislation until you have acquired 12 months' service. Therefore you are statutorily barred from bringing a claim for unfair dismissal or constructive dismissal. You mentioned you were unhappy about some issues in the workplace and therefore, as you do not have 12 months' service completed, your employer can simply decide that you are not right for the organisation and terminate your employment. An employer does not have to give you any reason to dismiss you when you are on probation.

The fact that employees are on probation or undergoing training has therefore no effect on continuity or status, and is entirely recognisable. Employers should at all times have regard to the statutory date of dismissal where employees are being trained or are undergoing probationary assessment in order to ensure that the employment does not extend to or beyond the one-year period. If they were then to terminate the employment, they might find themselves having to show that substantial grounds existed to justify the termination in circumstances where they believed otherwise.

The position at common law seems to be that the employer has an implied right to terminate during the probationary period on the giving of specified or reasonable notice (*Dalgleish v Kew House Farm Ltd*, (1982) IRLR 251 (CA) 2.93, 15.26). A prudent employer will provide that, during a probationary period, the employment may be terminated on specified notice, often shorter than the notice required to terminate the contract when employment has become permanent. In *Doyle v Grangeford Precast Concrete Ltd* ((1998) HC ELR 260) the employer sought to impose a probationary period in a written document produced to the employee for his signature after he had commenced employment. The High Court held that there was a breach of trust and that the employer was not entitled unilaterally to impose a new contractual provision. The employee obtained an interlocutory injunction pending the outcome of his claim for damages. The employee subsequently obtained damages measured at six months' remuneration in lieu of notice.

DIPLOMATIC IMMUNITY

I was dismissed from my job at the embassy. Can I bring an unfair dismissals claim against my employers?

Employees of embassies and foreign governments in Ireland cannot bring dismissal claims against their employers where the employer is entitled generally to diplomatic immunity, which is not provided for or referred to in the unfair dismissals legislation (*Government of Canada v Employment Appeals Tribunal* ((1991) ELR 57)).

APPRENTICES

I served as an apprentice for four years and one month. I learned a lot and received great training from my employer. I was hoping he would keep me on when the apprenticeship was completed. I was disappointed when my employer terminated my contract just one month after I completed the apprenticeship. Can I take a dismissals claim?

Section 4 of the 1977 Unfair Dismissal Act provides that apprentices are not protected for the first six months of their employment and for a period of one month following completion of the apprenticeship. This means that once an apprentice has completed six months of an apprenticeship, he is covered by the legislation where otherwise he might be thought to require the one year's continuous service (*MacNamara v Castlelock Construction & Development Ltd* (UD 1984/808)). This relates only to statutory apprenticeships. Section 1 of the 1977 Act defines a statutory apprenticeship as being an apprenticeship in a designated industrial activity, within the meaning of the Industrial Training Act 1967. Non-statutory apprenticeships should be treated as specified-purpose contracts where the employer wishes to be adequately protected from unfair dismissal claims. The general view is that an employer may terminate an apprenticeship if the apprentice's conduct is such that the employer can no longer instruct him.

A contract of apprenticeship may be defined as one in which the apprentice agrees to serve the employer and to learn from him, and the employer agrees to instruct the apprentice in his trade, profession or business and to maintain him during the continuance of that relationship.

In *Boal v IMED Ireland Ltd* ((1995) ELR 178), the employee was employed under a statutory apprenticeship for six years. His contract was terminated one month after the completion of the apprenticeship. The employers claimed that they had informed the claimant on a number of occasions during the six years of the apprenticeship that they would not be retaining him on the end of his apprenticeship. The Employment Appeals Tribunal held that the employee was employed under a contract of statutory apprenticeship, and was therefore excluded from cover under the Unfair Dismissals Acts 1977 as amended and his claim was dismissed.

ABSENT FROM WORK DUE TO ILLNESS

I am an employer and one of my business associates recommended that I draw up a sick leave absence management policy and procedure plan, setting out the procedure when an employee is absent a lot through illness and a dismissal may be necessary. Is there any legislation in place to deal with this?

A high level of absence due to illness may lead to a dismissal in some cases, even when such absence is covered by medical certificates. In such cases, a court or tribunal will have to balance the employee's welfare against the demands of the business. The employer must act reasonably.

An employer may be afforded statutory protection in dismissing a persistently absent employee due to illness. Section 6(4) of the Unfair Dismissals Act 1977 provides that

> "without prejudice to the generality of subs (1) of this section, the dismissal of an employee shall be deemed for the purposes of this act, not to be an unfair dismissal, if it results wholly or mainly from one or more of the following: (a) the capability, competence or qualifications of the employee for performing work of the kind which he was employed by the employer to do".

Under s 6(6), it is for employer to show that the dismissal resulted wholly or mainly from one or more of the matters specified in subs (4).

When considering absence dismissal due to illness, one must also look at case law and the requirements of the Employment Equality Acts 1998-2008 which afford protection to employees suffering from disability. Before dismissing an employee, the employer must afford the employee all reasonable opportunities to improve on the attendance record and allow fair procedures to the employee, afford the employee an opportunity to be heard and warn the employee of the possibility that the employment may be terminated (*Bolger v Showerings (Ireland) Ltd* ((1990) HC ELR 184). A decision to terminate employment is not a decision to be made by a doctor but is one to be made by management in light of medical evidence (*Bergin v Easons Cash & Carry (Wholesale) Ltd* (UD 1981/669)). The employer should nonetheless have an up-to-date medical opinion prior to making a decision to dismiss (*McLoughlin v Celmac (Ireland) Ltd* (UD 1984/799)). Abuse of sick leave by working or otherwise acting inconsistently with being out sick and on sick leave may justify dismissal for misconduct and dishonesty.

There may be instances where the employers are able to make alternative arrangements and can tolerate high levels of absence. The employer must show that the dismissal was necessary for good commercial reasons (*McGrane v Mater Private Nursing Home* (UD 1985/369)).

In *Reardon v St Vincent's Hospital* (UD 1979/74) Reardon was employed as a kitchen porter in St Vincent's Hospital. He had many prolonged absences, all due to illness and all covered by medical certificates. The employers wrote to him stating that, if he did not improve, the question of his continued employment would be reviewed. Reardon's sick leave record did not improve and his employers decided to terminate his employment. It was argued that this was an unfair dismissal, as his absence was due to illness and covered by medical certificates, and that, if his employers had offered him a change of duties away from the kitchen, this might help. The employers submitted that they did not have any alternative suitable vacancy. The Employment Appeals Tribunal held that the dismissal was not unfair. Reardon was not capable of doing the work he was employed to do (s 6(4) of the 1977 Act). The employers did not have an alternative vacancy for him, and therefore they had acted reasonably in dismissing him.

An employer can put a policy in place setting out the procedures to be adopted when an employee is absent through illness, and give a copy of it to all employees (a sick leave absence management policy and procedure). The policy would make it clear to everyone what to expect when an employee is absent because of an illness. The policy would include direction on whether there is a sick pay scheme and what the notification and certification requirements are when an employee is out sick. The policy could refer to medical certificates and provide for when and how often they must be furnished to the employer during absence from work, information on the nature of the illness, expected return to work date, temporary return to work and any other issues the employer may feel is relevant to the nature of the work involved. Make it clear that an employee can be requested to attend the employer's doctor for a medical report or examination, and that the employer is entitled to see a copy of this medical assessment. If an employee is returning to work after a long-term absence due to illness, request a "fitness to resume" doctor's note by the resumption date, or not later than one week thereafter. The employee should not be allowed to return to work without one.

4. Employment Law

If an employee's work contract is going to be terminated on the grounds of capacity, the employee should be invited to make a submission to influence the decision and fair procedures must always be followed. The medical report should support a decision to terminate by indicating that there is no reasonable prospect of a return to work within a reasonable timeframe (see Terry Gorry *Employment Rights Ireland*).

A Worker (represented by SIPTU) and A Company (in Receivership represented by Homes O'Malley Sexton Solicitors), Decision DEC-E2014-066 26 December 2014 EE/2011/795 involved a claim by Mr A that the respondent discriminated against him on the ground of disability contrary to s 6(2)(g) of the Employment Equality Acts 1998 to 2011, in terms of failure to provide reasonable accommodation and discriminatory dismissal.

The complainant submitted that he commenced work as a general operative for the respondent, a quarry business, in 2004. He held a variety of positions before he had to undergo surgery for a brain tumour in November 2009. The operation was successful, and the complainant made a full recovery. In October 2010, he was advised by his doctor that he would be fit to return to work for 20 hours per week. This request was initially implemented by the respondent, but by December 2010, the complainant was informed by the Operations Manager that he would have to return to work full time or he would lose his job.

In January 2011, the complainant was absent from work on sick leave, as the respondent would no longer accommodate him with a 20-hour work week. In June 2011, the complainant attended a doctor named by the respondent for a medical assessment. The complainant was then dismissed on 5 August 2011 on the ground that the respondent was not in a position to offer him a 20 hour work week on an ongoing basis. The complainant appealed this dismissal, but the appeal was unsuccessful. The reason given for his dismissal was again that he was not in a position to work full-time for the respondent. The Equality Tribunal found that pursuant to s 79(6) of the Employment Equality Acts 1998 to 2011, that the respondent company discriminated against Mr A by not providing him with reasonable accommodation on his return to work after he had recovered from a brain tumour, contrary to its obligations under s 16 of the Acts, and that it subsequently discriminatorily dismissed Mr A on the ground of his disability contrary to s 8(6) of the Acts. In accordance with s 82 of the Acts, as amended by s 25(1) of the Civil Law (Miscellaneous Provisions) Act 2011, they ordered that the respondent pay the complainant € 40,000 for the discriminatory treatment endured, and for his discriminatory dismissal.

Please note that many employers have insurance policies to cover their employees during a period of prolonged absence due to illness. It is normally a condition of these policies that the employee remains an employee while in receipt of payments. Once accepted under the policy, the insurer pays the money to the employer, who processes it through the payroll in the normal way and passes the net amount to the employee.

Retirement

I work in the canteen in a local mart. Friends are always enquiring about my retirement. However, I am fit and healthy and I love my job. I am not planning to retire any time soon. There is nothing set out in my contract of employment forcing me to retire from employment. Can my employer force me to retire?

The Employment Equality Acts 1998, as amended, set out grounds on which you cannot be discriminated against, and one of these grounds is age. There are some exceptions to this under the Acts, including that it is not discriminatory *per se* to set a retirement date for employees in the contract of employment. You stated that there is no such clause in your contract of employment forcing you to retire. Therefore if your employer were to try forcing you to retire, you may have had a good claim for discrimination on the grounds of age under the employment equality legislation above. However, s 10 of the Equality (Miscellaneous Provisions) Act 2015 provides that s 34 of the 1998 Act is amended by the substitution of the following subs for subs (4):

> "(4) Without prejudice to subsection (3), it shall not constitute discrimination on the grounds of age to fix different ages for the retirement (whether voluntary or compulsorily) of employees or any class or description of employees if – (a) it is objectively and reasonably justified by a legitimate aim, and (b) the means of achieving that aim are appropriate and necessary".

Therefore, under s 10, an employer can impose a retirement age for employees, provided he or she can objectively justify it and provided the means are appropriate and necessary.

EU Directive 2000/78/EC provides that any differences in treatment on the ground of age must be objectively justified and reasonable. The Equality Tribunal has held that this directive only has direct effect when it involves a State body as an employer.

The Labour Court decision in Connaught Airport Development Limited t/a Ireland West Airport, Knock and John Glavey, (Labour Court Decision, 30 June 2017) highlights the importance of specifying retirement ages in contracts of employment. The Labour Court found that dismissing an employee for their age was an act of discrimination. Mr Glavey had worked for the airport as a senior bartender from 1991 until his dismissal. Mr Glavey's employment contract with Campbell Catering did not include a retirement age. In 2006, nearly three years after the transfer, following negotiations between management and the union, Mr Glavey was issued with a new contract of employment. This contract did not specify a retirement age either. It came as a complete surprise to Mr Glavey when he was informed that he would have to retire in January 2016 on his 65th birthday. Mr Glavey argued that, due to the increase in the age of receipt of the state pension from 65 to 66 years, there was still a requirement on him to be available for work and that there was no justifiable objective reason for the employer to terminate his employment. He also argued that no legitimate aim or objective could be served by not allowing him to remain in work until he reached 66. Mr Glavey pointed to two employees who had remained in employment following their 65th birthday. The employer argued that the age of retirement of 65 years was justified within the meaning of s 34(4) of the Act and Art 6 of European Directive 2000/78/EC "Establishing a General Framework for Equal Treatment in Employment and Education" (the "Directive") and that the means chosen by the respondent were both appropriate and necessary for achieving that aim. It argued that it was an express term and condition of Mr Glavey's employment that his employment would not continue past his 65th birthday. The employer contended that it had one universal retirement age for all of its staff, ensuring consistency amongst all of its employees and creating certainty and succession planning. The employer argued that, although the contract did not contain a mandatory retirement clause, such a clause should be implied as it had been the accepted custom and practice of the employer since 1986 for employees to retire when they reached the age of 65, except in the most limited and exceptional circumstances. It argued that exceptional circumstances had applied in the case of the two employees who had worked beyond their 65th birthdays.

Section 34(4) of the Employment Equality Act 1998 allows an employer to fix a retirement age without contravening the prohibition of discrimination on grounds of age. Article 6(1) of the Directive provides that difference of treatment on grounds of age shall not constitute discrimination, only where it is objectively and reasonably justified by a legitimate aim and the means of achieving that aim are appropriate and necessary.

The Court found that there was no express term in his conditions of employment requiring Mr Glavey to retire at the age of 65, noting that the employer had numerous opportunities to include such a provision. The Court found that the employer had not provided any evidence to demonstrate that Mr Glavey had been informed of the retirement age or provided with any documentation from which this could be discerned. The Court did not accept that a retirement age of 65 had been implied or incorporated into Mr Glavey's contract of employment.

The Court held that the employer had not fixed a retirement age and that Mr Glavey had been dismissed because of his age. In view of this, there was no requirement for the Court to consider any of the employer's arguments of objective justification for a retirement age of 65. The complainant was awarded a sum of €6,500 for the effects of the act of discrimination, having clarified to the court that he did not seek reinstatement.

In *Porter v Donegal County Council* ((1993) ELR 101), the Department of the Environment introduced a requirement that all firemen should retire at the age of 55. The employees at the time they were taken on had a normal retirement age of 60. The county council forcibly retired some employees, who then claimed unfair dismissal. The justification for the forced retirement was the Department of Environment requirement and the practice that, given the nature of the work, firemen should not be required to work after the age of 55. In holding that the dismissals were unfair because of the unilateral imposition of a new retirement age, Flood J held that the employer could have resolved the problem of possible unfitness by requiring the employees to undergo regular medical examinations. An employer cannot normally oblige an employee to undergo a medical examination but, in this case, it was accepted that the employer might be in a position to suspend the employee from duty until the employee had satisfied the employer as to his fitness.

In *Buckley v Ceimici Teo* (UD 528/1980), at the time the claimant commenced employment, there was no contractual provision and the normal retirement age was 70 years. His employment was terminated when he reached 65, which was the pension age. The claimant maintained he was entitled to continue working until the normal retirement age of 70. The respondents, however, were in a position to produce documentary evidence that the normal retirement age had changed to 65 years, and that the claimant was aware of this. The dismissal was held to be fair. The retirement age for a company pension is not the same as being forced to retire from employment.

O'Neill v Fairview Motors (2012) EAT 093(adarehrm.ie-employment law) involved a claim that the Complainant was discriminated against by the Respondent when he was dismissed in circumstances amounting to discrimination on the grounds of age. The Complainant advised that he never received a contract of employment or Employee Handbook, and consequently, was never informed that he would be required to retire on his 65th birthday; The Complainant was approaching 65 when the Respondent approached him and advised him he would have to retire on reaching 65. The Complainant advised the Respondent he felt fit and well and capable of continuing to work and did therefore not want to retire.

The Respondent stated that the terms and conditions of employment were well understood, including the condition that he was required to retire on reaching the age of 65. The Equality Officer found that the Respondent's assertion that the Complainant's performance had slipped were not brought to the Complainant's attention at that time and occurred after the Complainant had raised considerable resistance to the Respondent forcing him to retire. The Equality Officer found that the Respondent discriminated against the Complainant on grounds of age when it denied him access to work related training courses, and the dismissal was discrimination on the grounds of age. The Equality Officer awarded the Employee €30,000 for the distress caused to him as a consequence of the discrimination he was subjected to.

In conclusion employers should be careful to ensure that contracts of employment have clear written policies and procedures/provisions in respect of retirement. The organisations policies on retirement should be clear to all employees. Employers should have a clearly thought out rationale for specifying the retirement age. Where no retirement age is specified and an employer seeks to rely on custom and practice, it will be difficult for the employer to defend a claim of discrimination if an employee can point to other employees who have remained in employment beyond that age.

4. *Employment Law*

How to Dismiss an Employee

I am an employer having grave difficulties with one of my employees. She clearly has no interest in her work and she has been dropping hints for years that she plans on leaving if she ever gets the opportunity - but regrettably that opportunity has never materialised. In any regard, she is not a particularly competent employee. What steps can I take in terminating her employment without risking her claiming against me for unfair dismissal?

Please contact an experienced employment law solicitors' firm for up to date advice regarding your query. An employee's employment can be terminated at any time but unless the dismissal is fair the employer may be found guilty of unfair dismissal by an Employment Tribunal. Section 6(4) of the Unfair Dismissals Act 1977 provides

> "that the dismissal of an employee shall be deemed for the purposes of this act not to be an unfair dismissal, if it results wholly or mainly from one or more of the following (a) the capability, competence or qualifications of the employee for performing work of the kind which he was employed by the employer to do, (b) the conduct of the employee, (c) the redundancy of the employee (d) the employee being unable to work or continue to work in the position which he held without contravention by him or of his employer of a duty or of a restriction imposed by or under any statute or instrument made under statute".

You must have substantial grounds justifying the dismissal (s 6(1) of the Unfair Dismissals Act 1977), and you must afford your employee fair procedures and natural justice.

You mention that your employee is not particularly competent. Before you could dismiss her on the grounds of lack of competence, you should first point out her shortcomings to her and your required improvements and give her a set time to make the improvements. Issue a warning regarding dismissal. An employee is entitled to fair procedures and natural justice, and that is why you should do the above first.

Redundancy is a defence to a claim for unfair dismissal if the redundancy is a legitimate one, that is, the role is being eliminated. If your employee lied at interview about her qualifications, dismissal may be legitimate. Gross misconduct can also justify summary dismissal, as can some lesser misconducts justify termination of employment. Dismissal on the grounds of capability would include issues such as persistent poor time-keeping or absence from the workplace because of illness or other reasons.

Direct and Indirect Discrimination

I am a woman in my late 50s and I have worked with the same company for years. I always thought I was paid the same as other employees working at my level. I was therefore very surprised to discover that the men working with me are paid more than I am paid. I am also required to carry out additional cleaning jobs at work that my male colleagues are never asked to do. When I recently complained about this my hours were reduced. I also feel intimidated and sometimes humiliated by a new employee that started working here a few months ago. He makes fun of the fact that I suffer from a very mild disability. Is there anything I can do about all this?

Discrimination is treating one person less favourably than another person on the grounds of gender, age, religion, disability, race/nationality/colour/membership of various ethnic communities, sexual orientation, family status, marital status or membership of the Travelling community. The Employment Equality Act 1998 prohibits discrimination in the workplace on any of these grounds. The sources of Irish employment equality law include the Employment Equality Acts 1998-2008, Article 141 of the EC treaty, the Irish Constitution, Social Welfare Act 2004 and various EU directives such as the Equal Pay Directive (75/117/EEC), the Equal Treatment Directive (76/207/EEC) and directives to cover harassment in the workplace and victimisation. In *Jenkins v Kingsgate (Clothing Productions) Ltd* [1981] IRLR 388, the Court declared that Art 1 of the Directive identifies both equal work and work of equal value on an equal basis to a claim for equal pay and gives an equal and independent right to found such a claim on either basis. Article 6 of the Equal Treatment Directive obliges Member States to introduce judicial remedies under their national legislation, so all persons who consider themselves wronged may pursue their claims by judicial process. Harassment is conduct that is unwelcome to the victim and may reasonably be regarded as intimidating, humiliating and offensive. Victimisation is where an employee is penalised for seeking redress in good faith under the relevant legislation. The main purpose of the equality legislation and directives is to prevent discrimination or inequality on the grounds of difference. The Employment Equality Acts established a legal right to equal pay for men and women engaged in "like" work by the same employer at the same time or during the previous or succeeding three years. Employers cannot discriminate in relation to access to employment, conditions of employment, training or promotion. Discrimination is against the law in collective agreements (with regard to access to and conditions of employment and equal pay for like work), employment agencies, advertising, professional and trade associations, trade unions (as regards membership and other benefits) and vocational training.

In Ms D (an employee) v An Employer (Workplace Relations Commission (WRC) 2016) a bar worker who suffers from an extremely painful medical condition causing her chronic pain won her discrimination case against her employer.

The Workplace Relations Commission (WRC) ordered that a publican pay €20,000 to the woman, referred to as Ms D, after the commission found he discriminated against her on the grounds of gender and disability.

In the case before the WRC, Ms D underwent a surgical procedure for her endometriosis in October 2015 and was supplied with a doctor's certificate stating that she was capable only of light duties and to not undertake any heavy lifting on returning to work.

However, on returning to work, Ms D found that her hours were reduced sharply.

Ms D asked why she could not continue with her normal hours as before in the bar and was told that the way her boss saw it, working in the bar and the reception involved heavy lifting.

Ms D was then handed her a letter which stated: "From a health and safety point of view, we will be unable to offer you any work until you inform us that you are fit for work."

The commission heard that prior to the surgical procedure, because Ms D was the only female on the staff, she was asked to carry out chambermaid duties at the business in addition to her bar duties.

Ms D told the hearing, which was held in Gorey, Co Wexford, that when the two other male bar workers came in to work she was sent off to clean rooms.

That work was physically much more demanding than her role as a bar worker.

Ms D said she found the work extremely demanding because of her endometriosis. She said her hours began to be reduced significantly in comparison to her two male employees.

The two male employees who took up employment after Ms D were consistently provided with full-time hours in their roles as bar staff, thus essentially leaving Ms D only with whatever remaining hours were available.

In her decision that Ms D was discriminated against on the ground of gender, WRC adjudication officer Niamh O'Carroll Kelly said that the employer provided no reasons which could objectively justify why Ms D was treated less favourably than her male counterparts.

Ms O'Carroll Kelly also found the publican discriminated against Ms D on the grounds of disability after finding he was fully aware she had undergone a small surgical day procedure and was certified fit to return to work, albeit restricted to light duties for a period of one week.

Ms O'Carroll Kelly also found the employer took no steps to consult with Ms D or her medical advisers in order to ascertain what reasonable accommodation or appropriate measures could have assisted her in maintaining her work role.

Ms O'Carroll Kelly recorded that without any knowledge, assessment, consultation, or even reading the certificate submitted, the employer made, "what can only be described as a bizarre decision" to take Ms D off the roster and Ms D resigned from her position shortly after that.

Awarding Ms D €20,000, Ms O'Carroll Kelly found she "has established a prima facia case of discrimination on the grounds of gender and disability".

She found the employer had failed to objectively justify the cutting of Ms D's hours and had failed to provide reasonable accommodation in relation to her disability.

Irish business owners can be held vicariously liable for the acts of their employees. Employers should take all reasonable steps to implement strict workplace policies to deal with all the aforementioned possible grounds of discrimination. Staff should be trained to ensure they fully understand and follow the policies in place. The burden of proof is on the employer to prove otherwise in a case where action is taken for discrimination on any of the grounds listed above. The Labour Court held in *Patrick J Lynch v Binnacle Ltd (trading as Cavan Co Operative Mart) Supreme Court* (2011) IESC 18 In that case the employer was held vicariously liable for the unsafe system of work which resulted in severe injury to a cattle drover. It was found that liability could be attached to the employer having regard to the fact that the otherwise safe system of work was not in operation on the day of the accident due to the absence of assistant drovers.

The Social Welfare (Miscellaneous Provisions) Act 2004 inserted a part VII into the Pensions Act 1990 which prohibits direct or indirect discrimination on any of the nine grounds specified in the employment equality legislation in all occupational pension schemes.

In *McCarthys v Smith* ((1980) C129/80), Mrs Smith was paid less per week than a man who had, until some four months before she took up the job, held the same position. The ECJ held that she could claim equal pay to that of her predecessor, but left it to be decided as a question of fact in every case whether or not a pay differential was due to sex discrimination or whether it could be explained by the operation of other facts unconnected with sex. In *Garland v British Rail Engineering Ltd* (1982) 2WLR918 House of Lords. European Court of Justice (case 12/81) (1982) 2 WLR 918, the ECJ held that the provision of travel concessions for retired male employees constituted discrimination against retired female employees, who did not receive the same facilities. However, an employer can pay a different rate of pay if the amount of work done by the person is less than normally done by a person without a disability. An employer must accommodate a person with a disability unless there is a disproportionate burden on the employer (2004 Act) and *An Employee (Mrs B) (represented by a public service union) v A Government Department (Instructed by the Chief State Solicitors Office) DEC-E 2005/034*.

In A Worker (represented by Ms. Grainne Fahy B.L. on the instructions of Coghlan Kelly Solicitors) v A Hotel (represented by IBEC) EAT DEC-E2013-094 (20 August 2013), Under the Employment Equality Acts 1998–2011.

This case involves a claim by a Worker against a Hotel that she was entitled to the same rate of pay as that paid to a named comparator in accordance with section 29 of the Employment Equality Acts, 1998 to 2008 and that the Respondent discriminated against her on the gender ground. The Respondent accepted that the Complainant and the named comparator were engaged in like work but submitted that there were grounds other than gender for the difference in pay. The Complainant also claims that she was subjected to discriminatory treatment by the Respondent in relation to promotion on the gender ground and that she was subjected to victimisation contrary to s 74(2) of the Acts.

4. Employment Law

The Tribunal in accordance with s 79(6) of the Employment Equality Acts, 1998 to 2008 found that the Respondent has failed to demonstrate that there were grounds other than gender for the difference in pay between the Complainant and the named comparator in accordance with s 29(5) of the Acts and that the Respondent discriminated against the Complainant on the gender ground contrary to s 29(1) of the Employment Equality Acts in relation to her pay. The Respondent discriminated against the Complainant on the gender ground contrary to s 8 of the Act in relation to access to promotion to the position of Leisure Centre Assistant Manager. The Respondent did not subject the Complainant to victimisation contrary to s 74(2) of the Acts.

In accordance with s 82 of the Act, it was order that the Complainant was entitled to arrears of remuneration constituting the difference between what she was being paid and the named comparator, Mr A was being paid. The Respondent was ordered to pay the Complainant the sum of €10,000 compensation for the effects of the discrimination in relation to access to promotion to the position of Leisure Centre Assistant Manager. This figure relates to compensation for the effects of the discriminatory treatment and does not include any element relating to remuneration (and therefore is not taxable).

Alcoholism has been held to be a disability (*A Complainant v Café Kylemore*, (6th March, 2003) DEC 52003-024 IET) as well as whiplash (*Customer Perception Ltd v Leydon (ED 21/2002) 178*). In *Sweeney v McHale Ltd* (2003) (DEC E 2003 /017) 180, the prospective employee, a member of the Travelling community, applied for a job in a saw-mill. His application was rejected. The equality officer agreed that the remark made by the employer that the prospective employee was one of the Sweeneys from Sligo and was not suitable to work with the employer indicated that the prospective employee did not get the job on the grounds of his membership of the Traveller community, and was therefore discriminated against.

The Irish Constitution 1937 may allow an aggrieved employee to seek redress under the terms of the constitution in addition to statutory and common law rights. In *Murtagh Properties v Cleary* ([1972] IR 330), Kenny J concluded that the framers of the Constitution intended that, in so far as the right to adequate means of livelihood was involved, men and women were to be regarded as equal. It was held in *Ryan v Attorney General* ([1965] 1 IR 294) that there exists a number of unspecified rights in addition to those found in Art 40.3 of the Constitution, including the right to bodily integrity.

Sexual harassment is defined in the 1998 and 2004 Acts and refers to any form of unwanted conduct related to any of the discriminatory grounds. References to sexual harassment are to any form of unwanted verbal, non-verbal or physical conduct of a sexual nature being conduct which in either case has the purpose or effect of violating a person's dignity and creating an intimidating, hostile, degrading, humiliating or offensive environment for the person.

The Acts provide a defence for the employer if he can show that he took steps which were as reasonable as possible to prevent the harassment and reverse the effects of it. Harassment can be carried out by any number of persons, not just the employer or fellow employees, and the employer may still be held vicariously liable as a result (s 15 of the Employment Equality Act 1998). An employer should always have workplace policies to deal with equality issues, as the presence or absence of such policies can be very important if a dispute is brought to the Workplace Relations Commission or the courts.

There are a few circumstances where an employer can lawfully discriminate, such as benefits conferred on an employee's family or on his/her marriage. In the operation of occupational benefits schemes, it is allowed to set ages for admission. Employers are not obliged to employ a person with a criminal record or a person who has a propensity to engage in sexual behaviour which is unlawful. A religious, medical or educational institution established for a religious purpose may discriminate where it is reasonable to do so in order to maintain the religious ethos of the institution.

Indirect discrimination occurs where the employer applies a condition to everyone in the workplace but it is a condition that fewer people of one gender (or other discriminatory ground) than another is able to comply with (Employment Equality Acts). The 2004 Act provides that "indirect discrimination occurs where an apparently neutral provision puts persons of a particular gender (or for whom a discriminatory ground applies) at a particular disadvantage in respect of any matter other than remuneration compared with other employees of their employer. The employer will be considered for the purposes of this act as discriminating against each of the persons referred to, unless the provision is objectively justified by a legitimate aim and the means of achieving that aim are appropriate and necessary". These provisions equalise the law on indirect discrimination on all nine grounds, making it easier for a candidate for employment or an employee to show that he or she has been disadvantaged by a provision applied to all, and putting a strict onus on the employer to justify any such provision. It will not be indirect discrimination if the employer can objectively justify (on grounds unrelated to the discriminatory ground) the condition or provision, provided that it is in pursuit of a legitimate aim, and the means of achieving that aim are appropriate and necessary to achieve a legitimate aim.

The Employment Equality Acts prevent indirect discrimination in relation to pay, and every contract of employment must have an equal pay clause. However, an employer can pay different rates of pay on grounds other than the discriminatory grounds.

THE DIFFERENCE BETWEEN AN INDEPENDENT CONTRACTOR AND AN EMPLOYEE

What is the difference between an independent contractor and an employee, and does it make any difference in taking an unfair dismissals claim?

There have been numerous cases deciding on whether a person was an independent contractor or an employee, in the courts and at the Employment Appeals Tribunal over the years.

4. Employment Law

Social welfare, tax and employment law statutes draw a distinction between an employee and an independent contractor. The employee works under a contract of service. The independent contractor provides a contract for services.

Knowing the difference between an independent contractor and an employee is important when bringing an unfair dismissals case under the unfair dismissals legislation because an employee must establish he or she is an employee in order to bring a claim. Only employees fall within the scope of protective legislation, such as unfair dismissal, minimum notice and redundancy.

There is a mutual obligation on the employer to provide work for the employee and on the employee to perform work for the employer. If mutuality is not present, then either there is no contract at all or whatever contract there is must be a contract for services or something else, but not a contract of service.

If an employer showed that the person was an independent contractor and not an employee, then the case for unfair dismissal could not be brought (*Murphy v Grand Circle Travel* (2014) IEHC 337).

Regardless of what label parties seek to put on their relationship the courts will look at the factual situation and decide as a matter of law what type of contractual relationship exists (*Henry Denny & Sons (Ireland) Ltd t/a Kerry Foods v Minister for Social Welfare* [1998] IR 34) (*Macken v Midland Community Radio Services Ltd* [1992] ERL 143 and *Phelan v Coillte Teoranta*, [1993] ELR 56). The wording of a written contract still remains of great importance. It can however emerge in evidence that, in practice, the working arrangements between the parties are consistent only with a different kind of contract - or at least are inconsistent with the expressed categorisation of the contract (*Castleisland Cattle Breeding Society Ltd v Minister for Social and Family Affairs* [2004] 4 IR 150).

The employment relationship can have a large range of possibilities. In *Minister for Agriculture v Barry* ([2009] 1IR 215), the respondents worked as veterinary surgeons in private practice and also were engaged in meat plants to assist the Minister's full-time veterinary staff and were an integral part of the meat inspection service. They were paid an hourly rate agreed between the Veterinary Union and the Minister. They were called part-time temporary veterinary inspectors. PAYE and PRSI was deducted. They were claiming statutory redundancy and statutory minimum notice. Edwards J said the Court must look at a wider range of possibilities that simply "whether the temporary surgeons were employed under a contract of service or a contract for services by the Department of Agriculture and Food". The possibilities were (a) the temporary veterinary inspectors worked under a single contract, which might be classified to fall under a contract of service or a contract for services, (b) on each occasion, the temporary veterinary surgeons worked, they entered into a new contract which might be classified as a contract of service or a contract for services, (c) on each occasion the temporary veterinary surgeons worked, they entered a separate contract governing that particular engagement which might be either a contract of service or a contract for service and that, by virtue of dealing over a period of time, it became "hardened or refined" into an enforceable contract, a kind of overarching master or umbrella contract to offer and accept employment which master or umbrella contract might be a contract of service or for services. Edwards J commented that the concept of "umbrella" contract had featured in cases concerning outworkers, casual workers and piece workers. (Supreme Court order July 2014: Employment Appeals Tribunal, April 2017 – case dismissed). In *Brightwater Selection (Ireland) Ltd v Minister for Social and Family Affairs* ([2011] IEHC 510), it was noted that "it is open to any court or tribunal to hold that an individual is engaged under neither a contract of service nor a contract for services, but instead under a contract *sui generis*, that is, a contract of its own type" (Francis Meenan Senior Counsel, the Employment Relationship, Employment Law 2014 and update 2017, Round Hall Press).

In *Re Sunday Tribune* ([1984] IR 505), Carroll J stated that "the court must look at the realities of the situation in order to determine whether the relationship of employer and employee in fact exists regardless of how the parties describe themselves". In *Young and Woods Ltd v West* ([1980] IRLR 201), the English Court of Appeal held that the legal relationship between the parties must be classified, not by appearance, but by reality.

In *Ready Mix Concrete v Minister of Pensions and National Insurance* ([1968] 2 QB 497), the court had to assess whether an owner/driver of a ready mixed concrete truck was an employee or an independent contractor. The court held that a contract of service exists if

> "(a) a worker provides his own work or skill for payment in performing some service for the employer. This element of personal service and the facility of assigning the duties to another person to perform is particularly inconsistent with the status of employee; (b) he agrees to be sufficiently subject to the other party's control to make that other party his employer. Clearly a genuine independent employer has more control over how, what, where, when and why he does the work; (c) the other provisions of the contract are consistent with it being a contract of service. This aspect is one that has particularly given rise to a widening of the test in modern times. The modern employee has more perks and benefits associated with his employment than was the case in the past and these will be assessed to see whether or not they are consistent with one status over another. Some of the matters that would be considered under this heading will be the right to paid holidays, sick leave, pension, trade union membership and staff concessions".

Look to see if there is a wage or other remuneration. Otherwise there will be no consideration, and without consideration, no contract of any kind.

In *Duncan v O'Driscoll* ((1997) ERL 38), a "share fisherman" was held to be a partner, and not an employee. It can be difficult to establish if a controlling shareholder is an employee of the company he owns. Ownership does not disqualify the person from being held to be an employee, but is a factor to be taken into account (*Philip Kirwan v Technical Engineering Union*, HC, 2005 and *Lee v Lee's Air Farming Ltd* [1961] AC 12).

4. Employment Law

An example of the Employment Appeals Tribunal approach may be seen in *Kirwan v Dart Industries Ltd and Leahy*, UD080/1. Dart Industries Ltd was an international organisation producing Tupperware. The Leahy's were distributors in a certain part of Ireland. Ms Kirwan worked for the Leahy's selling Tupperware through an organised dealership. The dealers organised Tupperware parties at the homes of members of the public. The products were transported by the dealers to the home of the member of the public and displayed at the premises to persons who had been invited. When goods were purchased, the dealer was paid and in turn paid the distributor, less a commission. In the case of the dealer, therefore, it was a case of no sale, no pay. Dealers were trained by distributors and, in order to assist in the training and running of the business, successful dealers were appointed managers. Ms Kirwan was a manager and she both acted as a dealer organising parties and assisted in the training and recruiting of dealers, in respect of which she was paid an overriding commission arising from her efforts. She was provided with a car, taxed and insured but she discharged the maintenance and running costs of the vehicle. She was under no continuing obligation to do any particular hours of work. PAYE tax was not deducted. Managers were at liberty to take whatever holidays they wished but to carry out their functions properly, it was necessary to take one week's holiday out of season and two weeks in season. Paid holidays were not given.

The EAT considered the relationship between the claimant and both of the respondents under the following headings: (a) control; (b) was the claimant carrying out the job on her own behalf? Was she in business on her own account?; (c) was there a personal obligation to perform the work?; (d) was the relationship between the claimant and the respondent such as would allow her to do other work in her spare time, which would be inconsistent with the status of employee?

Having considered these tests, the EAT held that the claimant was an employee of the second-named respondent but not the first-named respondent (*Employment Law*, Law Society of Ireland, (2nd edn, OUP 2007)).

A starting point for all the more recent cases and a case well-cited in this jurisdiction is *Autoclenz Ltd v Belcher* ((2011) ICR 1157). Here, the claimants carried out car cleaning services on behalf of the appellant company. In order to obtain work, the claimants were obliged to sign contracts (very elaborate contracts) which stated that they were sub-contractors and not employees, that they had to provide their own materials, that they were not obliged to provide services to the company and nor was the company obliged to provide work to them and that they could provide suitable qualified substitutes on their own behalf. The claimants maintained that they were workers for the purposes of employment legislation. The UK Supreme Court considered that the relative bargaining power of the parties had to be taken into account and that the written documentation might not take into account the reality of the relationship, that the true agreement will often have to be gleaned from all the circumstances of the case, of which the written agreement is only part.

You may also like to refer to the code of practice for determining the employment or self-employment status of individuals at www.revenue.ie The code of practice sets out in summary form criteria on whether an individual is an employee or otherwise.

While all the following factors may not apply, an individual is normally your employee if you control how, when and where the work is carried out, they supply labour only, you pay them a fixed hourly, weekly, or monthly wage, they cannot sub-contract their work, you supply the materials for the job, you provide all equipment other than the small tools of the trade, they are not exposed to personal financial risk in carrying out the work, they do not assume any responsibility for investment and management in the business, they cannot profit from the management, scheduling or performance of the work, you set the work hours, they carry out work for you or your business only, you pay expenses to cover subsistence or travel and they are entitled to extra pay or time off for overtime (www.revenue.ie).

In summary, a self-employed person will usually have professional indemnity insurance, own their own business, be exposed to financial risk, can take control and can delegate tasks or work. An employee generally cannot control or give direction, will be on a fixed wage and cannot sub-contract, does not supply materials, has no financial risk and has no opportunity to profit from sound management.

In the Competition (Amendment) Act 2017, two new categories of worker were provided for, namely the "false self-employed worker" and the "fully dependent self-employed worker". This Act provides for the removal of certain obstacles to categories of self-employed individuals being represented by a trade union for the purposes of collective bargaining. Such workers are de-classified as "undertakings" for the purposes of competition law.

EMPLOYERS' LIABILITY IN NEGLIGENCE

What must an employee prove in order to succeed in a claim for negligence against his or her employer? I was physically injured in the workplace as a result of what I believe to be the negligence of my employer. Can I also be compensated for stress or psychiatric injury I suffered as a result of my employer's actions?

An employer owes a duty of care to his employees. The employer will have discharged his or her duty if he or she does what a reasonable and prudent employer would have done in the circumstances. The employer's duty is not unlimited and varies according to the employees' circumstances. If you wish to pursue a claim in negligence against your employer, you must prove how and why your employer was in breach of his duty of care. The courts have laid down guidelines as to the extent of the duty of care. Reasonable care is required but there is no obligation to warn of obvious risks. It is not enough to show that your employer was negligent; you must also show that the negligence caused the injury complained of and the injury was reasonable foreseeable.

4. Employment Law

Bradley v An Post (unreported, High Court, (1998)) involved an employee of the defendant company, who sustained a back injury while delivering letters to low-level letterboxes in June 1993. He reported the matter to his supervisor and subsequently attended the company doctor. The injury resulted in an absence of two months from his employment. His injury and consequent vulnerability were well known to his employers yet, in October 1993, he was dispatched on non-emergency overtime to deliver mail to a development where some 350 houses had low-level letterboxes. During the course of this delivery, the plaintiff again suffered a back injury. McGuinness J held that the employer's duty of care towards the employee included a duty to ensure that, at least in the short term after his illness, he did not assume duties which would place undue and extraordinary strain on his back. Consequently, the employer was held liable, as it did not properly discharge the employer's duty of care in the case of the plaintiff's second injury.

An employer has a duty of care to provide competent staff, a reasonably safe place of work, proper equipment maintained in a proper condition and a safe system of work. The employer must ensure that the safe system of work is adhered to. These duties in expanded form were enacted into legislation in part II of the Safety, Health and Welfare at Work Act 1989. The employer would have to be aware of the staff incompetence. Where an employer supplies a standard tool with a latent defect which he had no means of discovering, the employer may avoid liability in negligence if the employee is injured. Ensuring a safe system of work would involve providing proper training.

The contributory negligence of the employee will be a factor in assessing any case but, in an employment situation, it will be the employer who will be setting the standard of care.

A claim for breach of statutory duty depends on the terms of the statutory provision and the duty set out therein (Safety, Health and Welfare at Work Acts 1989 and 2005).

An employer's duty of care to look after the health and safety of employees includes the reasonable prevention of bullying and stress-related injuries in the workplace. Breach of this duty may be treated as a breach of the contract of employment, enabling the employee to claim constructive dismissal. Constructive dismissal should only be availed of where an employee is left with no option other than to resign and where the employee has first exhausted any grievance procedure. In *Liz Allen v Independent Newspapers (Ireland) Ltd*, (2000), the EAT awarded the claimant €70,500 compensation. Significantly, the EAT included compensation for stress suffered as a result of constructive dismissal.

Employers have both a statutory and common law duty of care to protect their employees against stress. In *Saehan Media Ireland Ltd v A Worker* (1999) E.L.R. 41, the Labour Court acknowledged work-related stress as a health and safety issue and held that "employers have an obligation to deal with instances of its occurrence which may be brought to their attention".

Health and safety law requires risks to be eliminated or reduced so far as is reasonably possible. The Safety, Health and Welfare at Work Act 2005 also requires employers to conduct risk assessments of activities that could cause unreasonable stress to workers. The distinction between physical and psychiatric injury is no longer legally defensible. Section 2 of the 2005 Act defines "personal injury" as including any injury, disease, disability, occupational illness or any impairment of physical or mental condition or any death. In Curran v. Cadbury (Ireland) Ltd. - Circuit Court: McMahon J. - 17/12/1999 - [2000] 2 ILRM 343 2000 WJSC - 7070 McMahon J held that the duty of the employer towards his employee extended to protecting the employee from non-physical injury, such as psychiatric illness or the mental illness that might result from negligence or from harassment or bullying in the workplace.

An employer who is (or ought to be) aware that an employee is working under such pressure as to cause psychiatric or psychological injury owes a duty to the employee to take reasonable steps to deal with the problem.

In *McCarthy v ISS Ireland Ltd* (COA, 227 13 August 2018), the court looked at the law in regard to an employer's duty of care in psychological injury cases. An appeal of the dismissal of the plaintiff's personal injuries claim was allowed and the matter remitted back to the High Court. The Court of Appeal upheld the plaintiff's argument that the High Court had erred in deciding her case on the principles involved in bullying and harassment cases, but that the case should be decided on the principles of vicarious liability and the employer's negligence in failing to provide a safe place of work.

The case involved five separate incidents over the course of a 20-month period in which the plaintiff (a cleaning supervisor) had been threatened by members of her team, or they had behaved in a manner towards her which was threatening and abusive. She resigned but was diagnosed with post-traumatic stress disorder. The first incident occurred in May 2009 and she reported this to ISS but claimed that no action was taken to prevent it re-occurring. In fact, she claimed that by virtue of the fact that her employer had not taken sufficient action, following all of her complaints, they allowed a situation to arise whereby her team felt able to behave in a manner towards her which was abusive, threatening and aggressive, without fear of consequence. She claimed that the atmosphere of fear and intimidation towards her led cumulatively to her suffering such fear, stress and anxiety that she was forced to leave her employment. She alleged that her employer was in breach of its duty of care to her to provide a safe place of work, as a result of which she suffered personal injury. The plaintiff also conceded that the incidents were not sufficiently connected (they involved separate staff members) so that there was no claim that they were acting in a manner which was co-ordinated. Contrast this with *Glynn v Minister for Justice Equality and Law Reform* (High Court, 21 March 2014) in which members of Garda management were found to have engaged in a campaign of bullying and harassment against the plaintiff.

4. Employment Law

The *McCarthy* case was dismissed in the High Court on the basis that the plaintiff had not made out a claim of negligence against her employer. In addition to the fact that the incidents were not sufficiently connected so as to come within the definition of bullying, the trial judge said that these temporal gaps between the incidents could not have been anticipated by the employer – so were unforeseeable. In her appeal, the plaintiff submitted that the trial judge had erred in characterising her claim as one of work place bullying and instead alleged that the employer was vicariously liable for their employees' tortious acts, and was negligent in failing to provide a safe place of work.

The Court of Appeal dismissed the appeal for vicarious liability on the basis that the incidents complained of (admittedly assaults) were not behaviour committed in the course of employment even though they happened while the employees were at work. The Court said that it was stretching the concept of vicarious liability beyond its intended limit if an employer was to be found vicariously liable for every individual aggressive verbal outburst by one employee to another during the course of a day's work.

However, the Court stated that all employers owe a duty of care to their employees while they are at work, both as a matter of common law and by way of regulation. The common law duty of care includes the provision of a safe place of work. The Court said that it was reasonable to expect an employer of a supervisor to anticipate that conflict between the supervisor and her team might occur, and to have procedures in place to minimise such conflict and prevent any recurrence so far as is reasonably possible. An investigatory report commissioned by the employer (but carried out by a third party) was very critical of the employer and pointed to 12 failures on its part (including issues around bullying, but more importantly, around the breach of the employer's duty to provide a safe place of work) to which the Court of Appeal had regard. The Court of Appeal ultimately stated that where the plaintiff made complaints about incidents of hostility, aggression and abuse by those whom she was supervising, the employer owed a duty of care to take some reasonable steps to address what occurred with a view to minimising the chances of recurrence. The duty of care does not extend to ensure that no recurrence ever takes place, which would be too high a standard to be expected, but they were obliged to take reasonable steps to protect her from a recurrence where it was evidenced to them that these were a cause of significant stress, anxiety and fear to the plaintiff. On that basis, it was found that the employer was liable in negligence for the injuries, loss and damage sustained as a result of that negligence.

This case follows on from the *Hurley v An Post* case (High Court, 16 March 2018), which is very similar, but one where there was a one-off incident between the plaintiff and her colleague. After she reported the incident, she was effectively "sent to Coventry" by her colleagues as a result of the action taken against the other employee. The plaintiff was a 53-year-old mother of two who had commenced working in a sorting office in Cork in 2003. In July 2006, her colleague became very aggressive towards her, to the point where he came so close to her that she thought he was going to head-butt her. She was very frightened and having reported the incident, was on sick leave for three weeks. Her colleague was suspended and, when she returned to work, she was ostracised and isolated by her colleagues, who she believed blamed her for the dismissal of her colleague. She reported the situation to management who did not take any action but advised her that it would likely quieten down. Prior to the incident, the plaintiff had not exhibited any significant long-term physical or mental health symptoms. Evidence before the High Court was that as a result of the accident she suffered from post-traumatic stress disorder, and numerous "chronic persistent" physical symptoms, such as muscle spasms in her neck, which were driven by stress. She had a number of absences as a result of these symptoms and was dismissed by An Post in 2011.

The High Court was satisfied that the conduct of the plaintiff's co-workers following her return to work "*was, on the application of an objective test, highly inappropriate repeated behaviour which must reasonably be regarded as undermining her right to dignity at work*" and was the very essence of the bullying and harassment contemplated in the legal definition set out in the Code of Practice appended to the Industrial Relations Act 1990 (approved in the case of *Quigley v Complex Tooling*). The plaintiff had been "*subjected to debilitating and humiliating treatment on a daily basis of a petty and mean kind*", and the Court accepted that this behaviour which was allowed to continue unchecked by her employer had a serious effect on her "*well-being, her mental health and ultimately her ability to return to her employment*". Finding that An Post was liable for the bullying and harassment of which it was aware and failed to address in any meaningful way, the Court also held that it was in breach of its common law duty of care to the plaintiff as an employee and under section 8 of the Safety Health and Welfare at Work Act 2005 and exposed her to damage and injury to her health ("*moderate form of PTSD*") which she suffered as a result. An award in the amount of €161,133.00 was made, including €50k for pain and suffering.

You might also note the Personal Injuries Assessment Board Acts 2003 to 2007 (PIAB). Section 3(a) of the 2003 Act states that the PIAB Act applies to a civil action by an employee against his or her employer for negligence or breach of duty arising in the course of the employment with that employer. Civil action means personal injuries (s 4(1)).

Cases from the courts continue to emphasise the duty of care on employers to take reasonable steps to protect their employees from the reasonably foreseeable harm which may arise as a result of treatment by themselves or other employees.

INSOLVENCY PAYMENT SCHEME

My employers are insolvent. A provisional liquidator was appointed. How are employees protected in this situation? I am owed arrears in wages and holiday pay. Who, if anyone, will pay the arrears owed to me?

4. Employment Law

The Protection of Employees (Employers' Insolvency) Acts 1984-2012 protect certain outstanding entitlements relating to the pay of employees in the event of their employer becoming insolvent. It provides that employees may claim for arrears in pay, sick pay, entitlements under the minimum notice and terms of employment, employment legislation, unfair dismissals legislation, court orders in respect of wages, holiday pay, pay in lieu of statutory notice entitlements and certain other employment-related entitlements from an insolvency payment scheme. Outstanding contributions to occupational pension schemes which an employer may have deducted from wages but not paid into the scheme are also protected. These claims are generally made through the receiver or liquidator, depending on the circumstances, who processes them through the insolvency payments section of the Department of Social Protection out of the social insurance fund. For an employer to be covered by the insolvency payment scheme, he must be insolvent, as defined in the Protection of Employees (Employers Insolvency) Act 1984. The main categories are bankruptcy, liquidation, receivership and deceased insolvent employer. An employer who ceases trading but does not go into official liquidation is not covered. The employer must become insolvent within the terms of the Act. There are limits in respect of payments for sick pay, holiday pay, pay in lieu of statutory notices and arrears of pay. The maximum weekly rate is €600 per week, with a maximum of eight weeks. Generally, the scheme only covers entitlements arising in the 18 months prior to insolvency or termination of employment. Payments under the insolvency payments scheme are generally taxable.

If a claim is disallowed, the employee may make a claim to the WRC within six weeks of the decision being communicated. A payment made to an employee under the insolvency payments scheme does not prevent an employee from making a claim to the redundancy payments scheme. This is a different scheme and, if an employer is unable to pay statutory redundancy payments, the redundancy payments scheme will pay out. Disputes regarding most entitlements under the Acts may be referred to the Workplace Relations Commission.

The European Communities (Protection of Employees Insolvency) Regulations, SI 630/2005 amended the Protection of Employees (Employers Insolvency) Act 1984 by including a provision to cover employees who are employed by an employer who has become insolvent under the laws of another Member State.

MEDIATION

My working relationship has broken down with my employer. I do not want to leave my job, but I would like to sort out my differences with my employer. A friend suggested mediation. What are the advantages of mediation? I would prefer not to have to go to court.

Mediation is provided for in s 39 of the Workplace Relations Act 2015, and the purpose is to attempt to resolve disputes between parties without the matter going to adjudication. It is non-judgmental and non-adversarial. Both parties must be agreeable to going to mediation, and a party can withdraw at any stage. An employment mediation agreement should be signed by the parties before the mediation commences which indicates the parties' willingness to engage in mediation to try to resolve their differences. This will include a confidentiality and without prejudice status clause, a clause dealing with the legal status and effect of the mediation and a settlement formalities clause. The mediator is impartial and it is the parties themselves who arrive at their own agreement. Mediation is often used in cases of relationship breakdown, including allegations of bullying or harassment and misunderstandings over rights or obligations. If it works, it prevents the referral of disputes to such bodies as the Workplace Relations Commission or the civil courts, and it is much less expensive. It is also a much quicker way of trying to resolve disputes. Records and notes are confidential and cannot be used in subsequent proceedings or claims, except where the parties actually agree terms to resolve their differences.

The early resolution service is a type of mediation service offered by the Workplace Relations Commission. It can be carried out over the phone or by a face-to-face meeting. If an agreement is reached, the terms of the agreement are recorded by the mediator and a record will be kept by the Workplace Relations Commission and given to both parties. Any subsequent breach of the terms is actionable in court as a breach of contract.

Redress Forums

Where can an employer or employee turn in order to enforce their employment law rights?

There are a number of forums to which an employer and employee can turn in order to enforce their rights under common law and legislation.

The civil courts are available to employees for the determination of common law actions such as wrongful dismissal, breach of contract and injunctive relief. The principal courts in this regard are the Circuit Court, the High Court (or, on some occasions, the Supreme Court) and the European Court of Justice.

Under the Workplace Relations Act 2015, the adjudication service (formally the Rights Commissioner Service) operates as part of the Workplace Relations Commission. The list of legislation under which complaints may be referred for adjudication is set out in Schedule 5 of the Workplace Relations Act. The Adjudication service investigates disputes, grievances and claims that individuals or small groups of workers make. The Equality Tribunal was set up under the Employment Equality Act 1998 and has been replaced by the WRC.

The Workplace Relations Commission (WRC) assumes the roles and functions previously carried out by the National Employment Rights Authority, Equality

4. Employment Law

Tribunal, Labour Relations Commission, Rights Commissioner Service and the first instance (complaints and referrals) functions of the Employment Appeals Tribunal. The Commissions services include the inspection of employment rights compliance, the provision of information, the processing of employment agency and protection of young persons (employment) licences and the provision of mediation, conciliation, facilitation and advisory service. (www.workplacerelations.ie)

The WRC provides information to members of the public in relation to employment. Complaint forms are available for downloading at www.wrc.ie (Workplace Relations Commission website). I would also advise reading the WRC's work programme 2018 available on their website.

CHAPTER 5

Defamation, Bullying and Harassment

(Please note that bullying and harassment are considered different matters within the Irish legal system).

What is Defamation?

My friend claims to be the subject of an alleged false and defamatory statement. Please briefly explain what defamation is and where I may access up to date rules governing defamation in this country.

The law of defamation in Ireland is governed by the Constitution, common law and the Defamation Act 2009. Under the 2009 Act, a defamatory statement is defined as one which tends to injure a person's reputation in the eyes of reasonable members of society. Defamatory statements can include accusations of unethical, illegal or immoral behaviour.

High-profile defamation cases in Ireland which many would be familiar with include *Reynolds v Malocco T/A/ Patrick* ((1999) 1 ILRM 289) where it was suggested that a nightclub owner tolerated the sale of drugs on his premises and was gay, or *DeRossa v Independent Newspapers* plc. ((1999) 4 IR 432) where it was wrongly suggested that a person tolerated serious crime. In *Captain Cullen v Michael O'Leary* (High Court, May 2010) Ryanair CEO Michael O'Leary apologised for wrongly describing a trade union official as a 'failed Aer Lingus pilot' during RTE's *Prime Time*. The apology formed part of a settlement of a High Court action against him by Captain Evan Cullen.

Defamation was traditionally divided into two forms, that is, libel and slander. The advent of modern technology has made those definitions obsolete. Media such as the internet means that a false statement can now be preserved in the same way as a newspaper cutting. As a result of this, the 2009 Act established the 'tort of defamation'.

A defamatory statement is only actionable if it is published, refers to the complainant and is false. A defamatory statement need not necessarily name anyone. It may suggest a person for example by that person's connections. A statement will be presumed to be defamatory until proved otherwise. The 2009 Act applies to companies, as well as individuals.

The statutory defences to defamation include truth, absolute privilege, qualified privilege, honest opinion and fair and reasonable publication on a matter of public interest. If a statement is privileged, a potential plaintiff has no cause of action. There are two types of privilege, absolute privilege and qualified privilege. Judges and barristers in court have absolute privilege, and a fair and accurate media report of Oireachtas or court proceedings also attaches absolute privilege. The 2009 Act lists those that attract both absolute and qualified privilege. Please refer to part 1 and part 2 of schedule 1 of the 2009 Act. Qualified privilege attaches to communications where the informant has a legal, moral or social duty to communicate the information, and the recipient has a similar duty to receive it. Qualified privilege is also granted for reports of certain public meetings and tribunals subject to explanation, that is the erroneous statement must be amended.

Damages in defamation cases are usually very high and therefore quite a lot of such cases are settled outside the courts. Excessive awards of damages by High Court juries led to a provision in the 2009 Act which provides that, on appeal, the Supreme Court may substitute an appropriate amount for any High Court jury award.

There are strict limitation periods for taking a defamation action. A person who claims to be the subject of a defamatory statement may apply to the Circuit Court for a declaratory order that the statement is false and defamatory. The jurisdiction of the Circuit Court in defamation actions ranges to €50,000 (s 41). Verifying affidavits are necessary in defamation actions.

The main defence to an action is the defence of truth, where a defendant proves that his statement is true in all material respects. A person accused of defamation may make an offer of amends in writing, offering to make a suitable correction and sufficient apology, to publish same in a reasonable manner and to pay agreed compensation, damages and costs. An apology is not an express or implied admission of liability and is not relevant to the issue of liability. Under the 2009 Act, if a plaintiff dies, the defamation action survives and special damages may be sought.

How much Compensation Can I Expect to Get in a Defamation Case?

I was defamed in a media report and I wish to seek vindication of my good name. I do not have very much money. I am unemployed. Would I have a reasonable chance of pursuing a defamation action through the courts?

A defamatory statement is one which "tends to injure a person's reputation in the eyes of reasonable members of society" (Defamation Act 2009).

Defamation cases are always difficult to advise on, simply because the outcome of a defamation action is often unpredictable. For example, you may be familiar with the TV3 case where the station accidentally broadcast a photograph of an innocent party in error. The Court of Appeal reduced the award from €140,000 to €36,000 (*Christie v TV3 Television Networks Ltd.* (unreported, Court of Appeal, 29 May 2017, (2017) IECA 128).

5. Defamation, Bullying and Harassment

A defamation litigation case is usually very expensive and therefore you would want to have sufficient funding to engage in such an action in the first place, which is often a barrier for people.

If you decide to proceed with a defamation case, then a jury in the High Court will decide if the statement in the media report is defamatory or not. The jury will also decide how much compensation you should get.

Despite cases such as the above mentioned *TV 3 and David Christie* defamation awards in Ireland are generally the highest in Europe and out of kilter with other continental countries.

Malta's Press Act currently caps compensation for non-pecuniary damage at €11,646.87. However, the Maltese government, as part of a reform package that would see the repeal of the country's criminal libel laws, has announced plans to increase the maximum amount to €20,000. The maximum amount is planned to be lower in cases in which the journalist apologises but the plaintiff continues to pursue legal action.

Awards average about €5,000 in the Netherlands.

An award of €75,000 for a defamation case in Portugal was subsequently ruled disproportionate by the European Court of Human Rights. Such awards, the court said, "inevitably risked dissuading journalists from contributing to public debate on questions of general interest". In its 2010 decision *Público – Comunicação Social, SA and others v Portugal*, the ECHR found that the Portuguese Supreme Court had violated the newspaper Público's right to freedom of expression when it ordered the paper to pay damages of €75,000 to the football club Sporting. In its decision the ECtHR observed:

> *"The sum of 75,000 EUR ... was without a doubt an unusually high amount, in particular with regard to other defamation cases decided by the Portuguese courts of which the Court is aware and if one takes into account that this case concerns the reputation of a legal person and not of an individual. Such compensation inevitably risks dissuading journalists from contributing to public discussion on questions relevant to public life."*

In Ireland the Supreme Court ruled that an award of €1.25 million to businesswoman Monica Leech was reasonable. (*Monica Leech v Independent Newspapers* SC (2014). Then again when the Sinn Fein councillor Nicky Kehoe took a defamation action against RTE earlier this year he was awarded just €3,500 in damages (*Nicky Kehoe v RTE* (2018) HC). In another action taken by Senator Paudie Coffey against *The People Newspaper* the High Court failed to reach a verdict in his libel case (*Coffey v The People Newspaper* (2018) HC)

The Court of Appeal, in the landmark judgment of *Kinsella v Kenmare Resources plc & Anor*(1) delivered on 28 February 2019, has set aside an award of damages of €10 million as being disproportionate, unjust and unfair in the circumstances.

This had been the highest award of damages for defamation in Ireland until it was set aside. The Court of Appeal substituted the original jury award of €10 million (€9 million in compensatory damages and 1 million in aggravated damages) for an award of compensatory damages of €250,000.

An award of 900,000 euro was made in the case of *Mc Donagh v Sunday Newspapers Ltd* 27/07/2017 SC (Appeal No. S: AP: IE: 2015:000092) by Ms Justice Dunne. The plaintiff in this case was the subject of an article which appeared on the front page and on inside pages of the edition of the *Sunday World* newspaper published on 5 September, 1999. The headline over the front page story which was the main story that appeared was "Traveller is new drug king". Underneath a sub headline said "the shark is arrested as huge haul of hash and ecstasy is found". The story was continued inside on pages 2 and 3 in a similar vein. While the plaintiff was not mentioned by name in the article complained of, he was readily identifiable from the article and accompanying photographs, albeit that they were pixilated. The plaintiff brought proceedings for defamation arising out of the article and claimed inter alia that it meant that he was a criminal, that he was a drug dealer, that he was a tax evader and that he was a loan shark. A defence was duly filed pleading inter alia that the words complained of were true in substance and in fact. Following the trial of the action in February of 2008, the jury in response to the questions on the issue paper reached the conclusion that the plaintiff was not a drug dealer and was not a loan shark. They did however accept that the plaintiff was a tax evader and that the plaintiff was a criminal. The jury could hardly have concluded otherwise given that this was accepted by the plaintiff from the commencement of the trial before the jury. In circumstances which have already been described in earlier judgments of this Court and which do not need to be further addressed in this judgment, the jury proceeded to assess damages in favour of the plaintiff in the sum of €900,000.

Please consult a solicitor's firm who have experience in taking defamations actions.

LIBEL — FREEDOM OF EXPRESSION V ONLINE DEFAMATION

How do the laws of libel pertain to online posts? Is the site-holder/publisher responsible for all posts made on its page, irrespective of who makes them? To what extent are online service providers themselves liable for hosting defamatory comments? And what about the operators of news websites or blogs where users are allowed to comment?

The laws of defamation are a legal minefield, not just for publishers but for potential complainants. Social media sites, such as Facebook and Twitter, play a prominent role in how we communicate. The reality that reputations can be destroyed by such sites is brought into sharp focus by the Twitter and Facebook defamation cases in the courts. In January 2014, the High Court ordered the Dublin-based Twitter to remove a false profile displaying grossly defamatory and offensive pictures and tweets of a young Irish school teacher. Mr Justice White said he had

5. Defamation, Bullying and Harassment

no doubt that the profile site was totally defamatory of the woman and the court felt it should have been taken down as a matter of urgency in view of the particular content (*A.C. v Twitter International* (January 2014) HC, *Irish Times*, December 2013). Therefore, defamatory statements made via the internet can and do have legal consequences. The EU legal framework governing online service providers' liability for hosting defamatory comments is governed by the "notice and takedown" mechanism. The online service provider may avoid liability when it reacts quickly to a complaint of defamatory content by removing it. This is known as "safe-harbour". However this may be changing. The European Court of Human Rights case *Delphi AS v Estonia* (2015) ECHR 64669/09 involved a ferry company altering its island routes. The online news portal "Delphi" published an article about this, to which numerous defamatory comments were added by readers. The ferry company sued, not on the basis of the article itself, but due to the defamatory comments made by the readers. The ECHR decided that the online news portal was liable in defamation for the comments, despite the fact that they had removed the defamatory comments as soon as they were made aware of them. The Court took the view that, given the highly controversial and provocative nature of the news article, it was reasonably foreseeable that the online readers would post defamatory comments. Therefore the online news portal was obliged to predict and proactively prevent such comments. So this went beyond the "notice and takedown" principle and is a serious blow to free speech online. It is at odds with the EU prohibition against compelling online service providers to monitor the content they post.

In recent times, there is a growing tendency to name and shame trolls and those who act in a defamatory manner towards others online. This will hopefully lead to a societal shift in how people use online media. If social media companies do not address the matter and operate a hands-off policy when it comes to what is published on their websites, it is then up to the media and politicians to highlight the behavior. The editor of *Gay Times*, Josh Rivers, was fired after online news website Buzzfeed published dozens of racist and anti-Semitic comments Rivers made on social media. All his articles were removed from their website (The Guardian.com Nov.2017, Pressgazette.co.uk Nov. 2017).

This whole area is evolving, and it will be interesting to see what changes are made or enforced in the next few years.

FALSE AND DEFAMATORY GOOGLE REVIEWS

My business was attacked online recently, possibly by another business in competition with us or a jealous individual, by posting a false and defamatory review on our Google business listing. What can I do? I own a well-established business and work so hard to offer a fair and honest service and then a competitor or nasty individual tries to undo all my hard work.

There are a number of approaches. First, I would advise you to notify Google immediately of the defamation.

You could try speaking to someone at Google Ireland or, if a business knows the identity of the author of a review, the business can either pursue the author of the review legally, naming that person as a defendant in a legal action, or seek to resolve the issue with that person outside the courts. This may first involve the issue of a subpoena to Google. To publish a Google review, one must first register a Google account. The author of a false and defamatory Google review will probably have created a unique Google account solely to publish the review and would probably not have provided his or her real name on registering the Google account used to publish the review. A business that is the victim of a false and defamatory review should subpoena Google for records pertaining to the account-holder associated with the post, in particular information relating to the URL of the Google-plus page affiliated with the account the person used and the internet protocol address used to create the account and the internet protocol log records.

Internet protocol addresses can be traced to the issuing internet service providers, which can produce subscriber information in response to a separate subpoena. Therefore, even if a person provided a fake name and no legitimate phone number or secondary email address, internet protocol addresses are sufficient to help identify the author of a review. Furthermore, a business can seek to obtain a judgment from a court declaring the statements in a review to be false, and then present the court order to Google with the goal of having the relevant URLs de-indexed from Google.

Google also have a "report a policy violation" link, which you could try, or you could click on the second link "this page" to submit a legal request. Complete a "report other legal removal issue" form and submit.

Contacting removals@google.com does not handle the preservation or production of user information. If you think that a crime has been committed, you may wish to contact the police and the police can contact Google Inc. If you have questions about obtaining this information in a civil matter, please contact internationalcivil@google.com that is, Google legal Investigations support for more information on how to serve Google removals with valid process.

Some websites advise that the victim of a false and defamatory review should respond to the review in a professional manner, for example, "Dear Jack. We have no record of any client experience fitting this account nor can we verify anything about your identity from your name in our records. If you were a client of ours, we would like to investigate this matter further. Please contact us immediately so we can resolve this matter".

It is a matter of opinion of course but, personally, I wouldn't reply. Each time you respond to a defamatory review, you make the review more visible on search results. Very often the review contains so many inaccuracies that responding would be unlikely to help and you don't want to waste valuable time engaging with a small-minded individual or indeed a competitor, if that be the case. You mention that you own an established business, therefore your customers know the value and

5. Defamation, Bullying and Harassment

quality of your work. They are not going to leave you because of some silly review on Google. Intelligent, clear minded and successful people seldom in my experience pay much attention to online reviews. They make up their own minds about who to do business with!

MISTAKEN IDENTITY REPORT DEALT WITH UNDER THE DEFAMATION ACT 2009

Can a mistaken identity report be dealt with under the Defamation Act?

The answer is yes, as was evident when Dublin lawyer David Christie (who was wrongly identified in an evening news report as a solicitor accused of fraud) was awarded €140,000 in damages by the High Court (*David Christie v TV3*, [2015] IEHC 694).

Christie sued TV3 after he was pictured in a news report about his client Thomas Byrne, a solicitor accused of 50 counts of theft and forgery. Footage of Christie walking alone to the Criminal Courts of Justice was broadcast alongside a narration detailing Byrne's charges. The report led to Christie being abused and harassed.

The matter was dealt with under the Defamation Act 2009, and Christie was awarded €140,000 in damages (Ms Justice Iseult O'Malley, High Court). The Court of Appeal, however, reduced the award to €36,000 ([2017] IECA 128).

BULLYING IN THE WORKPLACE AND NON-PHYSICAL PERSONAL INJURIES CLAIMS

I hold an administrative position in an office in the city center. I enjoyed my job initially but, as time went on, my boss became more and more critical of me. I am experienced at my job and I am always careful to do everything right. He has even started blaming me for the mistakes of other employees. Yesterday he asked me to go to the local café and get a coffee for him with no sugar. I did as requested, but when I returned with the coffee, he spat it out and complained that I hadn't put any sugar in it. I am so stressed. I cannot sleep at night and I feel nervous all the time in work because I do not know what to expect from my boss from one moment to the next. Is there anything I can do? I cannot financially afford to leave this job, but I feel at this stage I may have to resign.

Everyone has a right to dignity at work. Many employees endure bullying at work or harassment, unaware of the protections afforded to them by the law. Bullying and harassment in the workplace can be physically and emotionally exhausting for the victim. Harassment at work can take many different forms, from being bullied to unwanted sexual approaches or being called racist or sexist names, or trying to shame the victim in some way or passive-aggressive behavior. A passive-aggressive person may appear very friendly but behave, for example, otherwise by excluding or isolating someone in the workplace. The Labour Relations Commission has defined workplace bullying as "repeated inappropriate behavior, direct or indirect, whether verbal, physical or otherwise, conducted by one or more persons against another or others, at the place of work and/or in the course of employment, which could reasonably be regarded as undermining the individual's right to dignity at work". An isolated incident of the behavior described in this definition may be an affront to dignity at work but, as a once-off incident, is not considered to be bullying. Examples of bullying and harassment may include spreading malicious rumors, gossip or innuendo that is not true, or excluding or isolating someone socially or intimidating a person. The effects of bullying and harassment may include stress, anxiety, sleeplessness, fatigue and trauma.

It is well established practice now that employers must meet their obligations to employees to create a work environment free of bullying and harassment by having a policy (or policies) designed to prevent such bullying or harassment occurring in the first place, and not just to deal with incidents when they arise. Failure to have such a policy can lead to liability being imposed on the employer the first time such an incident arises. Policies of this sort are rarely included in the text of a letter of appointment or contract, but rather are contained in a separate document which is appended to or referred to and incorporated in the contract.

Remedies for bullying and harassment can include among other things making a claim under the Unfair Dismissals Acts to the Employment Appeals Tribunal and bringing a claim to the civil courts for damages for injuries suffered as a result of bullying or harassment. A claim to the civil courts must by brought within two years of the injury.

The High Court case of *Una Ruffley v Board of Management of St Anne's School, 2014 HC 254* restates certain principles and proofs required to win a case for a personal injury arising from alleged bullying in the workplace. It is not enough to show that you have been bullied. You must also prove you suffered a personal injury as a result. This High Court decision was overturned on appeal December, 2015. The basis of this decision was the Court of Appeal's finding that the behavior and conduct in this case, no matter how ill-judged and inappropriate, did not amount to bullying within the legal definition. The Court of Appeal recognised that it was a "botched" disciplinary process. However it was not a case of repeated offensive behavior designed to destroy her dignity at work, which describes bullying. The Court of Appeal stated this case did not bring the board's conduct within the definition set out in the Supreme Court case of *Quigley v Complex Tooling and Moulding Limited, 2008, IESC 44*. In that case, Lyndon McCann, Senior Counsel, accepted, on behalf of the defendant that an employer owed a duty of care to his employees at common law not to permit bullying to take place. Both parties accepted the definition of "workplace bullying" at para 5 of the Industrial Relations Act 1990 (Code of Practice detailing Procedures for Addressing Bullying in the Workplace) (Declaration) Order 2002 (SI No 17/2002) as an accurate statement of the employer's obligation for the purposes of this case. That definition is "Workplace bullying is repeated inappropriate behavior, direct or indirect, at the place of work and/or in the

5. Defamation, Bullying and Harassment

course of employment, which could reasonable be regarded as undermining the individual's right to dignity at work. An isolated incident of the behavior described in this definition may be an affront to dignity at work but, as a once-off incident, is not considered to be bullying".

In an appeal to the Supreme Court, the Court agreed that the test for bullying as set out in *Quigley v Complex Tool and Moulding Limited* (2008) IESC 44 was still the correct test. Each part of the test must be fulfilled on each occasion of behavior, which is argued constitutes a pattern of bullying, and found against Ruffley.

Therefore in conclusion, the conduct complained of must be repeated, inappropriate and undermining of the dignity of the employee at work.

The type of behavior you must prove must be outrageous, unacceptable and exceeding all bounds tolerated by decent society. A certain degree of robustness is required of the employee in the workplace. Instruction, direction and robust management are sometimes all necessary in the workplace to ensure efficiency, that the work gets done, and health and safety in the workplace is maintained. The treatment you may endure may upset you from time to time, but it is not necessarily bullying. The test for bullying is of necessity set very high in order for workplaces to function without facing frequent court proceedings for perceived slights (Mr Justice Charleton in the Supreme Court, *Ruffley v Board of Management of St Anne's School*, Supreme Court Record Number 2016/24, 20 December 2016).

I think it is worth reading the judgment of O'Donnell J in the Supreme Court below (*Ruffley v Board of Management of St Anne's School*, Supreme Court Record Number 2016/24, 20 December 2016).

This case came before the Supreme Court after a detailed hearing in the High Court and three considered judgments in the Court of Appeal.

The significance of the case in Irish law was demonstrated by the hearing of the appeal by a seven person sitting of the Supreme Court on the 20 December 2016 and as stated by O'Donnell J. "At some level this novel case will set a benchmark for all bullying claims."

O'Donnell J delivered the majority judgment during which made the following comments and findings:

> "1. The Court of Appeal was correct in my view to identify the core issue as to whether a claim for unfair procedures leading to an unfair result could in itself amount to bullying.
> 2. During the hearing of the appeal it became apparent that to address only those issues [i.e. the grounds upon which the leave to appeal was granted] might not result in a complete resolution of the case since even if both questions were answered positively that would not necessarily lead to the overturning of the decision of the court of Appeal.

3. Here the complaint relates to unfair procedures in a disciplinary process including what was alleged to be the unfair singling out of the plaintiff for punishment. This is not to say that such matters cannot constitute bullying but rather it compounds the difficulty of this case that it involves conduct which on any view is at the margins of conduct alleged to be bullying.
4. At some level this novel case will set a benchmark for all bullying claims. One justification therefore for the law of torts and the stresses and costs it entails is that it provides a potent incentive to alter general behaviour. It is necessary therefore to have regard to the impact well beyond this case, of any finding or rejection of liability.
5. However, it is not necessary to establish a breach of fair procedures to succeed in a bullying claim, and conversely, the presence of unfair procedures does not establish bullying.
6. Bullying often involves a question as to how something was done rather than what was done.
7. I also accept for the purposes of this judgment that such a finding of conduct [i.e. denigration, belittling, and humiliation] even occurring at a private meeting between only two individuals is capable of constituting conduct which is inappropriate, and capable of undermining the plaintiff's dignity at work, and therefore if repeated, capable of constituting bullying.
8. There may also be so called 'corporate bullying' involving a superior, or indeed management more generally in the treatment of the individual.
9. I consider that the statement of law, accepted without question in this case, that no separate tort of bullying is or can exist, that bullying is in a sense a subspecies only of an employer's duty of care but that there can be nevertheless a concept of 'corporate bullying' for which the employer is directly responsible.
10. I agree with Finlay Geoghegan J. in particular that this issue involves a careful focus on at least three terms used in the 2002 Order:
    - Repeated behaviour;
    - Inappropriate behaviour; and
    - Behaviour reasonably capable of undermining dignity at work.

    Inappropriate behaviour does not necessarily need to be unlawful, erroneous or a procedure liable to be quashed or otherwise wrong in law: it is instead behaviour which is inappropriate at a human level. The test looks to the question of propriety in human relations rather than in legality.

    More importantly I consider that the requirement that the procedure be repeated inappropriate and undermining of dignity is a test which uses language deliberately intended to indicate that the conduct which will breach [i.e. human dignity] it is both severe and normally offensive at a human level" (*Ruffley v Board of Management of St Anne's School*, Supreme Court Record Number 2016/24, 20 December 2016).

The legal redress for workplace bullying include bring a claim that a tort (civil wrong) has occurred or bring a claim to the Workplace Relations Commission for constructive dismissal. Going to the WRC on a constructive dismissal claim will involve you quitting your job and only being able to recover your financial loss for

5. Defamation, Bullying and Harassment

being out of work between jobs. Going to court has potentially high legal costs, a high burden of proof to prove bullying and you must be able to prove you have suffered a recognised injury of a psychological or psychiatric nature.

Most employers are great but, if you are a victim of bullying, please contact your solicitor immediately.

BULLYING AND STRESS IN THE WORKPLACE AS A HEALTH AND SAFETY ISSUE — STATUTORY AND COMMON LAW DUTIES

I feel stressed at work. My manager does not communicate with me, except when he wants to verbally insult or undermine me, and my work roles are ill-defined. I deal directly with the public, and this can be highly demanding. There is a substantial turnover of staff and high absenteeism. I am tired all the time and I drink excessively as a result of this. I reported my manager's behaviour to my employer but he didn't do anything about it. What should I do?

A person may claim for psychiatric injuries sustained through harassment at work. Stress often accompanies instances of bullying and harassment; they all overlap somewhat and that is the reason I will address all three areas in answering your question. Bullying may cause an employee to experience occupational stress which, in turn, may result in injuries to mental health.

An employer's duty of care to look after the health and safety of employees includes the reasonable prevention of bullying and stress related injuries in the workplace. Breach of this duty of care may be treated as a breach of the contract of employment, enabling the employee to claim constructive dismissal after exhausting any grievance procedure in the workplace first. The Safety, Health and Welfare at Work Act 2005 (the 2005 Act) underlines the importance of an employer having an integrated safety management system which is relevant in identifying bullying, harassment and stress in the workplace. Employers and managers are required to prevent "improper conduct" likely to put the safety, health or welfare at work of employees at risk. Employers must conduct risk assessments on an ongoing basis (sections 8(2)(b)(d)(h) of the 2005 Act). There is no legal distinction between physical and psychiatric injury (s 2 of the 2005 Act) and *Cross v Highlands and Islands Enterprise* (2001) SLT 1060, IRLR 336.

In *Michael Shanley v Sligo County Council* (2001) HC, the plaintiff, a fireman, was systematically abused, bullied and belittled for over eight years by a superior officer. The abuse had been so severe that the employee had contemplated suicide. It was noted that the employee had filed complaints with senior management, who failed to act. In evidence he said the matter was investigated by the Anti Bullying Centre at Dublin's Trinity College which had vindicated his complaints.

He had been so pre-occupied with trying to survive at work that he had missed out nine or 10 years of rearing his children and being with his wife who suffered a brain tumour.

The county council admitted liability.

Mr James Nugent SC, for Mr Shanley, said his client over an eight year period was subjected to systematic bullying and abuse.

According to the Anti Bullying Centre report Mr Shanley's perception of the working relationship between himself and Liam O'Donnell was one of intimidation, humiliation, undermining and attempting to isolate him from colleagues.

Mr Shanley was subjected to frequent abuse and obscenities; open aggression and threatening behaviour; constant humiliation; undermining of authority; criticism, false accusations; rumours and goading.

From the beginning of his employment in Sligo fire station in 1991, the report stated, Mr Shanley feared Mr O'Donnell and his power.

Mr O'Donnell exerted his control often using obscene language. Mr Shanley was made to repeat demeaning jobs such as cleaning toilets.

Other firemen saw Mr Shanley as an excellent officer who handled them well in a non-threatening manner.

In evidence, Mr Shanley said he filed complaints but nothing happened.

Following a holiday in 1999 he genuinely feared for his own safety when returning to work as the chief and assistant chief fire officers were on a day off. He contacted his union. An inquiry was attended by the county secretary, county engineer and a SIPTU officer.

Mr Justice Butler said it was an unusual case and concerned post-traumatic stress disorder.

Butler J assessed damages at €65,000, the employer having admitted liability.

The Health and Safety Authority (HSA) defines workplace stress as arising when the demands of the job and the working environment on a person exceed their capacity to meet them, and the HSA identifies situations that can cause stress in the workplace as including, *inter alia*, poor communication at work, poor working relationships, ill-defined work roles, lack of personal control over work, highly demanding tasks, dull repetitive work and dealing directly with the public. Employers have both a statutory and common law duty of care to protect their employees against stress. In *Saehan Media Ireland Ltd v A Worker* ((1999) ELR 41) the Labour Court acknowledged work-related stress as a health and safety issue, and held that "employers have an obligation to deal with instances of its occurrence which may be brought to their attention".

The Code of Practice for Employers and Employees on the Prevention and Resolution of Workplace Bullying was issued in 2007. It defines bullying as "repeated inappropriate behaviour, direct or indirect, whether verbal, physical or otherwise,

5. Defamation, Bullying and Harassment

conducted by one or more persons against another or others, at the place of work and/or in the course of employment, which could reasonably be regarded as undermining the individual's right to dignity at work". The code provides a non-exhaustive list describing patterns of behaviour which are examples of bullying, including exclusion with negative consequences, verbal abuse/insults, physical abuse, intimidation, being treated less favourably than colleagues, undermining behaviour, humiliation, withholding work-related information or blaming a person for things beyond their control. An isolated incident is considered an affront to dignity at work, but as a one-off incident is not considered to be bullying. Physical assault is not covered by the code. The code distinguished bullying from harassment, which is covered by equality legislation. The code outlines that bullying in the workplace does not include the reasonable and essential discipline arising from the good management of the performance of an employee at work, or actions taken which can be justified as regards the safety, health and welfare of the employees. The code sets out guidelines for developing bullying prevention policies, and highlights a number of factors which may signal a risk of bullying such as high turnover of staff, high absenteeism or poor morale, changes in the workplace, such as a change in ownership, new manager or supervisor, not having an effective management system, personality differences, age or gender imbalance, lack of procedures to deal with bullying or professional employees bullying non-professional employees.

As the definition of bullying is huge, employers must have bullying prevention policies in place to deal with it.

Harassment may be carried on by a fellow employee, the employer, client, customer or other business contact, and the circumstances are such that the employer ought reasonably to have taken steps to prevent it. Harassment is defined in the Acts as being any act or conduct, including spoken words, gestures or the production, display or circulation of written words, pictures or other material. It constitutes harassment if the action or other conduct is unwelcome and could reasonably be regarded in relation to the relevant characteristic of the person harassed as offensive, humiliating or intimidating.

In *A Complainant v A Company* (2002) , a young lady alleged that an older male colleague who reported to her was hostile and extremely aggressive in his manner towards her. She alleged that he told her on many occasions that it would be wise for her to leave him alone and not interfere with his work, but that she could not do so because of the nature of her job. She said he repeatedly told her that she was only a young foolish girl, more inexperienced that he. The equality officer held, *inter alia*, that the nature of the verbal abuse was intended to intimidate the complainant, and that is was offensive and humiliating to her. The equality officer found that it constituted harassment and the employer failed to adequately investigate the complaints made by the complainant, and they failed to put in place adequate systems to deal with possible future complaints of that nature. The equality officer ordered the employer to pay monetary compensation for the stress suffered as a result of the harassment, to draft an equality policy and to draft a code of practice on harassment, which should be made available to all staff members.

In *Maher v Jabil Global Services Ltd* (2005) IEHC 130 and *Berber v Dunnes Stores Ltd* (2009) IESC 10, the courts considered negligently-inflicted psychiatric harm resulting from stress, bullying and harassment in the workplace, and they set out the main questions to be answered as whether the employee suffered an identifiable psychiatric injury, as opposed to just ordinary occupational stress and, if so, whether that psychiatric injury was attributable to the workplace. There must be proof (for example, other employees giving evidence) that excessively stressful conditions, bullying or harassment occurred, and that there was a causative link between the behaviour and the injury. Consider what the employer knew or ought reasonably to have known about the individual employee, that is was the harm suffered by the employee concerned reasonably foreseeable in all the circumstances? It is also necessary to consider what the employer not only could have done, but should have done, in the circumstances. The standard is that of a reasonable and prudent employer.

In *Shortt v Royal Liver Insurance Ltd* ([2008] IEHC 332) the plaintiff claimed damages for stress arising from a disciplinary inquiry which he alleged was unfairly conducted. Laffoy J rejected the claim and stated that stress in such circumstances is an ordinary consequence not amounting to an injury over and above medically recognised occupational stress or psychological injury. Even if the plaintiff's stress was recognised as a psychological injury this was not reasonably foreseeable. Judge Laffoy emphasised that an employer is entitled to assume that an employee is able to withstand such stress. In this case 'management were not aware of the problem. Furthermore, there was no reason why the management personnel ought to have known the Plaintiff was vulnerable or likely to succumb to psychiatric or psychological injury because of the implementation of the disciplinary process'.

In conclusion it should be noted that Employers can be held liable for an employee's bullying of a colleague, which may result in mental health problems, and an employer should take urgent action to rectify such a situation. Even where the behaviour complained of may not amount to bullying, an employer will likely be found to be liable on the basis of a breach of the duty of care to provide a safe place of work and failure to take all reasonable steps to protect an employee where it is reasonably foreseeable that when carrying out their work, there is a risk to which they may be exposed (*McCarthy v ISS Ireland Ltd* (13 August 2018 COA 227).

Employers should ensure that they have appropriate policies and procedures in place to deal with issues of this nature even if the behaviour does not come strictly within the definition of bullying (*McCarthy v ISS Ireland Ltd* (13 August 2018 Court of Appeal). These policies should be kept up to date, and be widely known throughout the organisation, so that employees are confident that their employer will deal with issues appropriately and in a timely manner. Regular training in this area should also be given to the entire workforce.

5. Defamation, Bullying and Harassment

EMPLOYERS' LIABILITY IN NEGLIGENCE FOR WORK-RELATED BULLYING AND STRESS CLAIMS

Can I be compensated for stress or psychiatric injury I suffered as a result of my employers' actions?

An employer's duty of care to look after the health and safety of employees includes the reasonable prevention of bullying and stress-related injuries in the workplace. Breach of this duty may be treated as a breach of the contract of employment, enabling the employee to claim constructive dismissal. Constructive dismissal should only be availed of where an employee is left with no option other than to resign and where the employee has first exhausted any grievance procedure. In *Liz Allen v Independent Newspapers (Ireland) Ltd*, (2000), the EAT awarded the claimant €70,500 compensation. Significantly, the EAT included compensation for stress suffered as a result of constructive dismissal.

Employers have both a statutory and common law duty of care to protect their employees against stress. In *Saehan Media Ireland Ltd v A Worker* ((1999) ELR 41), the Labour Court acknowledged work-related stress as a health and safety issue and held that "employers have an obligation to deal with instances of its occurrence which may be brought to their attention".

Health and safety law requires risks to be eliminated or reduced so far as is reasonably possible. The Safety, Health and Welfare at Work Act 2005 also requires employers to conduct risk assessments of activities that could cause unreasonable stress to workers. The distinction between physical and psychiatric injury is no longer legally defensible, that is, in law, physical and psychiatric injury are both treated the same. Section 2 of the 2005 Act defines "personal injury" as including any injury, disease, disability, occupational illness or any impairment of physical or mental condition or any death. In *Curran v Cadbury (Ireland) Ltd*, (2000), McMahon J held that the duty of the employer towards his employee extended to protecting the employee from non-physical injury, such as psychiatric illness or the mental illness that might result from negligence or from harassment or bullying in the workplace.

An employer who is (or ought to be) aware that an employee is working under such pressure as to cause psychiatric or psychological injury owes a duty to the employee to take reasonable steps to deal with the problem.

In conclusion the test outlined by Laffoy J in *McGrath v Trintech Technologies Ltd* ([2005] 4 IR 382) and refined by Clarke J in *Maher v Jabil Global Services Ltd* ([2005] IEHC 130) (adopted by the Supreme Court in *Berber v Dunnes Stores Ltd* ([2009] IESC 10) identifies the following main questions to be addressed in any case for personal injury arising out of bullying, harassment and stress at work:

Has the employee suffered an injury to her health as opposed to what may be described as ordinary occupational stress? Personal injury must be an identifiable psychiatric injury. In order to satisfy this element of the test, it would appear that the Plaintiff would have to rely on a medical report to establish a recognised psychiatric condition, capable of amounting to an identifiable psychiatric injury.

If so, is that injury attributable to the workplace? This element requires proof that excessively stressful conditions, bullying or harassment occurred and that there was a causative link between that behaviour and the injury. Work place bullying is repeated inappropriate behaviour which could reasonably be regarded as undermining the individual's right to dignity at work. An objective analysis of the treatment complained of is undertaken.

It appears that an employee should keep a diary of the conditions in the workplace and keep precise details of any complaint made to the employer. Supporting evidence or corroboration by colleagues would also be necessary. It also appears that the medical report would have to make a causal link between the bullying or stress and the injury claimed (as per *Quigley*).

If so, was the harm suffered by the employee concerned reasonably foreseeable in all the circumstances?

In this regard it is necessary to analyse the factual background in light of what are known as the "Hatton propositions". These put a good deal of responsibility on the employee to draw to the attention of his employer: (a) the nature of the difficulties; and (b) that the difficulties are having an adverse effect on their health.

The employer owes a duty of care to each individual employee and foreseeability therefore depends on what the employer knew or ought reasonably to have known about the individual employee.

It would be necessary to outline the details of what, if any, complaint the employee made to the employer and what steps the employee took to highlight the issue, bringing it to the attention of her employer.

If so, did the employer fall below the standard of a reasonable and prudent employer in addressing the needs of that particular employee?

It is necessary to consider what the employer not only could have done but should have done in the circumstances. With regard to the issue of standard of duty of care, it appears from the Berber case that even if stress was foreseeable, if the employer acted reasonably then injury was not so foreseeable.

The standard is that of a reasonable and prudent employer. It is necessary to consider what steps were taken by the employer to ascertain and address any issue that the employee may be having.

BULLYING IN SCHOOL

(Nasty comments, exclusion and aggression by other children)

Our daughter is being continually bullied in school by a number of girls in her class. The bullying consists of nasty comments and repeatedly excluding our daughter from taking part in their games. They can be quite aggressive towards her at times,

5. Defamation, Bullying and Harassment

and they take or break her personal belongings. Our daughter is a very pretty and talented girl, and we suspect the other girls in her class are jealous of her. We contacted the school and we were assured by the class teacher that everything would be fine. However a week later everything is not fine and our daughter is clearly very distressed. Please advise.

Bullying is defined as unwanted negative behaviour, verbal, psychological or physical conducted by an individual or group against another person (or persons) which is repeated over time. This includes cyber-bullying and identity-based bullying (Anti-Bullying Procedures for Primary and Post-Primary Schools, 2013).

The law imposes obligations on schools and those running them to deal with bullying in terms of having adequate policies and procedures to deter such behaviour and to act properly and promptly to deal with it when it does happen, and to act according to fair procedures.

Initially, I would advise you to forward continued written complaints about the bullying to the classroom teacher, and insist on meetings after every incident of bullying. Send letters and e-mails detailing the bullying, for example, "I would like to let you know that the bullying has increased. (Give dates and times and details of what happened). I would like to put this on file so if something happens again, we can show that there were past bullying situations". A properly-run school should already have a record of the incident and should have subjected the bully in question to a form of discipline, if appropriate Make it clear to the school that there will be a series of strongly-worded complaints and meetings. Do not let the school dismiss you. Let them know you are a force to be reckoned with, and that you are not going away. Request a formal investigation into your complaint. If schools are not tough enough on bullies, then the bullies are not afraid to bully.

If there is no improvement in the situation, you will have to escalate the complaint to the school principal and request an appointment with him or her. At the meeting, you can insist that anti-bullying initiatives are put in place and, most importantly, that direct sanctions are imposed on the bully. Ask directly what measures have been taken to stop the bullying (and any past incidents of bullying in the school) and insist on getting proof. Bring a copy of the school's anti-bullying policy to the meeting with you, and quote from it if necessary. Record everything that takes place. Every meeting at the school should be followed up by a letter. Some teachers appear kind and sympathetic, but they can be completely ineffective in dealing with the bullies. Some schools have a bullying culture and, as a parent, you might need to become your child's advocate in certain circumstances (Stella O'Malley, Bully proof your kids (Gill Books 2018). See also Joel Haber, Bullyproof your child for life (Penguin Putnam Inc 2007)).

Bullies come from all sorts of social backgrounds. Some children come from families where there is a history of bullying, that is, the bullies' parents may themselves have been bullies in school. Approaching such parents is a waste of time because they don't see anything wrong with their own child's behaviour, or they may know about it and still not address it, or they may themselves become aggressive and defensive. However, parents and guardians may be penalised by the courts for the criminal offences of their children, which can include bullying behaviour, and they can be liable under the civil law for failing properly to control their children's behaviour.

Sections 111-114 of the Children Act 2001 as amended gives the "children court" power to impose a number of orders on the parents or guardians of a child found guilty of an offence, including a parental supervision order of up to six months, ordering them to undergo treatment, participate in a parenting skills course, adequately and properly control or supervise the child and comply with any other instructions to prevent the child from committing further offences (s 111). Failure to observe such an order may be treated as contempt of court (s 112), for which a fine or a jail term (or both) may be imposed. The court can also order the payment of compensation (s 113) by those it feels showed a "wilful failure" to care for or control the child, contributing to his or her criminal behaviour, or order instead (or as well) that a parent or guardian enter a recognisance (a promise to the court) to exercise proper and adequate control over the child (Section 114). Refusal to make this promise can be seen as contempt of court. Section 115 gives the court power to impose a number of orders, including a community sanction on a child found guilty of an offence. They include a day-care centre order (s 118), probation orders (ss 124-126) and a restriction of movement order (s 133).

Some of the most serious types of bullying behaviour overlap with matters covered by the criminal law. While minors are not liable to the full force of the criminal law, they are not immune from its effects. The Criminal Damage Act 1991 (s 2(1)(2)(3)(4)) and s 3 refer to damaging property and the threat to damage property. See also the Criminal Justice (Theft and Fraud Offences) Act 2001.

There are six offences dealt with in the Non-Fatal Offences against the Person Act 1997 that bullying overlaps with, namely assault, assault causing harm, causing serious harm, threats to kill or cause serious harm, coercion and harassment. There are a number of defences for a person intervening in a violent situation, in terms of protecting persons or property and preventing crime, saving that person from being accused of assault in certain circumstances, something to be taken into account in a school member of staff's dealing with a violent student.

The Education Act 1998-2007 as amended deals with the regulation of primary and post-primary education. Section 15(d) provides that the board of management has the function of publishing the policy of the school, including the policy of the school relating to the expulsion and suspension of students. While there are no explicit provisions dealing with bullying, ss 28-29 are important.

Bullying can be subtle, just a comment or a look. Exclusion is a most nasty form of social bullying. Bullies can be interpersonally devious. They can lie (and they

5. Defamation, Bullying and Harassment

tend to be particularly good at telling lies)' so that it looks as though the target has made things up or misunderstood the situation. Parents who are in denial of their child's bullying behaviour may believe their children or turn a blind eye to such lies.

The dual-personality type or charismatic bully will often be especially attracted to competitive sports, because of the win-lose dynamic. "As a competitor on a social playing field, one who strives not only to win but to triumph over the social losers and destroy their sense of self, as in competitive sport, where winners and losers exist in a binary relation to one another, the bully is yoked in identity to his victims. The bully's self-image depends upon having those losers to persecute. I am a winner, you are a loser." (Dr Joseph Burgo, The Atlantic Psychologist (2013)).

An abuser will often position himself as a victim. Remember the cyclist Lance Armstrong's conduct? He tried to humiliate witnesses who first spoke up about his performance-enhancing drug use. To shore up his winner status, Armstrong tried to make them look like contemptible losers and he tried to turn public opinion against them.

Being undermined, made look like a contemptible loser, intimidated, ignored, excluded, shouted at, publically humiliated, physically or verbally abused are all forms of bullying.

You are entitled to see your child's record, so insist that the school forwards the records to you immediately. The case is not closed until you, the parent, says it's closed. The principal or class teacher cannot say the case is closed. The board of management, the patron, the religious order running the school, the Department of Education and the Gardaí can be contacted if you feel the principal is not properly engaged in resolving the situation.

You may contact the schools reporting inspector at the Department of Education and Skills and an inspector will be sent to the school for a few days to monitor the school environment.

Chapters 10, 11 and 12 of Developing Codes of Behaviour: Guidelines for Schools deal with the issue of suspension and expulsion from primary schools, including the legal and procedural requirements. The guidelines acknowledge the occasional need for schools to suspend or expel pupils where serious misbehaviour occurs.

Request a copy of the school's policy and procedures around the use of suspension and expulsion, or a copy of the school's code of discipline. A school's code of conduct will show the procedure it follows in dealing with bullying.

A single incident of misconduct may be grounds for suspension. The board of management will sometimes delegate the authority to suspend to the school principal. Some school principals are excellent at stamping out bullying in their school and will suspend the offending parties but, for various reasons, some principals do very little to help, preferring not to bring what they may consider to be negative attention to the school or smaller schools may fear losing numbers.

The board of management of a school has the authority to expel a student, and this should be invoked in extreme cases of unacceptable behaviour. Many parents don't seem to realise that their bullying brats can be suspended or expelled from primary school. Children are suspended or expelled from primary schools around the country every year.

If your child is absent from school as a result of the trauma associated with bullying, then bring your child to the doctor and get a written report stating the effects the bullying is having on your child. You may require this report for court later if it goes to that. Your child's doctor may report the matter to the Health Service Executive. That's absolutely fine. Keep a record of everything. If your child is referred to a councillor or psychologist, keep a record of that. Make the school aware of all this in writing by email or registered post so they cannot say they were unaware of the effects the bullying was having on your child.

Bullying is all about the need for a quick shot of power. Bullies often have a jealous personality type. Bullies and their sidekicks may target a child that stands out for some reason, for example, a child with special needs, a child that is quite brilliant in some way or a child that is visually different. Very attractive or good-looking and musically or otherwise gifted children are often bullied. Children with strong personalities that are not easily assimilated into the narrow confines of the bullies' life are often targeted, as are quiet passive types. Victims are usually targeted because they stand out as being different from their peers and therefore bullying could be considered a form of discrimination. Cook *et al* (2010) describes the typical bully as one who *inter alia* has social competence and academic challenges, comes from a family environment characterised by conflict and poor parental monitoring and tends to be negatively influenced by his peers. Bullying is both a sociological and a psychological problem.

Please do not be a bystander to bullying. Stand up for your child. If you don't stand up for your child, then who will?

And last but by no means least, you can issue legal proceedings against the school. Schools have a duty of care towards their students. Bring a school bully injury compensation claim if the school fails to comply with anti-bullying policies and procedures and protect one of its students from injury or the threat of injury. You can take legal action against the school for the psychological or physical trauma your child suffered at the hands and mouths of the bullies. It is a breach of the legal duty of care where damage is caused to a party to whom the duty is owed. The standard of care imposed by the courts on schools is that of a prudent parent (Irish Supreme Court case of *Lennon v McCarthy*, unreported, 13 July 1966). In the High Court case of *Mulvey(a minor) v Martin McDonagh* ([2004] IEHC 48) the judge accepted that "the degree of care to be taken by the school was that of a prudent parent exercising reasonable care and that that must be taken in the context of a

5. Defamation, Bullying and Harassment

prudent parent behaving responsibly with a class of 28 four year olds having their first experience of mingling socially with other children".

McCracken J in *Kenneth Murphy v County Wexford VEC* ([2004] IR 202) stated that school authorities are not insurers of the pupils in their care. However they do owe a duty to those pupils to take reasonable care to ensure that the pupils do not suffer injury. To do this, some degree of supervision is clearly required. The extent of such supervision will depend on a number of factors, for example, the age of the pupils involved, the location of the places where the pupils congregate, the number of pupils which may be present at any one time and the general propensity of pupils at that particular school to act dangerously". In this case, the school was found negligent because they had not provided such supervision and the plaintiff was struck in the eye by a chocolate bar and seriously injured.

The duty of care depends on the circumstances of the case. The duty of care owed by a school where there has been a history of disruptive and violent behaviour by a pupil or group of pupils would extend to taking appropriate account of these known circumstances when deciding on the appropriate level of supervision in the school, particularly during break time when pupils are outside of the more controlled environment (Peart J in *Wayne Maher (a minor) v The Board of Management of Presentation Junior School, Mullingar* [2004] IR 211). *Veronika Trjasunova v Guardian Angels National School Blackrock* (2017), Circuit Court Dublin related to school bullying and the court took into account the level of 'awareness' by the schools of the bullying complained of.

For further help or guidance, your child can also contact Childline on 1800 66 66 66 or 0800 11 11 or log on to www.childline.ie or www.childline.org.uk.

In my opinion, the anti-bullying policy offered by some schools is insufficient, for example, the "care strategy". This is a four-step procedure which is triggered on disclosure by any member of the whole school community. On its implementation, each student will receive a care credit card with three care credits, and will sign a care promise. It is each student's responsibility to keep their three care credits by continuing to be as caring as they can in the school environment. If there is a disclosure of bullying behaviour by anyone in the school community, four further steps are triggered involving the filling out of an anti-bullying referral form. A checklist is then given to the peer or group in question and students are asked to re-familiarise themselves with the various manifestations of bullying behaviour highlighted on the form. Each student will then be given an anti-bullying class survey to complete. Finally, students who have been named as engaging in bullying behaviour will be asked to fill out an anti-bullying interview form. This form is to help the students in question to recognise where they may have used bullying behaviours, how this has affected the victim of the behaviour and how to begin to empathise with the discomfort of the victim.

In my opinion, the above is all very well for the infant classes, but is not really a sufficient deterrent to older children of a bullying disposition. I would advise you to ask your school for evidence of the effectiveness of their care strategy (if they have one) or any other strategy they may have as a proposed deterrent to bullying, and request that they revise their policy if you feel this is necessary.

Bullying is behind all forms of harassment, discrimination, prejudice, abuse, conflict and violence, and therefore it is important that the offenders (or potential offenders) are addressed as early as possible in childhood. Bullying is always wrong and is unacceptable behaviour which should never be overlooked or ignored.

Finally, just a note on "relational aggression". This is the use of friendship and social status for manipulation. By teaching children that tactics like social exclusion, threatening to take away friendship and spreading rumours are unacceptable, children can make a conscious choice to move away from friends who use these behaviours (Signe Whitson LSW, Psychology Today). Two excellent books for young people addressing relational aggression that I would recommend are My Secret Bully for age's five to eight and Trouble Talk for age's six to nine, available at https://www.amightygirl.com/my-secret-bully. Stand Up for Yourself and Your Friends, for age's seven to 12, is a fantastic resource for children that addresses bullying of all types and is available at https://www.amightygirl.com/stand-up-for-yourself-and-your-friends.

In conclusion, I must say that I am truly sorry to hear your daughter is being bullied in school. It is the most horrific thing to happen to any child. At the end of the day, a well-run school with a good principal would not tolerate bullying. I think local knowledge is great. Speak to other parents attending the school, perhaps parents with children in the higher classes, and enquire if any of their children were the victims of, or did they hear of any incidents of, bullying in the school. Schools with a zero-tolerance approach to bullying in the area are generally well-known and popular schools. Regrettably, in my opinion it is sometimes the ego of the school principal that prevents action being taken against the bullies. The school principal may want to create an artificial front to the public and potential new students that everything is perfect in the school. An admission that there is bullying in the school would dent that artificial picture of perfection, and some school principals will allow the bullying to continue, rather than address the matter.

BULLYING IN SCHOOL – WHEN THE TEACHER IS THE BULLY

Our daughter informed us that her classroom teacher is always picking on her. She said her teacher told her that she was immature when she got upset about not being chosen as one of the competitors for an athletics event. Everyone in the class laughed at her when she cried as a result of this. Our daughter felt humiliated. The teacher is undermining our daughter's self-confidence. The teacher also ridicules and berates our daughter in front of the whole class any time she is late for school. Our daughter gets very anxious about this. We live 20km from the school and we admit we are sometimes a little late.

Most teachers are very altruistic, committed and do a great job. They have a very important and responsible role in educating our future work force and most

5. Defamation, Bullying and Harassment

teachers do this very well. Nevertheless, bullying is a risk and can in a small number of cases be a hazard of teaching. Regrettably, in a small number of cases, it is the teacher who is volatile or has the cruel streak. It is the teacher who is the bully and screams, threatens or uses biting sarcasm to humiliate a child in front of the class, and the problem may be more common than people believe. It is on a different level than child-to-child bullying because the child has no power. Stuart Twemlow MD, a psychiatrist who directs the Peaceful Schools and Communities Project, defines teacher bullying as "using power to punish, manipulate or disparage a student beyond what would be a reasonable disciplinary procedure". I would advise you not let the matter drag on for months. If you suspect there is a problem, meet the teacher in a non-adversarial manner first. After all, a child may have misinterpreted a teacher's behaviour. If this does not resolve the problem, continual written complaints from the parent and an insistence on meetings after every incident should ensure that the bully "in authority" learns to refrain from picking on your daughter because he knows there will be a series of strongly-worded complaints and meetings about it if he doesn't. Do not let the school dismiss you as an overly-protective parent. Complain by email each time there is an incident with the teacher and request a meeting. Let them know you are a force to be reckoned with, and that you are not going away. Request a formal investigation into your complaint. The child may not be removed from the bullying teacher's class, but the principal should warn the teacher to stop immediately. After all, your taxes pay the teacher's wages. When abuse is physical, most parents don't hesitate to report the offending teacher, but parents may see emotional or verbal bullying as a grey area. They worry that speaking up could cause a teacher to take revenge on the child. Don't ignore the problem. Make some discreet enquiries among the parents of your child's friends. Overt unpleasant remarks are likely to be remembered by other children and reported to their parents. If other parents also have concerns about the way their children are being treated, then that might indicate a problem. A meeting will sometimes resolve the problem, but often a master bully will rationalise and nothing may change until the matter is taken to a higher level, that is, the principal, or filing a complaint with the board of management and the superintendent. Keep good records of all communications and incidents. Obtain a copy of the school's policy on teacher bullying so that you can point out that your child is not being treated with respect or courtesy. Ask for a copy of the school's complaint policy.

Children are often afraid to speak up about bullying. All too often, when a child reports on bullying, a reversal occurs and they (the victim) become the ones who are in trouble. They are seen as a problem. If the bully is the teacher, the child may be shamed or humiliated for daring to jeopardise the adult's reputation. This is why, in my opinion, we need to change the way these complaints are handled in schools and in the law and why it is most important for parents or guardians to step in immediately and protect their child.

When a child is bullied at school, people will often ask why the child did not change schools. Expecting the victim to leave suggests that the victim is at fault. If your house is robbed, people don't usually ask you why you didn't move house!

Bullying by teachers can take many forms in order to harass and intimidate, such as swearing, yelling, direct personal attacks, comments targeting a child's disability or difference, humiliating, berating, ignoring, raging, expressing disgust at the child through gestures or facial expressions or shunning.

If a child is late for school, the issue should be privately addressed with the child's parents and never the child. A child should never be berated over something outside the child's control.

The procedures for boards of management/Education and Training Boards (ETB's) in relation to the suspension and dismissal of teachers and principals are set out in circular 0071/2014 ETB Procedures and circular 0060/2009 Primary/Post Primary Procedures.

Teachers should be reminded of sections 2 and 4 of rule 130 of the Rules for National Schools as superseded by Developing a Code of Behaviour – Guidelines for Schools. Section (2) provides that "Teachers should have a lively regard for the improvement and general welfare of their pupils, treat them with kindness combined with firmness and should aim at governing them through their affections and reason and not by harshness and severity. Ridicule, sarcasm or remarks likely to undermine a pupil's self-confidence should not be used in any circumstances. Section (3) provides that the use of corporal punishment is forbidden. Section (4) provides that any teacher who contravenes section (2) and (3) of this rule will be regarded as guilty of conduct unbefitting a teacher and will be subject to severe disciplinary action".

Bullying by the teacher happens more than parents realise. Some teachers may use bullying as a way of controlling the class, and the bullying tactic is used as a warning to other children that the same will happen to them if they step out of line. Some school authorities tacitly allow bullying to take place, but a continued stream of formal complaints will help keep the situation in check. Disciplinary action can include suspension of the teacher and, in cases of gross misconduct, summary dismissal.

Teachers are human, and it's unfair to expect them never to utter a hurtful word, but some teachers do bully for various reasons. A student may remind them of someone they dislike or insecure teachers may bully bright students out of envy. Some teachers may have personal problems or job burnout, and they take out their frustrations in class. They may require further training in effective classroom management. Supporting your child through this is very important, as your child may become anxious about going to school or become really upset about the situation. Some children may feel like they are causing issues, but reassure them that this is not the case and, if they are feeling bullied, you are there for them and will get this sorted out. Never assume the bullying will end without intervention. Have your child checked by a paediatrician for signs of depression, anxiety and sleep problems. Build your child's self-esteem and help him or her to focus on things they are good at. Talk to your child first before

5. Defamation, Bullying and Harassment

attempting to resolve the issue. Follow the chain of command, that is, talk to other parents and staff before going to the principal or board of management. Request a meeting with the teacher. Express your concerns. Take your complaint higher if the situation doesn't improve or the bullying is severe in nature. Request a classroom transfer at this point. Not all principals will honour such requests, but some do. Some principals may let teachers who bully go unchallenged or deny that bullying is taking place. File a formal complaint with the superintendent or school board. Keep records of all communications, including letters, emails and telephone calls. If the principal, superintendent or school board drags their feet in responding to you, then consider getting legal counsel and contact your solicitors as soon as possible.

Thankfully gone are the days when teachers beat children unconscious in schools, made them bleed from the nose or mouth and inflicted physical punishment on children who were left handed (I have spoken with men and women in their 80s who were beaten to such extremes by teachers in their schools). However, it is still up to us as parents to ensure that our children are protected from any possible wrongdoing.

If the Principal of the school is bullying a class teacher then that is a matter to be addressed by the class teacher as soon as possible. This would have an adverse effect on the children in the classroom if they were to witness the principal coming into the classroom and bullying or besetting the teacher in the course of her teaching. In *Sweeney v The Board of Management of Ballinteer Community School* [2011] IEHC 131 the plaintiff complained that the principal had subjected her to a deliberate and continuous campaign of bullying and harassment during her work and that she had suffered mental injury, in the form of clinical depression as a result. She was urgently summoned to an inspection by the Department of Education, subject to unwarranted requests to attend the office and her office was forced open during the summer vacation, with her belongings and confidential files moved. The Teacher had a history over the previous three years of absence from work due to work related stress which were found to be 'uncharacteristic'. On all the evidence, the plaintiff had been subjected to deliberate and continuous bullying and harassment by the principal as a direct consequence of which she had suffered mental injury in the form of clinical depression, a result which had been reasonably foreseeable. The defendant had been negligent in causing or permitting the plaintiff to be harried, watched and beset in the course of her employment.

In my opinion the above could have inadvertently caused stress to the students in the class and effected their ability to study. Young children need continuity of teaching staff to help them thrive and feel secure at school. Various different substitute teachers coming and going throughout the course of the academic year could in my opinion lead to instability in the classroom setting and may have an adverse effect on their ability to learn.

BULLYING VERSUS MEAN AND UNKIND BEHAVIOUR

I befriended a lady from my bridge club some months back. Everything was going well until she verbally put me down at a coffee morning. Her comments were mean, spiteful and unkind, and I was quite shocked at the time. I keep away from her now because I suspect she is perhaps a bully. Are there any legal remedies available for this type of behaviour? Can this type of behaviour be classed as bullying?

Bullying is meanness from someone with more power than you that is repeated over a period of time. There is a fine line between bullying and bad behaviour. However being mean or unkind or behaving badly cannot be classed as bullying unless it happens repeatedly and the perpetrator has more power than the target. Bullying is repeated intentionally aggressive behaviour by someone with more power. Bullies are sometimes physically bigger than their targets and they will have the intention of inflicting harm. Having a sustained conflict or disagreement with someone isn't bullying. Taunting isn't bullying although it can be traumatising for some people. Some allegations of bullying are misguided and do a disservice to genuine victims of bullying. Try to distinguish between hurtful or unkind behaviour and bullying behaviour. Expressing negative thoughts and feelings is not bullying, being left out is not always bullying, experiencing conflict is not bullying, a fight or disagreement is not bullying, teasing is not bullying, unless it is cruel, unkind and repetitive and there is a conscious decision to hurt another person. Bossiness is not the same as bullying.

Psychologists like to group a target's response to aggressive or unkind behaviour into different modes such as "fight, flight, freeze or appease". Having the emotional intelligence to sever connections with unkind people and not leaving yourself open to becoming an aggressor's repeated target is sufficient in my opinion in a situation such as you described. Be resilient and self-protect.

Some people clearly have a chip on their shoulder. They lack empathy and understanding and the best way forward in my opinion is to sever connections with them instinctively and robustly. Some behaviour is mean, rude and unkind (and indeed may have some of the traits of bullying, for example, a deliberate and premeditated verbal put-down) but, if the person doesn't have any power over you and they are never going to be given the opportunity to speak to you like that again, their behaviour cannot be classed as bullying.

Many of the cases of bullying that were shared with me over the years are unspeakably cruel and horrifying. However, some people are crying "bullying" when it isn't bullying at all. It is important to be able to distinguish the difference between behaviour that is rude, behaviour that is mean and behaviour that is characteristic of bullying. Rudeness is often unintentional. Mean behaviour very much aims to hurt or deprecate someone, such as criticising someone's appearance or intelligence or just about anything they can find to denigrate, and is often motivated by the misguided goal of propping themselves up in comparison to the person they are putting down. Mean behaviour can also be a random comment or

5. Defamation, Bullying and Harassment

act of unkindness. Meanness and rudeness is different from bullying in ways that should be understood and differentiated when it comes to intervention.

LIABILITY OF PARENTS FOR STUDENTS WHO BULLY

Can parents of students who bully be liable in negligence?

There is no general rule for parents being liable for the torts of their children due to being parents. However, parents may be held negligent for allowing their minor child the opportunity to injure another (McMahon and Binchy, Law of Torts (4th ed, Bloomsbury Professional 2013) p 631). When parents fail to control a child properly, they may be liable for the child's injuries or the injuries their child causes to another. In the Supreme Court case of *Curley v Mannion* ([1965] IR 543), Chief Justice Ó Dálaigh stated that a "parent may be liable if negligent in failing to exercise his control to prevent his child injuring others". This can also extend to cyber-bullying.

A parent can also be liable if he or she knows or ought to know of a "dangerous propensity" of a child and fails to reasonably protect others against an injury resulting from it, for example, if a child previously attacked another person. Parents will not be liable if their reasonable best was not enough to prevent an injury (McMahon and Binchy, Law of Torts (4th ed, Bloomsbury Professional 2013) pp 632-633). It may also be negligent for a parent to leave dangerous things within the reach of a child where it is foreseeable that this could cause injury to that child or another child (*Sullivan v Creed* [1904] 2 IR 317).

ELDER ABUSE

My elderly neighbour confided in me recently that her adult daughter who lives with her is mistreating her. I got the impression that she is frightened of her daughter. I would like to help her. Please advise.

Elder abuse is defined as any act, or failure to act, which results in a breach of a vulnerable person's human rights, civil liberties, physical and mental integrity, dignity or general well-being, whether intended or through negligence, including sexual relationships or financial transactions to which the person does not or cannot validly consent, or which are deliberately exploitative.

The Report of the Working Group on Elder Abuse: Protecting our Future (2002) defines elder abuse as the abuse of someone aged 65 or over. It occurs within a relationship where there is an expectation of trust. It is a single or repeated act, or a lack of appropriate action that causes harm or distress to the older person or that violates their human and civil rights.

It can take place when an older person lives alone or with a relative, within residential or day care settings, in hospitals, home support services or public places.

In cases of elder abuse, parents may seek protection of the courts in securing a protection order, safety order or barring order against their adult children over the age of 18. You could help by arranging a meeting between your neighbour and a solicitor to discuss the various legal options open to her. You could also put your neighbour in touch with the Health Service Executive or local health office, as they have an elder abuse service with senior case workers in elder abuse or take them to a medical practitioner, public health nurse or the Garda Síochána.

Elder abuse can include discrimination, physical abuse, financial abuse, sexual abuse, psychological abuse and neglect. Leaving an elderly person who is immobile alone for long periods or not providing an elderly person with sufficient food, drink and clean, warm clothing would all constitute neglect. Putting an elderly person under pressure to give you or someone else money and spending an elderly person's money inappropriately would constitute financial abuse, as would an elderly person feeling under pressure to allow someone else access their accounts. If your neighbour is afraid in her own home or feels in any way intimidated by her daughter, then this also would be considered abuse. Further information is available from the HSE information line at infoline1@hse.ie.

CYBERBULLYING

My child was bullied on social media. Girls from her class in school used their school i-pads to set up a hate video 'to destroy her' and they posted this on Facebook and YouTube and other social media sites. My little girl is devastated. Is there anything I can do to help her?

Cyberbullying by definition is an aggressive, intentional act carried out by a group or individual, using electronic forms of contact, repeatedly over time against a victim who cannot easily defend himself or herself. However insisting that a cyberattack has to be repeated over time to be defined as cyberbullying is open for debate, in view of the fact that a single abusive message or image can stay online indefinitely and can be seen by multiple viewers (Kirwan and Power 2012).

Cyberbullying often involves written attacks using demeaning words, insults, name-calling and defamation of character, for example broadcasting lies about a person's character over social media. It includes anything offensive and humiliating directed at you in an electronic form of communication. Cyberbullying generally takes a psychological, rather than physical, form but is often part of a wider pattern of traditional bullying. It often occurs among young people. Once-off posting of nasty comments or uploading photographs intended to embarrass someone is not nice, but it is not by itself bullying. Bullying is behaviour that is sustained or repeated overtime. Bullying and mean children have been around forever, but technology now gives them a new platform for their actions. When an adult is involved, it may meet the definition of cyber-harassment or cyberstalking, a crime that can have legal consequences and involve jail time (Non-Fatal Offences (Amendment) Bill 2017). Sadly, internet

5. Defamation, Bullying and Harassment

bullying and personal attacks online are on the increase in Ireland and many cases of cyberbullying have found their way to the courts due to the extreme nature of the attacks. Cases have reached the courts where physical violence has been threatened over the internet and people have been convicted and jailed. Garda research has shown that a child carrying out cyberbullying at 12 years of age is twice as likely to have a criminal conviction by the age of 24.

Acts of cyberbullying include impersonating a victim online or posting personal information, photos or videos designed to hurt or embarrass another person. A fake account, webpage, or online persona may have been created with the sole intention to harass and bully. In the old days, we did crosswords; now kids are keeping their memories strong by trying to remember their 102 fake account passwords. Many cyberbullies go to the extent of setting up several fake accounts on various social media platforms to subject the victim to mental torture repeatedly. As long as children have access to a phone, computer or other device, including tablets, they are at risk.

As a parent of a child being bullied, you should find out when it started, notify the school, report to the website, that is, contact the service provider through its customer care or report abuse facility. Request that all information be removed and that the usage policy is enforced against the perpetrator. Insist on a takedown of offending material and have all evidence ready to hand to back up your request. Responsible websites provide ways for their users to report things such as bullying content. Take records and contact the Gardaí; if any illegal activities are apparent contact the Gardaí immediately. Illegal activities include persistent bullying that is seriously damaging to the victim's well-being.

The Irish case of *Damien Tansey v John Gill (a bankrupt), and Vogelaar, Dotster Inc and (by order) Ann Vogelaar* ([2012] IEHC 42) is particularly interesting and important with regard to the legal responsibilities in defamation of those controlling websites. The judge, Peart J, granted interlocutory injunctions under s 33 of the Defamation Act prohibiting the publication or further publication of the defamatory material/comments in question, and ordering the removal of such material from the internet. Those involved in running such websites, in particular social networking sites, could find themselves the subject of defamation cases.

You will need to gather the necessary evidence of bullying messages on the social media sites the bullies used by capturing the messages from your computer screen and saving them as images to show parents, teachers or the authorities. Print screenshots of these to have for the future. You don't have to read the content but keep a record that outlines the details, dates and times of bullying to help the school and the Gardaí with their investigations. Block the bully if you can. Ask for help from friends you trust and family.

You could apply for an injunction, which is a court order that can either prohibit the publication of certain information or force its removal.

Advise your child not to reply to any of the messages or comments.

Investigate how such incidents of cyberbullying are handled in your child's school. Call an emergency meeting with the school principal and request a copy of the school's anti-bullying policy. Demand to know what action the school has taken in handling this issue. Were the students involved in the cyberbullying suspended? Were their parents informed? If the matter cannot be resolved by the school staff, you may report the matter to the chairman of the school's board of management for attention. The board of management is legally responsible for the day-to-day running of the school, and has a duty of care to its schools students. The school's board of management is in turn responsible to the school's patron for the exercise of its duties under the Education Act 1998. The Department of Education and Skills can advise you on how to proceed with a complaint, but the department itself does not have any power to investigate complaints. Contact the Parents' and Learners' Section, Schools Division, or email childprotection@education.gov.ie or telephone 090 648 4099. Do not leave the meeting without answers. Arrange for mediation with a therapist or counsellor at school who can work with your child and/or the bully.

Schools have a duty of care to those in their care. Culpability for cyberbullying can attach to the school in some circumstances. Those running schools should have adequate policies and procedures to deter such bullying, and act properly and promptly to deal with it when it does occur (and when dealing with such behaviour, act according to fair procedures, particularly where long term suspension or expulsion is an issue). Liability can arise due to the non-implementation of school policies which would allow unmonitored access to the internet through computers or smartphones. A school could be held liable for damage caused due to negligence and/or breach of its statutory duty to look after pupils. Schools have a duty not to allow bullying or harassment to take place and to take all reasonable steps to prevent it. Schools are becoming more and more liable in recent times. Schools should have a full and complete school policy in relation to such activities, and avoid pupils having unfettered access to the internet via broadband and other means. However as shown in the *Wayne Maher (A Minor) v The Board and Management of Presentation Junior School, Mullingar* [2004] 4 IR 211 case, the courts will not expect perfection of a school and those running it, as long as the standard of a prudent parent is kept. Peart J said "the school is expected to be no more and no less vigilant of those in its care than a prudent parent would be in his or her own home".

In civil cases, parents may be held liable or accountable for the actions and conduct of their children in certain circumstances, depending on the facts of each case. Parents and guardians may be liable for the actions of their minor children if they allow "dangerous things" within their reach that can foreseeably cause harm to them or another, or if they know of a "dangerous propensity" of a child and fail to reasonably protect others against an injury resulting from it, or they fail to control a child properly. The last two categories, in particular the failure to control, as outlined by the Supreme Court in *Curley v Mannion* (1965) IR 543, are particularly

5. Defamation, Bullying and Harassment

relevant in the area of cyberbullying. If a parent or guardian allows a child to use his or her own electrical device, such as a computer, gives that child an electrical device or both, in each case setting conditions on how it is to be used, and fails to exercise proper control in ensuring that these conditions are adhered to, that parent or guardian could be held liable for defamatory statements posted or sent by the child. This would be particularly the case if it could be shown that the child had a "dangerous propensity" to post or send such statements.

The primary legislation protecting individuals are the Non-Fatal Offences Against the Person Act 1997 and the Offences Against the Person Act 1861. These laws are designed to safeguard individuals from abuse and to provide appropriate sanctions to those who are found guilty. Section 2 of the Non-Fatal Offences against the Person Act 1997 sets out the offence of assault. Section 2(1) provides as follows: "A person shall be guilty of the offence of assault who without lawful excuse intentionally or recklessly (a) directly or indirectly applies force to or causes an impact on the body of another or (b) causes another to believe on reasonable grounds that he or she is likely immediately to be subjected to any such force or impact without the consent of the other". Section 5(1) of the 1997 Act provides that a person "who, without lawful excuse, makes to another a threat, by any means intending the other to believe it will be carried out, to kill or cause serious harm to that person or a third person shall be guilty of an offence". Therefore, force does not actually have to be used; merely causing an apprehension of force is sufficient for assault under the law (providing the victim reasonably believes that the threat is real and imminent).

Therefore, if social media messages, tweets, texts or emails were to contain threats of physical violence such as "I hate you" or "You are going to die" or other such words, and the recipient has reason to believe the threat is real and that death or injury will occur imminently, then the person issuing the threat has committed an offence.

Section 10 of the 1997 Act outlines the offence of harassment. Any person who "without lawful authority or reasonable excuse, by any means including by use of the telephone, harasses another by persistently following, watching, pestering, besetting or communicating with him or her shall be guilty of an offence".

People can be prosecuted for cyberbullying under the Defamation Act 2009. Defamation of character over social media is a form of cyberbullying. You can take legal action to defend your reputation and to recover damages for any adverse event you have experienced. However, there are number of conditions that must be fulfilled before claiming compensation for defamation. Such cases can be costly to run and you would need to know the defendant was able to pay your costs and damages to make it worthwhile. A defamatory statement means a statement that tends to injure a person's reputation in the eyes of reasonable members of society. Defamatory statements made online including email, Twitter and other social media accounts are not immune to the laws of defamation, and civil redress can be claimed through the courts.

The Law Reform Commission's report detailed a number of new harassment offences to reflect advances in technology. The report proposes jail terms of up to seven years for anyone guilty of publishing online revenge porn, or engaging in serious internet-linked harassment or cyberstalking.

Bullies often know their targets but hide their own identities, however online bullies can often be traced. You can put a stop to it.

In the meantime, keep computers in a family room so activity is visible. Ensure social network accounts are private. Install filtering and anti-malware software. Most websites and smartphones include parental control options that give parents access to their children's messages and online life.

Barnardo's can be very helpful at a time like this. Contact them at www.barnardos.ie/cyberbullying and ask for their schools speaker to give a talk on cyberbullying in your daughter's school. Cyberbullying can have serious emotional consequences for our children including anxiety, depression and other stress-related disorders and even, in some cases, suicide. It is potentially criminal behaviour that must be dealt with.

In April 2012, the Herald reported on a ten-year-old boy who was being terrorised online by bullies who had gone as far as creating a Facebook page entitled "Everyone Hates (child's name)". The abuse became so bad that his parents opted to switch their son into a different school. The boy's father said "We were not aware of the page because we do not allow our youngest son on Facebook." Facebook has a rule that children under 13 should not use their site. However statistics have revealed that 75% of eight-year-olds creating Facebook accounts are aided by their parents, to bypass the age restriction controls.

Tragedies surrounding cyberbullying in Ireland include the deaths of three young teenage girls in Counties Kildare, Donegal and Leitrim.

To report cyberbullying content on YouTube, go to http://help.youtube.com/support/youtube/bin/request.py.

You can report any illegal or inappropriate behaviour, such as harassment or threats on MSN Messenger by notifying Microsoft at https://support.live.com/eform.aspx?productKey=wlmessengerabuse&ct=eformts.

Contact Skype at http://support.skype.com and Yahoo Messenger at http://help.yahoo.com/I/us/yahoo/abuse/.

See also www.02.ie/blockit and www.webwise.ie.

The Irish Society for the Prevention of Cruelty to Children (ISPCC) has compiled the Safe Click Code as a support and information guide for staying safe online. Cyberbully Ireland was established in 2016 to provide resources in the area of internet communications and cyberbullying. Bully 4U is an anti-bullying service for Irish schools. The Tackle Bullying website is a national website designed to

5. Defamation, Bullying and Harassment

help tackle cyberbullying. You might like to view campaigns such as "Connect with Respect" or "Think B4U Click" or "Watch your Space".

Irish-based websites with up-to-date information on cyberbullying are very useful resources. You might like to refer to the following: http://www.dcya.gov.ie/viewdoc. asp?DocID=120 Department of Children and Youth Affairs http://abc.tcd.ie/Anti-Bullying Centre, Trinity College Dublin http://www.scoilnet.ie/pdf_website/07_cyber-bullying.pdf Scoilnet (great for schools) http://www.citizensinformation.ie/en/education/primary_and_post_primary_education/attendance_and_discipline_in_schools/bullying_in_schools_in_ireland.html Bullying in Schools in Ireland http://www.isfsi.ie/#/teacherbom/4553400194 Internet Safety for Schools http://www.hotline.ie/documents/Cyber-bullying.pdf A guide to cyberbullying.

The Data Protection (Amendment) Act 2003 brought Ireland into line with EU Data Protection Directive 95/46/EC. This legislation covers data protection on computers, emails and all types of platforms. It allows for remedies where a breach of information has occurred. Please note the EU have brought in strict rules regarding the protection and use of personal data under the General Data Protection Regulation (GDPR) which was introduced in May 2018. Most organisations have found GDPR compliance to be a very worthwhile exercise in terms of information governance and organisations are continuing to develop so as to manage data protection risks.

FREE SPEECH V HATE SPEECH

Can online bullying ever be justified? How do the laws of libel pertain to online posts? Is the site-holder/publisher responsible for all posts made on its page, irrespective of who makes them? To what extent are online service providers themselves liable for hosting defamatory comments? And what about the operators of news websites or blogs where users are allowed to comment on same?

The laws of defamation are a legal minefield, not just for publishers but for potential complainants. Social media sites play a prominent role in how we communicate and the reality that reputations can be destroyed by such sites is brought into sharp focus by the Twitter defamation cases in the courts. In January 2014, the High Court ordered the Dublin-based Twitter to remove a false profile displaying grossly defamatory and offensive pictures and tweets of a young Irish school teacher. Defamatory statements made via the internet can and do have legal consequences. Under the EU legal framework governing online service providers, liability for hosting defamatory comments is governed by the "notice and takedown" mechanism. The online service provider will avoid liability if it reacts quickly to a complaint of defamatory content by removing it. This is known as "safe harbour". However, this may be changing as we saw earlier in the European Court of Human Rights in *Delphi AS v Estonia* (2013) ECHR 64669/09 where the ECHR decided that the online news portal was liable in defamation for defamatory comments posted despite the fact that it had removed the defamatory comments as soon as it was made aware of them.

You may remember Milo Yiannopolous who was banned from Twitter for stoking racist and sexist abuse against the actress Lesley Jones. People were quick to point out that online bullying could not be justified. Milo removed the tweet and apologised. "I now understand the difference between free speech and hate speech," he said. Hopefully others have learned from this too.

LEGAL RESPONSIBILITY OF THOSE CONTROLLING WEBSITES

Are those controlling websites liable in defamation?

In an effort to answer this question, I will look at the Irish case of *Damien Tansey v John Gill (a bankrupt), And Vogelaar, Dotster Inc andnd (by order) Ann Vogelaar* ([2012] IEHC 42). This case is important with regard to the legal responsibilities in defamation of those controlling websites. Damien Tansey is a solicitor and he brought a case against the defendants because they were alleged to be involved with a website called www.rate-your-solicitor.com. He claimed that defamatory statements were posted on that website alleging him to be engaged in corrupt, unprofessional and incompetent conduct. The first defendant repeated a number of earlier allegations against the plaintiff, as well as against other solicitors. He also fronted a campaign against the solicitors' profession which included establishing the website allowing others to make complaints. Tansey did not seek relief against the second defendant, as she denied any involvement in the website. The third defendant had a registered office in the USA and leave had been given to serve notice of the case's proceedings at that address. The fourth defendant was a daughter of the second, who stated that she was an unpaid volunteer for the website and denied any involvement in running or controlling the website.

The judge, Peart J, granted interlocutory injunctions under s 33 of the Defamation Act against the first and fourth defendants, prohibiting the publication or further publication of the defamatory material. He stated that the material in question was "seriously defamatory" of the plaintiff, and ordered the removal of such material from the internet. The defendants were ordered to end the operation of the website. The judge ordered the defendants to give up the names and addresses of the people involved in publication of the defamatory material.

This case shows that, even being an unpaid volunteer for such a website, confined to answering questions sent to it, will not exempt such a person from being liable for defamatory comments posted on it. It also shows that those involved in running such websites, in particular social networking sites, could find themselves the subject of defamation cases.

LIABILITY OF PARENTS/GUARDIANS FOR DEFAMATORY COMMENTS MADE BY THEIR CHILDREN ONLINE

Can parents be held liable for defamatory comments posted by their children online?

In civil cases, parents may be held liable or accountable for the actions and conduct of their children in certain circumstances depending on the fact of each case. Parents and guardians can be liable for the defamation committed by their minor children if they allow "dangerous things" within their reach that can foreseeably cause harm to them or another, or if they know of a "dangerous propensity" of a child and fail to reasonably protect others against an injury resulting from it, or they fail to control a child properly. The last two categories, in particular the failure to control, as outlined by the Supreme Court in *Curley v Mannion* ([1965] IR 543), are particularly relevant in the area of cyberbullying. If a parent or guardian allows a child to use his or her own electrical device, such as a computer, gives that child an electrical device, or both, in each case setting conditions on how it is to be used, and fails to exercise proper control in ensuring that these conditions are adhered to, that parent or guardian could be held liable for defamatory statements posted or sent by the child.

LIABILITY OF SCHOOLS FOR THEIR PUPILS' DEFAMATORY COMMENTS POSTED DURING SCHOOL HOURS

My child was attacked online by other children in his class during school hours. Is the school liable for this?

Schools have a duty of care to those in their care. Culpability for cyberbullying can attach to the school in some circumstances. Liability can arise due to the non-implementation of school policies which would allow unmonitored access to the internet through computers or smartphones. A school could be held liable for damage caused due to negligence and/or breach of its statutory duty to look after its pupils. Schools have a duty not to allow bullying or harassment to take place and to take all reasonable steps to prevent it. Schools are becoming more and more liable in recent times. Schools should have a full and complete school policy in place in relation to such activities and avoid pupils having unfettered access to the internet via broadband and other means.

HOW TO HAVE AN OFFENSIVE IMAGE REMOVED FROM GOOGLE, FACEBOOK OR SNAPCHAT

I want to get an offensive image of my 15-year-old daughter removed from social media. How do I do this?

It is relatively easy to make a complaint to Google, Facebook and Snapchat, but it can take a long time for a response to be returned. Google may remove an image if it contains sensitive personal information, that is, information that, if lost, compromised or disclosed, could result in substantial harm, embarrassment, inconvenience or unfairness to an individual. If the offending image is covered under Google's "removal policies", then the complainant needs to ask Google to remove the image from the search results. If the offending image should be removed for legal reasons, then the complainant needs to visit the Google "legal removals" page. If the image is not covered under either of these removal policies, the complainant needs to contact the site's webmaster to ask him to remove the image. Give reasons why the image should be taken down. Send an email to whoever is in charge of managing the website and bring it to their attention that your daughter is under 18 and the image is illegal. If they have a policy against removing the image, then ask them to block the content from being indexed by using robots or removing her name from the image. If this doesn't work, then you could try posting a plethora of positive posts so that a person would have to search very hard to find the negative post. You could try instructing digital reputation management companies, and pay them to "game" Google so that negative stories and images can be hidden by swamping the online identity with positive stories and images. To report offensive behaviour on Facebook, the complainant should go to the "community standards" page and follow the appropriate link. The Facebook standards show what is and is not allowed on Facebook. Issues such as threatening behaviour, self-harm, bullying behaviour and exploitation are covered on this page. Most messages from Snapchat automatically expire; however, there are ways to save snaps, chats and stories on Snapchat, and you can follow their guidelines for removal. Most civilised countries have laws about "hate speech". In Ireland, complaints are often made with the support of the Irish Council of Civil Liberties and the Incitement to Hatred Act 1989 protects citizens from nasty behaviour. Speed is of the essence in a case such as this one as every day that goes by with this image floating around online is causing emotional harm to your child.

You may be familiar with the Irish broadcaster Miriam O'Callaghan. In a recent high profile case Ms O'Callaghan secured a High Court order requiring Facebook to provide her with information aimed at identifying those behind alleged defamatory adverts on the social media platform.

Facebook neither consented nor objected to the orders made by Ms Justice Leonie Reynolds. The orders require Facebook to give Ms O'Callaghan's lawyers basic subscriber information, payment method details and business manager account information, to the extent such information exists, about those behind the adverts. Ms O'Callaghan intends to seek damages over the alleged false and malicious adverts containing her image and name on Facebook and Instagram in May 2018. She wants to bring proceedings against both Facebook, which owns Instagram, and those behind the adverts. As her lawyers do not know who the latter are, she sought orders requiring Facebook Ireland Ltd to provide information it allegedly has about those who paid for the adverts to be placed on the platforms. When the matter was mentioned before Ms Justice Reynolds recently Paul O'Higgins SC, for Ms O'Callaghan, said "progress has been made" and an order was being handed

5. Defamation, Bullying and Harassment

into the court. He said Facebook's ordinary protocol in such applications is that it will notify customers before providing details of their accounts but, in this case, his side wanted that bypassed. The account details "may be phoney anyway", but he did not want the account holders to be informed in advance, he said. Joe Jeffers, for Facebook, said it was neither objecting nor consenting to the order. The judge said she would make the order and returned the matter to April 30th.

Previously the High Court was told the adverts contained misleading and defamatory headlines wrongly suggesting Ms O'Callaghan has left her job with RTÉ's Prime Time to promote skincare products. Ms O'Callaghan says she has "nothing to do" with the adverts, linked to offers for skincare products, and is most distressed at being associated against her will with what has been described as "a scam product". She claims the adverts have exploited the trust placed in her by the Irish public and damaged her good name and reputation. The advertisements appear on social media users' newsfeeds and are designed to encourage the user to click on the adverts. Those who click on the adverts are offered various skincare products, which she says are falsely stated to be owned or endorsed by Ms O'Callaghan. It is also claimed users who avail of an offer of free trials of the skincare products have reported they had unauthorised money debits from their bank accounts. Ms O'Callaghan intends to seek a permanent injunction restraining publication of the adverts, plus damages for malicious falsehood, unlawful appropriation of personality, various breaches of her constitutional rights and defamation. (Miriam O'Callaghan v Facebook Ireland (2019) High Court) (Mary Carolan, The Irish Times Friday, 5 April 2019).

GARDA JUVENILE DIVERSION PROGRAMME

My son is just 10-years-old. He is a high-spirited child and he has been involved in a bit of regrettable behaviour, including the theft of a bicycle, public order offences and damage to property. He was cautioned by the Gardaí and they are dealing with him through the Garda Juvenile Diversion Programme. I do not know very much about this programme. Please advise.

The aim of the Garda Juvenile Diversion Programme is to prevent young offenders in Ireland from entering into the full criminal justice system by offering them a second chance. When a young person comes to the notice of the Gardaí because of criminal activity, he or she may be dealt with through the Garda Juvenile Diversion Programme. This allows for young people who commit criminal offences to be dealt with by means of a caution (that is, a warning by the Gardaí against committing certain types of behaviour), instead of the formal process of charge and prosecution. Children under 10 years of age are not dealt with within the criminal justice system. Their behaviour is considered to be as a result of welfare needs, and they are dealt with by the Health Service Executive.

The Garda Juvenile Diversion Programme facilitates young people who are under 17 years of age and can be extended to those under 18 years of age. The Criminal Justice Act 2006 raised the age of criminal responsibility to 12 years, but it also allows the programme to cater for children as young as 10 or 11 years. The Children Act 2001defines a child as a person under the age of 18 years.

The Garda Juvenile Diversion Programme is administered by specially trained Gardaí called Garda Juvenile Liaison Officers (JLO) who are specially-trained to deal with young people and their families in relation to crime prevention and the operation of the diversion programme. The final decision as to whether or not a person is cautioned lies with the director of the National Juvenile Office. If it is a serious crime, then consent to issue a caution lies with the Director of Public Prosecutions.

To be eligible for the programme, the child must accept responsibility for his or her criminal behaviour and must consent to be cautioned and, where appropriate, to be supervised by a JLO. The JLO is directed to give notice in writing to the parents or guardian of a child who is admitted to the programme. The identity of the child is not disclosed publicly. Every child who receives a formal caution is placed under the supervision of the JLO for 12 months. A key part of the programme is the Juvenile Diversion Programme Conference which is held to discuss the welfare of the child, to mediate between the child and the victim and to formulate an action plan for the child. An action plan is drawn up, which may include an apology by the child to the victim, participation by the child in sport or a training course, the child being at home at certain times, the child staying away from specific places or people or other initiatives which would help the child avoid criminal behaviour. Most importantly, the programme pays regard to the needs of the victims of youth offending.

The types of offence committed by children under the age of 18 years are primarily theft, alcohol-related offences, criminal damage including damage to property and the environment, assault, traffic offences, drugs possession, public order offences and burglary. Close to one in 10 of all crimes reported in Ireland are committed by children, with under 18s responsible for more than half of all car and bicycle thefts, trespass offences, arson, unlawful collections, fireworks offences and robberies from the person.

The Garda Juvenile Diversion Programme has been shown to be successful in diverting young people away from crime by offering guidance and support to young people and their families.

THREATENING, ABUSIVE OR INSULTING BEHAVIOUR

I was walking towards my car when a group of young men started insulting me verbally. They followed me and I felt very threatened by them. Would this be defined as a public order offence?

Section 6 of the Criminal Justice (Public Order) Act 1994 covers insulting words and abuse, which can lead to more serious offences. Section 6(1) provides that it shall be an offence for any person in a public place to use or engage in any threatening, abusive or insulting words or behaviour with intent to provoke a breach of the peace, or being reckless as to whether a breach of the peace may be occasioned. Section 6(2) provides that a person who is guilty of an offence under this section shall be liable on summary conviction to a fine not exceeding €1,000 and/or three months' imprisonment.

Non-Fatal Offences (Amendment) Bill 2017

What is the Non-Fatal Offences (Amendment) Bill all about?

Digital technology has facilitated such trends as intimidating and threatening online messages directed at private persons and public figures. We have all heard the stories of celebrities closing their Twitter or other social media accounts because of the constant online abuse they receive at the hands of trolls and intimidating bullies. There are many instances of online and digital harassment, stalking and abuse issues, such as cyberbullying and revenge porn, which was huge in media discussions in the last few years. Up to recently, loopholes in Irish legislation have allowed revenge porn to go unpunished, causing untold emotional damage.

Two new criminal offences are proposed to deal with this. The first is to deal with the intentional victim-shaming behaviour of posting intimate images without consent. The second offence also deals with posting intimate photos or videos, and is to deal with a new kind of voyeurism often called 'up-skirting' or 'down-blousing'. Under the proposals, offences such as revenge porn, online harassment/cyberbullying and cyberstalking would lead to an unlimited fine and/or a jail sentence of up to seven years. For less serious cases of these offences, a fine of €5,000 and/or up to 12 months in prison are applicable.

Any potential threats or issues pertaining to online harassment should be notified to all relevant parties immediately. This includes parents of all children, teachers and Gardaí where necessary.

The Role Played by the Irish Constitution in Bullying

Do any provisions of the Constitution of Ireland deal with bullying in the Irish education system?

The Irish Constitution was enacted in 1937 and, for the first time, certain fundamental rights were set out in writing. These rights are generally set out in Arts 40-44. Throughout the years since the passing of the Irish Constitution, there have been a number of judgments in Irish law which have established that there are also a number of unenumerated constitutional rights. These rights are not expressly written in the Constitution, but have been accorded constitutional protection by the Irish courts.

Article 40 deals with the personal rights of the citizen, including the right to a good name (Art 40.3.2°). This has led to the development by the Irish courts of the right of a citizen to fair procedures, that is, no one can be a judge in his or her own cause, and persons against whom allegations are made should be given an opportunity to answer them. Chief Justice Cearbhal ÓDálaigh said that "a person whose conduct is impugned as part of the subject matter of the inquiry must be afforded reasonable means of defending himself" (*In re Haughey* [1971] IR 217).

Article 42 deals with the education system. While the law allows parents to educate their children at home if they wish, the State will insist that the child receives a certain minimum education under the Education (Welfare) Act 2000, as amended. The State will intervene in the case of an appeal from an expulsion or long suspension of a student from a recognised school, or the refusal of such a school to enrol a student.

The father of 15-year-old teenager Phoebe Prince, who took her own life after being bullied, said he wanted to see a change to the Irish Constitution to protect other children and parents. He said a fitting tribute to his deceased daughter would be to see every child in Ireland given the right to be educated free from bullying under the Irish Constitution. He said lives were being damaged every day, and it should not be difficult for schools to stop bullying. (The suicide of Phoebe Prince, on January 14, 2010, led to the criminal prosecution of six teenagers for charges including civil rights violations, as well as to the enactment of stricter anti-bullying legislation by the Massachusetts state legislature. Phoebe was an Irish teenager who moved to Massachusetts and she was bullied in the school she attended there).

It will be interesting to see what changes are made in this area over the coming years.

A School's Duty of Care Towards its Students (Outside School, Outside School Hours)

A number of students from my daughter's school were involved in a fight outside school. They bullied another student from the same school outside of that school, outside of school hours. Does the school have any power over this?

The school may discipline a student who bullies outside school hours and outside school in certain cases. The case *State (Derek Smullen and Declan Smullen) v Duffy and Others* ([1980] ILRM 46) involved the High Court upholding a principal's decision to suspend a number of students involved in a fight outside school "in order to maintain peace and discipline within the school". In another High Court case, *Student A and Student B v Dublin Secondary School* ([1999] IEHC 47) the judge held that exceptional circumstances, such as danger to life and property, could justify immediate or long-term suspension without notice or procedure. In the Supreme Court in *Shane Dolan v Timothy Keohane and Michael Cunningham* (Unreported, 8 February 1994), Judge O'Flaherty

5. Defamation, Bullying and Harassment

stated that, while there were clearly cases where the duty of the school to supervise did not end at the school, this was not one of them. In this case, an accident occurred outside the primary schools grounds. In the Supreme Court case of *Christina Hosty v Patrick McDonagh, Canon Hyland and Another* (Unreported, 29 May 1973), the school was held 25% liable for an injury to a pupil. The case involved a 10-year-old schoolgirl who left her school with three other girls at 12.30pm through a double gate. She was struck by a car, both her legs were broken and her scalp lacerated. She recovered well and had no permanent disability. Fitzgerald CJ held the student to be 30% liable, the driver of the car 45% liable and the school 25% liable for not having a suitable exit from the school, not having it supervised and allowing the girl onto the road unattended. In the English case of *R v London Borough of Newham and Another* ([1995] 1 FCR 248), the judge stated that it would be "a very sad thing if head teachers did not have authority, in an appropriate case, to use disciplinary action in relation to the behaviour of pupils of the school towards each other off the school premises". However, in the Court of Appeal's judgment in *Leah Bradford-Smart v West Sussex County Council* ([2002] EWCA Civ 07 and 2002 ELR 139), it was held that the school could not owe a general duty to its pupils, or anyone else, to police their activities once they have left its charge. This is principally the duty of parents and, where criminal offences are involved, the Gardaí.

You may refer to Sinead Kanes PhD thesis (January 2018) 'An exploration of Irish second level teachers perceptions of bullying and duty of care: an educational and legal analysis, PhD Thesis, Dublin City University. This is available online at doras.dcu.ie/221 70.

PLAY THERAPY

What is play therapy?

Play therapy is a form of therapy for children with a wide range of emotional and behavioural difficulties, including anxiety, aggression and difficult life experiences, such as family breakdown and trauma. Play therapy can help children develop confidence and positive self-esteem and it can help them find healthier ways of communicating. Some children cannot help fighting because they feel bad about themselves or are scared about something. Play therapy has its roots in child psychotherapy.

Schools can refer a child to play therapy. I know quite a number of schools who have referred children with behavioural issues, or children who are acting up in some way, to play therapy sessions, and the outcome was very successful. It is generally used for children aged three to 12 years.

It involves a referral meeting and discussion with the parents and child. The sessions last under an hour (usually 50 minutes) one day a week for eight to 10 sessions, depending on progress. There are regular review sessions with the parents and school teacher. There is an assessment process undertaken prior to professional play therapists accepting referrals. The Irish Play Therapy Association is a professional association open to play therapists who have successfully completed a professional play therapy training course accredited by the British Association of Play Therapists (Play Therapy Ireland, www.playtherapy.ie).

CHILDREN WITH ADHD OR SPECIAL NEEDS IN THE CLASSROOM

Can a school suspend or expel a student who suffers from Attention Deficit Hyperactivity Disorder (ADHD) and is extremely badly behaved, deliberately hitting other children or fighting with them?

I'll start by saying that, in my opinion, this is an area in which a lot more research is required. I do not personally see ADHD or, for example, autism as a disability, but rather a valuable neurological difference, and neurologically different minds should be accepted, valued and celebrated for themselves. If necessary, in some cases we may need to change the environment to fit the child, rather than trying to change the child to fit the environment. What is perceived as normal to one person may not seem normal at all to another person, and who is to decide who is right or wrong? (The psychologist Dr Devon Mac Eachron has in my opinion some very interesting thoughts on this and you may also like to research her work in areas such as neurodiversity, the academic underachievement myth, challenging neuromyths). Please refer to www.tiltparenting.com/2019/06/11/episode-161-dr-devon-maceachron or www.ffacebook.com/2Egifted/posts or www.parentfootprint.com/podcast/neurodiversity-De.Devon Maceachron

However, this is not a research psychology thesis and, for now, I'll just look at case law in this area. A balancing act is at play here, that is, balancing the rights of one student in the class with the other students in the class.

Certainly not all children with ADHD have behavioural problems, but some may behave differently to others in the classroom environment because this restrictive environment may not suit them. Primary school teachers are trained in this area (that is, how to deal with or teach a child that has ADHD) within the classroom, but teachers cannot diagnose ADHD.

In the High Court case of *Richard Clare v Minister for Education and Science, the South Eastern Health Board, Ireland and the Attorney General* (2004) IEHC 350, Richard Clare claimed that the defendants failed to provide appropriate education for his needs as a boy suffering from Attention Deficit Hyperactivity Disorder.

In a questionnaire to the health board in 1993, the plaintiff's mother said her son was not suffering from any behavioural problems. The primary school principal and teachers failed to notice that there was anything wrong with the boy, despite the fact that his mother was called to the school every year to discuss his behaviour. In sixth class, the teacher told Mrs Clare that her son's behaviour was inappropriate and unacceptable but brushed it off as low-key misbehaviour. The principal said there was nothing to lead him to believe the boy needed psychological assessment.

5. Defamation, Bullying and Harassment

Clare then went on to secondary school where he was disruptive in class, disrespectful to a teacher, deliberately hit another child with a school bag, used bad language, had homework missing and he was suspended. While the mother later admitted that she suspected her son might have ADHD, there was no evidence that she contacted the school about this. It was not until 1999 that he was diagnosed with ADHD, the school then being told.

In 2000, the plaintiff's year head wrote to the boy's parents stating that he had been involved in a fight, and that they were extremely lucky the other boy's parents didn't take legal action. He was then suspended from school indefinitely. He was later allowed to return to the school on agreement that he behaved, and that he would be expelled if he did not behave. He was eventually expelled.

The judge held that the school "did not discriminate unfairly, unreasonably or at all" in the context of s 7(10)(d) of the Equal Status Act 2000 in expelling him. The school was "entitled to balance the rights of Mr Clare with the other students in his class", which was not discrimination under s 7(4)(b).

The judge went on to say that the school principal and class teachers should not be faulted for failing to ascertain that the boy had ADHD. His mother should have made the authorities aware that her son had a defined problem.

Some parents may not want to know about their child's problem, and treatment cannot be sought without parental consent. Some parents will deliberately try to hide the fact that their child has a problem so that their child can attend secondary school with a clean slate.

In my opinion, the whole area of diagnosis of ADHD is a huge problem in primary schools. We have the parents in denial that there is something wrong with their child and they won't have their child assessed by a consultant, and then we have some teachers brushing off a child's behavioural problems as "boisterous behaviour". Some teachers may have a lack of interest in getting involved, or fear falling out with the child's parents. Young and inexperienced teachers may simply not know any better. There is no single test for ADHD, which can make it more difficult to diagnose.

Symptoms of Attention Deficit Hyperactivity Disorder include, *inter alia*, impulsiveness, poor attention span and hyperactivity. A child psychologist will base the diagnosis on a number of things, including observations by parents and teachers and direct observations of the child involved.

NEPS, the national educational psychological service, is a free service available to primary schools. A psychologist will come to the school, assess the child, determine what the child needs and consult the parents and teachers involved. If a diagnosis has been missed in primary school, there is a major chance that it will not be picked up in secondary school. You may wish to refer to the Department of Education website www.education.ie and click on the NEPS link at the top of the page for more information.

Chapter 6

Farming and Agricultural Law

Turbary Rights – An Important Role in Modern Rural Life

I recently relocated from Dublin to Leitrim. I purchased a beautiful home overlooking Lough Scur. I recall my solicitors at the time of the sale mentioning something about turbary rights. However, I was so excited about getting the keys to my new home that I forgot to ask them what turbary rights actually are. What are turbary rights and are they of any use to me?

Congratulations on the purchase of your new home. If we are to understand turbary rights, we first must put them into the context of how the law sees property rights. In theory, people do not own land in Ireland, they own a right to use the land. The level of the right to use the land can range from freehold title – where one traditionally could use the land for anything to more ethereal rights to use land for certain restrictive purposes. Examples of these latter rights would include hunting rights and turbary rights. In legal terms, they are referred to as incorporeal hereditaments or *profits à prendre*. A right of turbary refers to the right to dig, cut and take away turf from another person's land in common with others to use as fuel for one's house. The right to take turf for fuel attaches to the dwelling house, and it does not attach to the lands. The right of turbary cannot be severed from the dwelling house. If some of the lands on which the right of turbary attaches are sold, the turbary right will remain attached to the portion of lands on which the house is situated and will not attach to the remaining sold lands which were severed from the dwelling house. If the house is replaced by another house on the same lands in continuance of the older house, the right of turbary automatically attaches to the new house. Turbary rights are limited to the fuel requirements of the house owner and do not extend to a right to cut and sell turf.

It may be thought that the controversial EU-inspired restrictions on turf-cutting have placed turbary rights in jeopardy of becoming little more than footnotes in dusty legal history books. However, as a property practitioner, I know a considerable amount of them still exist and they are ubiquitously associated with old country cottages. While a considerable amount of turf cutting has been banned from many bogs, there is still plenty of bog in Ireland that has fallen outside the remit of the restrictions. While turbary origins may be lost in time, they still have an important role in modern rural life.

MEDIATION – FARM DISPUTES

I am a farmer and I am involved in a dispute with my neighbour who is also a farmer. I dread the thought of going to court to resolve this matter, as the costs of going to court in Ireland are well documented. I understand that mediation could be a cost-effective alternative way of helping us dissolve this dispute or come to our own solutions. What is involved in mediation?

You have the option of appointing an independent mediator from a panel appointed by a professional body, or a person who both parties trust to undertake the role. A mediator does not have to be legally qualified, but many of them are. The mediation would usually take place within seven days of the appointment of a mediator, with the hope of finding a solution to the dispute. First there is a joint "without prejudice" meeting of the parties, followed by separate meetings between the parties to the dispute and the mediator. "Without prejudice" means you cannot use any information that comes out of the mediation in any future litigation case or court proceedings. The parties try to agree a resolution. The mediation is voluntary, which means either party can walk away at any time. If this doesn't work, then you have the option of going to court. However, mediation would be a good way of reducing your legal costs.

To summarise, mediation aims to help parties involved in a dispute to reach an agreement that is acceptable to both sides. The mediator acts as a go-between to help re-open channels of communication and broker agreement. Mediation can be a time-saving and cost-effective alternative to legal action. Community Law and Mediation, based in the Northside Civic Centre, provides a mediation service which is available to people countrywide, as well as having a branch in Limerick City. You can also avail of private mediation services where you pay by the hour.

HEALTH AND SAFETY LEGISLATION

My son was badly injured while working on our neighbour's farm. Our neighbour is a lovely man, but I feel he is somewhat oblivious to farming dangers. Is there any particular code of practice farmers should implement to avoid the risk of injury or death on their farms?

The Safety, Health and Welfare at Work Act 2005 imposes a legal duty on employers to prepare and work to a safety statement. The code of practice for preventing injury and occupational ill health in agriculture incorporates a risk-assessment document and plan for a a safe system of work. If the farmer follows the code of practice and an accident occurs on his farm, he can rely on the fact that he followed the code of practice in defending himself in proceedings. The code of practice helps farmers identify and assess the risk of hazards on the farm and identify measures that can reduce the impact of an accident, such as putting up danger signs or providing training for workers. The safety statement should be given to all people who work on the farm. A farm inspector may look at how the statement is being implemented.

6. Farming and Agricultural Law

Legal requirements also apply to children. The Safety Health and Welfare at Work (Children and Young Persons) Regulations 1998 require farmers to identify what work is suitable for children. Children under 14 are not allowed to drive or operate tractors or machinery, and children over 14 are only allowed to do so if they received training. It is on a regular basis, and especially during the summer, that I see very small children in the cabs of tractors around the countryside, usually standing beside the driver. When children are carried in a cab, it must be fitted with properly-designed and fitted passenger seats with seat belts. The 2005 Act places a duty of care on self-employed farmers and farm workers to do what is reasonable to ensure safety on the farm.

SINGLE FARM PAYMENTS – THE TIPPERARY FARMER CASE

With reference to the Single Farm Payment, please explain the landmark judgment in the High Court involving a Tipperary farmer who challenged a Department of Agriculture decision to withhold his Single Farm Payment.

The Department of Agriculture lost a landmark case brought by a Tipperary farmer. White J in the High Court ruled in favour of a Tipperary farmer who challenged a Department of Agriculture decision to withhold all his Single Farm Payment after it was discovered that 46 hectares of commonage showed no evidence of farming activity (the 46 ha accounted for over 20% of the farmer's application). Mr Justice White ruled that the Department's inspection was procedurally flawed, and that the farmer was entitled to the Single Farm Payment on all his eligible land, less a 5pc penalty for a cross-compliance breach on his cattle. The farmer had initially appealed the Department's decision under the Agricultural Appeals Act and the appeal failed. Mr Justice White stated that an interest rate of 2% per annum should apply from the date that the Agricultural Appeals Office upheld the review of the Department's findings. The judge awarded O'Connor a refund of €124,431 for his eligible land, plus all his legal costs and interest amounting to nearly €10,000 (*O'Connor v Minister for Agriculture* (2016) IEHC 336 White Michael J).

It is not often we see a case like this in the High Court and it is good news for farmers appealing decisions of the Department of Agriculture, as well as farmers who have lost appeals in the past. Farmers may be able to request the director of appeals for a review of their case. As a result of this case, some potentially very significant issues around the Department's compliance with EU regulations, which relate to the inspections process, have come to light. A "control report" will now have to be furnished to the farmer, prior to any conclusions being drawn by the Department, which makes it possible to review the details of the checks carried out. The farmer then has a chance to rebut the findings of the inspectors, and respect must be had for fair procedures before an automatic penalty is applied.

However, the Department appealed the case to the Court of Appeal as most likely they were afraid of a flood of claims from farmers in similar positions. The department considered that some farmers would now be seeking a review of their appeals of inspection decisions, as the "control report" in many of these cases may not now be valid.

The court of appeal allowed the Minister's appeal, set aside the payment order and dismissed the cross appeal. Mr Justice Michael Peart said the SPS is an EU scheme, implemented by each member state, which rewards farmers who conduct their farming activities to a minimum standard. (*O'Connor v Minister for Agriculture, Food and the Marine and Others* (2018) IECA 376 Peart J).

AGRICULTURAL RELIEF – LAND AND TAX MATTERS

I will inherit my father's farm and house after his death. The farm is worth a substantial amount of money. Will I have to pay a lot of tax on my inheritance? I previously received a gift of €40,000 from my father.

The amount of tax you may have to pay to Revenue depends on a number of factors. Farmers may qualify for a tax relief referred to as agricultural relief. This relief is similar to business relief, in reducing the taxable value of your inheritance by 90%. This can provide up to 90% tax relief on gifts/inheritances of relevant agricultural property. To qualify for this agricultural relief, you must pass two tests, that is, be a "farmer" and an "active farmer", as defined by the Revenue Commissioners. The "farmer" test requires that 80% of your assets must be agricultural assets at the date of the transfer. To qualify as an "active farmer", you must either hold an agricultural qualification (e.g. the Green Cert or an agricultural science degree), or you must obtain that qualification within four years of the farm being transferred to you, and you must farm the land for the next six years. If you don't have the agricultural qualifications, you must spend at least 20 hours a week farming the land for at least six years from the date of transfer. If you don't satisfy these conditions, you may still claim agricultural relief if you lease the land for a minimum of six years from the date of transfer to an "active farmer".

The amount one can receive tax-free depends on one's relationship to the person who died. The highest tax-free threshold applies to inheritances and gifts from one's parents. The tax-free thresholds that apply in other cases, for example, to inheritances from other relatives or from friends, are much lower. If the value of what you receive exceeds the relevant threshold, you will pay tax at 33 per cent on the excess amount. Exemptions and reliefs from inheritance tax include business relief, agricultural relief and dwelling house relief. Inheritances of a house or apartment can be exempt from tax in certain circumstances. There are very detailed rules and conditions applying to these reliefs and Revenue regularly carries out detailed checks on relief claims. It is very important to get professional tax advice from a chartered tax advisor or accountant. Where a family business is concerned, your tax bill may be downsized. If you inherit your family's business, you may qualify for this relief, which reduces the taxable value of what you receive by 90%. Currently, children may each inherit €310,000 from their parents without being

6. Farming and Agricultural Law

liable for tax. Any inheritance valued in excess of this amount will be taxed at a rate of 33%. This tax is called Capital Acquisitions Tax (CAT), or gift or inheritance tax. If you qualify for agricultural relief, then the CAT will be calculated on 10% of the market value of the agricultural property you receive. Therefore if you inherit a farm worth €800,000 and you qualify for agricultural relief, the value of the farm you are inheriting will be valued at €80,000 for tax purposes. That is below the tax threshold and you will not be liable for any tax. It's always best to discuss these issues with your accountant.

An inheritance is a gratuitous benefit taken on a death, and a gift is a gratuitous benefit taken otherwise than on a death. Recipients of any gifts or previous inheritances must factor those into account when calculating their threshold. So, if you previously received gifts or inheritances, you must take account of these in considering whether you have used up the relevant tax-free threshold. Calculating the tax you owe can be quite complicated. This is because there are lots of different rules determining, for example, the date you inherited the property, that is, whether it was the date the person died or the date probate was granted.

The recipient of the inheritance is the person responsible for paying the tax. Inheritance tax is a self-assessment tax which could prove to be a difficult area for people who have never had to submit tax papers, so please get further assistance if necessary.

AGRICULTURAL RELIEF – CASH INHERITANCE

I made a will leaving everything, that is, my farm and cash savings, to my only son. My son qualifies for agricultural relief on the farm. Will he also qualify for agricultural relief on the cash he will inherit?

Whether or not your son will qualify for agricultural relief on the cash inheritance will depend on how you draft your will. If you include a clause in your will providing for the bequest of this cash to your son on the condition that the whole, or part thereof, be invested in agricultural property within two years of the date of issue of the grant of representation in your estate, then your son will qualify for agricultural relief on the cash inheritance. Therefore if your son complies with this condition, the cash bequest will be written down accordingly for tax purposes.

The valuation date for tax purposes will be the date of investment in agricultural property. Perhaps have a meeting about this with your son first. He may not wish to invest this cash in agricultural property, and may have already made plans of a different kind for the future investment. Perhaps it might be better to provide for an alternative clause in your will to protect your son's cash inheritance. As with all conditional bequests, the bequest will fail if your son invests the cash elsewhere. It is always advisable to consult a tax consultant or accountant to avail of good tax-planning advice in these circumstances.

You did not confirm the amount of cash you are bequeathing to your son. A child may inherit up to €310,000 from their parents without being liable for tax. Therefore the above only applies if you are bequeathing over €310,000 to your son. Again, I would always recommend a meeting with one's accountant in these circumstances to clarify the correct up-to-date thresholds.

Marriage Breakdown in the Farming Community

My only son was killed in a farming accident a few years back. He had one son. I own a lovely farm and, on my death, I would like to pass it on to my grandson. My grandson is a wonderful young man. The problem I have is his girlfriend. I really don't like her or trust her at all. I suspect she's a gold digger. What will happen if I make a will leaving everything to my grandson and he marries this person and their relationship ends soon thereafter? I don't want my land sold. Could I get my grandson to do up a pre-nuptial agreement or something like that?

At present, there is no legislation in the area of pre-nuptial agreements, despite a demand from the farming community. However, I would advise you to do one anyway because, although the Irish courts are not bound to accept the contents of a pre-nuptial agreement as the terms of a separation or divorce, there is significant case-law to show that, where these agreements are in place, the courts are having regard to them in some circumstances. There is nothing in Irish law preventing couples entering into pre-nuptial agreements. Furthermore, I see no reason why Irish courts should not take pre-nuptial agreements into account when making provision for spouses. Even if your grandson does not marry this girl and decides to live with her anyway, they become qualified co-habitees if they have been living together and are parents of one or more dependent children of the relationship after a period of two years. In most other cases, they must be living together for five years or more. In this case, they have the option of entering into a trust agreement which is binding in law and which would prevent the farm being sold if the relationship broke down. Under a trust, you could give your grandson the use of the land for his lifetime while devising the land to a later generation, even if they are not yet born. A trust can be created in a will or it can be created *inter vivos* or during the life time of the land owner. You can appoint a trustee and ensure that he or she is properly carrying out your wishes. The benefit of a trust is to prevent the sale of the land for a generation, and this might well suit the situation you describe.

Pre-nuptial Agreements, Wills and The Family Farm

My father has transferred the family farm to me. My mother is deceased. I made a will recently and stated therein my intentions for the family farm should anything happen to me. I am happy to leave it at that but my fiancée wants to sign a

6. Farming and Agricultural Law

pre-nuptial agreement. Would a pre-nuptial agreement have any bearing on my will? What would happen in terms of the pre-nuptial agreement if my spouse died?

Pre-nuptial agreements are not binding on a judge in this country, and a pre-nuptial agreement does not have any bearing on your will.

However, in the case of a separation or divorce, they may have a somewhat persuasive effect in judgments. Couples sometimes draft a pre-nuptial agreement to help make their intentions clear regarding the distribution of assets in the case of separation. It is an agreement between two future spouses in contemplation of being married to each other.

If your spouse died, the existence of a will is most important. If a spouse who owns a farm dies without a valid will, then the rules of intestacy apply. This means that the surviving spouse will be entitled to inherit two thirds of the estate and if there are children, they get the other third. If you do not have any children, your surviving spouse will get the entire estate. It is always better to make a valid will clearly stating your wishes for the family farm after your death.

Pre-nuptial agreements usually just deal with what you would like to happen to your assets in the event of a separation or divorce. However, you could enter into a pre-nuptial agreement, clearly making provision therein for what you wish to happen on the death of one of the spouses. Fairness must prevail towards your spouse in such an agreement. Once again, such an agreement may have a somewhat persuasive effect in judgments but, as stated previously, are not binding on a judge in this country.

AGRICULTURAL LEASE

I own a substantial amount of land which I lease on a short-term basis to my farmer friend. He would like a longer lease. Are there any tax advantages of entering a longer term lease agreement?

A land owner is exempt from income tax on lease rental income up to various exemption limits. The lease term and the maximum tax exemption limits are as follows: (a) 5 to 7 year lease, up to €18,000 rental income per year; (b) 7 to 10 year lease, up to €22,500 rental income per year; (c) 10 to 15 year lease, up to €30,000 rental income per year; (d) 15 year-plus lease, up to €40,000 rental income per year. The rental income eligible can include income from both land and agricultural entitlements. The lease must be in writing and stamped by the Revenue Commissioners in order for the lessor (that is, the land owner) to avail of these income tax incentives. The Universal Social Charge and **PRSI** still apply to the lease income. The tax reliefs do not apply to leases to a spouse, son, daughter or sibling.

STAMP DUTY AND OTHER TAXES ON AGRICULTURAL LAND

I live in a country house. An excellent opportunity has now presented itself in that the owner of adjoining land has put 30 acres up for sale. I was hoping to purchase llamas for their wool, and this land would be perfect for them. Will I have to pay stamp duty and Capital Gains Tax or any other taxes on the full market value of the purchase?

The purchase of agricultural land currently attracts stamp duty at a rate of 6% of the land value. Interest and penalties will be payable if the stamp duty is not paid within the requisite time period. You are liable to pay stamp duty. You are not however liable to pay capital gains tax (CGT). The seller is liable for CGT because this is a tax payable on the profit made on the disposal of investment property. You are not receiving a gift of the land, and you are not inheriting it. Therefore, capital acquisitions or capital gains tax does not apply to you.

CONTROLLED BURNING AND CUTTING OF LAND, VEGETATION AND HOUSEHOLD WASTE

I am hoping to cut hedgerows and tidy up my land at the weekend if good weather conditions prevail. I'll probably just burn any unwanted trimmings. What is the law around burning or removal of vegetation? I live close to a wooded area and my land is designated as a 'Special Area of Conservation'.

Under s 40 of the Wildlife Act 1976, as amended, it is forbidden to cut or remove hedgerows or destroy other vegetation during the bird nesting season, from 1 March to 31 August each year. There are some exceptions to this law, including removal or cutting of hedgerows during routine agriculture or forestry practices, for public safety (such as roadside hedges), for the development of land (such as building houses) and for maintenance of waterways. The Heritage Act 2018 includes proposals to change the dates for hedge-cutting and land-burning. The Minister is proposing a two-year pilot programme with a rollover clause, which would allow hedge cutting in August and burning in March. Under s 39 of the Wildlife Act, as amended, it is prohibited to burn vegetation growing within one mile of a wood which you do not own without giving written notice seven days in advance to the owner or your local Garda station. The Waste Management (Prohibition of Waste Disposal by Burning) Regulations 2009 make it an offence to dispose of waste by uncontrolled or unregulated burning. Waste refers to trees, tree trimmings or similar waste. Exemption is provided for certain agricultural practices, but only as a last resort and after steps are taken to reduce and recycle waste. Under s 74 of the Wildlife Amendment Act 2000, fines for breaches of the Act range from €635 to €63,490 and prison terms for three months to two years, or both a fine and prison term.

6. Farming and Agricultural Law

You mention your land is designated as an SAC (Special Area of Conservation), so you must consult the NPWS in advance of any burning.

I understand it is necessary to burn land in some circumstances, particularly in the management of plant disease and invasive species or to remove old, unproductive vegetation from land, and controlled burning is legal and encouraged in such cases. But as the fires in Galway showed, one must be very mindful that the fire does not get out of control, because it can have devastating effects on wildlife and forestry.

Burning household waste at home or in your garden is illegal and can incur a fine of up to €3,000 or 12 months in prison (or both) on summary conviction in the District Court. It is an offence under waste management legislation, air pollution Acts and the Waste Management (Prohibition of Waste Disposal by Burning) Regulations 2009.

Cutting Trees on My Land

Can I legally cut old apple trees on my own land? They are huge and very close to my house. I fear that, if we get a bad storm, they might fall over and damage my house.

The Forestry Act 2014 replaces the Forestry Act 1946 and it sets out revised requirements in relation to tree felling, as discussed in the next question on liability for trees, both fallen and overhanging.

Section 19(1) of the Forestry Act 2014 sets out the list of exempted trees and includes at s 19(1)(0) apple, pear, plum and damson trees.

The legislation on the whole area of tree felling is quite clear.

Forestry Act 1946: under s 37, it is illegal to uproot any tree over 10 years old or to cut down any tree of any age unless a notice of intention to fell or uproot trees has been lodged at the Garda station nearest to the trees at least 21 days before felling commences. On receipt of a completed felling notice (that is, a form you get in the Garda station), an order prohibiting the felling of trees is issued. This protects the trees in question while consideration is given to the issuing of a felling licence. The Act refers to two types of felling licence, that is, a general felling licence and a limited felling licence.

You refer to the felling of apple trees and therefore you appear to fall into one of the exemptions, as the requirement for a felling licence under the Act for the cutting down of trees does not apply where the tree in question is a plum, hazel, apple, damson, cherry or pear tree. The tree is standing within 100 feet of any building other than a wall or temporary structure. There are various fines/penalties for the illegal felling of trees.

Forestry Act 2014: where a person wishes to fell or otherwise remove any trees, he or she shall apply to the Minister for a licence to do so (s 17(1)). The licence shall be valid for such period as the Minister decides, which shall not exceed 10 years (s 17(3)). A person who fells or otherwise removes trees without a licence shall be guilty of an offence and be liable to a fine not exceeding €200 for every tree in respect of which the offence was committed (not exceeding €5,000 in total), or imprisonment for a term not exceeding six months or both, or on conviction on indictment, to a fine not exceeding €1,000,000 or imprisonment for a term not exceeding five years or both (s 17(6)(i)(ii)). Every application for a licence must be determined within four months (s 18(1)).

Section 19(1) sets out a list of exempted trees, and includes a tree in an urban area, within 30 metres of a building (other than a wall or temporary structure), but excluding any building built after the trees were planted that is, in the opinion of the Minister, required to be removed to control or prevent the spread of fire or pest or disease, to protect the integrity of the forest gene pool, for forest-survey purposes, to mitigate a threat to a habitat or important environmental resource, Christmas trees, a tree dangerous on account of its age, condition or location, required to be removed after an accident, less than five years of age that came about through natural regeneration and was removed from a field as part of the normal maintenance of agriculture, of the willow or poplar species and maintained solely for fuel under a short rotation coppice, removed for scientific purposes, outside of a forest within 10 metres of a public road and which, in the reasonable opinion of the owner, is dangerous to persons using the public road on account of its age or condition, on an agricultural holding and removed by the owner for use on that holding, provided it does not form part of a decorative avenue or ring of trees, its volume does not exceed three cubic metres and the removal of it, when taken with the removal or other trees, would not exceed 15 cubic metres in any 12 month period, is of hawthorn or blackthorn species, in a hedgerow and felled for the purposes of its trimming, provided that the tree does not exceed 20 centimetres in diameter when measured 1.3 metres from the ground, in a burial ground maintained by a burial board, of the apple, pear, plum or damson species shall be an exempted tree.

A tree over 150 years old, within the curtilage of a protected structure, within the area subject to a special amenity area, within a landscape conservation area, a historic monument or archaeological area or natural heritage area shall not be an exempted tree, except in some limited circumstances (s 19(2)). Nothing in this section shall be construed as removing any restriction on the felling or removal of trees under the Planning and Development Acts 2000 to 2013 or the Wildlife Acts 1976 to 2000.

Where trees have been felled or removed within a licence under s 7 or seriously damaged, the Minister may issue a replanting order in respect of the owner requiring him or her to replant or to fulfil any or all of the conditions attached to the licence (s 26). The Minister may issue a preservation order prohibiting the felling or removal of trees, including exempted trees, and anyone who then removes such trees will be guilty of an offence (s 29(1)).

LIABILITY FOR FALLEN AND OVERHANGING TREES

My land abuts a roadway and the trees on my land are very mature, with large branches reaching out over the road. I am considering cutting the trees because they pose a risk to drivers in that they may obstruct the drivers' view. Do I require a tree felling licence to do this?

You need a licence to cut certain types of trees. The Forestry Act 2014 replaces the Forestry Act 1946 and sets out the requirements in relation to tree-felling licences. It includes an expanded list of exempted trees to allow felling without a tree felling licence of trees outside of the forest in certain circumstances. The Act allows for a single licence process for tree felling and allows for felling licences of up to 10 years in duration.

If trees or branches are reaching near enough to the road to pose a risk of danger, you should take action by seeking a licence to cut. You are also responsible for ensuring that drivers' views are not negatively affected by bushes or trees if your land abuts a roadway.

You must exercise a standard of reasonable care when maintaining trees or hedges. Hedges should not be cut back any later than 1 March, due to birds nesting. The law allows the cutting of isolated bushes and gorse, as well as the mowing of isolated growths of fern in the ordinary course of agriculture at any time of year, with a few exceptions. Contact the felling section of the Department of Agriculture for details.

Landowners or occupiers (which would include a farmer renting land) are responsible for ensuring that trees and hedges do not encroach on their neighbour's land. The local authority and Electricity Supply Board (ESB) have powers to deal with trees which may overhang the roadway or which are near power lines. They can give notice to the owner requiring them to cut or prune the tree. If the ESB or local authority direct the owner to remove the tree and the owner fails to comply, they have the authority to carry out the work and charge the owner. If the tree is on your neighbour's land, do not cut it as this could raise liability issues for you.

DOGS AND LIVESTOCK: THE ANIMALS ACT 1985

Our pet terrier went missing on Tuesday night. We searched everywhere, but we could not find him. He is a companion dog and he usually never leaves our house. We were therefore shocked when we received a telephone call to say he was caught

in a field with sheep, and the owner of the sheep shot him. Can a livestock owner legally shoot a dog? Our dog may have wandered in to a field with sheep, but he would never harm a sheep. He loves sheep and is used to playing with them at home.

The Animals Act 1985 makes the owner of a dog liable in damages for any injury to a person or to livestock by the dog. There is no onus on the injured party to prove that the dog had a previous propensity to cause such injury, or that the owner knew this. Therefore it is not a defence to say that "my dog loves sheep" or "would never harm a sheep". It is essential that you know where your dog is at all times. A livestock owner may legally shoot a dog which is caught worrying livestock. Under the Control of Dogs Act 1986, all dogs must be kept under effective control at all times in a public place, regardless of breed or temperament. A dog warden may seize any dog he finds unaccompanied by a person in a public place. After five days, the dog may be re-homed to a new owner. The Control of Dogs (Restriction of Certain Dogs) Regulations 1998 has a list of restricted breeds of dog that must be kept under control at all times. They must be kept muzzled and on a short, strong lead when in a public place. Examples of such breeds are the English bull terrier, American pit bull terrier, Staffordshire bull terrier, rottweiler, doberman pinscher and bull mastiff.

EMPLOYMENT CONTRACTS FOR FARM WORKERS

I came to Ireland four years ago and initially I got part time work helping out with machinery. My most recent job is on a farm and I love it. My boss said he is going to give me full-time employment, and this will include food and accommodation. He said he will have an employment contract for me to sign next week. Is there anything I should look out for in the contract? I was also asked if I would work on Sundays. I would prefer to work a five-day week, but I will work on Sundays if I have to.

An employer must issue employees with a written statement of terms and conditions relating to their employment within two months of commencing employment. The contract should include details such as the title of the job and the nature of the work. It should also include the date of commencement of employment and whether there is a probationary period and for how long, terms of pay, hours of work, notice periods, holidays, redundancy, dismissal and safety statements or code of practice if same applies. The Safety, Health and Welfare at Work Act 2005 places a legal duty on employers to prepare and work to a safety statement. You are enquiring about Sunday work. If an employee does Sunday work, in the absence of any specific agreement, an employer must give an employee a reasonable allowance for this or a reasonable pay increase or reasonable paid time off work. An employer must keep a record of his employees' working time. The maximum average working week for most employees cannot exceed 48 hours, and that can be determined over six months for employees working in agriculture. An employer must pay at least the minimum wage. You mention that your employer is going to provide food and accommodation. The maximum value that can be

6. Farming and Agricultural Law

attributed to these in terms of the minimum wage calculation is €54.13 per week. Please ask your employer for a pay slip which should include a breakdown of gross pay, hours worked, hourly rate of pay, holiday pay, sick pay and any deductions from gross salary, such as tax, PRSI, board and lodgings. As an employee, you are entitled to holidays. A worker who has eight or more months of service is entitled to take an unbroken period of two weeks' annual leave, or four working weeks in the leave year in which the worker works at least 1,365 hours. An employee who is in continuous employment for 13 weeks or more is entitled to certain minimum notice in the event of dismissal. Dismissal can be justified on the grounds of competence or qualifications. An employee who has been employed for a year or more may claim unfair dismissal if he should be dismissed or feels obliged to leave by reasons of the conditions of work being made so difficult. An employee who is employed for two continuous years or more is entitled to statutory redundancy amounting to two weeks' pay for each year of continuous service up to €600, plus one further week's pay. So, as you can see, it is very important to ensure you have a contract of employment. Read the contract well and be sure you are happy with all the terms and conditions before you sign it. It is important to start a new job with a clear understanding of what is expected of you and equally to know and understand what you can expect from your employer.

CREATION OF A TRUST TO PRESERVE ASSETS

I am an elderly farmer and I am contemplating making a will. I have a large family and many grandchildren. My eldest grandchild uses the land for his cattle and I would like him to continue doing so. I would not like to see the land being sold. The land was in our family for several generations, however I would like my younger grandchildren to get a share also.

Typically in the countryside, farm lands are left to one person in the family, usually a son with an interest in farming, as the owner may not like to see the land being sold or, if it's a large farm, it may be divided and made into two or three viable farms. One issue you could consider in your circumstances is the creation of a trust. With a trust, you could give your grandson use of the farm for a set number of years, while devising the lands to your other grandchildren at a later date. The creation of a trust requires careful consideration and should be carried out by a legal professional, as the courts will not uphold a trust if it is not properly constituted. One or more trustees must be appointed for a trust, and the trustee will have responsibilities and duties regarding the running of the farm. The trustee should be someone you trust to fulfil their obligations under the trust. A trust can be created in a will. The benefit of the trust is that it can keep your land secure from sale according to your wishes.

DAMAGE TO PUBLIC ROADS BY LANDOWNERS

I have noticed a lot of slurry, muck and fodder on the country road where I live. Are landowners allowed to transport these materials on public roads?

The Roads Act 1993 introduced certain provisions making it an offence for landowners to allow any material such as slurry or fodder to fall onto a public road where such material is (or could be) a hazard to road users or interferes with the safe use or maintenance of a road. Landowners must ensure that the transport of winter fodder over public roads is on the basis that there is no alternative off-road means of access, and adequate measures must be taken between gateways and storage locations to minimise the amount of clay that is carried onto the public road. Fodder or plastic should never be left on grass margins, and livestock should be fed away from the road so that road drainage is not interfered with. Slurry should never flow onto the public road. If soil accidently spills onto the public road, it must be removed as soon as possible. Tyres of farm machinery should be washed often to keep them clean so that soil is not carried onto the road.

CONSERVATION WORK ON OLD FARM BUILDINGS

I am planning to carry out conservation work on an old farm building I own. I hope also to repair the stone wall around the building, and fix some of the gates thereon. Are there any grants available to help me fund this project?

The GLAS Traditional Farm Buildings Scheme reopened for applications in January 2019. Please refer to the department of agricultures website for details of this scheme or similar schemes. Only farmers approved in the Green Low-Carbon Agri-Environment Scheme (GLAS) are eligible to apply. This scheme is jointly funded by the Department of Agriculture, Food and the Marine and the European Union, and is administered on behalf of the Department by the Heritage Council. The financial allocation to the scheme is €6 million for the lifetime of the 2014-2020 Rural Development Programme. All applications are assessed individually to identify the best and highest priority projects. Under the scheme, grants are available to GLAS participants to carry out approved conservation works to traditional farm buildings and associated landscape structures, such as historic yard surfaces, walls, gate pillars and gates. The principal objective of this scheme is to ensure that traditional farm buildings and other structures that contribute to the character of the landscape and which are of significant heritage value are conserved for agricultural use. The grants available range from €4,000 to €25,000, and can cover up to 75% of the cost of the works.

Chapter 7

Consumer Rights

The Sale of Goods and Supply of Services Act 1980

I have an issue with an item I purchased. Can I ask the seller to refund the cost to me?

The purchaser of goods has a number of rights under the Sale of Goods and Supply of Services Act 1980 which include (a) the goods should be of reasonable quality, taking into account what they are meant to do, their durability and their price, (b) the goods must do what they are reasonably expected to do and (c) the buyer must not be misled into buying something by the description of goods or services given orally by a salesperson or an advertisement (s 10 of the 1980 Act).

If you have an issue with an item that you have bought, it is always the seller who should put things right by repairing or replacing the item or refunding the cost. It is not good enough for the seller to say it is the responsibility of the manufacturer to replace or repair an item. The act is clear in that the responsibility falls on the seller (Section 10 of the 1980 act).

When you buy goods in a sale, you have the same rights as when you pay full price for the goods unless a specific defect is brought to your attention. If you are not satisfied with the quality of goods, you can return them to the supplier who sold them to you as soon as you can. Do not try to repair the item yourself and make sure you keep the receipt.

You cannot return the item if you were told about the defect before you bought it, or you should have noticed the defect before you bought the item, you broke or damaged the item, you changed your mind, you made a mistake when buying the item or you bought the item knowing it was not fit for what you wanted it to do.

One should act as soon as possible, since delay in returning a good can be seen as acceptance.

What is a Contract?

How will I know for sure if I have entered into a binding contract?

In order for a contract to be binding, there must be an agreement made as a result of an offer, an unequivocal acceptance of that offer and there must be consideration (that is, money or actions taken). The terms of an offer must be set out clearly and completely to avoid any confusion. The offer may be by written or spoken words or be inferred by the conduct of the parties. There are some exceptions to the rule that contracts can be both oral or written. The most famous of these is in regard to land/houses where the contract must be evidenced in writing. There must also be an intention to create legal relations, and all the parties to the contract must consent to the terms of the contract. The terms must be legal and capable of performance. The parties must also have the capacity to contract, that is not a minor or a person with diminished mental capacity. An agreement without legal effect will be deemed voidable by the party whose rights have been infringed. That is, the wronged party will not be bound by such an agreement.

A statement of intention or an invitation to treat is not an offer (*Fisher v Bell* (1961) QB 394) that is, a seller asking someone whether they are interested in buying a product at a certain price does not mean a contract has been agreed. Simply stating the price of something or supplying information is not an offer (*Harvey v Facey* (1893) UKPC 1; AC 552).

The offeror may revoke the offer at any time before it is accepted (*Routledge v Grant* (1828) 4 Bing 653). An offer will terminate at the end of the time specified in the offer. If no time limit is specified, it will terminate after a reasonable time.

A voidable contract is different to a void contract. A voidable contract is where the law allows one of the parties to withdraw from the contract if they wish, making it void. It remains valid unless the innocent party chooses to terminate it.

Finally, an unenforceable contract is a valid contract which will not be enforced by the courts because of the lack of legal evidence (or written evidence in a property transaction) or because it would breach the law/public policy considerations to enforce same (such as prostitution or drug dealing).

CONSUMER RIGHTS – FAULTY CLOTHING

I considered purchasing a dress I liked online, but at the last minute decided it might be quicker to drive to the actual shop that stocked it. It was a three-hour drive but worth it. I would have had to wait two weeks for the online delivery. The first time I wore the dress it split up the side. I returned to the shop with my receipt and said I wanted a refund. They said they can have the dress repaired for me but that they cannot give me a refund. I would prefer a refund.

I would advise you to make a formal complaint in writing to the shop, stating that you are not happy with the offer of a repair and that you would like a refund. Any item you buy should be of an acceptable standard, fit for the purpose intended and as described. You are very well protected by consumer legislation in Ireland. You are entitled to look for a refund if the dress was faulty because of the way it was manufactured, and the shop should have made a better effort to accommodate your request of a refund. The consumer helpline in Ireland has template letters on its website if you feel you require help drafting the letter. If the shop owner or shop manager doesn't respond to you or if you are unhappy with the response, then your next step is to use the small claims process. This is done through your local district court and it is only €25 to make a claim using this process. It accepts cases up to the value of €2,000. You cannot claim the cost of application. (s 10, Ord 53A, District Court Rules, SI No 17 of 2014).

You do not mention in your query whether the shop you went to was in Ireland or Northern Ireland (if we leave Brexit aside for the moment). Under EU consumer law you can make a claim in your local district court for goods and services purchased in another EU country for goods and services up to the value of €5,000 (SI No 315 of 2018 District Court, European Small Claims Procedure, 2018).

Consumer Rights in Ireland

I bought a dress in a boutique in the city. The boutique owner only sells her own labelled clothes and jewellery with some other high end brands. The boutique owner advertised her labelled clothes and jewellery in the shop unit as "exclusive designer wear" and therefore I didn't mind paying a rather high price for the dress. I later discovered that these were generic products that the seller had just labelled and I could have purchased the same dress at a fraction of the price online. The same dress was available on numerous websites and was not advertised therein as being "exclusive" or "designer". When this came to my attention, I felt misled. Is there anything I can do?

The Consumer Protection Act 2007 established the National Consumer Agency, which has the power to protect consumers and enforce consumer law. The National Consumer Agency may refer cases to the DPP and investigate consumer complaints. Section 41 of the Consumer Protection Act 2007 states that a "trader shall not engage in an unfair commercial practice". Under the 2007 Act, traders will be penalised if they provide misleading information about the nature of the product, price, servicing, replacement or legal rights of the consumer, or if they coerce the consumer, causing them to make a decision they would not otherwise make. Prohibited practices are also listed, such as claiming that a product is only available for a limited time.

There are of course the implied terms in the Sale of Goods and Supply of Services Act 1980. Under the Act, it is implied that goods shall correspond with the description given and that the goods are fit for the purpose intended.

The European Communities (Misleading Advertising) Regulations 1988 give the director of the National Consumer Agency the power to request any person engaged in misleading advertising to discontinue. A person may also apply to the High Court for an order prohibiting the publication of an advertisement, and it is not necessary to prove actual loss or damage (or even negligence) on the advertiser's behalf.

Under the European Communities (Cancellation of Contracts Negotiated away from Business Premises) Regulations 1989, consumers must be given a seven day "cooling off" period within which they may withdraw. There is no penalty for withdrawing in these circumstances.

As a consumer, you may also bring a civil action for damages.

In regard to your case the passing off of cheap generic products as exclusive designer wear would definitely be sharp practice and fall under the above legislation. At first instance I would return the goods and approach the boutique owner for a refund. If that does not work, as you can see from the above there are many avenues open to you.

Consumer Rights – Defective Products and Guarantees

I purchased a coffee machine a few months ago. It worked perfectly until last week when it started leaking and I got a nasty burn on my arm, which necessitated me going to hospital. I found my receipt as proof of purchase, brought the coffee machine back to the shop where I had bought it and requested a refund. The shop manager said that the coffee machine came with a manufacturer's guarantee and therefore I should contact the manufacturer directly. I was a little disappointed with this but decided nonetheless to follow his advice. I contacted the manufacturers and they said that my guarantee was invalid because I had not registered my coffee machine with them within the first month of purchase. Now I'm left with a very expensive and broken coffee machine. Do I have any other option?

It's correct to say that some guarantees are conditional in that they must be registered within a certain time in order to activate same; if it's not activated, it becomes invalid. You didn't register on time and therefore your guarantee is invalid.

However, the good news is that you also have consumer rights, and consumer protection is very strong in this country. You mentioned it was an expensive machine and you don't have it very long. It should not have leaked so quickly. Therefore, I would advise you to take the coffee machine back to the shop you purchased it in and enforce your statutory rights. If the shop manager is not accommodating, then I would suggest you communicate with him in writing outlining when you purchased the machine, providing a copy of the receipt, what you were using it for and all relevant details, to include how you would like the matter resolved, for example, repair or replacement of the machine or your money back.

Legislation such as the Liability for Defective Products Act 1991 and the Civil Liability Act 1961 will provide relief to the consumer in relation to defective products. Under the Liability for Defective Products Act 1991, the consumer does not need to prove negligence on behalf of the supplier or retailer. One just needs to show that the product caused the consumer damage because of a defect in the product. Section 2(1) of the 1991 Act provides that the producer shall be liable in damages in tort for damage caused wholly or partly by a defect in his product. It is a strict liability rule, therefore the consumer does not need to show any negligence on the part of the manufacturer. You just need to show a link between the product and the damage suffered.

The Sale of Goods and Supply of Services Act 1980 provides that the supplier has a contractual duty to the consumer in respect of defects in his product.

The European Directive on Product Liability and the European Communities (General Product Safety) Regulations 2004 also provide protection to the consumer in relation to defective products.

The Statute of Limitations is also important in these cases, that is the time within which an action must be brought.

Common law protects the consumer against tort or civil wrongs, such as negligence.

You may find the National Consumer Agency helpful, as they have powers under the Consumer Protection Act 2007.

In regard to the burn you suffered to your hand, you normally have two months to notify the person who is responsible for your injury. In your case it would be advisable to notify both the manufacturer and the shop owner. You have two years from the date of the accident to make a claim with the personal injuries assessment board.

Consumer Rights – Changing Your Mind about a Purchase

I bought a pair of leather jeans recently at the full cost of €250. I also bought a belt which cost €50. I tried them on when I got home and I didn't look anything like the biker chick I imagined I would look like. I returned to the shop with my receipt for the jeans and asked for a refund. I lost the receipt for the belt but nonetheless asked for a refund for the belt also. By then, the jeans were reduced to €170 and the store manager would only refund me the €170 sale price. He refused to accept the return of the belt, because I had no receipt.

If a shop is prepared to offer a refund, rather than a repair or replacement, then your entitlement is to a refund of the full price you paid, and not the reduced sale price. When a consumer purchases an item in Ireland, the goods must be of merchantable quality, fit for purpose and as described. If they are not, then you are entitled to a repair, replacement or refund (s 10 of the Sale of Goods and Supply of Services Act 1980).

If you change your mind about a purchase because you don't like the style when you get home, a shop is not obliged to take the item back or refund the money. Some shops might have a goodwill policy of a refund in change of mind situations, but that's up to the individual shop. It would usually just refund the sale price if the item had come on sale.

With regard to the belt you purchased, you will have to find the receipt or some other evidence of purchase if you want a refund or replacement. A good example of this would be a credit /debit card statement or bank card statement proving that you paid the shop a certain amount of money on that date.

Consumer Rights in the EU

I purchased goods from another EU Member State that were advertised in Ireland. Am I protected under Irish consumer law?

All consumers purchasing goods in any EU Member State are entitled to basic consumer rights. These basic consumer rights are provided for under the European Directive on certain aspects of the sale of consumer goods and associated guarantees (1999/44 EC) which was passed into Irish law in 2003 (SI No 11 of 2003).

These rights include (a) if you purchase goods or services from another EU Member State and they were advertised in your country, you are protected under the consumer law of your own country, (b) if you purchased goods or services from a representative of the business in your home country, national consumer law of your home country protects you, (c) if you buy goods or services while you are visiting another EU Member State, the law of the country in which you bought the items applies.

National consumer laws may provide supplemental rights. Your basic right as a consumer is to have a product replaced, repaired or to have a refund or reduction in price for any fault in the product that you were not made aware of at the time of purchase.

To conclude if you bought a product in Ireland believing same as being sold in Ireland as a result of a representation made to you by the seller you are protected by Irish consumer law. If in the alternative you purchased the goods knowing that they were coming from another EU country you can still make an application in your local district court for redress up to the value of €5,000 (SI No 315 of 2018 District Court, European Small Claims Procedure).

Mistakes in Pricing and General Pricing Rules

Clothing I was interested in was marked at €70. However, when I went to pay the €70 at the check-out in the shop, the assistant said there was a mistake in the pricing and the actual price was €95. Can the shop do this? I also noticed that there was not any price at all marked on some of the clothing for sale.

If a business incorrectly labels something with the wrong price, and it is lower than the price charged at the cash register, you do not have an automatic right to buy the goods at the marked price. As long as the business tells you before your money is taken that the higher price applies, you can decide not to buy it. The Consumer Protection Act 2007 affords protection to a retailer who makes a mistake. Under the Act, the buyer does not have the automatic right to demand that the goods be sold to them at the marked price.

Businesses and service providers must display their prices, and there are rules on how they must be displayed. You have the right to clear and accurate information on the prices of goods and services, so that you can compare prices and make informed choices. Prices for goods sold in shops in Ireland are not controlled by law. This is to allow competition between businesses. All prices must be displayed in euro, and businesses can also display prices in other currencies alongside the euro price. Prices should be accurate, and not misleading. The price displayed must be the same as the price charged at the till (the Competition and Consumer Protection Commission).

While a shop owner is protected against once off mistakes, if it is deemed that they are deliberately displaying misleading prices this is an offence that they can be prosecuted for. Quite regular examples of such systematic sharp practice would be for a shop owner to mark a tag on an item with a fictitious normal price and a marked down lessor sale price on the same tag.

The Competition and Consumer Protection Commission (CCPC) was established on 31 October 2014 and took over the functions and powers of the National Consumer Agency. The CCPC is an independent statutory body that enforces competition and consumer protection law in Ireland. It promotes consumer welfare and is responsible for investigating, enforcing and encouraging compliance with consumer law. Please refer to https://www.ccpc.ie for further details.

In conclusion in the absence of any evidence that the shop owner was deliberately marking down prices, there would be no redress for you in this situation in that at the cash register you are told about the mistake and given the correct price.

FLIGHT CANCELLATIONS

I booked a flight with Ryanair, however my flight was cancelled due to Ryanair's cancellation programme. Am I entitled to a refund of the cost of my ticket?

If your flight has been cancelled, you have rights under EU Regulation (EC) No 261/2004. You are entitled to choose between a full refund of the cost of your ticket or re-routing to your destination, either as soon as possible under comparable transport conditions, or at a later date, if that is more convenient for you. This applies regardless of when you were due to travel. If you choose to be re-routed, Ryanair must provide you with meals and accommodation as necessary while you wait on your alternative flight. As your flight was cancelled as a result of Ryanair's cancellation programme, you are entitled to receive compensation. You may wish to refer to the Commission for Aviation Regulation's websites for more detailed information at www.flightrights.ie and www.aviationerg.ie (EU Regulation 261/2004).

The Consumer Protection Act 2007
The Competition and Consumer Protection Act 2014
EU Unfair Commercial Practices Directive
(Directive 2005/28/EC of 11 May 2005)
The Sale of Goods and Supply of Services Act 1980

As a consumer, what consumer rights am I afforded in legislation?

The Consumer Protection Act 2007 provided for the establishment of the National Consumer Agency. Under the Competition and Consumer Protection Act 2014, the National Consumer Agency and the Competition Authority were replaced by the Competition and Consumer Protection Commission (CCPC). The Commission took over the function of the two agencies.

The CCPC is the statutory office with responsibility for providing advice and information to consumers on their rights. It is responsible for the enforcement of a wide range of consumer protection laws. The CCPC does not become involved in individual issues or disputes between consumers and sellers of goods or service providers. The CCPC can, however, advise you if you have a particular consumer problem.

The 2007 Act also put the EU Directive on unfair commercial practices (Directive 2005/28/EC of 11 May 2005) into national law, and it made various changes to our consumer laws. The directive deals with unfair business-to-consumer commercial practices. It does not apply to dealings between businesses.

The Consumer Protection Act 2007 bans trading practices that are unfair, misleading or aggressive and that are likely to distort the consumer's choice. The Act gives the Minister the power to make regulations requiring that the pricing of certain products are displayed in a specific manner. The Act bans participation in pyramid schemes and inducing others to participate. Under the Act, the CCPC may serve a compliance notice on a trader whom it considers to have engaged in a prohibited activity. The CCPC also has the power to impose on-the-spot penalties for offences relating to the display of prices. The Central Bank of Ireland has a role in enforcing the provisions of the Act in the financial services area.

A person may apply to the Circuit Court or the High Court for an order prohibiting any practice which is unlawful under the Consumer Protection Act 2007. If a person takes such an action, notice must be given to the trader and to the CCPC. It is not necessary to show loss or damage as a result of the trader's actions. A compensation order may be issued instead of or in addition to a fine or penalty imposed by the court on the trader. Consumers may sue the trader for damages. The Act offers a range of penalties for the various offences (Department of Business, Enterprise and Innovation, Competition and Consumer Protection Commission, http://www.isitfair.eu).

7. Consumer Rights

Under the Sale of Goods and Supply of Services Act 1980, the purchaser of goods has a number of rights. The goods must be of merchantable quality, taking into account what they are meant to do, their durability and their price. Goods must do what they are reasonably expected to do. Goods must be as described. The buyer must not be misled into buying something by the description of goods or services given orally by a salesperson or an advertisement. When you buy goods in a sale, you have the same rights as when you pay the full price for the goods. If you have a contract with the supplier of services, you can expect that the supplier has the necessary skill to provide the service, the service will be provided with proper care and diligence, the materials used will be sound and that goods supplied with the service will be of merchantable quality. If you have a problem with an item that you have bought, it is always the seller who should put things right. As a general rule, the seller can either repair or replace the item. Alternatively, it can refund the costs of the item or service to the consumer. If you are not satisfied with the quality of goods or services, you can return the goods to the supplier who sold it to you. Act as soon as you can. A delay can indicate that you have accepted faulty goods or services. Do not attempt to repair the item yourself. Always keep your receipt, cheque stub or credit card statement. You have no grounds for redress if you were told about the defect before you bought the item or if you examined the item before you bought it and should have seen the defect, or you broke or damaged the item, you changed your mind or you made a mistake when buying the item. If you are not satisfied with a seller's response, you may be able to take a claim to the Small Claims Court. If you made your purchase using your credit or debit card, you may be able to get your bank or credit card company to reverse the transaction. This is called a chargeback. (The Sale of Goods and Supply of Services Act 1980 as amended).

BUSINESS GOES INTO LIQUIDATION

I paid a deposit for goods and the seller went out of business (the business went into liquidation) before the goods were delivered. I am having difficulty in getting my money back. I was informed that the seller owed money to a large number of people.

There are rules for the priority to be given to the various debts in the case of a business going into liquidation or receivership. Generally, the individual customer who has just paid a deposit on an item is low in the order of priority. If you pay a deposit using a credit or debit card and the shop goes out of business, your card provider can reverse the transaction. This is called a chargeback.

Purchasing with a credit card may also provide some other protection in that some provide insurance in regard to goods purchased but not delivered. You should talk to your credit card provider in regard to the specific terms associated with your card.

As the business has gone into liquidation, you will be treated as an unsecured creditor. A creditor is someone the company owes money to. As an unsecured creditor, you rank behind other types of creditors such as Revenue, employees who are owed wages and banks that are owed money. If a company changes ownership, the new owners may not have purchased the previous owner's liabilities. The new owners may not be responsible for fulfilling orders placed with the previous owner which have not yet been delivered (Companies Registration Office).

Other options open to you include contacting the liquidator to see if you can get the goods you ordered. Your contract is with the business you buy from. If a supplier of that business closed down, the liquidator should sort out the issue for you. Contact the official appointed to look after the affairs of the business for further details.

It may be that the seller was an intermediary or an agent for the manufacturer and may have passed on your deposit in full or part to the manufacturer. If this is the case there would be a remedy against the manufacturer.

TRAVEL CLAIM FRAUD

I was on holiday with my friend in Spain. We had a great time. When we returned home, I was surprised to hear that she was making a holiday sickness claim for compensation on her travel insurance. She was not sick at all during our trip but she is claiming she had gastric illness. She said there is a pile of money waiting around to be claimed by holidaymakers just like her. She is my friend and I don't wish to name and shame her, but I also feel really uncomfortable about this fraud.

Pursuing a fraudulent claim is illegal, and you might advise your friend against making such a claim. Fraud is the premeditated commission of a serious criminal offence which merits trial on indictment before a judge and jury in the criminal courts.

As a result of bogus claims, holiday prices are on the rise to mitigate future pay outs. Opportunistic fraudsters are abusing the system and innocent holidaymakers will ultimately pay the price in their premiums if action is not taken to prevent fraudulent claims. Of course, not all claims are fraudulent ,but regrettably some are. Insurance fraud costs insurance companies in Ireland an estimated €200 million annually.

In the UK, a couple who made a £20,000 fraudulent claim against Thomas Cook were jailed. The couple lied about getting sick on two holidays to Majorca. Paul Roberts and Deborah Briton were jailed for 15 months and 9 months respectively after pretending that two of their annual trips to Majorca ended in diarrhoea and vomiting. Liverpool Crown Court heard that the scam could have cost the travel agent £19,958 in damages and £28,000 in legal costs (*Roberts and Briton v Thomas Cook Travel* (2017) LCC 254).

Insurance fraud is a crime and offenders face a maximum fine of up to €100,000 and/or up to 10 years in prison. Convictions are under the Civil Liability and Courts Act 2004.

7. Consumer Rights

TRACKER MORTGAGE SCANDAL

I was offered a fixed-rate mortgage with my lending institution. I was promised that I could move on to a tracker rate at the end of the fixed-rate period. However, in 2008 my lending institution did away with tracker mortgages for new customers and failed to take into account that I would be entitled to a tracker rate after my fixed-term ended. I cannot remember what I signed regarding this at the time. I don't know if I'm due compensation. What steps should I take in order to find out what redress if any is available to me?

This is a complicated issue for thousands of people. The first step I would advise you to take is to contact the bank. If you are unhappy with the banks response then review your original loan offer, in particular you should read the special conditions in your loan offer. If you retained any correspondence at the time you took out your loan from the bank that makes representations to you in regard to (a) the benefits of a fixed rate over a tracker (b) the ability for you to switch back to a tracker after the term of the fixed rate had expired (c) the applicable tracker rate that you would get on the end of a fixed term mortgage, you should retain same so that you can use it as evidence against the lending institution.

You mention that you think you may have been promised something that the bank did not deliver on, and therefore you could fall into the "impacted category" and you would accordingly be entitled to redress.

Contact a financial advisor with experience in this area if there is an issue in the loan offer. You may also contact your solicitor in regard to this matter to appropriate legal advice in regard to the mortgage contract.

You might also consider writing to your lending institution's complaints department.

According to Central Bank figures at the end of December 2018, c39,800 tracker mortgage accounts across 15 banking institutions had been identified as being victims of this scandal, and several families have lost their homes. It is currently unknown how many people will be affected by this scandal since the number is continuously rising as the investigation progresses.

The largest fine ever imposed by the Central Bank has been given to Permanent TSB for regulatory breaches that affected thousands of tracker customers.

The regulator has reprimanded and fined Permanent TSB €21m.

It said this was due to "serious failings to 2,007 tracker mortgage customer accounts which were impacted for the period between August 2004 and October 2018".

The debacle caused 12 families to lose their homes, and 19 buys-to-let were repossessed as a result of the tracker scandal.

The Central Bank said the bank did unacceptable harm to its tracker mortgage customers.

Along with the fine, Permanent TSB has had to pay €54.3m in redress and compensation and put the 2,000 customers back on the attractive tracker rates.

It is the first of six banks to be fined over the handling of tracker cases.

Bank of Ireland, AIB and its subsidiary EBS, Ulster Bank, KBC Bank can also now expect hefty fines, which could mean up to €100m will be paid by the lenders.

The Central Bank said the original fine for Permanent TSB was €30m, but this was reduced by 30% as the bank made a settlement with the regulators, effectively accepting the fine

Permanent TSB failed to warn some of its customers about the consequences of decisions they might make relating to their mortgage. This was when customers choose to opt out of their tracker rates for a period but were not told they might lose the valuable tracker rate.

The bank was also accused by the Central Bank of operation and systems failings.

The Central Bank said: "PTSB made a decision to deny certain customers their entitlements to the correct lower tracker rate between 2009 and 2010 unless the customer specifically requested it or queried or complained." (*Central Bank v Permanent TSB* (2019) reported by Charlie Weston, 30 May 2019, Independent.ie).

There were also some out of court settlements in the tracker mortgage scandal cases (*Marie Page v Roscommon Circuit Court* (2017) RCC 22).

IMPORTING A CAR INTO IRELAND

I was on holiday abroad and I was very impressed by the range of cars available. Can I import a car into Ireland from another country? Will I have to pay any additional taxes? What happens if I don't pay any taxes due?

If you bring a vehicle into Ireland from another country, the first thing you will have to do is pay the Vehicle Registration Tax (unless you are exempt) and get new registration plates from your local National Car Testing service. Bring your PPSN and the chassis number of the car with you. Vehicle Registration Tax is a tax you must pay when you first register a motor vehicle in Ireland. Your vehicle will be examined to ensure that you are paying the correct Vehicle Registration Tax. The amount payable is based on a percentage of the recommended retail price, that is, the open market selling price, and it is also based on the level of CO_2 emissions from the car. They will look at the market value, engine size, year, model and condition of the vehicle. You can get an estimate of the Vehicle Registration Tax due from the Revenue Vehicle Registration online enquiry system. The Revenue Commissioners will guide you if you have any queries and you may appeal to Revenue if you think you are being overcharged.

7. Consumer Rights

You will no doubt be aware that you must have motor insurance, motor tax and a valid driving licence.

When you pay the Vehicle Registration Tax, you will receive the vehicle's registration certificate showing that you have paid the tax. Do not delay in paying or you will be liable to penalties, such as forfeiture of your vehicle and prosecution. When you register and pay the Vehicle Registration Tax, a registration number will be assigned to your car. You must display the registration number within three days. Failure to display the new registration number is an offence and you can be fined by the gardaí. Your local motor factors will have registration plates.

If you are exempt from Vehicle Registration Tax, you must still register your vehicle in Ireland.

If you are importing a new car from another EU country, you have to pay Value Added Tax when registering the car. If you are importing a new or second hand car from outside the EU, value added tax and customs duty is payable. Customs duty is paid when the vehicle first enters the EU at the point of entry, and you must have proof of payment of this duty.

If your vehicle is four years old or more, it will have to go through the National Car Test immediately. Since September 2016, all new motor vehicles being registered for the first time in Ireland are required to have an electronic certificate of conformity.

ONLINE PURCHASES

I ordered a set of drums for my son online. Is it possible for me to cancel the order and return the drums to the trader if my son changes his mind about drum lessons?

When you enter into a contract with a trader online, you have the right to the same consumer protection as you would if you had bought the goods in a shop. The goods should be of merchantable quality, fit for the purpose intended and as described. The Consumer Rights Directive also offers you protection. This Directive aims to ensure that consumers can expect the same level of protection, regardless of where the trader is based in the European Union (European Union (Consumer Information, Cancellation and Other Rights) Regulations 2013).

The trader must make certain information available to you, including the price of the goods with all taxes, delivery costs, the trader's complaints handling policy, whether a right to cancel exists and the conditions, time limit and procedures for doing so, whether you will bear the costs of returning the goods, the estimated cost of returning the goods if you have to bear the cost and they cannot be returned by normal post, conditions of after-sale customer services, the duration of the contract, the conditions for terminating it if it is extended automatically and the minimum duration of your obligations under the contract.

Read your contract carefully when purchasing online products. The trader must provide confirmation of the concluded contract to you by letter or email. You are entitled to a cooling-off period of 14 days, which begins on the day that you receive the goods.

During the cooling-off period you can cancel your order without giving a reason and without incurring charges, other that the charges incurred in returning the goods. To cancel the contract, you must inform the trader of your decision to cancel using the prescribed cancellation form or other method listed.

On cancellation, the trader is obliged to repay all payments you made, including delivery charges, within 14 days.

Of course, it should be noted that the EU laws will not cover purchases from countries outside the EU. When buying a product or service, one should try and ascertain where the seller is based and, if possible, confirm the seller is covered by the EU legislation.

In conclusion it is possible to cancel your order without penalty if you are within the cooling off period. If the purchase has gone beyond the cooling off period one does not have this added protection. If you had purchased the drums in a shop and you did not like the product or you changed your mind about the product, you would have no redress. Similarly, you cannot return the drums you purchased online just because your son has changed his mind after the cooling off period has expired.

THE SMALL CLAIMS COURT

I bought goods for private use at a cost of €1,870 from a local business. The goods are damaged. The business owner refuses to engage with me and he has not returned my calls. My friend recommended that I go to the Small Claims Court to have the matter resolved. What does this involve?

The small claims procedure is a simplified way of bringing someone to court. It is specifically set up for disputes like yours. Hearings take place in the District Court. The court will hear claims up to the value of €2,000. In some cases where the claim is just over the small claims limit it may be more cost effective in bringing a small claim and forfeiting the possibility of getting the full reward. This is due to the fact that normally in the small claims court you advocate your own case without the assistance of a solicitor or barrister. The court is specifically geared towards lay litigants. While we understand that you are a consumer in this case the small claims procedure is not just limited to consumers, in fact, businesses can make claims against other businesses using this procedure. While your claim being for damaged goods would fall within the category of claims allowable to avail of this procedure, if your claim was for debts owed or personal injury or the breach of a leasing or hire purchase agreement you would not be able to make this claim under the small claims procedure.

The application form can be completed either online or in person at your local District Court office. The form is straightforward in that it allows you to set out your claim in full. When doing so you should explain where and when you bought the goods, who the claim is against, what went wrong, how much you are claiming for and why you are taking court action.

There are some specifics that you will need to fill out your claim, for example, the shop owner may be trading under a business name that is different to himself or his company and you will need to find out this before filling in the form. When your application is complete the registrar will notify you of same and he will send a copy of the claim to the business owner that you are claiming against. The business owner has fifteen days to do either of three things (a) admit the claim (b) dispute the claim (c) make a counter claim or (d) simply ignore the claim.

If the respondent admits the claim, he can either agree to pay the amount claimed immediately or consent to judgment. In your case, the respondent will only pay when judgment is issued in the District Court. The respondent may propose paying in instalments, and the claimant has the option of agreeing or not to the terms proposed. If the respondent disputed the claim and a settlement cannot be reached between the parties, then the matter is set down for a hearing in the District Court. If the respondent does not reply, then he is held to have admitted the claim. This is the same as if the respondent has consented to judgment. If the claimant obtains judgment, there is a possibility that the respondent will not comply with this order of the court. Therefore the claimant will have to enforce the judgment by giving the decree to the Sheriff or County Registrar for execution. They then seize goods or money to the value of the amount set out in the decree.

If your case has been referred to a hearing in the District Court, you will receive a letter from the District Court Office telling you the date and time of the court hearing and the location of the court (www.courts.ie).

THE COMPETITION AND CONSUMER PROTECTION COMMISSION IN IRELAND (CCPC)

I went to purchase a new car from a main car dealership. He told me the price for the make and model would be €23,435. I decided I would try another main car dealership to see if I could get a better price but the price was the exact same. I tried a number of other dealerships and all the dealers had the exact same price. I thought this was quite suspicious. Who should I consult to have this investigated?

The Competition and Consumer Protection Commission (CCPC) was established in October 2014 and it is the statutory body responsible for enforcing consumer protection and competition law in Ireland. The aim of the CCPC is to use its statutory powers to increase compliance with competition and consumer protection law, taking enforcement actions where appropriate. It can conduct investigations and can take civil or criminal enforcement action if it finds breaches of competition law.

The CCPC has a consumer helpline and website which gives consumers information on their rights. The contact details are as follows: Competition and Consumer Protection Commission, Bloom House, Railway Street, Dublin 1 DO1 C576, and the telephone number is 01 402 5555 or Lo-call 1890 432 432). The CCPC has responsibilities in relation to product safety, Alternative Dispute Resolution and the regulation of business relationships in the grocery sector.

In fact the CCPC and its pre-deceaser the competition authority have run a number of investigations against car dealerships with successful convictions against certain Citroen car dealerships for price fixing (*DPP v Paddy Duffy and Duffy Motors (Newbridge Limited)* [2009] IEHC 208.

There may of course be an objective reason for the similarity in price between all the dealerships but it's highly unusual that all of them came back to you with the same price and we would recommend that you speak to the CCPC in regard to same.

PAYING A DEPOSIT TO A SHOP TO HOLD A PRODUCT

I paid a deposit to a shop to hold a product for me but I later changed my mind about it and decided not to pay the balance. The shopkeeper is refusing to give me my deposit back. Can he do this?

When you pay a deposit, it becomes part of a legal contract. Such contracts give rights to and impose duties or obligations on you and the supplier. When you pay a deposit, you are paying in part for a product or service. It shows that you intend to buy the item. When you pay a deposit, you and the business should agree in writing as to the exact product or service that you are buying, the amount of deposit you pay, when the balance has to be paid and when the product or service will be provided. A verbal contract is also enforceable.

Deposits are usually non-refundable. If you pay a deposit for a product or service and then change your mind, the business may not have to return your deposit. For example, if you pay a deposit to a shop to hold an item for you and you decide not to pay the balance, the shop may not have to refund the deposit.

If a business delays the delivery date or if the product is not what you ordered, then you may ask for your deposit back, but only if you cannot agree a new reasonable delivery date and the business fails to meet the new delivery date, or if the business cannot provide you with the item you agreed to buy.

You may be asked to pay a deposit for products or services, such as ordering something from a shop, booking a hotel room, hiring equipment or getting building work done.

In conclusion, you entered into a contract to buy a product and put down a deposit to buy the said product. You then decided not to buy the product. In these circumstances it would be very unlikely for you to be able to get your deposit back unless the shopkeeper did something wrong. You have entered into a contract and you have not fulfilled the contract. In fact the shop-keeper if he was minded could bring you to court for breach of contract. Nevertheless the shop-keeper as a gesture of good will may transfer or off-set your deposit against another product you buy from him. We would feel this is probably your best avenue of relief in the circumstances.

Unfair Terms in Consumer Contracts

I have agreed to buy broad band for my house. I live in a rural area where there is only one supplier. I got a copy of a contract to sign. There are a few very vague terms and there are some terms in the contract I am happy with as follows: (a) while I only agreed to sign a contract for one year, I note the term in the contract is for 5 years; (b) the price agreed was €40 per month for the duration of the contract. While this is stated at the front of the contract I notice that when I read the small print the price changed to €120 after six months; (c) I am still liable to pay the monthly fee even if I don't get broadband all the time.

I want the internet in my house and will probably have to sign this agreement since I have no other option. What else can I do?

You should contact the consumer and competition authority since some of the above terms may be considered unfair in accordance with the unfair terms in the European Communities (Unfair Terms in Consumer Contracts) Regulations (SI No 27 of 1995).

Contracts are made up of terms and conditions, including implied terms, core terms and mandatory terms.

An unfair term in a consumer contract is a term that can cause a significant imbalance in the parties' rights and obligations, to the detriment of the consumer - for example, a term that limits the liability of the supplier of goods or services (for example in your case the clause that you are still liable to pay the broadband fees without receiving the services with no rebate) or a term that puts an unfair burden on the consumer (for example, the clause in your agreement that obliges you to sign up for five years). Other examples would be inserting a term into the small print of a contract where the consumer cannot see it easily (for example, the small print which raises the monthly price of the broadband from €40 to €120), or a term that gives the supplier of goods or services the right to change the terms of the contract.

If there is a doubt about the meaning of a term, the meaning that is most favourable to the consumer will prevail. If one term or condition in a contract is found to be illegal, the remainder of the contract remains in force. If you come across an unfair term in a contract, you may contact the Competition and Consumer Protection Commission.

Under the European Communities (Unfair Terms in Consumer Contracts) Regulations (SI No 27 of 1995), consumer contracts are open to a test of fairness. Any term found by a court to be unfair is ineffective (SI No 160 of 2013). The regulations take into account the circumstances surrounding the conclusion of a contract. However, the 1995 Regulations do not include core or mandatory terms.

In conclusion, I think the CCPC in a monopoly situation like yours would be very mindful of adverse terms placed upon a consumer and I would think if you made them aware of what your broadband provider is trying to make you sign or agree to, action would be taken against them.

The Right to Make a Complaint

We holiday in Bilbao every year. We are an elderly couple and our usual tour operator/company books and manages everything for us. However, this year we were disappointed, as many of the activities we had paid for were cancelled or rescheduled to dates conflicting with other arrangements we had made. Is there anything we can do about this?

You should contact your tour operator directly to make a complaint. When you buy goods or services in another EU Member State, you have rights under consumer legislation, including the right to make a complaint. First check the complaints mechanism and follow this. If you are then unhappy with the firm's actions or lack of action, you should seek advice from the European Consumer Centre in Ireland. It is there to support you if you have an issue with a supplier of goods or services in another EU Member State. The ECC will try to resolve your issues with your tour operator but, if this fails, it will refer your case to an Alternative Dispute Resolution body. Remember to keep all your receipts or credit card statements and booking documents to prove your case, that is to prove you actually paid for the activities that were cancelled. The consumer laws of Spain would apply in your case. Try to deal with the matter as soon as possible as, in some cases there are time limits for taking certain actions.

Chargebacks

I am a credit card holder. I noticed a transaction on my statement from a particular shop that I do not recognise. I am concerned that I may be the victim of a fraud. Are there any consumer protection mechanisms?

As a customer, you may ask your credit card issuer to reverse the charge (return the funds to your account) and this is called a chargeback. A chargeback is a transaction reversal, that is the reversal of a credit card payment that comes directly from the bank.

7. Consumer Rights

It serves as a form of consumer protection from fraudulent activity committed by commercial agents or individuals. It is a demand by a credit-card provider for a retailer to make good the loss on a fraudulent or disputed transaction.

Chargeback is used in circumstances where a buyer pays for an order but never receives it, a buyer receives an item that is considerably different than expected when placing the order or a purchase was made without the account holder's consent.

Rather than contacting the business for a refund, the consumer is asking the bank to take back the money from the business's account. An investigation follows and, if the cardholder's request is found to be valid, funds are returned to the cardholder's account.

Cardholders cannot be expected to pay a charge that should not have been made at all. The ability to claim a chargeback on fraudulent credit card transactions is imperative for consumer protection.

CUSTOMER RIGHTS AND RESPONSIBILITIES IN A TAXI

At a taxi rank, may I choose to travel in a taxi other than the one at the head of the queue if I think the one at the head of the queue looks dirty? May a taxi driver refuse service for short journeys? I asked a taxi driver for a receipt recently and he said he didn't give written receipts. What are my rights as a passenger in a taxi?

The answer to your first question is yes, a passenger may travel in any taxi in the queue. Drivers must display their driver identification card and passenger information card in clear view of the customer. The vehicle should be clean and the driver should have a good knowledge of the various routes/roads. Drivers may not unreasonably refuse service for journeys of less than 30km, and they must issue a written receipt to the customer when requested to do so. They may not charge more that the metered fare and they cannot charge an extra fare for guide dogs. Customers must not smoke or consume food or drinks in the taxi.

Chapter 8

Personal Injuries, Accidents and Negligence*

Car Crash

Recently I was injured as I was driving to work. The driver of another car drove out from a junction without stopping, and crashed directly into the side of my car. The insurance company approached me within days after the accident to reach a quick settlement. Should I settle with them?

Settling at this stage may not be in your best interest, and you should seek legal and medical advice to ensure you have the best chance of receiving appropriate compensation for your current and future needs. If you want to make a claim, you have two months from the date of the accident to correspond in writing with the driver of the other car (or their agent) setting out details of the accident and the cause of action. You then have two years from the date of the accident (or the date you were aware that there was a connection between the injuries and the matters you believe to have caused the injuries) to bring a personal injuries claim. The courts and the injuries board are the two routes open to you. While in neither case you are obliged to engage a solicitor, we would nonetheless recommend that you do so to ensure you receive the compensation you deserve. The Personal Injuries Assessment Board (PIAB) is the first route you must follow when making a claim for compensation. When making the application, you must get a medical assessment (form B) completed by your doctor and fill in the application form (form A). Send in all your receipts for any financial loss you may have incurred and a €45 fee. PIAB will only assess a claim for compensation if the other party does not dispute liability and consents to the assessment. If, after 90 days, the other party declines to have the claim assessed by PIAB, then an authorisation will be issued. At this stage you can instruct a solicitor to commence court proceedings on your behalf. If the other party does not dispute liability and consents to the assessment, then the injuries board has nine months to assess your claim. This may be extended to 15 months in some cases. Claims are assessed using all the medical evidence. They also have regard to the level of compensation awarded for particular injuries known as the book of quantum. Once the award is decided, you have 28 days to accept or reject it. If accepted, the claim is settled. An order to pay is provided to the other party, which has the same effect as a court judgment. If the award is rejected, then you are entitled to go to court immediately. Finally it should be noted that, even

[*In contentious business, a solicitor may not calculate fees or other charges as a percentage or proportion of any award or settlement. Before acting or refraining from acting on anything in this guide, legal advice should be sought from a solicitor.]

in a relatively minor car accident, it is best to contact the police. If the gardaí do not attend the scene, make sure you report the accident to the nearest station in order for the incident to be recorded. It is important that you do not admit liability at the scene of the accident, because this may invalidate your insurance policy. Make a note of the registration number of the other car, insurance policy, if it has a valid NCT, valid road tax and use your mobile to take photographs of the scene of the accident and the damage done. I would recommend contacting a solicitor. Solicitors in Ireland are not allowed to advertise "no win, no fee" arrangements, but most firms would be amenable to such arrangements. In any event, normally a consultation fee with a solicitor would cost little more than a visit to a doctor, but may save you a lot in the long run.

Personal Injuries on Holiday

I recently took my girlfriend on a trip to Berlin. I booked a nice hotel and all was going well until a little incident in the sauna resulted in my girlfriend breaking her ankle. We ended up in the emergency department of the local hospital. Unfortunately, my girlfriend has been left with lingering pain and is now attending a physiotherapist for treatment, which is giving her some pain relief. She is considering looking for compensation for her injuries. I guess she will have to instruct a German lawyer to sue the hotel in Berlin to get compensation. We live in Roscommon.

Not necessarily. Legal proceedings may be brought before the courts in the country where the injured party resides or where the incident occurred. For obvious reasons, it is preferable to bring proceedings in one's own country. The law in Ireland determining the time limits in which one may claim compensation for injuries following an accident is called the Statute of Limitations (the Courts and Civil Liability Act 2000).

Under existing legislation, one normally has two years from the date of an accident to bring a compensation claim for personal injuries, which is submitted to and assessed by the Personal Injuries Assessment Board (PIAB). One may not fully appreciate the full extent of injuries sustained until several weeks or months after an accident occurs. All claims submitted to PIAB are assessed using the medical evidence provided by the claimant's doctor and, if necessary, a report provided by an independent doctor appointed by PIAB. PIAB will inform the person held responsible for the injuries about the claim. The respondent has 90 days to consent to the board assessing your claim. If the respondent does not consent, the board will issue you with an authorisation, a legal document allowing you to proceed with your claim through the courts. Out of general interest, you might like to note that a total of 119 awards were made in County Roscommon by the Personal Injuries Assessment Board in a one-year period.

In conclusion, your girlfriend may bring legal proceedings before the courts in Germany or initiate legal proceedings in Ireland. It is important to engage a solicitor as soon as possible to advise you.

8. Personal Injuries, Accidents and Negligence

PERSONAL INJURIES ON A BOUNCY CASTLE

My child was injured while playing on a bouncy castle. It was a children's bouncy castle but adults were also using it. Can my child be compensated for his injuries?

Minors are not allowed to employ a solicitor or commence legal action until the age of 18 years old, but it is permitted for minors to seek compensation for an accident through a parent or legal guardian. If you (the parent/guardian) choose not to pursue a claim, then your child can choose to do so themselves from the age of 18. The Statute of limitations doesn't commence until a person's 18th birthday. From that date, they have two years to pursue a compensation claim. Although, there are advantages to pursuing a case before then. Gathering evidence is more efficient and witness statements needed would be fresher in people's minds.

The number of people suffering personal injuries on bouncy castles is rising. An eight-year-old Waterford girl died after a freak fall from a bouncy castle after celebrating her First Holy Communion at her family home. Amy Byrne's death is the latest in a series of reported bouncy castle fatalities in recent years (The Irish Times, Monday, 16 May 2011 and *The Irish Examiner*, Monday, 16 May 2011).

Another bouncy castle injury compensation case in Ireland involved a five-year-old girl who broke both wrists on an inflatable slide. The girl was awarded €20,000 damages in the Circuit Civil Court. Circuit Court president Mr Justice Matthew Deery heard that Lily Parsons was sliding down the castle when she collided with a woman sitting at the bottom of the slide. Barrister David Conlan Smyth told the court that Lily Parsons had been playing at the David Lloyd Riverview gym and leisure centre in Clonskeagh when the accident happened. Mr Conlan Smyth said the Personal Injuries Assessment Board had recommended €20,000 as suitable damages. Judge Deery approved the figure. (*Lily Parsons v David Lloyd Riverview Ltd* (CC 2010)), (*Irish Independent*, 28 April 2010).

In another case, a mum of three who suffered a severe back injury after playing on a bouncy castle slide with her son at her nephew's First Holy Communion party was awarded €14,000 in damages by the High Court in Sligo. The mum sued the owner of the bouncy castle, along with her sister-in-law and her husband in whose garden the castle was erected, for personal injuries arising from the accident. The court held the mum 80% responsible for the accident, saying the slide was not designed for jumping in the manner she did. The judge found that the owner of the bouncy castle and the householders were each 10% liable. Costs were awarded on Circuit Court costs to the plaintiff. (*Aisling McGowan v S and G Bouncing Castles and David and Roisin Kavanagh*, (2016) High Court) (Reported in *The Sligo Champion*, 12 November 2016).

A four-year-old girl was playing on a bouncy castle at an attraction centre in County Clare when her baby tooth was damaged because the left side of her face was struck. The child's mother took her to the dentist when the tooth became discoloured after three days, and the damaged tooth was extracted. The mother then brought a claim for a personal injury on a bouncy castle against the owners of the centre, as the bouncy castle had been unsupervised at the time of the accident. Liability was admitted by the attraction centre and the injuries board assessed the value of the injury at €5,000, plus €1,624 for costs incurred. At the Circuit Civil Court, Groarke J approved the settlement for compensation for a personal injury on a bouncy castle commenting "What always astonishes me is having seen children on these bouncy castles, they are terrifying. How they don't come out with broken noses and broken teeth and everything else is quite astonishing" (*Aimee Turner v Craggaunowen Living Past Experience*, 2011, www.injuriesboardadvice.com, www.independent.ie, www.personalinjuryireland.ie, Gordan Deegan, *Irish Independent*, 29 May 2013).

In conclusion it is always advisable to check with your home insurance provider prior to hiring or purchasing a bouncy castle to check what you are covered for, especially if friends and neighbours will be invited to use it.

Check if the company you are hiring the bouncy castle from holds public liability insurance. If you hired a child's bouncy castle then adults should keep off it. If on the day of booking the bouncy castle you are asked to sign a terms and conditions agreement which includes a term stating that you are liable if an injury occurs while the bouncy castle is in your possession, you should make absolutely sure any users of the castle abide by the terms and conditions of the agreement. If someone is severely injured using a bouncy castle then the person who fired the bouncy castle could be held liable in negligence.

While there haven't been many cases involving bouncy castles that I'm aware of in this jurisdiction, it certainly is possible and parents should be careful.

Companies renting out bouncy castles should have an up to date safety certificate in compliance with European safety standards. Parents who hire bouncy castles should normally be covered by their household insurance policy (home contents), although it is wise to check the details to find out exactly what is covered and contact their insurance company if they are in any doubt.

Operators should carry adequate public liability insurance cover in case of faulty equipment.

PERSONAL INJURIES AND MINORS

Our ten-year-old boy was knocked down by a passing car and injured. We ended up in the emergency department of the local hospital. Unfortunately our child has been left with lingering pain and we have also noticed behavioral changes which may or may not be attributed to the accident. We are considering looking for compensation for his injuries.

It is not uncommon for people to bring compensation claims for injuries sustained in an accident until many months after the accident, because one may not fully appreciate the full extent of injuries sustained at the time of the accident. The good

8. Personal Injuries, Accidents and Negligence

news is that a child may bring a claim for injuries sustained as a child up until their 20th birthday. When a personal injury incident occurs and the injured party is a minor, it is up to the parent or guardian of the minor to start the claim process if the injury requires immediate compensation. A minor is considered as someone who is under the age of 18. The Statute of Limitations specifies the time limit within which an injured party can issue proceedings. This timescale for a minor differs from that of a person over the age of 18. The date of knowledge for a personal injury claim involving a minor is the victim's 18 birthday. The Statute of Limitations for personal injury claims in Ireland for children does not start running until the child reaches 18 years of age. Under existing legislation, the injured party then has two years in which to submit an application for assessment to the Personal Injuries Assessment Board, or to issue proceedings in court. The assessment of damages owed to the injured party is decided on the particular injuries the person sustained and the circumstances surrounding the incident. When the board makes its assessment, the claimant then has 28 days to decide whether to accept or reject the award. If you don't reply in writing within 28 days, it is deemed that you have rejected the assessment.

In conclusion from the facts you outline, it would appear your son may have a case against the driver. Your son may wait until he reaches the age of 18 years to take a legal action or he may act through you his parent. While acting through you will cause a risk in that the monies will be lodged in court and the interest rate may not keep up with inflation, bringing the action yourself will allow you easier ascertainment of facts. Witnesses for example may be available now but not be around in 10 or 15 years' time. Furthermore, the uncertainty of the situation will be relieved in that the case will be run and won or lost and an award made rather than it hanging over a child until they reach the age or 18 or beyond. If you have to pay for any special treatment for your son the court may allow this to be taken from any award. In some serious cases of medical mal-practice the High Court has approved intermittent payments to ensure that a child will get all the care they need on an ongoing basis for the rest of their lives.

Please contact your solicitor who will fully advise you of your rights further.

PERSONAL INJURIES: SCAR TISSUE

I work as a hand model for an upmarket jewellery store. I am 20 years old. Last year, I was involved in a car crash; thankfully, I was not seriously injured. However, when I put my hand out to save myself from the impact of the crash, glass from the mirror broke and cut my hand. I got a few stitches and now I notice I have a scar. The driver of the other car was responsible for the crash. Can I be compensated for this?

As with all personal injuries actions, strict time limits apply so please contact your solicitors immediately as regards bringing a claim. You have two months from the date of the accident to correspond in writing with the driver of the other car or their agent setting out details of the accident and the cause of action. You then have two years from the date of the accident (or the date you were aware that there was a connection between the injuries and the matter you believed to have caused the injuries) to bring a personal injuries claim.

The courts and the injuries board are the two routes open to you. The injuries board is the first route you must follow when making a claim for compensation. It will only assess a claim for compensation if the other party do not dispute liability and consents to the assessment. If, after 90 days, the other party declines to have the claim assessed by the injuries board, then they will issue an authorisation. At this stage, you can instruct a solicitor to commence court proceedings on your behalf. If the other party does not dispute liability and consents to the assessment, then the injuries board has nine months to assess your claim. This may be extended to 15 months in some cases. Claims are assessed using all the medical evidence. They also have regard to the level of compensation awarded for particular injuries known as the book of quantum. Once the award is decided, you have 28 days to accept or reject it. If accepted, the claim is settled. An order to pay is provided to the other party, which has the same effect as a court judgment. If the award is rejected, then you are entitled to go to court immediately.

I would advise that, if the scar is as a result of the negligence of another, you would be entitled to compensation. Scar tissue is complex, in the sense that the scar will not form until after the injury heals and that can take some time. In your circumstances, you may not be in any physical pain but the fact that you are a hand model would affect your claim. It is possible you may be out of work as a result of this injury, and this may indeed lead to emotional trauma for you. Perhaps you may also have to consider corrective surgery. Your age would also be taken into consideration. Expert medical advice from medical practitioners and your plastic surgeon (if you have one) will be assessed. Please keep any receipts you may have for medical treatment, pain killers, scar reduction aids you may have.

How Much Should I Expect to get in Damages in a Minor Personal Injuries Case?

I suffered moderate shoulder, neck and back injuries in a road traffic accident. I am taking legal action. How much should I expect to get in damages for my pain and suffering?

It really can vary considerably. Such rewards were very generous in the past but, in more recent times, I have noticed reduced levels of awards in the more modest personal injury cases. If the case goes to appeal, it may be reduced even further, as was evident in *Cronin v Stevenson* (2016) IECA 186, Court of Appeal, where the plaintiff suffered modest neck and back soft tissue injuries arising from a road traffic accident. The Court of Appeal reduced the original High Court award for general damages by 42%, from €180,000 to €105,000. It was noted that the injuries were not catastrophic and that the prognosis was that the victim would eventually recover over time.

8. Personal Injuries, Accidents and Negligence

In another road traffic accident (*Shannon v O'Sullivan* (2016) IECA 93, Court of Appeal), a couple who suffered modest neck injuries and psychological injuries had their High Court award reduced from €130,000 to €65,000.

The case of *Nolan v Wirenski* [2016] IECA 56 came before Judge Barr in the High Court in July 2014 and resulted in a total award of €120,000. The personal injury claim arose from a road traffic accident in September 2010 where the plaintiff, Mrs Nolan, was the passenger in a car driven by her husband. The plaintiff claimed to have suffered significant injuries to her right shoulder, hand and thumb which resulted in approximately 60 sessions of physiotherapy and, at the time of the hearing — some four years post-accident — she still required daily pain killing medication. Judge Barr accepted her evidence that she was unable to lift her right arm above shoulder level and had difficulty finding a comfortable sleeping position. Ultimately, he found that the plaintiff was restricted in her ability to perform certain activities and was satisfied that it was unlikely that she would return to her pre-accident status.

In making his award, Judge Barr relied on that fact that the plaintiff remained symptomatic four years after the accident. The plaintiff was awarded €90,000 in damages for pain and suffering up to the date of the trial and a further €30,000 in respect of pain and suffering into the future.

The defendant appealed and the case came before the Court of Appeal in February 2016 when Judges Ryan, Irvine and Peart were sitting. The court found that the sum awarded by the trial judge was wholly disproportionate to the plaintiff's injuries and significantly reduced the award to €65,000, consisting of €50,000 in respect of damages for pain and suffering up to the date of the hearing and €15,000 for pain and suffering in to the future.

The case of *Payne v Nugent* [2015] IECA 268 concerned a plaintiff who suffered moderate shoulder, neck and back injuries in a road traffic accident. The court reduced the award from €65,000 to €35,000.

In *Woods v Tyrrell Junior* [2016] IEHC 355 the High Court awarded €120,000 in general damages to the plaintiff, who suffered physical injuries and significant psychological injuries.

In *Andaloc, Sheila v Iarnrod Eireann/Irish Rail, Federal Securities Ltd (in receivership), Caraher and Ward Ltd* [2014] IEHC 637, 2010 No 1114P the plaintiff was awarded damages of €60,000 by the High Court for loss of consortium and servitium suffered by reason of negligence and breach of duty of the defendants in causing serious personal injury to her husband. In this case the plaintiff's husband suffered serious physical injury as well as a traumatic brain injury through the course of his employment which resulted in him developing a significant change in personality. His wife (the plaintiff) suffered loss of consortium and servitium as a result. As a consequence of the permanent brain damage and associated change of personality suffered by her husband, the plaintiff's marriage to her husband came to an end and he ultimately moved out of the family home in February 2008 and thereafter he was made a Ward of Court. The question for the court to decide was whether a valid, real and subsisting marriage existed at the time of accident. Justice Hunt in the High Court held, that the accident was a highly probable proximate cause of the marriage breakdown, it was legally foreseeable that such consequences would flow from the extensive injuries of the type inflicted on the Plaintiff's husband by the negligence of the defendants. Damages in the sum of €60,000 were awarded to the Plaintiff.

In *Anna Fogarty v Michael Cox* [2017] IECA 309 the plaintiff was awarded €121,000 in the High Court for injuries sustained when another driver backed into the side of her car. Delivering judgment in the Court of Appeal, Ms Justice Irvine found that the amount awarded was excessive to the point that it must be considered a legal error and she reduced the amount of damages to €69,000.

Another case involving a soft tissue injury is that of former garda Edel Dore. She was assaulted by a woman whom she was attempting to arrest in Dublin in June 2003. She suffered damage to her left arm and shoulder, and the development of a numbness throughout her left arm and into the fingers in her left hand prevented Dore from being able to return to work full-time until November 2004 with the assistance of pain-relief medication. She continued to experience flare ups, culminating in an acute episode in 2009.

In court, medical reports from various medical professionals were admitted in evidence. The court found as a matter of probability that the symptoms and condition for which Dore was investigated and treated was caused by the assault and awarded her €50,000 for pain and suffering to date and into the future (*Garda Edel Dore, An Garda Síochána, Minister for Justice* (HC 2017)) (*Irish Legal News*, 29 August 2017)

Ultimately, Dore's career as a member of An Garda Síochána was brought to an end following an incident in 2013 when, in the course of assisting in an arrest, she sustained very serious injuries for which she had several operations.

In the High Court case of *Jacqueline Whelan v Castle Leslie Equestrian Holidays Ltd*, [2018] IEHC 12 the plaintiff claimed damages for the injuries she had suffered in an accident while participating in a horse-riding exercise on the premises of the defendant's hotel. The plaintiff contended that she had suffered severe pain and swelling in her lower-back area and left buttock. The plaintiff also showed the evidence of medical examination to prove that the plaintiff would be in discomfort for a prolonged period of time and she suffered serious cosmetic blemishes which she will have to live with for the rest of her life. The plaintiff also contended that she was undergoing IVF treatment at the time of accident that had to be postponed due to the injuries sustained in the accident.

Mr Justice Barr awarded the plaintiff a sum for pain and sufferings together with general damages for pain and suffering and in respect of cosmetic aspects of her injuries into the future and held that the sum must be added with the agreed sum

8. Personal Injuries, Accidents and Negligence

for special damages in favour of the plaintiff. The Court found that the plaintiff had to postpone the IVF treatment due to the injuries sustained in the accident and that would have caused frustration and disappointment during that period to the plaintiff. The Court also noted that the plaintiff had been left with serious cosmetic blemishes, which would remain with her for the rest of her life. On a finding of facts the High Court awarded her a total of €52,122 in general and special damages.

Another case involving a member of the gardaí was that of Garda Justin Brown, who was awarded €52,000 in respect of a road traffic accident that occurred in the performance of his duties. On 17 March 2002, the stationary patrol car in which Garda Brown was sitting was struck from behind by another vehicle. The court heard that the physical injuries sustained, whilst essentially soft tissue in nature, also involved the aggravation of a pre-accident chronic lower back pain condition which had resulted from a very serious assault in 1998, following which Garda Brown had also suffered a post-traumatic stress disorder. In 2005, Garda Brown brought proceedings arising out of the assault, in which he was awarded €100,000. In the months subsequent to the accident, apart from the physical pain Garda Brown also suffered fatigue, sleep disturbances, nightmares, flashbacks and anxiety.

Specialist physician Dr Pat Slattery was of the opinion that the back injuries arising from the assault had been aggravated by the road traffic accident, and that approximately 20% of the ongoing back pain was attributed to the road traffic accident. Dr Slattery also said Brown would be able to continue working until retirement, despite his injury.

In assessment of general compensation, Brown was awarded €50,000 for the soft tissue back injuries and aggravation of the pre-existing back condition, together with the soft tissue and psychological injuries otherwise arising as a result of the road traffic accident. Adding to this the pecuniary expenses agreed between the parties, the total award was €52,556.59 (*Garda Brown, An Garda* Síochána, *Minister for Finance*).

There are numerous cases on this topic and if you are interested in reading further about the amount of damages awarded in personal injuries case you might like to visit www.injuriesboardadvice.com or the accident claims and advice bureau. Information is also available on www.personalinjuriesireland.ie

In conclusion, there is great uncertainty as to what one can expect in an award from a court. While we have briefly reviewed all the above cases we have not had sight of the medical reports and the strength of the prognosis by the medical professionals. Awards are normally very specific to a particular case and while there may be similarities between cases these do not tell the whole story. To add to the mix of uncertainty alongside general damages for the injuries sustained, special damages are awarded to cover expenses and loss of income. A relatively minor injury to a foot would result in different awards depending on one's profession, for example, if a premier league footballer was no longer be able to function because of this injury it would equate greater special damages than if a surgeon had a foot injury. Therefore, you should take the above awards listed with a 'pinch of salt'. All awards are specific to the damages caused to include physical, emotional and economic.

WHAT FACTORS DOES THE JUDGE TAKE INTO ACCOUNT WHEN ASSESSING DAMAGES?

What factors will the judge consider when making a decision regarding the pay-out or general damages I will receive to cover pain and suffering resulting from an accident I was involved in?

It is difficult to accurately value a claim, and every claim is different. However, the Court of Appeal, in various personal injuries cases, has identified some guidelines or general principles that may be applied by trial judges when assessing the level of general damages in personal injuries cases, such as setting out the effect of the injuries sustained by the plaintiff on his or her lifestyle.

The plaintiff's accuracy, reliability and credibility is important. The trial judge should carefully evaluate the evidence and also have regard to the type of personal injury. Any general damages awarded must be reasonable with regard to the injuries sustained and proportionate to the awards made in respect of similar injuries.

Minor injuries should attract appropriately modest general damages, severe injuries significant damages and extreme or catastrophic injuries damages in or around €405,000. It may be more than that depending on the injuries.

General damages are intended to compensate a person for pain and suffering resulting from the injuries sustained from the accident. The Injuries Board works from a book of quantum which outlines the type of damages which a particular injury might yield. On the Injuries Board website there is also an estimator which essentially contains an online version of the booklet of quantum. General damages will compensate you for general pain and suffering and inconvenience, loss of life expectancy, Loss of amenity, Loss of consortium (compensation for sexual dysfunction/loss of a partner or spouse due to an accident).

Compensation for pain and suffering would include compensation for a physical injury and the pain associated with that injury. It would also include factors such as lack of enjoyment of life and psychological and psychiatric illness and symptoms in respect of the accident. General damages are normally divided in to two categories, that is, a Court or the Injuries Board will take in to account the pain and suffering of a person to date and the Court will take in to account the pain and suffering of a person in to the future.

Special damages are damages for loss of earnings and out-of-pocket expenses, such as medical expenses. Special damages are assessed separately to general damages.

8. Personal Injuries, Accidents and Negligence

Therefore to summarise, an award must be: (a) fair to the plaintiff and the defendant; (b) objectively reasonable in light of the common good and social conditions in the State; and (c) proportionate within the scheme of awards for personal injuries generally *(MN v SM* [2005] 4 IR 461).

Higher Financial Awards for Serious Injuries

I suffered catastrophic injuries after an accident at work. My whole life has changed as a result and I may not be able to return to work. I feel anxious and depressed. My personal injuries case is due before the courts shortly. I was advised by my friend that, as my injuries are extreme or catastrophic, I may be awarded around €400,000 in general compensation.

It may be more or less than that, depending on the injuries. Every case is different. You may also be entitled to special damages. Special damages are damages for loss of earnings and out-of-pocket expenses, such as medical expenses. Special damages are assessed separately to general damages.

In *Gardiner v Zinc Processors Limited t/a Shannonside Galvanising* (2017) IEHC 230, the High Court awarded a man €675,100 for serious injuries sustained while working as a supervisor in a galvanising plant. The defendant company accepted liability for the accident. They also created a non-physical job for the man to return to after he recovered. On return to work, he suffered heightened anxiety and became frightened for his own safety. He had a strong work ethic but, nonetheless, in the end he had to give up work.

There were a number of issues in this case, but I'll not go into detail as they are not all relevant to your question.

The court awarded Gardiner €140,000 for pain and suffering and loss of amenity to date and €95,000 in respect of pain and suffering and the continuing disabilities which will continue for the rest of his life. The court allowed €25,000 in respect of future expenses. In addition to various medical and treatment costs, loss of earnings to date and loss of earnings into the future, the total award to Gardiner was €675,116.72.

As you can see from the above case, the court can take all matters into account when making an award.

€5 Million Awarded in Hospital Negligence Case

I read a brief report about Bernadette Surlis, a 60-year-old woman who suffered terribly due to the negligence of her local hospital. She was awarded €5 million in compensation. Is this an excessively high award and what were the circumstances that led to this level of compensation?

The award was not, in my opinion, excessive when one considers the ongoing care that Surlis will require for the rest of her life. The money will enable her hopefully to be in a position to live out her life comfortably in her own home. Bernadette Surlis from Strokestown in Co Roscommon was left almost completely blind and partially paralysed due to negligence in her care and treatment at Sligo General Hospital. She is confined to a wheelchair and is in a nursing home. Senior Counsel Michael Cush told the High Court that her "only ambition" was to go home. Liability was admitted in this case, and the court approved a settlement of €5 million in her action against the Health Service Executive over negligence in her care and treatment in November 2013. Cush said it was accepted that, had Surlis been appropriately and promptly diagnosed and treated, she would not have suffered the injuries.

Basically, the hospital should have immediately transferred Surlis to Beaumont Hospital when she first presented in Sligo and she probably would have been treated successfully and made a full recovery. The delay resulted in her suffering a brain haemorrhage. (*Bernadette Surlis, the Health Service Executive, Sligo General Hospital*, 13 December 2017, Mr Justice Cross) (reported in the *Irish Times* Wednesday, 13 December 2017). Please note the Hospital Negligence Ireland website www.medicalirishlaw.ie provides up to date details of hospital negligence cases in Ireland. See also https://www.medicalnegligenceie.com/news/category/hse-hospital-medical-negligence. www.iriishexaminer.com (article by Ann Loughlin December 2017), www.mlaw.ie.

€500,000 Awarded in Road Traffic Accident

Adeola Ozoruchi was involved in a road traffic accident and suffered significant injuries. I was reading about this case in the newspaper, but it did not explain how damages were assessed. Please advise.

In January 2013, Ozoruchi was crashed into as she drove home to Sligo from her job as a carer. She was admitted to Sligo General Hospital and then transferred to Tallaght Hospital in Dublin where she underwent two operations. She was left with two significant large operation scars and suffered from ongoing low back, hip and thigh pain. As a result of the accident, she was unable to return to her pre-accident work.

The parties were in agreement as to the out-of-pocket special damages, which were assessed at €68,786.

Ozoruchi was earning €799 gross per week before the accident, and would have continued working in that job were it not for the accident. Noting the demand for carers in Ireland and the UK, Mr Justice Cross awarded her €100,000 for loss of earnings to date.

Taking certain factors into consideration, such as social welfare payments, Ozoruchi's loss of earnings into the future was assessed at €175,000.

8. Personal Injuries, Accidents and Negligence

Given the severity of the injuries, Mr Justice Cross awarded €100,000 for pain and suffering to date and €50,000 in relation to future pain and suffering for the permanent scarring and ongoing physical and psychological pain.

Therefore, in total she was awarded €493,785 in the High Court (*Adeola Ozoruchi v Kilcawley Building & Civil Engineering (Sligo) Ltd, Kilcawley Building and Civil Engineering Ltd, Martin Tuffy* (HC, 2016) (*Irish Legal News*, 16 November 2016).

You might note that, in making an award in personal injuries cases, the court will consider special damages, loss of earnings to date, loss of earnings into the future, pain and suffering to date and into the future.

PHYSICAL AND PSYCHOLOGICAL INJURIES

Can compensation be awarded for both physical and psychological injuries in the same action? I was physically injured in an accident and thereafter suffered anxiety and depression as a result of my injuries.

Compensation may be awarded for both physical and psychological injuries, as was evident in a recent case where the High Court awarded €195,000 to a garda with 33 years of experience who suffered persistent physical and psychological harm as a result of a vicious and violent prolonged assault that occurred in the course of arresting a member of the public (*Maguire v The State* (2017) High Court) (Roise Connelly for the *Irish Legal News*, published 19 August, 2016).

Maguire did not recover and over time his "physical and psychological status deteriorated to a point where he felt compelled to retire early at the age of 53.

The physical pain had a profound psychological effect and Maguire gradually developed a low self-esteem and when he experienced flare ups he experienced increased anxiety and low mood as well as pain, describing the combination of physical and psychological symptoms as taking the whole soul out of him in relation to work, social life, recreational facilities and family relationships" with "poor medical prognosis contributing to feelings of depression".

In deciding on a level of compensation in this action, Mr Justice Barton stated that the purpose of an award of compensation was to put the applicant into the same position, insofar as that can be done by a money award, which he would have been in but for the wrong committed against him and that such an award must be fair, reasonable and commensurate with the injuries sustained. Mr Justice Barton considered that a fair and reasonable sum to compensate Maguire was €100,000, comprising €65,000 for injuries to date and €35,000 in respect of the future.

Maguire was also awarded €62,246 in respect of past loss of earnings, €11,000 for future loss of earnings to age 60 and €21,824 for future loss of earnings from age 60 to 65, making a total of €195,070.60.

Therefore, as you will note from the above one can be assessed for both physical and psychological injuries resulting from a single injury. See also https://ie.vlex.com/vid/vernon-v-colgan-66298860 *Vernon v Colgan* [2009] IEHC 86 where the plaintiff suffered some physical injuries as a result of the collision but the long-term sequelae were of a psychiatric and psychological nature.

In *Loughnane v Doreen Smith* [2019] IEHC 374 a personal injuries case arose out of a road traffic accident which occurred in 2013 when Ms Loughnane was stationary at traffic lights and her motor vehicle was struck from behind by a motor vehicle being driven by Ms Smith. Negligence was admitted by Ms Smith and the matter in dispute was whether Ms Loughnane suffered injuries as a result of the accident and, if so, the extent of those injuries. As a result of the accident, Ms Loughnane suffered physical, psychological and dental injuries. The medical report of an independent Accident and Emergency Consultant before the court noted that she had suffered a moderate degree of musculo-ligamentous injury to her neck, back, left shoulder, left elbow and left wrist. It was noted that she was in the process of recovery and would continue to experience neck, back, left shoulder, left elbow and left wrist pain but that same should lessen with the passage of time. A psychologist report before the court noted that the trauma associated with the accident was still ongoing in the form of panic attacks, forgetfulness, anxiety, sleep disturbance, physical distress and that Ms Loughnane was suffering from post-traumatic stress. A dental report before the court noted that Ms Loughnane may lose all of her root canal treated teeth and conventionally crowned teeth which would require replacement with dental implant supported crowns. Mr Justice Keane of the High Court awarded the sum of €55,000.00 general damages for pain and suffering to date and €30,000.00 for pain and suffering into the future, being a total of €85,000.00. He held that he would hear the parties on the appropriate figure for special damages, in light of the conclusions reached, before making a decree.

Dublin Bus Cases

I was injured when the bus I was on travelling stopped suddenly. I fell backwards and injured my back. I am hoping to take legal action. However, my friend told me that Dublin Bus really fight their cases, and that I am unlikely to succeed with my case.

Dublin Bus has a huge responsibility for the safety of the large number of passengers who use bus services on a daily basis. However it cannot - and indeed should not - be held responsible for opportunistic plaintiffs or the negligence of passengers. It could not run its service if it was always handing out awards.

In *McGarr v Dublin Bus /Bus Atha Cliath* (2015) IEHC 277, COA (2017) the Court of Appeal dismissed a claim brought by a woman who fell down the stairs of a double-decker operated by Dublin Bus. Peart J found that the woman was the author of her own misfortune by letting go of the handrail before she reached the top of the stairs, and that it was unreasonable and unrealistic to expect bus drivers to ensure all passengers were secure before moving off.

Mr Justice Peart stated that this case raised an important question as to the extent of Dublin Bus's duty of care to passengers whom it carried on a double-decker bus. The question for the Court was whether it could be fair and reasonable that the company's general duty of care towards its passengers should extend to the driver having to satisfy himself or herself that any passengers who have got on were actually seated. The duty of care is one which requires the driver to take reasonable care in all the circumstances.

McGarr argued that the driver was obliged under the Drivers' Safety Handbook to have ensured that she was in some way secure before he drove away. Mr Justice Peart stated this standard of care was too high, that it was unreasonable and completely ignored the realities of modern day bus travel.

He concluded that McGarr's actions alone in letting go of the handrail were what caused her to lose balance when the bus moved off, and there was no breach of the duty of care owed to her by Dublin Bus.

This is not to say your friends claim won't succeed. It will depend on all the facts of the case. Other avenues that may be explored in your case would be the speed the bus was travelling at and the reason behind the sudden stopping of the bus. The driver may well have been driving negligently.

Another avenue to explore is whether a third party can be joined to the action, for example if the driver braked suddenly because someone crashed into him or pulled out in front of him from a side road. Circumstances such as these could lead to the liability of a third party.

OPPORTUNISTIC PLAINTIFF

I am rather accident-prone and, as a result, I have made several accident claims for damages over the years. I am usually successful in my claims. I was regrettably injured again recently in a road traffic accident and I am going to make another claim for personal injuries I suffered as a result of this. My friend stated jokingly that my claim was slightly exaggerated. I am concerned that the judge may feel the same way. Will the judge know about my past claims?

All the facts and evidence of the case will be examined in detail. You will have to disclose details of any previous settlements you received in replies to particulars, which your solicitor will explain to you. The court may take the view that your previous claim history is relevant to your credibility and your current accident claim.

In *Thomas Moore v Mary Carroll* [2017] IEHC Mr Justice Twomey dismissed an appeal from the Circuit Court to the High Court finding that the plaintiff, Thomas Moore, was not credible and awarded 100 percent of the Circuit and High Court costs against him. The plaintiff was described as "somewhat accident prone", and the Court was advised of "at least five accident claims" that he had made previously. Moore sought to sue an elderly lady for personal injuries that he allegedly suffered as a result of a road traffic accident. On the facts, it was shown that their cars barely touched and the damage amounted to no more that scuff marks. Mr Justice Twomey stated that it was regrettable that the defendant had to attend Court to face what was at best an exaggerated claim and at worst an opportunistic attempt to manufacture a personal injury claim against an innocent motorist.

Moore's previous claim history was looked at. He had previous settlements of €30,000 for an accident at work, €10,000 from a separate car accident which he did not disclose in replies to particulars, €31,150 for a car accident and €16,330 for another car accident. The Court was of the view that Moore's claims history was relevant to his credibility and that it was clear he was "well experienced at claiming for damages".

Moore's claim was dismissed.

You should note also that the Judge may look at the viability of any expert opinions you rely on. In *Byrne v Ardenheath Company Ltd* ([2017] IECA) the Court of Appeal held that caution needs to be exercised by a court in relying on experts that have been retained by one of the parties to litigation, particularly where the experts' opinion is based only on information provided by the plaintiff. Looking at the plaintiff's medical report, Twomey J concluded that in this instance the doctor had based his conclusions "*on the evidence which was provided to him by his patient*" and that the plaintiff may not have mentioned any pre-existing problems.

While the claims history of a plaintiff might be relevant, it will not invalidate a perfectly good claim. The previous accident history may be taken into account in regard to the damage done if a person has sustained a previous injury in an area and has been compensated for same. The plaintiff will have to prove the current injury in the area is not just a recurrence of the old injury, but a new injury - or at the very least, an inflammation of the old injury.

This is not to say an inflammation of the old injury itself is not actionable.

THE DUTY OF OWNERS AND OCCUPIERS OF LAND IN PERSONAL INJURIES CASES

I was recently injured when I fell over a protruding piece of low shelving that was jutting out of the isle as I was shopping in my local supermarket. I sprained my wrist and could not go back to my job as a typist for a number of weeks. Even now I get intermittent pain which is exasperated by my work. What right of action do I have against the owner of the shop?

Your case would have similarities with a number of recent cases, for example, in a recent High Court case, a plumber who fractured his shoulder when he

8. Personal Injuries, Accidents and Negligence

tripped on a stone block projecting from a Luas bridge was awarded €67,500 for disability and loss of function to his right arm (*James O'Shaughnessy v Dublin City Council, Irish Rail, the Railway Procurement Agency and Veolia Transport Ireland Ltd* [2017] IEHC 774). In 2007, while walking under a Luas bridge, O' Shaughnessy tripped and fell when his right foot came into contact with part of a stone block which was projecting from the right hand side of a Luas bridge at ground level. O'Shaughnessy sought damages in the High Court. The Court heard that he now lived in sheltered local authority accommodation because he had a permanent disability (unable to use his right arm).

Mr Justice Barr, in considering liability, stated that it was settled law that even a small impediment on the public highway could constitute an actionable nuisance, and he was satisfied from the evidence that the piece of stone which jutted out from the foot of the wall constituted a nuisance on the public highway. Barr J was also satisfied that, having regard to the provisions of the Transport (Railway Infrastructure) Act 2001, the third- and fourth-named defendants were the owners and occupiers of the lands consisting of the Luas line, and in particular of this bridge. In allowing the stone to project out onto the footpath, they had failed to extend the common law duty of care as defined in the Occupiers Liability Act 1995, to persons using the footpath, who were visitors on their property. O'Shaughnessy was not held contributorily negligent because the area was badly lit and the projecting stone was the same colour and material as the wall surrounding it.

In reply to your query, a shop owner has a duty of care to its customers. This duty would include the duty to remove of a hazard like the one you encountered. The damages that you have suffered are as a direct result of your fall. This was a foreseeable event and the shop owner should have prevented it happening. He would have a similar liability to the defendants in the O'Shaughnessy case above.

Personal Injuries Claim Dismissed

I was out socialising last Saturday night and after a few too many drinks I decided to take a short cut home across a football pitch which is fenced off. I fell getting over the fence and twisted my ankle. I heard it is easy to get compensation for an injury such as mine. How much will I get for my claim?

The court will consider the merit of your case before reaching a decision. There is always the possibility that you may not get any compensation at all.

In 2012, Amy Walsh sought damages in respect of personal injuries she suffered when she tripped and fell while crossing the car park area at Wexford Wanderers rugby club. Walsh alleged that her accident and resulting injuries were caused by the negligence and breach of duty of the rugby club, for failure to maintain the area in a safe and proper condition. Walsh stated that there was a hole in the car park with which her foot came into contact and, as a result, she fractured her ankle.

The rugby club did not dispute that Walsh had fallen in the car park, but they contended it was in a different area to that alleged and they denied that there was any defect in the surface of the car park. They also argued that Walsh was highly intoxicated, and therefore she was not in a position to take reasonable care for her safety. Walsh said she had only one vodka and 7-Up in the house prior to going to the club. However, her friends stated in evidence that they consumed two bottles of vodka, two bottles of peach schnapps, a bottle of Mickey Finns and a bottle of strawberry and cream shots before leaving the house. Further vodka was consumed in the toilets of the rugby club. Mr Justice Barr said this did not touch on the issue of liability as such, but nonetheless highlighted the issue of Walsh's credibility. The crux of the case concerned where in the car park Walsh had fallen and what caused her to fall. There was stark conflict between Walsh's evidence and that of her two former friends regarding the area in which she allegedly fell. The Court also had regard to the fact that Walsh had told her engineer that she had slipped on loose stones and did not mention any hole.

Having considered all the evidence, Mr Justice Barr dismissed the case. He concluded that Walsh fell in a different area than that which she had contended in Court and that, as she did not make any complaint about the surface of the car park in that area, that was the end of the case (*Walsh v Wexford Wanderers Rugby Club* (2017) IEHC 228.

In *Elizabeth Lavin v Dublin Airport Authority* [2016] IECA 268 the Court of Appeal overturned a €40,000 award for damages in a Dublin Airport personal injury case made in favour of a woman who fell while using an escalator at the airport. Mr Justice Peart stated that the trial judge had erred when concluding that there was a breach of duty to the plaintiff. He said that Dublin Airport Authority did not have a duty to "spoon feed" members of the public when considering what reasonable steps it should take to protect those likely to use the terminal.

As you can see from the above cases, it is not a matter of just turning up in court and showing one was injured to get compensation. One must show that the other side were responsible for your injury in that they owed you a duty of care and they breached this duty in some way.

Just because you fell when you were drunk in a fenced off football pitch and received an injury does not mean you are automatically entitled to compensation. As you can see from the above case law the court will take into account all the circumstances of your injury and in particular whether you contributed to your own injury. Without any other evidence furnished by you there would not seem to be any wrong done against you by the owner of the property. The duty of care owed by the owner of the football pitch towards you is not to intentionally harm you. There is nothing to say he did anything of the sort. You were a trespasser on the football pitch and the court would take this into consideration.

8. Personal Injuries, Accidents and Negligence

THE JOGGER WHO TRIPPED ON A HOLE IN THE FOOTPATH

I tripped on a hole in the footpath while I was out jogging. I injured my arm and hand. I understand I am not the first person to have found myself in this predicament. Do I have a case against the county council?

The High Court awarded a young man €60,000 in damages after it found that South Dublin County Council had breached the common law duty of care it owed to the man by failing to repair the footpath (*Martin Stokes v South Dublin County Council*, [2017] IEHC 229). Stokes was living with his parents in a caravan park at Bawnogue, Dublin 22, owned by South Dublin County Council, when he tripped and suffered a fracture to his hand in 2011. He was jogging up a footpath leading from the entrance to the site when he alleged that he tripped over a depression or hole in the surface of the footpath causing him to fall to the ground and suffer a fracture to the knuckle on his right hand.

The council argued that Stokes was putting forward a fraudulent claim. The council argued that he was a boxer, and that he sustained the injuries boxing. It also argued that the hole was clearly visible and that he should have seen it while jogging. It argued that Stokes was frequently trying to blame the council for things. It was submitted that, as Stokes was engaged in jogging when the alleged incident occurred, he was a "recreational user" within the meaning of the Occupiers' Liability Act 1995 and therefore the council only owed him a duty not to act with "reckless disregard" for his safety. There was no evidence it had so acted in this case.

Mr Justice Barr stated that the essential question was whether the council, as occupier, breached the common law duty of care which it owed to Stokes on the day in question. The judge was satisfied that the depression on the footpath constituted a danger to people using it. In failing to repair the footpath, the council had breached the common duty of care which it owed to the plaintiff.

Stokes was also entitled to be compensated for the upset caused to him by virtue of the fact that the council had accused him of putting forward a fraudulent claim.

PIAB – PERSONAL INJURIES ASSESSMENT BOARD

I hope to be compensated for personal injuries I suffered in the course of my employment and my solicitors advised me that I should make a claim for assessment to the Personal Injuries Assessment Board. What does this involve?

The Personal Injuries Assessment Board (PIAB) was set up under the Personal Injuries Assessment Board Act 2003 to enable, in certain situations, the making of assessments without the need for legal proceedings and to allow compensation for personal injuries and property damage.

Section 3 of the Act states that it applies to a civil action by an employee against an employer for negligence or breach of duty arising in the course of the employee's employment with that employer. It also applies to a civil action by a person against another arising out of that other's ownership, driving or use of a mechanically-propelled vehicle and a civil action by a person against another arising out of that other's use or occupation of land or any structure or building. In essence, the only personal injuries not dealt with by PIAB are those arising from alleged medical negligence.

Where a person is making a claim for assessment of damages, he or she must furnish a letter notifying the other side of the claim and seeking compensation, copies of any correspondence between the parties, medical reports in respect of the personal injury, receipts, vouchers or other documentary proof in relation to the loss or damage. (s 11(3)(a)).

The board has discretion not to arrange for the making of an assessment if, in its opinion, there is not a sufficient body of case law or settlements to which the assessors could refer for the purpose of making an assessment, or if, in its opinion, it would not be appropriate to do so because of the particular complexity of the issues that would require to be addressed or the injuries consisted wholly or in part of psychological damage, the nature or extent of which would be difficult to determine by the means assessment available to the assessors (s 17).

Where a respondent states in writing that he or she does not consent to an assessment being made, or where an assessment has been made which is not accepted by either party in writing, the board will authorise the claimant to bring proceedings in respect of the claim. (s 14(2)).

One of the functions of the board is to publish a book of quantum containing general guidelines as to amounts that may be awarded in respect of specified types of injury. (s 54).

Where a claimant rejects an award of damages by the PIAB which has been accepted by the respondent, and that award is not exceeded in subsequent proceedings, no award of costs may be made to the claimant. In such proceedings, the court may, at its discretion, order the claimant to pay the defendant's costs. This will not apply if a formal offer is made and the amount is not equal to the PIAB award or if a payment of a lessor amount of money into court or an offer of tender is made (s 51(a) of the Personal Injuries Assessment Board Act 2007) Please also refer to the PIAB (Amendment) Act 2019 for an update on the changes introduced in that Act. (See Mary Faulkner, *Essentials of Irish Labour Law*, (3rd edn, Clarus Press 2018)).

CONTRIBUTORY NEGLIGENCE

Does the fact that I was not wearing my seat belt prevent me from claiming against my neighbours' car insurers for serious injuries I sustained as a passenger in my neighbour's car when she crashed into a tree as a result of speeding?

8. Personal Injuries, Accidents and Negligence

You contributed to your injuries because you were not wearing your seat belt in accordance with law, and this is called contributory negligence. However, you did not contribute to the actual accident itself and therefore the fact that you were not wearing your seat belt does not prevent you from pursuing a personal injury claim. You mention that your neighbour was speeding, that is driving her car negligently, and therefore some of your injuries can be attributed to her actions. Your neighbour's car insurers will try to reduce your compensation claim on the basis that some of your injuries were exacerbated by reason of you not wearing your seat belt. Remember to keep any medical or engineers' reports you might have, photographs and receipts. Your solicitor will advise you on time limits, the courts system and PIAB applications.

An example of a personal injuries case where the court looked at the plaintiffs own negligence and dismissed the case is *Edward O'Connor v Wexford County Council* [2018] IEHC 232 where Edward O'Connor filed a claim for damages against Wexford County Council the defendant, after sustaining injuries to his back when he slipped on a steep grassy bank at the Ferns water reservoir. The plaintiff alleged that the defendant had failed in its duty to provide a safe place and system of work under the Safety Health and Welfare at Work Act 2005. The defendant alleged that the plaintiff himself was responsible for his injury as there was no need for the plaintiff to go up the steep incline to reach the manhole cover.

Mr Justice Twomey dismissed the plaintiff's claim. The Court held that the plaintiff did not take reasonable care for his own safety by using the steep incline to access the manhole when there was a flat route a modest distance away. The Court further held that the route taken by the plaintiff for fulfilling his duty was not approved by the defendant in any way.

A good website with examples of up to date cases where the court allowed claims of contributory negligence and examples of cases where the courts have dismissed claims of contributory negligence is www.injury_compensation.ie (injury claims advice Ireland).

The Duty of Care Owed by a Defendant to an Injured Party Under The Occupiers' Liability Act 1995

I am a tenant in a county council house. Regrettably, I was injured when I fell on slippery tiles on an exterior porch at the house. I am not entitled to carry out any works on the house. Am I entitled to compensation for my injuries? Can I take legal action against the council?

In answering your query, I will refer to a case similar to yours. In 2013, Thomas Keegan slipped on a wet, exposed porch at the front of his house that he rented from Sligo County Council and broke his ankle. He later developed osteoarthritis in the ankle joint. He was awarded €105,650 in damages. Mr Justice Barr accepted the evidence of the man's engineer that the tiles used on the front porch were inappropriate for exterior use, and that the council was liable to the man pursuant to the Occupiers' Liability Act 1995. It was accepted that Keegan was not entitled to carry out works to the property and was instructed to report any problems to the council. The council's engineer submitted that the tiles were perfectly adequate for use at the house. There was plenty of disagreement between the engineers about the tiles but, in the end, Mr Justice Barr held that the tiles were inappropriate for use in an exterior porch. Most importantly, Mr Justice Barr was satisfied that the council had to be seen as the occupier of the premises within the meaning of the Occupiers' Liability Act 1995. Keegan, as a tenant, was a visitor on the property within the meaning of the Occupiers' Liability Act 1995 and the use of the incorrect tiles constituted a breach of the common law duty of care owed by the defendant to Keegan under the Act.

The use of the tiles also rendered the house unfit for human habitation and, as such, the council was in breach of the implied covenant in such tenancy agreements (*Siney v Dublin Corporation* (1980) IR 400) *(Dublin Corporation v Burke* (2001) IESC 81) (*Thomas Keegan v Sligo County Council* (2017) IEHC 722).

To answer you query, a council has a duty of care to its tenants. If the tiles are deemed inappropriate for a porch, then the duty of care owed to you by the council is breached. The council may have breached its duty to you. From this breach you suffered an injury. It would follow then that you would be most likely entitled to damages for your injury.

MEDICAL NEGLIGENCE

I had an operation three years ago. Recently I attended a specialist and he confirmed, after a series of tests, that the operation had been unsuccessful. He advised that the operation had, in fact, caused further damage and that I would need to undergo it again. My friend mentioned that I have only two years from the date of the incident to make a claim.

While you are over the time limit for a normal personal injury claim where it is virtually immediately apparent that an injury has occurred, your case may fall within an exception to this general rule. The exception you may rely on is that the time limit will only start to run from the date you are aware of the injury, or should have been aware of it. This means you may still have the possibility of a claim if you act within two years from the date you became aware, which you mention was only recently. Time is of the essence in your case.

You may have a clinical negligence action against the specialist. Such claims are very complicated, and you should contact an expert solicitor with experience in this area. Your solicitor will carry out investigations to determine if a medical negligence action exists. He will gather extensive legal and medical evidence to prove that the negligence caused the injuries which have been sustained. These

8. Personal Injuries, Accidents and Negligence

cases take a considerable amount of time to process. Normally, both junior and senior counsel are instructed to draft and settle the detailed claim.

If the claim is to proceed you may instruct your solicitor and he or she will require the following information: name and speciality of the specialist, the date of your operation, personal details, such as loss of earnings, your inability to carry out certain activities, copies of your medical records to include the doctor's clinical records, nursing notes, blood pressure, fluid, heart and temperature charts, drug administration chart, surgeon's operating notes, anaesthetic records, consent forms, laboratory test results. A letter will be served by registered post on your specialist stating the nature of your claim. Your solicitor will also need to forward all your medical records to the UK for an independent medical opinion, which is crucial in a medical negligence case. Since to win a medical negligence case, it must be proved that, but for the specialist's negligence (which was peer reviewed by your independent specialist), you would not have suffered these injuries. In other words, you must establish on the balance of probabilities that there was a causal connection between the alleged negligence and the injury sustained.

This is done by proving the medical professional has not carried out the procedure on you in accordance with standard practice or a standard level of care that such a specialist should have.

It would seem from the facts of your case that something has gone wrong that should be investigated immediately.

MEDICAL NEGLIGENCE CLAIMS AFTER DEATH

Can an action for damages for alleged medical negligence survive the plaintiff's death for the benefit of the estate?

A recent case addressing this issue was that of *Doyle v Royal Victoria Eye and Ear Hospital* (2017) (*Irish Legal News*, 21 November 2016). In January 2010, Doyle underwent surgery at the Royal Victoria Eye and Ear Hospital to remove a cataract from her left eye. The surgery was not a success and post-operative complications necessitated removal of that eye in February 2010 in order to prevent damage to her right eye.

Doyle passed away on 11 July 2014 after an unsuccessful High Court hearing, but before the conclusion of the hearing of her appeal before the Supreme Court. It was asserted in the Supreme Court that the cause of action survived for the benefit of the estate.

The case made on behalf of Doyle was that the legislature did not succeed in sweeping away the rule that a personal action dies with the person, and that some aspect to the exception to that rule survives and that the exception should extend to personal injury actions.

Ms Justice Iseult O'Malley stated that an appeal from the High Court to the Supreme Court was not a *de novo* hearing and the appellant had to establish error by the trial judge.

She said that the intention of the Oireachtas was clear, that is a claim for general damages for pain and suffering may not be maintained after the death of the person who sought compensation for that pain and suffering. The beneficiaries of the estate could not complain that they had been unfairly denied compensation for the suffering of another individual.

In conclusion, the Court ruled that Doyle's action for damages for alleged medical negligence could not survive her death, and the claim was dismissed.

Therefore, it is clear that an estate cannot continue a claim on behalf of an individual for pain and suffering.

NEGLIGENCE CLAIMS AGAINST PRISON OFFICERS

I visited my brother in prison last week, and he informed me that one of the prison officers had assaulted him. I noticed he had swelling around his eyes and his hands were scratched. Is there anything my brother can do? Can a prisoner take legal action against a prison officer?

Depending on all the circumstances of the case, your brother may be able to sue the State for assault or negligence. Please refer your brother to a solicitor.

In the Court of Appeal in *Savickis v The State* ((2016) *Irish Legal News*), a convicted rapist was awarded €17,225 after he sued the State for assault, negligence and breach of constitutional rights arising from an assault when he was a prisoner at Castlerea Prison, resulting in him being taken to hospital.

Overturning the finding of the High Court that had awarded him just €225, Mr Justice Hogan in the court of appeal stated that "it was very difficult to avoid the conclusion that some of the witnesses tendered by the State told lies in the course of their evidence".

Looking at the facts of the case, a prison officer confronted Savickis and placed him in a headlock while Savickis clung to the railings in an effort to resist being moved towards the exercise yard. At that point, four or five prison officers quickly arrived and prised Savickis from the railings and subdued him. Savickis did not respond to the actions of the prison officer in an aggressive manner. He did not attempt to strike out at the prison officer. It was clearly evident in the CCTV footage that, as he was being subdued by the prison officers using control and restraints techniques, he was struck three or four times by a particular prison officer with punches to the chest. Savickis was subsequently brought to Roscommon County Hospital and the medical notes showed bruising on his face and forehead, trauma injury to his chest and traces of blood in his urine consistent with a blunt blow to the patient.

8. Personal Injuries, Accidents and Negligence

The High Court found that, although Savickis was assaulted, he was guilty of 95% contributory negligence and awarded him €225.

The Court of Appeal held that, although the State authorities were entitled to use appropriate force against Savickis once he had refused to obey a lawful direction from a prison officer and that the use of control and restraint techniques were appropriate, these techniques had nonetheless been applied in a negligent fashion, due to inadequate training.

Mr Justice Hogan found that Savickis was unlawfully struck three or four times by a prison officer while he was subject to a restraint. This was backed up by CCTV evidence and medical evidence. Hogan J set aside the finding of contributory evidence.

Savickis was awarded €17,225 (*Savickis v The State* [2016] IECA 310.)

CONSENT TO VIOLENCE AGAINST THE PERSON

With the controversy in rugby and other sports regarding concussion and injury, the EL James movies and the high-profile trial of Graham Dwyer, I was wondering where does Irish law stand on the issue of violence against the person? Can one consent?

There is little Irish case law on the matter. However in other common law countries, such contracts as are outlined in EL James' famous book would not be valid. A defence against criminal liability may arise when a defendant can argue that, because of consent, there was no crime, but public policy requires courts to lay down limits on the extent to which citizens are allowed to consent, or are to be bound by apparent consent given. In the context of sadomasochism, Lord Mustill in *R v Brown* [1993] UKHL 19 has set the limit just below actual bodily harm. Therefore, no consent can be given for relationships that expose one of the parties to excessive violence. In *R v Emmett* [1999] EWCA Crim 1710, the court applied *R v Brown*, and ruled that a woman's consent to events that put her at risk of death or bodily harm did not provide a defence for her partner. The general rule, therefore, is that violence involving the deliberate and intentional infliction of bodily harm remains unlawful. These cases are considered to be violent crimes, and it is not an excuse that one partner consents.

The general rule is that, once an *actus reus* (a prohibited action) with an appropriate *mens rea* (mental element, for example, intent) has been established, no defence can be admitted, but the evidence may be admitted to mitigate the sentence. This was confirmed by the ECHR in *Laskey v United Kingdom* (1997) 24 EHRR 39 on the basis that, although the prosecution might have constituted an interference with the private lives of those involved, it was justified for the protection of public health.

The basic principle that makes violence in sports legal is consent. Consent is valid in a range of circumstances, including contact sports such as boxing or martial arts, where the participant consents to run the risk of injury arising within the rules of the game being played. This does not give sport a licence to enact rules permitting acts that are excessively or maliciously violent. Sports using implements such as bats and hard balls can injure and kill. Phillip Hughes died after a fist-sized object was thrown towards him, and no one was prosecuted. As a batsman playing cricket, he fell victim to an accident, not a crime (*The Irish Times*, 27 November 2014). In 2001, James Butler, an American boxer, approached his opponent after losing a fight, ostensibly to congratulate him. Instead, he punched him in the jaw with his ungloved hand and his rival collapsed. Butler served four months in jail (The tragedy of the Harlem hammer, written by Bernard Fernandez and published in 'the sweet science' on 21 November 2014. TheSweetScience.com is an excellent boxing news website). As more injured players turn to the courts, judges will increasingly have to rule on which sporting risks - and perhaps even which sports — are acceptable. Judges may be more willing to hear claims for civil liability. Players could find themselves legally liable for injuries once regarded as routine and, if the public turns away from dangerous games, huge industries such as American football could vanish. Super Bowl Sunday would be a distant memory. In 2006, Jarrod McCracken, a rugby player in Australia, was awarded AUD97,500 in a suit against two players and their team who ended his career with a spear tackle (*The Sydney Morning Herald*, 23 February 2005). This course of action could have been open to our own Brian O'Driscoll after the infamous spear tackle that ended his Lions Tour (www.independent.co.uk, 23 June 2017). In 2013 America's National Football League reached a $765 million settlement with former players over brain damage, setting a precedent that leagues can be held liable for previously unknown health risks to which players could not have consented. With the current controversy in rugby in regard to concussion and the increase in injuries that are affecting both GAA and rugby players during and after their careers, due to possible overtraining and more aggressive combative games with larger, stronger opponents, there is an obligation on those associations and all other sporting bodies to study the injuries occurring in their sports with a view to implementing plans to minimize such injuries. If nothing is done, sporting bodies may be leaving themselves open in the future to possible legal action. This is especially the case where those playing the sport are minors who cannot meaningfully give their consent.

VICIOUS DOG ATTACK AND POST-TRAUMATIC STRESS DISORDER

I was attacked by two dogs while I was going for a walk in the countryside. I suffered horrific injuries. I have still not recovered from the incident, and I am terrified to walk alone now. I seldom leave the house and I take antidepressant medication. I understand that my claim for damages will probably be uncontested.

Looking through the caselaw I noticed there was a case in 2012 that has some similarities to your own.

In 2012, a woman was attacked by two dogs while walking on a public road in Co Kildare. It was a vicious attack. The dogs repeatedly bit the plaintiff in the head, face, arms and legs. Portion of her left ear was partially torn away. She was left with significant scarring and will require extensive dental surgery in the future. As a result of the attack, the plaintiff was diagnosed as suffering from Post-Traumatic Stress Disorder.

Liability was not an issue in the proceedings. The court accepted in evidence the profound change which the plaintiff suffered in her personality, in her appearance and in her mental state since the accident.

In assessing damages, Mr Justice Barr accepted that some of the victim's scars were permanent and represented a serious cosmetic blemish. He also accepted evidence that the victim suffered a moderate PTSD, requiring ongoing treatment, and it was unlikely she would return to her pre-incident state due to nightmares and an avoidance of walking in the countryside. Dental implants would also be necessary.

Mr Justice Barr made an overall award in favour of the plaintiff in the sum of €234,557 made up of general damages of €110,000 for pain and suffering to date, general damages of €70,000 for pain and suffering into the future and special damages of €54,557 (*JT v AM and FM* [2017] IEHC 516).

In conclusion, I would advise that you have presented a strong case and your claim will hopefully be uncontested and successful. I am sorry to hear about the frightful ordeal you went through and I hope, with good medical assistance, that you will make a speedy recovery.

PERSONAL INJURY ON A PACKAGE HOLIDAY

My daughter sustained a serious injury while on a package holiday in Portugal. She broke several bones after slipping on a wet floor in the hotel she was staying at. She had booked the package holiday through a tour operator and it seemed great, with even the transport included. Can she make an injury compensation claim against the tour operator?

Yes, your daughter could possibly make such a claim against the tour operator, but we will have to look at all the evidence before reaching a decision. First, we should look at the legal definition of package holiday. It's defined under the Package Holidays and Travel Trade Act 1995 as a combination of two or more of the following, when sold or offered for sale at an inclusive price: (a) transport, (b) accommodation and (c) other significant elements of a tourist service nature. Under the Act, a tour operator may be held responsible for all of the services provided as part of a package holiday. Therefore your daughter's tour operator may be held liable if the hotel she was staying at as part of the package deal failed to comply with the health and safety standards set down in Portugal.

In conclusion, as your daughter booked her holiday as a package holiday through a tour operator, she may be able to make an injury compensation claim against the tour operator for the injuries she sustained. Please advise her to speak to her solicitor as soon as possible.

In conclusion we have seen in the recent case law a demise of the compensation culture. €171,201 was the average award in 2018 and most awards were between €60,000 and €200,000. Please see the following cases: *Nolan v Wirenski* (2016) IECA 56, *Gore (A Minor) v Walsh and Another* (2017) IECA 278, *Cronin v Ardkeen Sales Ltd T/A Londis* (Twomey J) (2017) IECH 406, *O'Flynn v Cherry Hill Inns Ltd* (Irvine J) (2017) IECA 211, *Fagan v Dunnes Stores* (2017) IEHC 430, *Wilcynska v Dunnes Stores* (2017) IEHC 305, *Ward (A Minor) v The CPW* (2017) IEHC 336, *O'Connor v Wexford County Council* (2018) IEHC 232, *Moloney v Templeville Developments Limited* (2018) IECA 47, *Dunnes v Trustees and Board of Management of St Pauls Secondary School* (2019) IEHC 22, *O'Grady v Abbott Ireland* (2019) IEHC 79, *Donnelly v Dunnes Stores* (2019) IEHC 347.

Chapter 9

Last Will and Testament, Probate Law, Trusts, Enduring Power of Attorney

The Civil Partnership Act provided the same rights to civil partners as were previously given to spouses in Irish inheritance law. Now with the advent of same sex marriage the law does not discriminate on the basis of gender/sex. If one is married ones inheritance rights are the same under the law.

THE 'HANDS-ON GUY' DRAFTING HIS OWN WILL

I am a houseowner with a wife and children. I am a fairly hands-on guy and I think I should be able to handle making a will myself. Would you mind setting out what is involved in drafting a will?

One of the shortest wills ever written simply stated "Being of sound mind I spent all my money." If this is it for you, then by all means handle it yourself.

If, however, you have a little finance or assets to pass on, then I would advise you to familiarise yourself with the rules of will-making first. A will is a legal document signed by you in front of two witnesses. These witnesses should not be receiving a benefit in your will. It should also be dated and all the provisions in the will should be set out before your signature, with your witnesses signing underneath you. Apart from the above, the will should have the following eight essential points:

1. It should expressly state that this is your final will and clear off previous wills.
2. It should state who you want to appoint to step into your shoes to fulfil your wishes (that is, gather your assets and distribute them). These people are called your executors.
3. It should set out who you want to give your assets to. These people are called your beneficiaries.
4. It should clearly identity significant assets that you want to give to specific people. A legacy is a gift of money or goods. A devise is a gift of real property. There are a number of different types of legacy.
5. It should contain a provision clearing off s 63 of the Succession Act, 1965 (unless you want distributions made during your life to be taken into account when dividing up shares in your estate)
6. It should contain what is called a residuary clause, that is a catch-all clause that sets out what happens to whatever you own at the date of your death that is not listed specifically in your will.

7. It should be dated and the testator's name and address clearly and correctly noted.
8. It should have the signature of two witnesses, with their addresses and descriptions.

The above is the barebones of a will, without taking into account the obligations imposed by law to make proper provision for your wife (enforceable by her legal right share) and children (enforceable by s 117 actions). The above does not deal with the potential tax implications of your gifts.

A will is a document that speaks from death and therefore it can fail, or the gifts given can fail, for a number of reasons. For instance, there can be virtually no ambiguity in it. There are very restrictive rules in regard to interpretation. A small deviation from the rules of execution can invalidate the will.

If the will is to fail for whatever reason, the consequences are that your assets will be distributed under the rules of intestacy. In essence, you may be setting up a battle between your wife and children (or the representatives of their estates) – where your wife will receive a two-thirds share and your children a one-third share. If you do not have significant assets other than your house, then the house may have to be sold under your wife's feet to pay off your children.

A will is revoked by marriage, but not by divorce. If there is a clause in your will revoking all previous wills, this will revoke foreign wills also. If you have young children, it may be necessary to insert a clause providing for the establishment of a trust or the appointment of trustees or guardians. A parent in a will can appoint another person to be guardian of the children after death. A testamentary guardian can act jointly with the surviving parent, provided the surviving parent does not object (s 7 of the Guardianship of Infants Act 1964).

An effective residuary clause is important in a will. If a beneficiary predeceases a testator, whatever was left to that beneficiary fails and that gift will be distributed as if the testator died intestate, unless there is an effective residuary clause in the will. There are some exceptions to this, such as where there is a bequest to someone on trust for another, bequests to children or where the bequest is in discharge of a legal or moral duty. Another option would be to state in the will, what will happen in the event of a beneficiary predeceasing the testator.

If you decide to make a will and later decide to alter it in some way, please note s 86 of the Succession Act 1965 which provides that "an obliteration, interlineation, or other alteration made in a will after execution shall not be valid or have any effect, unless such alteration is executed as is required for the execution of the will; but the will, with such alteration as part thereof, shall be deemed to be truly executed if the signature of the testator and the signature of each witness is made in the margin or on some other part of the will opposite or near to such alteration, or at the foot or end of or opposite to a memorandum referring to such alteration, and written at the end of some other part of the will".

9. Last Will and Testament, Probate Law, Trusts, Enduring Power of Attorney

While you are no doubt a hands-on guy and very capable, please remember that a will is the largest transaction that you will ever do. You are in essence giving everything you have away. If you get it wrong, it can have dire consequences for the people you love. We would respectfully advise that you consult a solicitor on this one.

Should I Make a Will?

I am a 36-year-old homeowner with four children. My wife and I own our home jointly. Recently, my wife made an appointment with our local solicitor to draft her will. She would like me to make a will also, but I am undecided. What happens if I do not make a will?

I understand that making a last will and testament is a very private and personal matter. I will however endeavor to explain briefly what is involved. A will is a legal, witnessed document in which the person making the will (called the testator if male or testatrix if female) expresses his or her wishes in writing as to how his property or possessions will be distributed after his death. It is important to make a will because, if you do not, the law on intestacy decides what happens to your property. A will can ensure that proper arrangements are made for your dependents. It is possible to make your own will but, to ensure the will is valid, it is advisable to consult a solicitor in the drafting.

The requirements for a valid will are set out in s 77 of the Succession Act, 1965. For a will to be legally valid, you must act of your own free will, be over 18 years and of sound mind. It must be in writing and the testator must sign it at the end, in the presence of two witnesses who must sign it at the same time. The two witnesses must not be beneficiaries. If they are beneficiaries, any gift to them will be rendered void, with the rest of the will remaining valid. The will must also contain the date it will was signed and an executor must be appointed. The executor's duty is to administer the estate. If no executor is appointed or the executor has predeceased the testator, the estate will then be administered by a person called an administrator. The executor named in your will has to get permission from the Probate Office after the death of the testator before the assets of the estate are distributed, that is before a will can take effect, a grant of probate must be made by a court. Always make it clear in the will, what gift is being given and who it is being given to. Check the spelling of the names of the beneficiaries. If you are giving someone a house under the will, consider whether you want to include the contents. If you want to include the contents, expressly state that in the will. You mentioned you were married, so therefore you will have to make provision for your wife. If for any reason she is unhappy with what she receives under the will, then she may under the Succession Act 1965 elect to take her legal right share. This share is one half of the entire estate if there are no children, and one third if there are children. Your wife may elect to take this share in preference to what you leave her in the will, and then the rest of the will is altered to reflect this.

As you own your home jointly with your wife, on your death, your interest will automatically pass to her as survivor of the joint tenancy outside your will. Of course, in extreme cases, like the one of Eamonn Lillis who was convicted of killing his wife, this will not happen. The joint tenancy will be severed and the estate will be divided in accordance with the contribution of parties - normally half of the estate to the deceased and half to the surviving spouse. This explains the reason behind Lillis receiving half of the proceeds of the joint assets held by him and his wife, rather than the whole amount. (*Cawley and Another v Lillis* (2011) IEHC 515, (2012) IEHC 70, I IR 281). Still, to the bystander it does appear unfair that he should receive anything. In essence the court is only giving him his share of the assets, rather than allowing him the whole of the estate, which he would have been entitled to. Where joint bank accounts are opened with a spouse/civil partner or child, it is presumed that one party will be fully entitled to the money in the account when the other party dies. For the sake of clarity, if you have a joint bank account you should make it clear with the bank and in the will what your intentions are for the money in such accounts.

If you fail to make proper provision for your children in the will, they may bring an application under s 117 of the Succession Act within six months from the first taking out of representation. The court will consider the amount left to the surviving spouse, the number of children and their ages and positions in life, the testator's means, the applicant" age, financial position and prospects and any other provision already made by the testator for the applicant. An exception to this rule is that, if you leave everything to your spouse who is the mother of your children, the court will consider that you are making provision for your children, in that your spouse at the time of her death will make adequate provision for your children.

If you do not make a will, then your next of kin becomes the administrator of the estate. The rules of intestacy are applied as outlined in the Succession Act 1965. These rules set out a fixed method of disposing of the assets, and they run in family lines. These rules will trace back to very distant relations if no close ones are alive or contactable. If there are no relatives, the State will inherit the assets. It should be noted also that property that passes under a will or intestacy may be liable to various forms of taxation. The personal representatives are responsible for paying the tax. With reference to the expenses incurred in administering your estate, these will be deducted from the estate (along with funeral expenses) before any gifts are given out under the will.

It is important to note that a will is revoked by a subsequent marriage. It may also be revoked by a properly-executed later will or codicil (additional document altering the will), a declaration in writing stating that you are revoking the will or its destruction by the testator or testatrix of the will. If a will is lost, advertisements should be placed in newspapers to try and find it.

Finally, you might like to leave a gift to charity in your will. Many charities are committed to working with the world's most vulnerable people, so why not leave a

9. Last Will and Testament, Probate Law, Trusts, Enduring Power of Attorney

legacy that lasts for generations and help to make the world a fairer place? It is also important that you make your next-of-kin aware of whether you want your organs donated well before the trauma of an accident. If you want to donate your body for medical purposes to one of the medical teaching colleges, you need to contact that college in advance, sign a form and again make your next of kin aware of it because, in the case of body donation, there are strict time limits with regard to receipt of the body (normally 48 hours).

Therefore by making a will, administration of your estate is quicker and less expensive than if you do not make a will. You get to decide who deals with your assets on death, rather than having the law do it for you. You can provide for the special needs of your loved ones by making your wishes clear in a legal document. Finally, by making a will, you are in a position to ensure that the minimum of Capital Acquisitions Tax is paid by beneficiaries. A person may make as many wills as they want, but the only relevant one is the last valid will made before their death.

DUTIES OF AN EXECUTOR

My best friend informed me that she is making her last will and testament and that she is appointing me as the executor of her will. What does this mean and will I have certain duties or responsibilities?

The executor is the person who is named in the will to deal with the estate. It is the duty of the executor to administer the estate of the deceased in accordance with the terms of the will or the provisions of the Succession Act 1965.

The powers and duties of the executor date from the date of death of the deceased. On the date of death, the whole estate devolves to the executor. Once you take on the role of executor, you cannot renounce the role at a later date. An executor has many functions including extracting the grant, gathering or controlling the assets, discharging the debts and distributing the assets and arranging insurance for the property and contents and clearing out any property that may be going for sale.

The executor's role is for life once it is accepted, and the duty is therefore ongoing. An executor must act to protect and administer the estate. It is a highly responsible role.

If you have instructed a solicitor, he or she will request the death certificate, names and addresses of beneficiaries, details of the deceased's accounts, including the funeral accounts, and receipts and details of any other insurance or fund he might have had.

Unless it is a relatively small estate, probate will have to be applied for to administer the estate. The duties of an executor are to identify and gather in the assets of the estate and to pay the lawful debts of the testator. The executor must identify all assets of the estate, such as houses, land, investments and any private company shares or assets that are not in the sole name of the deceased and swear an Revenue affidavit for filing with the Revenue Commissioners. Prior to making an application for a grant of probate, the executor must identify all debts and liabilities of the deceased. Proper procedures should be followed, as the executor could be held personally liable for the debts if proper procedures are not followed. The executor must distribute the estate according to the wishes of the deceased. In most cases, the will is unambiguous.

An executor must follow the instructions as written in the will. If there is any potential for conflict, especially within the family, the executor must be capable of acting objectively and impartially to avoid disputes. Executors are also required to keep clear and accurate accounts of their dealings with the deceased's assets and liabilities and beneficiaries are entitled to inspect them. Where an executor has no experience of the preparation of accounts, he is under a duty to delegate the task to a competent person. On completion of the administration of the estate, the executor must produce final administration accounts to the residuary legatees which must show the value of the estate at the date of death, all financial transactions which occurred during the administration of the estate, including all payments made and received and all income earned during the administration of the estate, such as rental income, bank interest income, share price increases and dividends.

It may take the personal representative some time to administer the estate, during which time income may be earned or capital gains may be made. The personal representative is liable to pay income tax at the standard rate on income earned during the administration period. There is no entitlement to personal credits or to any of the reliefs otherwise available to individual taxpayers. Death does not give rise to Capital Gains Tax liability. If, however, the personal representative sells any property during the administration period, there may be a liability to Capital Gains Tax, but only to the extent that the value of the property in question has increased between the date of death and the date of sale.

Note that if there is no will made, the person who steps forward to deal with the estate is called an administrator. The law sets out in priority the close relatives or who among the deceased's beneficiaries are entitled to act as administrators. The executor and administrator are sometimes referred to as personal representatives of the deceased.

Executor's Role in Preserving an Inheritance

I collect old vintage tractors and I was due to receive an inheritance of a 1936 Angleworm 10 from my neighbour, who was aware of my hobby. The probate of the estate was not completed and the tractor was left in my neighbours garage pending completion. However, the tractor has now mysteriously disappeared and it's looking doubtful that it will ever be recovered. I'm very upset.

9. Last Will and Testament, Probate Law, Trusts, Enduring Power of Attorney

The rather unfortunately named Angleworm 10 by the Bradley Tractor Company was a small tracked tractor weighing 2,600 pounds and was only 37 inches high. It was not popular at the time and disappeared the same year it was introduced. I understand how excited you must have been to inherit this rare gem. When a person makes a will, they appoint an executor to carry out the directions of the will. The executor is obliged by law to preserve, protect and administer the estate of the deceased person strictly in accordance with the terms of the will. The obligation to preserve and protect the assets of the estate means that the executor is obliged to ensure that all assets are adequately protected until they are distributed. The Angleworm 10 should have been left in a safe, secure locked unit and, furthermore, in fulfilling his legal obligation, an executor should make sure that all assets required to be insured are insured for their market value. The Angleworm 10 would be worth quite a bit, due to the limited number of them available worldwide. Hopefully, the executor took out an insurance policy to cover the assets of the estate, to include the vintage tractor. Talk to the executor, who must ensure that any relevant claim form is filed with the insurance company. You may receive the market value of the vintage Angleworm 10.

ENDURING POWER OF ATTORNEY

I recently executed my last will and testament. What happens if I no longer have the mental capacity to look after my affairs?

There is a legal document called an enduring power of attorney (EPA) which has built-in safeguards which ensure that the power vested in the attorney cannot be used without legitimate reasons. Basically, you appoint someone you know well and trust, such as your spouse or adult children (referred to as the attorney) to look after your affairs if you become incapable of doing so. You also nominate two people who are known as notice parties. They are informed by registered post at the beginning of the process that you have signed this EPA. Your doctor and solicitor must also sign certificates stating that you fully understand what you are signing at the time. If at some stage in your life your attorney decides that you are no longer capable of looking after your own affairs, then he/she must register the EPA with the High Court and the two notice parties are informed immediately by registered post. If they do not agree with this assessment of your capacity, then they will object on your behalf.

MAKING A WILL PRE-AND-POST MARRIAGE

I made a will years ago while I was still single. I am getting married soon. My will was not made in 'contemplation of the marriage'. Should I make another will or will the will I have made be revoked as a result of the marriage? Must I provide for my spouse in the will? She said she only wants my love.

If you were to die after getting married without having made a new will after the date that you got married, you would effectively die intestate and the rules of intestacy would apply. Therefore, I would advise you to review your will after you get married to ensure that it reflects the change in your circumstances and to ensure that the will is valid on your death.

It is always possible for a person to revoke their will. This can only be challenged if your mental capacity when you revoked your will is called into question.

If you marry, your will is automatically revoked unless your will was made in contemplation of that marriage. If you make another will, the first will you made will be superseded by the second will and normally a common clause in most wills is to revoke the previous wills.

You are free to dispose of your estate as you wish, but your will is subject to certain rights of your spouse called a legal right share, courtesy of s 111 of the Succession Act 1965. If you make a will, your spouse's legal right share is one half of your estate if you do not have children, or one third of your estate if you do have children. In contrast if you die without having made a valid will your wife shall receive all of your estate if you do not have children and two thirds of your estate if you have children (the other one third going to your children). Your spouse would not have to go to court to get this share, as an executor is obliged to grant this share, where applicable. You can also make a bequest in your will that increases your spouse's legal right share if you so wish. will

It is possible for a spouse to renounce her rights to the legal right share. This can form part of an agreement prior to marriage, or the spouse may set aside her rights to favour any children. However, any such renunciation may be ignored if there is evidence of undue influence or evidence that the spouse did not understand what she was doing or she did not have independent legal advice. If a couple is separated, a renunciation of each other's right to the legal right share is usually included in any separation agreement. Divorce automatically ends succession rights. A spouse can cease to be a spouse by renunciation (s 113, Succession Act 1965), by separation (Judicial Separation and Family Law Reform Act 1989 and Family Law Act 1995), by divorce (Family Law (Divorce) Act 1996) or by unworthiness to succeed (s 120, Succession Act 1965).

LIVING GRANDCHILDREN AND S 98 OF THE SUCCESSION ACT 1965 (MY SON'S CHILDREN)

My wife is deceased and I have two adult sons. I made a will leaving my sons my entire estate. One of my sons is very ill. He has three children. What will happen to the bequest in my will if my son dies before me?

Normally, in circumstances such as yours the bequest/gift would lapse and fail. However, an exception to this rule is contained in s 98 of the Succession Act 1965.

Section 98 provides that, where a child pre-deceases a testator (that is the person who makes the will) leaving children, and such children are living at the time of the death of the testator, the gift shall not lapse but shall take effect as if the death of that person happened immediately after the death of the testator. Therefore if your son dies before you, the benefit that would have been received by your son is preserved and will pass to his estate. The bequest will then be divided in accordance with the terms set out in your son's will. So to clarify, if you leave a benefit in your will to your child who predeceases you, the benefit will go to his estate, not to his children. You can prevent this happening by making provision in your will that the benefit will go to your child's children. if you so wish.

Inheritance Tax

My parents died and they left me a significant amount of property in their will. The property is valued at around €600,000. Am I liable to pay a substantial tax bill on my inheritance?

Inheritance tax does not apply if the value of the property falls within the tax-free thresholds. The parent-to-child threshold is €310,000. However, if you go over this threshold, tax at a rate of 33% will apply. Therefore, a property worth €600,000 inherited by you alone will incur a tax bill of €95,700, that is, 33% of €600,000 less the €310,000 threshold.

You did not say whether the property was a dwelling house. If it was, you may be able to avail of the dwelling house exemption, but the use of this exemption is restricted.

If the property is a farm you may avail of a discount on inheritance tax called agricultural relief. Again the conditions in availing of such relief are quite strict. It is best to get professional advice in regard to possible ways of avoiding inheritance tax. A good place to start is to look at the guides on the revenue commissioners' website in regard to inheritance tax.

Young Children

We are unmarried parents of very young children. We were not considering making a will until our friend suggested that we should do so, in case anything happened to us. She was concerned about who would care for our children.

Under the Succession Act 1965, children include marital and non-marital children and adopted children. Failure to plan your affairs can have unhappy consequences for your loved ones. The whole process of preparing a will offers great peace of mind, ensuring that loved ones are provided for in the manner that you want, and whether any other lifetime planning is appropriate for your circumstances. It also means that the responsibility for administering your estate can vest in people whom you have chosen. Who do you want to raise your children if you die suddenly? Will your assets be available to fund your children's schooling if you die suddenly? What age do you want your children to inherit at? In my opinion, your friend is right to be concerned. If you die suddenly without having made a will, there can be traumatic disputes over who should raise your children. It is better to leave clear instructions as to who you want to raise them. By making a will, you can leave your property, money and assets to the people or charities you want. If you have children under the age of 18, you can appoint or choose your children's trustees and/or guardian. Your children's future is protected if you choose a legal guardian to be responsible for their upbringing in the case of your death. You must tell them, of course, and it is important that you give your children's guardians power to deal with your assets, in order that there is sufficient resources for them to pay for your children's needs. If you are a guardian of a child in Ireland, by law you have a duty to maintain and properly care for the child and you have a right to make decisions about the child's religious and secular education, health requirements and general welfare. So choose a guardian for your child wisely, someone you have known a long time, a very close friend or family member. In the will, you can specify whether you would want your children to inherit at 18 or a little order, perhaps after they complete their third-level studies. Any other concerns or plans you may have for your child's future care can be written into a will. It is imperative that you both make a will as soon as possible.

TRUSTS AND TRUSTEES

I am thinking about setting up a trust fund for my young children. What are the benefits of a trust in a will? What is the role of the trustees?

Setting up a trust in your will is a good way of handling the assets of your estate for the benefit of your young children. It is though froth with difficulties and traps created by the archaic nature of trust law in Ireland and the cat and mouse games played between some wealthy individuals and their advisors on the one hand and the revenue commissioners on the other.

Trusts can be created during a person's lifetime or they can be created by will, taking effect after a person's death. There are many reasons why a testator might want to include a trust in a will. Trusts are sometimes set up where the testator wants to make arrangements for someone with a disability, for taxation reasons or where there are minor children or grandchildren who will be beneficiaries in the will, to keep property from spendthrift children or where the testator or beneficiary has debt problems and they want to try to keep the assets out of reach of their creditors. I would advise you, the testator, to review the terms of your will in line with any changes in taxation, that is regard should be had to tax provisions in relation to the type of trust the will creates. For example, in the case of a discretionary trust, discretionary trust tax may also apply, in addition to the usual taxes. All property in the State is liable to gift/inheritance tax. A CAT (inheritance

9. Last Will and Testament, Probate Law, Trusts, Enduring Power of Attorney

tax) return to the Revenue must be made and any tax due paid within a specified period. The valuation date is the date on which the market value of the property comprising the gift/inheritance is established.

There are various different types of trusts used in drafting a will. The most common are discretionary trusts and a trust for sale. A discretionary trust means any trust whereby property is held on trust to accumulate the income (or part of the income) of the property or where property is held on trust to apply the income or capital (or part of the income) or capital of the property for the benefit of any person, whether at the discretion of the trustees or any other person and notwithstanding that there may be a power to accumulate all or any part of the income.

A discretionary trust gives trustees the property to use at their discretion for a particular purpose for instance 'John in his will gives all his property to be held in a discretionary trust for the benefit of his children until they reach the age of 18'. He appoints Mary and Jack as trustees. He gives Mary and Jack wide powers to use the property as they see fit for the benefit of his children. In this case the children are potential beneficiaries and do not have an interest in the property of the estate until the last of his children reach the age of 18. Since it is uncertain what they will receive they cannot be taxed as if the whole asset of the estate was given to them. An example would be where Mary and Jack who have absolute discretion may give all the benefit of the estate to a single child. This may be appropriate where that child has an immediate medical need that requires specialist treatment abroad. As you can see it does not follow in a discretionary trust that just because a certain amount is given in a trust fund for the benefit of three children that each child will get an equal share.

Beneficiaries do not have an absolute right to the trust fund, so do not have an interest in property. A discretionary fund could be used where the education of young children or grandchildren. The bequest can state the purpose for which the fund is being set up, or it can be left to the trustees in a general way to be distributed among the testator's children. The trust fund, the details of the beneficiaries and the trustees must be clearly defined and set out in the will. A trust fund can include a specific sum of money, property or the residue of the estate. A testator can create a residuary trust over a fund and instruct the trustees to distribute the fund as they, in their absolute discretion, shall think fit. In the case of a discretionary trust, the powers given to the trustees should be as extensive as possible having regard to the assets that will probably comprise the estate of the testator.

A trust for sale is where the trustees are under an obligation to sell, invest the proceeds and hold the proceeds on the terms of the original trust. This type of trust puts the trustees in control of the timing of any sale of trust property, and they cannot be forced to sell, even if a beneficiary wants them to do so. If a property is not held on trust for sale, then a power of sale must be given to the trustees in the will. The advantage of the trust for sale is that it removes any doubt in respect of the trustee's power of sale. The will should provide that the obligation to sell under the trust for sale may be postponed at the discretion of the trustees. There is no need to create a trust for sale where the persons who will become entitled are of full age, not suffering from an incapacity and absolutely entitled to the property.

The statutory powers given to trustees are set out in s 58 of the Succession Act 1965 and s 20 of the Land and Conveyancing Law Reform Act 2009. Section 18 of the 2009 Act provides for a trust of land which covers all forms of trust of land, including where land is vested in a minor. Under s 20(1) of the Act, subject to the duties of a trustee or any court order or statutory duty, a trustee of land has the full power of an owner to convey or otherwise deal with it and to permit a beneficiary to occupy or otherwise use the land on such terms as the trustee thinks fit, or sell the land and reinvest the proceeds. Trustees are allowed to hold property vested in them under s 57 of the 1965 Act.

When inserting a trust in a will, one might consider giving additional powers to the trustees. For example, the power to run a business might also require the power to insure the business property, purchase assets, the power to maintain the property of the business, the power of investment or the power to borrow money.

If no trustees are appointed, the personal representatives are deemed to be trustees for the purposes of s 57. Section 57 only applies to the share of a minor. We would recommend Bracken and Campbell, *The Probate Handbook* (Clarus Press 2012), Terry Gorry, *Business Ireland*, and Brian Spierin, *Will Precedents and Drafting* (Bloomsbury Professional 2013) for further information in this area.

CREATION OF A TRUST TO PRESERVE ASSETS

I am an elderly farmer and I am contemplating making a will. I have a large family and many grandchildren. My eldest grandchild uses my land for his cattle, and I would like him to continue doing so. I would not like to see the land being sold. The land was in our family for several generations. However, I would like my younger grandchildren who are all still minors to also get a share.

Typically in the countryside, farmlands are left to one person in the family, usually a son with an interest in farming, as the owner may not like to see the land being sold. If it's a large farm, it may be divided and made into two or three viable farms. One issue you could consider in your circumstances is the creation of a trust. With a trust, you could give your grandson use of the farm for a set number of years, while devising the lands to your other grandchildren at a later date. The creation of a trust requires careful consideration and should be carried out by a legal professional, as the courts will not uphold a trust if it is not properly constituted. One or more trustees must be appointed for a trust and the trustee will have responsibilities and duties regarding the running of the farm. The trustee should be someone you trust to fulfil their obligations under the trust. A trust can be created in a will. The benefit of the trust is that it can keep your land secure from sale, according to your wishes.

CREATION OF A TRUST TO PREVENT THE SALE OF LAND

My only son was killed in a farming accident a few years back. He had one son. I own a farm and, on my death, I would like to pass it on to my grandson. My grandson is a wonderful young man. The problem I have is his girlfriend. I really don't like her or trust her at all. I suspect she's a gold digger. What will happen if I make a will leaving everything to my grandson and he marries this person and their relationship ends soon thereafter? I don't want my land sold. Should I get my grandson to do up a pre-nuptial agreement or something like that?

At present, there is no legislation in the area of pre-nuptial agreements, despite a demand from the farming community. However, I would advise you to do one anyway because, although the Irish courts are not bound to accept the contents of a pre-nuptial agreement as the terms of a separation or divorce, there is significant case law to show that, where these agreements exist, the courts are having regard to them. There is nothing in Irish law preventing couples entering into pre-nuptial agreements. Furthermore, I see no reason why Irish courts should not take pre-nuptial agreements into account when making provision for spouses.

Even if your grandson does not marry this girl and decides to live with her, they become qualified cohabitees if they have been living together and are parents of one or more dependent children of the relationship after a period of two years. In most other cases, they must be living together for five years or more. In this case, they have the option of entering into a "trust agreement" which is binding in law and which would prevent the farm being sold if the relationship broke down. Under a trust, you could give your grandson the use of the land for his lifetime, while devising the land to a later generation, even if they are not yet born. A trust can be created in a will or it can be created *inter vivos* or during the lifetime of the land owner. You can appoint a trustee and ensure that he or she is properly carrying out your wishes. The benefit of a trust is to prevent the sale of the land for a generation, and this might well suit the situation you describe.

TESTAMENTARY CAPACITY

My elderly father is quite ill in hospital. I was informed on a recent visit that my brother had brought a solicitor to the hospital to help my father draft his will prior to my visit. I am shocked because I do not think my father is well enough to make a will and he is taking strong pain medication. He is vulnerable at this time. Can I challenge my father's will at a later date if needs be?

I am often called to hospitals and nursing homes by family and relatives (and, in one particular case, a carer) to assist an elderly relative or sick person in drafting their will. I usually make a point of contacting the hospital or nursing home in advance and I meet the consultant, doctor or nursing director (and sometimes all three) to discuss the patient's testamentary capacity, that is whether or not they are of sound mind, what medication they are on and how it could influence their decision-making. I also of course use my own judgment in such cases and I may, depending on the circumstances, request a written medical report or a sworn statement from the medical personnel in attendance.

> The factors to consider were first set out in *Banks v Goodfellow* (1870) LR 5 QB 54 which provided that the testator must understand he is making a will and what a will is, that it will dispose of his or her assets after they die. The testator must be capable of knowing the extent of his estate and must be able to give consideration to those people who might expect to benefit and decide whether or not to benefit them. This was restated in the Supreme Court by in *Blackwell v Blackwell* (1929) AC 318, 335 where Barron J stated that sound testamentary capacity means the testator must understand that he is giving his property to one or more objects in his regard, he must be able to recollect the extent of his property and he must also understand the nature and extent of the claims on him, including those he is including or excluding from the will.

The more recent case of *James v James* (2018) EWHC 43 (Ch) affirmed the above test.

When a testator is elderly or in ill health, there is sometimes a presumption of undue influence, that is the testator may be unduly influenced by someone in whom they placed trust and confidence. Independent legal advice should always be recommended in such circumstances to rebut the presumption of undue influence.

Your father's solicitor would have a legal duty to ensure that your father was capable of giving instructions, and that he was able to read the will - or at least have it re-read to him. There should be two independent witnesses to your father's will. Witnesses must attest by their signatures the signature of the testator in the presence of the testator, but not necessarily in the presence of each other.

If you think that you may have to challenge your father's will at a later stage on the basis that you think your father was of unsound mind when he executed it, then it is up to you, the challenger, to prove that your father was of unsound mind. The courts will decide on the evidence presented whether or not your father had the testamentary capacity to make his will at the time. In *Glynn v Glynn* [1990] 2 IR 326, two doctors were of the opinion that the testator was disorientated on the day that he executed the will and concluded that he was unable to communicate his own ideas. However, the evidence of the attesting witnesses was to the effect that they were both satisfied that the testator knew what he was doing and was capable at that point of making a will. The court was impressed by both of the attesting witnesses, who had no private or personal interest in the estate of the deceased and, despite the reservations of the doctors, the court upheld the validity of the will.

The above case law would seem to be contradicted by the recent case where it would now appear that to prove testamentary capacity if it is in doubt then a medical professional must certify same at the time the will was made.

Conditional Bequests

I made a will leaving everything, that is my farm and cash savings, to my son. My son qualifies for agricultural relief on the farm. Will he also qualify for agricultural relief on the cash he will inherit?

Whether or not your son will qualify for agricultural relief on the cash inheritance will depend on how you draft your will. If you include a clause in your will providing for the bequest of this cash to your son on condition that the whole or part thereof be invested in agricultural property within two years of the date of issue of the grant of representation in your estate, then your son will qualify for agricultural relief on the cash inheritance. If your son complies with this condition, the cash bequest will be written down accordingly for tax purposes.

The valuation date for tax purposes will be the date of investment in agricultural property. Perhaps have a meeting about this with your son first. He may not wish to invest this cash in agricultural property, and may have already made plans of a different kind for the future investment of the money. Perhaps it might be better to provide for an alternative clause in your will to protect your son's cash inheritance. As with all conditional bequests, the bequest will fail if your son invests the cash elsewhere. It is always advisable to see a tax consultant or accountant to avail of good tax planning advice in these circumstances.

You did not confirm the amount of cash you are bequeathing to your son. A child may inherit up to €310,000 from their parents without being liable for tax. Therefore the above only applies if you are bequeathing over €310,000 to your son.

Various Types of Legacy

I wish to leave money and jewellery to my daughter and a car to my wife in my will. Perhaps I might also leave a few euro to the North West Simon Community. It was mentioned to me that I should consider the various types of legacies first.

Since the passing of the Succession Act 1965, property vests on death in the executors of the will (where there is a valid will), and in the President of the High Court in the case of intestacy, where the executors appointed have died or where there is a will but no executors have been appointed. It is important when a person is drafting a will to know the difference between the various types of legacies.

A general legacy is usually a pecuniary legacy (money) which is payable out of the testator's general estate as in all the assets that have not been specifically given to anyone in the will. An example is "John has a car, house and bank account and he gives the car in his will to Tom and gives 10k to Mike. This 10k is taken out of the proceeds of sale of the house and/or the bank account after the debts of the estate are paid (funeral expenses)".

There will either be funds to meet a general legacy or there will not. It is a gift out of the rest of the estate after the payment of debts, outstanding taxes owed by the testator and specific legacies. If the estate is insufficient to meet the pecuniary legacies, then they will abate on a *pro rata* basis or entirely. A general legacy may also be an item of personal property which is not specified, such as a legacy of a book without specifying which book from the testator's collection. For example, "I GIVE all my clothing, jewellery, books and articles of personal use to my daughter, Mary Smullen of 37 Dakota Drive, Sunnyroad, Dublin".

A specific legacy is a legacy of a specific item of personal property, and may be given away during the lifetime of the testator, in which case the gift will be adeemed. This would not happen in the case of a general legacy, therefore it is sometimes better to try to avoid specific pecuniary legacies and instead to use general legacies in the case of bequests of money. A specific legacy would be for example the proceeds of a specified bank account, jewellery, paintings, furniture or shares in a particular company. The specific legacy should be properly and clearly described. It is important that the testator gives full and complete instructions in relation to all the testator's estate, so that the will can be as comprehensive as possible. A specific legacy will only abate after the residue and the general legacies have abated in full. If the specific legacies are abating, they will abate on a *pro rata* basis, so that the various items would have to be independently valued and they would then abate *pro rata*. An example of a specific legacy to a spouse, in addition to his or her legal right share, would be "I GIVE AND BEQUEATH to my wife Elizabeth Gorby of Moon City, Moonsville, County Laois, my motor car, registration number 213-D-09, which said bequest is in addition to my wife's legal right share in my estate, if she elects to take such share".

An adeemed legacy is where the testator gives away during his lifetime the item referred to in the will. An abated legacy is where the residue of the estate is insufficient to meet the testator's debts and liabilities.

A demonstrative legacy is a mixture of a general and specific legacy. This is where there is a particular fund designated for the payment of the legacy concerned, for example "€2,500 from my account with the Bank of Ireland". It will not abate. It will adeem and is payable out of the testator's general estate.

A conditional legacy has a condition attached which will see the bequest forfeited if the condition is not fulfilled. For example, "I GIVE the sum of one thousand euro (€1,000) to each of my executors, provided they act as my executors and take upon themselves the burden of the administration of my estate".

When leaving a gift to charity, describe the charity clearly and explicitly so that the property or pecuniary legacy passes to the intended beneficiary. Give the

9. Last Will and Testament, Probate Law, Trusts, Enduring Power of Attorney

correct name and address of the charity. The Simon Community has branches all over Ireland. Therefore, make it clear that you want the gift to go to the North-West branch of the Simon Community. Some charitable organisations will not be incorporated and therefore a gift to the charity is in fact a gift to all the members of the charity. The bequest should state that the receipt of the treasurer or some other proper officer of the charity would be sufficient discharge to the executors in respect of the payment of the legacy Brian Spierin, *Will Precedents and Drafting* (Bloomsbury Professional 2013).

MY WISHES MAY NOT BE PROPERLY CARRIED OUT

My wife passed away several years ago and I have now made a will leaving all my assets to one of my sons. At the time, I trusted his good nature and felt that he would do the right thing and divide my property and money with my other children after I die. I am quite wealthy. However, my son has changed a lot and I am concerned now that, if anything happened to me, he would not share his inheritance with his siblings.

If your will states that your entire estate is to go to your son after your death, then he will inherit everything. He is under no obligation to share his inheritance with your other children. There will be inheritance tax implications for him, of course, and he will be liable to Revenue if the inheritance is particularly big.

When making a will, you would usually appoint an executor to administer your estate after your death. The executor is obliged to ensure that your estate passes to the beneficiaries named in the will. I would respectfully suggest that you make another appointment with your solicitors and review your will. Appoint an executor and state clearly in the will how you want your assets distributed. Please also liaise with your solicitor regarding the current tax thresholds for parent-to-child gift/inheritance tax. If you divide your assets equally between your children, they may be able to avoid a tax liability or have their liability considerably reduced.

If you do not make proper provision in your will for all your children a disappointed child can bring an action against the estate in accordance with s 117 of the Succession Act. Fighting such a case can dissipate the assets of the estate not to mention the fractured family relations that it leaves behind.

DECEASED LEAVES AN INSOLVENT ESTATE

I am a beneficiary under my father's will. However, my father was a gambler and his debts far outshine any assets he had. Will I have to pay my father's debts?

Creditors can only bring a claim against your father's estate. They cannot bring a claim against you or anyone in your family or the executor, except you or members of your family at any stage personally guaranteed your father's debts. If your father was a known gambler, it's unlikely any members of your family guaranteed his debts. Any assets your father left must be used to pay his debts. His funeral and testamentary expenses will be paid first. Any creditor who had security against any property owned by your late father will be paid next. Taxes due are paid after that. All creditors in due course receive a share if there is anything to give but usually in such a case all creditors debts will not be satisfied and sadly there will be nothing left over for the beneficiaries.

Ademption

What does ademption mean?

Where a specific thing designated in a will no longer exists or is not the property of the testator at his death, it is said to be "adeemed" and the beneficiary or legatee will take no substantial benefit or receive nothing. A specific bequest is one where a specific item of property is left to the beneficiary, for example, "my entire collection of Lord of the Rings DVDs". A general legacy would be "all my DVDs". A general legacy will not adeem. Therefore, in order to avoid ademption in the case of bequests of money or investments, it is sometimes better to try to avoid specific pecuniary legacies and instead to utilise general legacies.

A way to try avoiding this would be for example bequeathing to a beneficiary "any dwelling house which I may own at the time of my death", rather than naming a specific dwelling house. However, if the testator owns a number of properties and wishes to give them to various people, they will have to be dealt with by way of specific bequest, and the doctrine of ademption would apply if any of the houses were disposed of by the testator prior to his death.

Treating All One's Children Fairly

I made my last will and testament and stated therein that it was my wish that all my property be left to my son. I also have three daughters but I do not want them to inherit. My sister advised me that my daughters may feel excluded from the will and take legal action contesting my will after my death. Can my daughters legally do this?

Under Irish law, children of a deceased person may challenge the last will and testament of their parent (or parents) under s 117 of the Succession Act 1965 on the basis that the parent failed in the moral duty to make proper provision for the child in accordance with his or her means. If a child is excluded from a will without good reason, there is a strong chance that the will can be successfully challenged under s 117 of the Act. But there is no guarantee that a court will uphold the challenge. Each case will be treated separately. The court will consider the situation from the perspective of a prudent and fair parent and must consider the position of the other children of the testator. There will be an assessment of the means of all parties to the dispute. There are strict time limits applicable to making a s 117 claim. If a claimant

9. Last Will and Testament, Probate Law, Trusts, Enduring Power of Attorney

leaves it too late, she may be statute-barred. The time limit for bringing an action under s 117 is six months, so it is vital that proceedings are issued quickly in order to protect the interests of the claimant.

When considering a s 117 claim, a judge will consider factors such as the number of children the testator has, their ages and their positions in life at the time of the testator's death, the means of the testator, the age of the child whose case is being considered and his or her financial position and prospects in life and whether the testator has already in his lifetime made proper provision for the child making the s 117 application, whether the parent positively failed in their moral duty to make proper provision for the child, and the child must establish that he or she had a need which the testator could have satisfied in making his will. A court cannot make an order which would interfere with the legal right share of the surviving spouse.

Section 63 of the Succession Act 1965 allows a child to bring a case against another child who has previously received an advancement during the testator's lifetime. This action will seek to have the previous advancement to a sibling taken into account in the distribution of the estate on death.

Another type of action may arise if you have promised one of your daughters some part of your estate and they have relied on this representation and altered their lives accordingly. This is called a proprietary estoppel action. It will aim to prove that the child acted to his or her detriment in the belief that he or she would be given a right to the deceased's property, and the deceased knew and encouraged this belief.

The court will not allow a testator to go back on their word in such circumstances.

INTESTACY — WHAT HAPPENS IF I DON'T MAKE A WILL?

I am an elderly farmer. I lost my wife to cancer four years ago. I own a large farm and, as is tradition in this part of the country, I want to pass on the farm to my son after my death. He is interested in farming and I don't believe he would sell the farm. I would hate to see the farm sold. It has been passed down and farmed from generation to generation. I have four daughters also. They'll be fine. I'm sure they'll just get married and move away. I informed them I was leaving the farm to my son. I do not plan on making a will. I have verbally set out my wishes and that is that. However, my brother is nagging me to make a will because he thinks my daughters might object to my wishes after I die. It seems like a lot of trouble.

Failure to plan your affairs in the form of a will can have unhappy consequences for your family and loved ones. Making a will allows you to choose your own executor, that is, the person who will wind up your estate and deal with your affairs after your death. A will also enables you to decide how your body will be dealt with after your death, for example, cremated or buried, the type of funeral service and whether your body parts can be used for medical purposes.

If a person dies without a valid will, they are said to have died intestate. Their belongings, including all money, property and possessions, are called an intestate estate. If you die without having made a will, your property will be divided in accordance with the rules of intestacy, as set out in the Succession Act 1965. For example, in a situation where a husband dies leaving a wife and children but no valid will, the wife is entitled to two-thirds of the estate and the children are entitled to share the remaining one-third. If the deceased is survived by a spouse but no children, then the spouse gets all of the estate. If the deceased is survived by parents and no spouse or children, then the parents get 100%. If the deceased is survived by children and no spouse, then the estate is divided equally between them.

In your situation, your next of kin are your five children and your estate will be divided equally among them. Your farm may have to be sold so that each of your five children receives their share. Alternatively, your five children may be registered as equal owners of the land. You have decided not to execute a will and therefore there is no obligation on your four daughters to give their share to their brother after your death.

PRE-NUPTIAL AGREEMENTS, WILLS AND THE FAMILY FARM

My father has transferred the family farm to me. My mother is deceased. I made a will recently and stated my intentions for the family farm, should anything happen to me. I am happy to leave it at that but my fiancé wants to sign a pre-nuptial agreement. Would a pre-nuptial agreement have any bearing on my will? What would happen in terms of the pre-nuptial agreement if my spouse died?

Pre-nuptial agreements are not binding on a judge in this country, and a pre-nuptial agreement does not have any bearing on your will.

However, in the case of a separation or divorce, they may have a somewhat persuasive effect in judgments. Couples sometimes draft a pre-nuptial agreement to help make their intentions clear regarding the distribution of assets in the case of separation. It is an agreement between two future spouses in contemplation of being married to each other.

If your spouse died, the existence of a will is most important. If a spouse who owns a farm dies without a valid will, then the rules of intestacy apply. This means that the surviving spouse will be entitled to inherit two thirds of the estate and, if there are children, they share the other third. If you do not have any children, your surviving spouse will get the entire estate. It is always better to make a valid will clearly stating your wishes for the family farm after your death.

Pre-nuptial agreements usually just deal with what you would like to happen to your assets in the event of a separation or divorce. However, you could enter into a pre-nuptial agreement, clearly making provision for what you wish to happen

9. Last Will and Testament, Probate Law, Trusts, Enduring Power of Attorney

on the death of one of the spouses. The only problem with such an agreement is that your spouse is by law entitled to certain percentages of your estate. In the case that you make a will your spouse has a legal right share to between one third and one half of your assets depending whether you have children. In the case of intestacy your spouse could be entitled to the whole of your estate if you don't have children.

One again such an agreement might have some sort of persuasive effect in a court battle over the remaining assets but it cannot obliterate the legal rights of a spouse which are created on marriage.

PROTECTION FOR SURVIVING SPOUSES OF DECEASED PERSONS

My husband died recently and we have three adult children of the marriage and one adopted child. I don't know if my husband made a will or not, and I am currently checking with solicitors in the area to see if he made a will with them. Can I continue living in the family home? What share of my husband's estate am I entitled to?

The testamentary freedom of a married testator is curtailed by the provisions of part IX of the Succession Act 1965 and will be restricted to a greater extent where the testator is both married and has children. Usually, if a testator is happily married, he or she will leave their entire estate to their surviving spouse but of course this is not always the case. In circumstances where a spouse has not made provision for another spouse in their will, certain sections of the Succession Act, 1965 enforce a minimum right for disinherited spouses. Section 111(1) of the Succession Act 1965 states that, if the testator leaves a spouse and no children, the spouse shall have a right to one half of the estate. If the testator leaves a spouse and children, the spouse shall have a right to one-third of the estate (s 111(2)). This only applies where the deceased person has made a will. This "legal right share" is calculated on the net estate of the deceased person. Brian Spierin, *Will Precedents and Drafting* (Bloomsbury Professional 2013).

If the testator left no will, the surviving spouse is entitled to two thirds of the estate if the deceased has children and the entire estate if the testator has no children. Children are referred to as issue and include marital and non-marital children, adopted children and their lineal descendants. Step-children and foster-children are not included but if a gift is made in a will to a step child or foster child the revenue will in certain circumstances take the step or foster children as if they are natural/adopted children for tax purposes. Section 112 of the Act states that the right of the spouse shall have priority over devises, bequests and shares on intestacy.

If the testator makes no provision at all for his spouse, then the spouse will be automatically entitled to the legal right share and that share will vest in the surviving spouse on death (s 111(1) of the Succession Act 1965 and *O'Dwyer and Another v Keegan* (1997) 2 ILRM 401

Where, under the will, a deceased person who dies wholly testate, there is a devise or bequest to a spouse, the spouse may elect to take either that devise or bequest or the share to which she is entitled as a legal right (s 115(1)(a)). If the surviving spouse does not elect to take either the bequest or the legal right share, she will be deemed to have taken the bequest and will lose the legal right share (s 115(1)(b)). Therefore where there is a bequest to the spouse, the legal right share only vests if the spouse elects to take same. If a spouse dies before an election is made, the legal right share does not form part of the spouse's estate (*Reilly v McEntee* [1984] ILRM 572). Where the spouse or civil partner is of unsound mind, the right of election may be exercised by the spouse's or civil partner's committee or, if no committee, by the appropriate court.

The surviving spouse has a right to request that the dwelling in which the surviving spouse ordinarily resides and the household chattels be appropriated, if the property is part of the estate of the deceased person. Appropriation in this instance means to take possession of the house or to set apart or take it for oneself. This appropriation will be towards the satisfaction of her legal right share. There are time limits on the right of appropriation, and the personal representative should be notified in writing of your wishes to appropriate the family home. If the legal right share if less than the value of the house, the right may also be exercised in respect of the share of an infant for whom the spouse is a trustee (s 56).

This right of appropriation can be exercised in respect of any benefit accruing to a spouse, as either a benefit under a will, a legal right share or a right accruing on intestacy. The personal representative is required under the Succession Act 1965 to give notice to the surviving spouse of the entitlement to elect to exercise the right of appropriation.

A spouse ceases to be a spouse under the Succession Act 1965 in certain circumstances, such as divorce. A will is revoked by the subsequent marriage of a testator (Family Law (Divorce) Act 1996. Regard should be had as to whether a foreign divorce would be recognisable by the Irish courts, or whether the person to whom the testator was married would still be regarded as a spouse under Irish law and therefore entitled to his or her rights under the Succession Act 1965. The Family Law Act 1995 provides for property adjustment orders and the extinguishment of succession rights. Section 113 of the Succession Act 1965 provides for renunciation before or after marriage by way of a written contract. Section 120 of the Succession Act, 1965 provides for the unworthiness of the surviving spouse to succeed, such as in a case where a wife murders a husband, or other unsavory behavior or offences against the family of the deceased. Children can seek a court order that provision should be made for them, where a parent has failed to provide for them what a prudent and just parent should (s 117). The court has an absolute discretion to make provision for the child as it thinks proper.

In conclusion, it is noted that legislation governing wills in Ireland provides unique protection for spouses of the deceased. Your husband cannot disinherit you. If your husband made a will, you are entitled to one third of his estate, as you had children. This entitlement is called a legal right share which ranks in priority after the rights of creditors of your husband and ahead of any other beneficiary. You do not have to go to court to get your entitlement, as the executor is obliged to grant this share to you. If your husband left no will, you are entitled to two thirds of the estate. Please contact your solicitors immediately and get legal advice, as time limits apply.

Unmarried Testators with Non-Marital Children

I had a brief fling with a woman years ago and apparently she had a baby as a result of this. She says it is my child, but of course it could be anyone's child. I have no interest in this woman or the child. I am quite wealthy. I am assuming this child will have no legal rights over my estate when I die.

One should never assume anything. Where an unmarried person has non-marital children, if he or she dies intestate, his or her non-marital children will be entitled to the entire of his or her estate. If he or she dies testate and fails to make provision or adequate provision for them, the non-marital children will have a right to bring an application pursuant to s 117 of the Succession Act 1965 which provides that, where a parent fails in his or her moral duty to make proper provision for a child in accordance with his or her means, then the court shall make such provision for the child as to the court may seem just. The courts will consider what provision has been made for the non-marital child during the course of the testator's life and what provision should have been made in a will Brian Spierin, *Will Precedents and Drafting* (Bloomsbury Professional 2013).

Therefore your child has a very strong claim under s 117 of the Succession Act 1965 because you have not provided at all for your child.

If your child was adopted by someone else, then that would afford you the testator an escape route. If a non-marital child has been legally adopted, the Status of Children Act 1987 provides that from the date of the adoption order, the child becomes the child of the adoptive parents and no other person. In those circumstances the adopted child could not bring a claim under s 117 of the Succession Act 1965 against the unmarried testator's estate.

You express concerns that perhaps this is not your child. Directions may be given for the taking of blood or tissue samples after your death for the purposes of DNA testing. When there has been an affiliation order made in respect of the child, that is conclusive evidence *vis-à-vis* the child's paternity.

If you, the testator, decide to make a will and disinherit your non-marital child, then please leave detailed instructions with your solicitors as to why you are disinheriting your child, as this may help in any future challenges to your will.

TAX EXEMPTION FOR DWELLING HOUSE

I wish to leave property (my home) to my son after my death. Will my son be able to avail of any tax relief?

Section 86 of the Capital Acquisitions Tax Consolidation Act 2003 provides that inheritances of a dwelling house taken on or after 25 December 2016 will be exempt from Capital Acquisitions Tax provided the following conditions are complied with: a) the donor must have occupied the house as his/her only or main residence at his/her date of death. This requirement will be relaxed in situations where the deceased person had to leave because of ill-health, for example, to live in a nursing home, b) the beneficiary must have continuously occupied the dwelling house as his/her only or main residence for three years immediately before the date of the inheritance. Where the dwelling house on which the exemption is claimed replaced another dwelling house within the three-year period, this condition will be satisfied where the beneficiary has continuously occupied both houses as his/her only/main residence for a total period of three out of the four years, immediately prior to the date of the inheritance, c) the beneficiary must not be entitled to an interest in any other dwelling house at the date of the inheritance, or d) the beneficiary must continue to occupy the house (except where such beneficiary is aged 65 or over) as his/her only or main residence for a period of six years from the date of the inheritance. The exemption will not be withdrawn where the recipient requires long-term medical care in a hospital or nursing home or is required by reason of his/her employment to reside elsewhere. Please always contact your tax consultant or accountant for the latest updates in this area. This is an area of law that changes a lot.

NURSING HOME SUPPORT SCHEME
(KNOWN AS THE FAIR DEAL SCHEME)

My father is elderly and in poor health. I am currently reviewing different nursing homes in the hope of finding somewhere nice that he will enjoy and be well cared for. I am also aware that many of the nursing homes are very expensive. My friend mentioned the Fair Deal Scheme to me, but I really don't know very much about this scheme and if it would apply to my father's situation.

Under the Fair Deal Scheme, he will make a contribution towards the cost of his care and the State will pay the rest, regardless of whether the nursing home is public, private or voluntary. There are three steps in applying for the scheme. First is an application for a care needs assistant, who identifies whether or not your father needs long-term nursing home care. Next is an application for State support. This will be used to complete the financial assessment which determines the contribution to your father's care and his corresponding level of State support. The financial assessment looks at all of his income and assets, including pensions, social welfare, earnings, commissions and rental income.

9. Last Will and Testament, Probate Law, Trusts, Enduring Power of Attorney

An asset is any material property or wealth, including property or wealth outside of the State. If he is part of a couple, the assessment will be based on half of the couple's combined income and assets. The assessment will not take into account the income of other relatives, such as you. Having looked at his income and assets, the financial assessment will work out his contribution to care. He will contribute 80% of his assessable income and 7.5% of the value of any assets per annum. However, the first €36,000 of his assets will not be counted in the assessment. Where his assets include land and property in the State, the 7.5% contribution based on such assets may be deferred and collected from his estate (that is, the HSE will pay the money to the nursing home on his behalf and it will be collected after his death). His principal residence will only be included in the financial assessment for the first three years of his time in care. The third step only applies to those who wish to apply for the nursing home loan. This is a loan advanced by the State which can be repaid at any time, but will ultimately fall due for repayment upon his death. If he was in a public or voluntary nursing home or in a contracted bed in a private nursing home before the start of the scheme, he can continue with his existing arrangements.

To summarise, the nursing home support scheme, known as the Fair Deal Scheme was introduced to help older people finance their nursing home care. It's supposed to be a fairer way of financing elder care. Private and voluntary nursing homes don't get to set their weekly price for residents who come in under the Fair Deal Scheme, the National Treatment Purchase Fund does. The NTPF, which sources private care for public patients, sets the price. The government has been reviewing the Fair Deal Scheme. Any additional charges for activities or social programmes are, in some cases, passed on to the resident. As this scheme is in review, please contact your solicitors before making any decision regarding your father's care.

EXTRACTING A GRANT OF PROBATE

My uncle died leaving a valid last will and testament. I was appointed the executor. What steps must I now take in order to distribute his estate in accordance with his wishes? I hold the original last will and testament and the death certificate.

When someone dies leaving a valid will, their property passes into the control of their executor. The executor must then apply to the Probate Office in the High Court to take out a grant of probate in order to administer their estate. The Probate Office gives authority to the correct person to deal with the deceased person's estate. As executor, you must ascertain the entire assets and liabilities of the deceased, that is everything from the cost of the funeral expenses and other debts or bills to the money held in your uncle's bank accounts, credit union or other institutions. Property held under a joint account is not included in the deceased's estate. The principal of survivorship applies to such property. Once all the assets and liabilities of the estate have been ascertained, a return to the

Revenue Commissioners must be made. This must be completed with the utmost care and honesty, as it is a sworn statement and it will be scrutinised by the Probate Office. When all the forms are ready, your solicitor will apply to the Probate Office for a grant of probate, which involves the submission of a number of forms, along with the original will. If you decide to prove the will yourself without the help of a solicitor, then you must ask the personal application section of the Probate Office for an appointment in the Four Courts in Dublin. If everything is in order, the Probate Office will issue a document called a grant of representation which authorises the executor to administer the deceased estate.

The documents necessary for the application to the Probate Office are (a) the Inland Revenue affidavit completed by the person acting in the administration of the estate, signed by the applicant and sworn, (b) the original will with the signature of the executor and witnessing solicitor/commissioner for oaths on the back and a copy thereof, (c) the oath of the executor and a copy thereof. Make sure the oath of the executor is correctly completed and that the gross value of the assets, as per the Inland Revenue affidavit, is detailed. The name and address of the deceased and the executors as contained in the oath must be as set out in the will. The oath is to be dated no earlier than six months prior to the application, and the same commissioner for oaths/practising solicitor is to witness the signature of the executor on the oath and back of the will, (d) the Probate Office fees based on the net estate, as certified in the Inland Revenue affidavit (see the Courts Service website for details), (e) the death certificate of the deceased, (f) the renunciation of the executor (if applicable) and (g) the resolution of trust corporation (if applicable).

In some circumstances, it may also be necessary to file an affidavit of an attesting witness (if the attestation clause is in any way defective), affidavit of plight and condition (if the will/codicil is damaged in any way) or affidavit of mental capacity (if the cause of death on the death certificate refers in any way to mental disease such as Alzheimer's Disease).

WARD OF COURT

Sadly, my brother is mentally incapacitated and our family is considering making an application to the courts to have him made a ward of court. This is a very difficult time for our family, and we would appreciate if you could clarify briefly what is involved.

When a person becomes unable to manage his/her assets because of mental incapacity, an application can be made to the courts for this person to become a ward of court. If the court decides, based on all the evidence, that a person cannot manage her/his own assets because of mental incapacity, a committee is appointed to control the assets on the ward's behalf. In some cases, a person can be taken into wardship for his/her own protection. This would normally only arise in the case of a person with a mental disability, rather than a psychiatric illness. Applications are

9. Last Will and Testament, Probate Law, Trusts, Enduring Power of Attorney

usually made to the High Court by a family member. The Office of Wards of Court is on the third floor, 15/24 Phoenix Street North, Smithfield, Dublin 7. The petition for wardship must be verified by an affidavit of the petitioner and supported by the affidavits of two doctors based on recent medical examinations. Signing an enduring power of attorney is, in our opinion, a much better system than being made a ward of court, but traditionally this was the only channel available to families when a loved one became mentally incapacitated, before the introduction of the nursing home support scheme (Fair Deal Scheme).

MY SOCIAL MEDIA ACCOUNT AFTER MY DEATH

I simply love social media, especially Facebook. I love to share pictures of my dog, selfies in my bikini, my vacuum cleaner, what I have eaten, what I have done the night before and with whom. I like to give an account of every single event I attend. I like to give every new acquaintance the thumbs up and tell them that I "like" them. Such a shame that one day I will die and the sharing will end. What will happen to my account when I die? Should I amend my will to express my wishes for my Facebook account? I know that Google allows users to select digital heirs for Gmail accounts and Cloud storage. will Facebook allow this?

I am pleased to advise that Facebook has an option whereby users may choose someone to manage their account after their death. Users can choose a "legacy contact" to post on their page after their death, respond to new friend requests and update their profile picture. Your legacy contact will not be able to see any of your private messages. Alternatively of course, you could have your account deleted but I doubt — having read your query — that you would like that. If you decide not to select a legacy contact but instead name a digital heir in your last will and testament, Facebook will designate the person you selected as a legacy contact. If you do not select a legacy contact or digital heir, then the named executor in your will or closest next of kin may contact Facebook and arrange for your account to be deactivated (*Roscommon People* newspaper). A special request must be submitted to Facebook, including a copy of your birth certificate, death certificate and proof of your executor being the lawful representative of your estate. I hope the above is of some help with what must be a very difficult decision for you.

UNDUE INFLUENCE

I was at the funeral recently of an elderly neighbour. The deceased was an alcoholic and she had suffered from a chronic illness. I suspect she may have also suffered from depression in her final years. After the funeral, many of her relatives were discussing the hearty fellow who inherited her property. Apparently this chap (that is, the beneficiary) had taken the deceased (who was sick, elderly and lonely at the time) to a solicitor, who did not know the deceased, so that the deceased could make a last will and testament. The beneficiary was present when the deceased

wrote a new will, leaving her property to him. The same "hearty fellow" was also (interestingly) appointed executor of her will. The will was not witnessed by any other close family relatives. What remedies are available to enable one to challenge a will that one suspects was made by a person in a weak and vulnerable state?

The courts would usually be wary of situations where testators make abrupt changes in their last will and testament while suffering from a serious illness, especially if the changes are at the behest of a beneficiary who stands to benefit from the new will.

In a situation like this, the will could possibly be challenged on the basis that the testatrix was acting under pressure or undue influence. "Undue influence" occurs when one party to a transaction is able to influence the decisions of another party to the transaction. Flattery, trickery and deception can all amount to undue influence. No physical force or threat thereof is necessary to prove undue influence. The courts will consider whether the testator received independent legal advice, and that he or she did not use the services of a solicitor in the will. The courts may address the witnesses to the will and whether the solicitor instructed obtained a medical opinion regarding the testamentary capacity of the testatrix.

The individual making the will (that is, the testatrix) must not have suffered from any condition which would compromise her ability to give full and rational instructions at the time of making the will. Being elderly of itself does not suggest that a person lacks capacity to make a will.

While there is a presumption in law of undue influence in circumstances where an elderly person is relying heavily on carers, due to age, frailty or illness, undue influence is difficult to prove or detect. Those who engage in such behaviour are usually very good at deception and covering their tracks, so such cases often fail due to lack of evidence supporting the claim.

However, if a will is declared to be invalid by the courts, the will is set aside, with any previous will being deemed to be the valid and binding will. If there is no previous will, the estate will be divided according to law.

In the English case of *Gill v RSPCA* (2009) EWHC 2990 (CH) an elderly woman left everything to the RSPCA and nothing to her daughter when she died. The woman had prepared the will some years previously with her since deceased husband. The daughter claimed that Mr Gill had forced Mrs Gill to prepare her will the way she did. The testatrix was a nervous woman who relied heavily on her husband. The court agreed that the testatrix was indeed coerced into leaving everything to the charity.

In answering your question, it would depend on the court's assessment of all the evidence presented to support a claim of undue influence. I would advise you to engage the services of a good probate solicitor if you wish to proceed with this matter.

9. Last Will and Testament, Probate Law, Trusts, Enduring Power of Attorney

BEST WILL IN THE WORLD WEEK

I am the parent of three young children living in Carrick-on-Shannon. Is it important for me to make a will? What is the Best Will in the World week? I would like to mention that I am divorced and hope to remarry in the summer. Does this affect my will?

In my opinion, it is very important that you make a will if you have children under 18 years, or if you have any long-term dependants. Making a will allows you to appoint a testamentary guardian to care for your children after your death, ensuring that custody of your children is granted to people you trust to care for them. When a person in Ireland dies without a will, their estate is divided on the basis of rules laid down in the Succession Act1965. If no beneficiaries can be found, the person's estate including property and savings revert to the State's intestate funds deposit account.

Congratulations on your forthcoming marriage. You should note that a marriage will revoke any will previously made, whereas a divorce will not. Best Will in the World week was launched by MyLegacy.ie. The idea behind it is to advise people about the importance of making a will and also to consider leaving a gift to charity, such as one of MyLegacy's 77 Irish charity members. Perhaps UNICEF, Concern, Temple Street Foundation, Irish Heart Foundation. Ireland ranked as the ninth most generous country in the world in the 2016 world-giving index.

THE RIGHT OF A COHABITANT TO BE PROVIDED FOR OUT OF DECEASED'S ESTATE

Marie and I lived together as a couple for seven years. Marie worked full-time as a teacher and I depended on her financially. I did not work outside the home because I was caring for our two children. Sadly, Marie has now died and I was wondering if I will be provided for financially out of her estate.

Section 194(1) of the Civil Partnership and Certain Rights and Obligations of Cohabitants Act 2010 entitles a person who claims to have been in an intimate cohabiting relationship with another to make application for financial provision to be made out of the estate of the deceased cohabitant. To succeed, the applicant must show that the parties have lived together as a couple for a period of two years or more where there are dependent children, or five years or more in any other case. The relationship must be between two persons, whether of the same or opposite sex, who have been living together as a couple in a committed relationship. Section 172(2) obliged the court in assessing cohabitation, to examine each of the following: (a) duration of the relationship, (b) the basis on which the couple lived together, (c) the degree of financial dependence of either adult on the other and any agreements in respect of their finances, (d) the degree and nature of any financial arrangements between the adults, including any joint purchase of an estate or interest in land or joint acquisition of personal property, (e) whether there are one or more dependent children, (f) whether one of the adults cares for and supports the children of the other and (g) the degree to which the adults present themselves to others as a couple (Civil Partnership and Certain Rights and Obligations of Cohabitants Act 2010)

Therefore, you and your children would be entitled to financial provision out of the estate.

THE RIGHTS OF A COHABITANT AFTER THE DEATH OF A PARTNER

I have lived with my partner for seven years. However, I do not wish my partner to have a claim over my estate when I die. It is my wish that all of my estate pass to my children. Am I legally bound to provide for my partner?

The Civil Partnership and Certain Rights and Obligations Act 2010 established a redress scheme for qualified cohabitants which may be activated on the death of one of the parties. The Act also allows cohabitants to opt out of the provisions of the Act if they so wish. They may agree not to seek provision from the estate of the other in the event of the death of either party.

I would advise you to discuss your intentions with your partner and draw up a written agreement or legal contract which must be signed by both of you. You must both get independent legal advice prior to signing the agreement in order for the agreement to be valid. You or your partner may confirm in writing that you have waived your right to independent legal advice if you so wish. However, a court can set aside such an agreement if the enforcement of the agreement would cause serious injustice.

MISSING BENEFICIARY – BENJAMIN ORDER

The beneficiary in my uncle's estate cannot be located. The personal representative has carried out exhaustive searches and advertised extensively in an effort to find him. In light of this, we were informed that the personal representative is now applying for a Benjamin Order. What is this?

This is an order which is sought when a beneficiary to an estate cannot be located and the personal representative seeks liberty, without further enquiries, to administer and distribute the estate of the deceased on the basis that the missing beneficiary did not survive the deceased, and as if the missing beneficiary was unmarried and without children. The personal representative must carry out exhaustive searches and advertise, and must lead this evidence on affidavit (Bracken and Campbell, The Probate Handbook (Clarus Press 2012)) (*Benjamin Neville v Benjamin* (1902) 1 Ch 723)). The application is commenced by special summons grounded on an affidavit. The Circuit Court has jurisdiction to deal with this type of application.

9. Last Will and Testament, Probate Law, Trusts, Enduring Power of Attorney

Property Abroad

I own a holiday homes in Spain and Portugal. Can I make a will in Ireland to dispose of my property abroad?

I would advise a person who owns property in various other countries to make a will in each of those countries, due to possible differences in succession law.

You can then limit your Irish will to dispose of assets you have in Ireland only.

*In contentious business, a solicitor may not calculate fees or other charges as a percentage or proportion of any award or settlement.

Index

A

Abated legacy 264
Abuse behaviour 180–1
Ademption 264, 266
Adoption
  parental leave and 97
  Philomena Project 73–4
  proposed new legislation 73–4
  voluntary contact register 73
Adoptive leave 102
Adverse possession 19–21
Age discrimination
  retirement 122–4
Agency workers 102
Agricultural lease 193
Agricultural relief
  cash inheritance 191–2, 263
  house/family business 190–1
  see also Farming/agriculture
Apartment purchase
  common areas 21
  freehold 21, 22
  house purchase compared 21–2
  leasehold interest 21, 22
  legal title 21
  management company 21–2
  patio/balcony 22
  second hand apartment 22
Apprentices 118–19
Assisted reproduction
  IVF financial aid 64
Attachment of earnings order 65
Attention Deficit Hyperactivity Disorder (ADHD) 184–5
Attic
  conversion of 8, 38–9
Au pairs 77–8
Auctions
  house purchase 11–12

B

Barring order 69
Benjamin Order 278
BER certificate and advisory report 3, 7
Best Will in the World week 277
Birth certificate
  adopted people and 73
  father named on 68
  father not named on 66
  re-registration of birth 66
Bouncy castles
  personal injuries claim 223–4
Building Control Regulations
  attic conversion 38–9
  generally 3
Bullying
  cyberbullying 170–5
  definition of 159
  elder abuse 169–70
  mean/unkind behaviour compared 168–9
  online bullying 170–6
  relational aggression 164
  school, in
    duty of care 182–3
    Irish Constitution and 181–2
    legal proceedings 162–3
    outside school/outside school hours 182–3
    parents' liability 169
    by pupils 158–64, 169
    relational aggression 164
    social exclusion 160–1, 164
    by teachers 164–7
  workplace, in
    definition of 150, 154–5
    employers' liability 136–8, 157–8
    generally 136, 138
    health and safety issue, as 153–6
    personal injuries claims 150–3
    policy on 150

psychological injury 136–8, 153–6
  remedies 150
see also Harassment; Victimisation
Business rates 43
Buying a property see Apartment purchase;
  House purchase

C

Capacity
  testamentary capacity 261–3
  ward of court 274–5
Capital acquisitions tax 272
Capital gains tax 46, 194
Car crash
  personal injuries claim 221–2
Car parking
  house purchase 8
Care orders 76
Cars
  competition law issues 215–16
  importing into Ireland 212–13
  taxis 219
  Vehicle Registration Tax 212, 213
Case progression hearings 66
Certificate of title 6
Chargebacks 209, 218–19
Charities
  bequests to 252–3, 264–5
Childcare
  au pairs 77–8
Children
  ADHD 184–5
  bullying in school see Bullying
  care orders 76
  divorce and 62, 63–4
  emergency care orders 76
  Garda Juvenile Diversion
    Programme 179–80
  guardianship see Guardianship
  holiday without father's consent 68
  home schooling 70–1
  maintenance for 62, 63–4
  one-parent family payments 66
  personal injuries 224–5
    bouncy castle 223–4
  play therapy 183–4
  special needs 184–5
  step-children 67
  supervision order 76
  trust fund 258–60

wills
  appointment of legal guardian 258
  child pre-deceases testator 256–7
  failure to make provision 252, 265,
    266–7, 270, 271
  provision for young children 257–8
  trust fund 258–60
  unmarried testator with non-marital
    child 271
Civil partners
  maintenance for 64–5
  sale of family home 24–5
Co-ownership agreements 46
Cohabitants
  death of partner 74, 75, 277–8
  guardianship of children 67
  rights of 74–5, 278
Collaborative law
  divorce/separation 62–3
Commercial leases
  breach of planning 52–4
  Café en Seine case 51–2
  fire safety 52–4
  notice of termination 54–5
  receiver sale 51–2
Commercial premises
  business rates 43
  Globe Bar and Rí Rá nightclub 55–7
  specific performance 55–7
Competition and Consumer Protection
  Commission (CCPC) 215–16
Compulsory purchase order (CPO)
  appeals 34
  dangerous land 34
  derelict/vacant sites 39–40
  generally 34
Conditional bequest 263
Conditional legacy 264
Conservation work
  old farm buildings 200
Constructive dismissal 91–4, 152–3
Consumer rights
  binding contracts 201–2
  business goes into liquidation 209–10
  cars imported into Ireland 212–13
  CCPC 215–16
  change of mind about purchase 205–6
  chargebacks 209, 218–19
  complaints 218
  cooling-off period 203–4
  credit card purchases 209, 218–19

Index

damages 208
defective products 204–5
deposits 216–17
display prices 206–7
European Union, in 206
faulty clothing 202–3
flight cancellations 207
guarantees 204–5
Ireland, in 203–4
legislation 201, 208–9
liquidation and 209–10
misleading information 203
mistakes in pricing 206–7
online purchases 213–14
passing off 204
pricing rules 206–7
refunds 201, 205
return of goods 201, 205
Sale of Goods and Supply of Services Act 1980 201
small claims procedure 203, 209, 214–15
taxi ranks 219
tour operators 218
tracker mortgage scandal 211–12
travel claim fraud 210
unfair terms in consumer contracts 217–18
Contract of employment
  implied terms 104–6
Contract of service 131–2
Corporation tax 46
Council housing
  in private housing estates 33–4
Credit cards
  chargebacks 209, 218–19
Cyberbullying 170–5
  hate speech 175–6

D

Damages
  consumer rights 208
  defamation 144–6
  Dublin Bus cases 234–5
  €5 million award 231–2
  €500,000 award 232–3
  general damages 230
  hospital negligence 231–2
  judge's assessment of claim 230–1
  minor injuries 226–30
  opportunistic plaintiff 235–6
  physical and psychological injuries 233–4
  road traffic accidents 232–3, 235–6
  serious injuries 231–3
  special damages 144, 230
  see also Personal injuries
Death
  cohabitant, of 74, 75, 277–8
  defamation actions and 144
  insolvent estate 265–6
  medical negligence claims after 243–4
  social media accounts 275
  see also Wills
Defamation
  absolute privilege 144
  actionable statements 143
  apology 144
  damages 144–6
  death of plaintiff 144
  defence of ruth 144
  freedom of speech/expression and 146–7, 175–6
  generally 143–4
  limitation periods 144
  mistaken identity reports 149
  offer of amends 144
  online see Online defamation
  qualified privilege 144
  statutory defences 143–4
  tort of 143
  verifying affidavits 144
Demonstrative legacy 264
Deposits
  booking deposit 4
  consumer rights 216–17
  rental contracts 47–8
Derelict sites 39–40
Diplomatic immunity 118
Disability discrimination 125–30
Disciplinary proceedings 94–5
Discrimination
  age discrimination 122–4
  direct 125–30
  disability discrimination 125–30
  equal pay 125–30
  generally 102
  indirect 130
  lawful 130
  retirement 122–4

283

Dismissal
    absence due to illness 119–21
    constructive 91–4, 152–3
    how to dismiss an employee 125
    lack of competence 125
    redundancy *see* Redundancy
    unfair *see* Unfair dismissal
Dissolution of marriage *see* Divorce; Judicial/
        legal separation; Separation agreement
Divorce
    children and 62, 63–4
    collaborative law 62–3
    decree of 60, 61
    farming community, in 192
    generally 60–1
    maintenance and *see* Maintenance
    mediation agreement 74
    proceedings 61
    wills and 250, 256, 268, 270, 277
Dogs
    livestock and 197–8
    personal injuries claims 246–7
    vicious dog attack 246–7
Domestic violence
    barring order 69
    court orders 69
    definition 69
    elder abuse 169–70
    generally 68–9
    interim barring order 69
    protection order 69
    safety order 69
Domestic workers 77–8

E

E-stamping 9
Education
    home schooling 70–1
    see also Schools
Elderly people
    elder abuse 169–70
    Fair Deal Scheme 272–3
Emergency care order 76
Employers' liability in negligence
    generally 134–8
    work-related bullying/stress 157–8
Employment
    absent from work due to illness 119–21
    agency workers 102

apprentices 118–19
au pairs 77–8
bullying *see* Bullying
childcare 77–8
contract of service 131–2
diplomatic immunity 118
direct discrimination 125–30
disciplinary proceedings 94–5
dismissal *see* Dismissal
domestic workers 77–8
employers' liability in negligence 134–8,
        157–8
employment status 130–4
equal pay 125–30
farm workers' contracts 198–9
fixed-term workers 102
harassment at work *see* Harassment
health and safety *see* Health and safety
implied contract terms 104–6
independent contractor and employee
        distinguished 130–4
indirect discrimination 130
insolvency payment scheme 138–9
maternity leave 78–81
mediation 139–40
minimum notice on termination
        108–9
minimum wage 77, 101, 109–10
notice periods 108–9
other people's homes, in 77–8
parental leave 97–8
part-time workers 102
probationary period 117–18
protected disclosures 112–17
redress forums 140–1
redundancy *see* Redundancy
rest breaks 101, 107–8
retirement 122–4
sick leave absence 119–21
statutory remedies 101–2
transfer of undertaking/business
        96–7
unfair dismissal *see* Unfair dismissal
victimisation 84, 126, 128, 129
whistleblowing 112–17
working time 101, 107–8, 111
WRC *see* Workplace Relations Commission
written statement of terms of
        employment 77, 90, 101, 106–7,
        108, 198
young people 110–11

Index

Employment contracts
  farm workers 198–9
  implied terms 104–6
Enduring power of attorney 255
Equal pay claims 125–30
Extensions
  generally 7
  planning permission 35–6

F

Facebook
  after death 275
  defamation and 146
  legacy contact 275
  removal of offensive images 177–9
  see also Online bullying; Social media
Fair Deal Scheme 272–3
Family home
  negative equity 32–3
  partition and sale of land co-owned by mortgagee 14
  protection 14, 24–5, 59–60
  sale of 24–5
  spouse's consent to sale 59–60
Family law
  adoption 73–4
  care orders 76
  case progression in 66
  cohabitants' rights 74–5
  death of cohabitant 74, 75
  divorce *see* Divorce
  emergency care order 76
  guardianship *see* Guardianship
  judicial/legal separation *see* Judicial/legal separation
  mediation agreement 74
  paternity leave and benefit 71–2
  polygamous marriages 75–6
  separation agreement 60, 61, 62, 256
  supervision order 76
Farming/agriculture
  adverse possession 19–21
  agricultural lease 193
  agricultural relief
    cash inheritance 191–2, 263
    house/family business 190–1
  capital gains tax 46, 194
  conditional bequests 263
  conservation work on old buildings 200

controlled burning 194–5
cutting vegetation
  hedgerows 194–5
  trees 195–7
damage to public roads 200
dogs and livestock 197–8
employment contracts 198–9
Green Low-Carbon Agri-Environment Scheme 200
health and safety legislation 188–9
intestacy 267–8
marriage breakdown 192
mediation 188
pre-nuptial agreements 192, 261, 268–9
  wills and 192–3, 261, 268–9
rights of way 12–13
Single Farm Payments 189–90
slurry 200
squatters' rights 19–21
stamp duty 194
taxes 46, 194
Tipperary farmer case 189–90
Traditional Farm Buildings Scheme 200
trees
  cutting 195–7
  liability for fallen/overhanging 197
  tree-felling licence 197
trusts
  to preserve assets 199, 260–1
  to prevent sale of land 192, 261
turbary rights 187
turf-cutting 187
Fathers
  child taken on holiday without consent of 68
  named on birth certificate 68
  not named on birth certificate 66
  paternity leave and benefit 71–2
  unmarried fathers' guardianship rights 67–8
Financial support *see* Maintenance
Fire safety 52–4
Fixed-term workers 102
Flight cancellations 207
Freedom of speech/expression
  defamation and 146–7, 175–6

G

Garda Juvenile Diversion Programme 179–80
General legacy 263–4

Google
   digital heirs 275
   false/defamatory reviews 147–9
   removal of offensive images 177–9
Grants
   Repair and Lease scheme 38
Green Low-Carbon Agri-Environment Scheme (GLAS)
   Traditional Farm Buildings Scheme 200
Ground rent
   residential property 34–5
Guardianship
   automatic rights of 67, 68
   cohabitants and 67
   step-children 67
   unmarried fathers' rights 67–8

H

Harassment
   definition of 155
   online 181
   policy on 150
   psychological injury 136–8
   sexual harassment 129–30
   threatening/abusive/insulting behaviour 180–1
   workplace 126, 129–30, 136, 138, 149, 155–6
   see also Bullying; Victimisation
Health and safety
   bullying/stress 153–6
   complaints respecting 102
   farming/agriculture 188–9
Hedgerows
   cutting 194–5
Help-to-Buy scheme 25
Holiday homes
   purchase of 32
   rights of way 13–14
   septic tank 32
Holidays
   flight cancellations 207
   personal injuries claims 222
      package holiday 247–8
   taking child without father's consent 68
   tour operator complaints 218
   travel claim fraud 210
Home insurance
   generally 6
   post-storm claims 41–2

Home schooling 70–1
Home-bond guarantee scheme 27
Hospital negligence 231–2
   see also Medical negligence
House
   attic conversion 38–9
   compulsory purchase order 34
   family home *see* Family home
   grant for vacant property repair 38
   ground rent 34–5
   history of 10–11
   local property tax 29
   map search 11
   planning permission *see* Planning permission
   pyrite damage *see* Pyrite damage
   Repair and Lease scheme 38
   repossessions 16–18
   selling *see* House sale
   title deeds 10–11
House purchase
   apartment purchase compared 21–2
   appointing a solicitor 3–4
   aspect 8
   attic-space conversion 8
   BER certificate and advisory report 3, 7
   booking deposit 4
   budget 1–2
   building control regulations 3
   buy-to-let mortgages 43
   car parking 8
   cash buyers 2
   certificate of title 6
   closing dates 9, 23
   company structure 46
   completion date 9–10
   contract for sale 5
   costs 1–2
   council housing in private estates 33–4
   deed of conveyance/transfer 9
   documentation 9
   e-stamping 9
   energy rating 3, 7
   exchange of contracts 5
   extensions 7, 35–6
   final inspection 10
   first-time buyers 42–3
   Help-to-Buy scheme 25
   holiday homes 13–14, 32
   home insurance 6
   independent survey 2–3

Index

instructing a solicitor 3–4
inventory 10
keys 10
lender, from 18
life insurance 6
light 8
loan offer 5–6
management company 7
mortgagee in possession, from 18
mortgages *see* Mortgages
multi-unit developments 7
new build property 22–3, 24
non-first time buyers 42–3
non-primary dwelling home 42–3
objections and requisition on title 5
planning permission *see* Planning permission
process 1–10
property chain 2
property in course of construction 9
property tax receipts 7
public auctions 11–12
pyrite damage *see* Pyrite damage
radon levels 3
receiver, from 18
registration of ownership 10
Residential Property Price Register 1
rights of way *see* Rights of way
searches 9
second-hand property 23–4
septic tank 8, 32
service charges 7
snag list 8
stamp duty 8–9
structural defects 27
structural survey 2, 4, 24, 26
tracker mortgages 32–3, 211–12
valuation 1
House sale
family home 24–5
generally 30–2
legal requirements 30–1
subject to contract 31–2

I

Independent contractor
employee distinguished 130–4
unfair dismissal 131
Indirect discrimination 130

Inheritance tax
agricultural relief 190–2, 263
dwelling house 272
generally 257
Insolvency
insolvency payment scheme 138–9
insolvent estate 265–6
personal insolvency arrangement 15
Insulting behaviour 180–1
Insurance
employee absent due to illness 121
home insurance 6, 41–2
life insurance 6
mortgage protection 6
post-storm claims 41–2
pyrite damage 27, 28
Interim barring order 69
Intestacy 252, 267–8
Irish Constitution
bullying in the education system 181–2
home schooling 70–1
IVF financial aid 64

J

Joint tenancy 45–6, 252
Judgment mortgages 14, 21
Judicial/legal separation
domestic violence 69
generally 59, 60, 61, 256
maintenance *see* Maintenance
mediation agreement 74
by way of court order 61, 62

L

Land
changes in zoning laws 40
derelict/vacant sites 39–40
partition and sale of land co-owned by mortgagee 14
rendered unsaleable 40–1
trust to prevent sale of 192, 261
Land Registry 10, 11, 12, 13, 30, 35
address 21
charges 1–2
Leases
agricultural lease 193
apartments 21, 22

commercial *see* Commercial leases
Repair and Lease scheme 38
see also Renting; Tenancy
Legal separation *see* Judicial/legal separation
Lender
  buying property from 18
  see also Mortgages
Libel *see* Defamation
Life insurance 6
Liquidation
  consumer rights and 209–10
  pyrite damage and 28
Livestock
  dogs and 197–8
Local property tax 29

M

Maintenance
  applications in District Court 65
  attachment of earnings order 65
  children, for 62, 63–4
  civil partner, for 64–5
  enforcement order 65
  father not named on birth certificate 66
  one-parent family payments 66
  spouse, for 62, 64–5
Management company 7
Map search 11
Marriage
  dissolution of *see* Divorce; Judicial/legal separation; Separation agreement
Married couples *see* Spouse
Maternity leave 78–81
  unfair dismissal and 79–80, 81–6
Mediation
  employment disputes 139–40
  farm disputes 188
Mediation agreement
  judicial/legal separation 74
Medical negligence claims
  after death 243–4
  generally 242–3
  hospital negligence 231–2
  time limit for claims 242–3
  see also Personal injuries
Minimum wage 77, 101, 109–10
Minors *see* Children; Young people
Mistaken identity reports
  defamation 149

Money Advice and Budgeting Service (MABS) 15
Mortgagee in possession
  buying property from 18
Mortgages
  'all sums due' clause 6
  buy-to-let mortgages 43
  certificate of title 6
  enforcement 16–18
  falling behind in payments 15–16
  family home in negative equity 32–3
  generally 5–6
  insurance protection 6
  judgment mortgage 14, 21
  loan offer 5–6
  loan-to-value (LTV) limits 43
  partition and sale of land co-owned by mortgagee 14
  repossessions 16–18
  tracker mortgages 32–3, 211–12
Multi-unit developments
  service charges 7

N

National Building Energy Rating certificate and advisory report 3, 7
National minimum wage 77, 101, 109–10
Negligence
  employers' liability in 134–8
    psychological injury 136–8
    workplace bullying/stress 136–8, 157–8
  medical negligence *see* Medical negligence claims
  parents' liability for bullying 169
  prison officers, claims against 244–5
  pyrite damage 27
Nursing homes
  Fair Deal Scheme 272–3

O

Online bullying
  cyberbullying 170–5
  hate speech 175–6
Online defamation
  controllers of websites 176
  freedom of speech/expression and 146–7, 175–6

Index

Google reviews 147–9
  hate speech 175–6
  legal responsibility 176
  parents' liability 177
  removal of offensive images 177–9
  schools' liability 177
  Twitter 146–7
  see also Defamation
Online harassment 181
Online purchases
  consumer rights 213–14
Overseas property
  wills 279

P

Parental leave 97–8
Part 4 tenancy 50–1
Part-time workers 102
Partition and sale of land co-owned by mortgagee 14
Partnership agreements 46
Paternity leave and benefit 71–2
Personal injuries
  bouncy castles 223–4
  car crash 221–2
  children 223–5
  consent to violence against the person 245–6
  contributory negligence 240–1
  council liability 239, 241–2
  damages *see* Damages
  dismissal of claim 237–8, 241
  dog attack 246–7
  on holiday 222
    package holiday 247–8
  hospital negligence 231–2
  medical negligence *see* Medical negligence claims
  minors and 224–5
  occupiers' liability 236–7, 241–2
  post-traumatic stress disorder (PTSD) 246–7
  prison officers, claims against 244–5
  recreational users 239
  scar tissue 225–6
  shop owners' duties 236–7
Personal Injuries Assessment Board (PIAB) 138, 221, 222, 225, 239–40
Philomena Project 73–4

Planning permission
  breach of term 52–4
  extensions 35–6
  generally 3
  self-builds 37–8
Polygamous marriages 75–6
Post-storm insurance claims 41–2
Post-traumatic stress disorder (PTSD)
  dog attack 246–7
Pre-nuptial agreements
  family farms and 192–3, 261, 268–9
  wills and 192–3, 261, 268–9
Premier Guarantee 27
Prison officers
  negligence claims against 244–5
Probate
  extracting grant of 273–4
Probationary period 117–18
Property chain 2
Property Registration Authority (PRA)
  charges 1
  generally 10, 20, 21
  ground rents purchase scheme 35
  rights of way 12, 13
Property tax receipts 7
Protected disclosures 112–17
Protection order 69
Psychological injury
  bullying in the workplace 136–8, 153–6
  damages 233–4
  employers' liability 136–8, 157–8
Public auctions
  house purchase 11–12
Public order offences
  Garda Juvenile Diversion Programme 179–80
  threatening/abusive/insulting behaviour 180–1
Pyrite damage
  breach of contract claim 27
  builder in liquidation 28
  Home-bond guarantee scheme 27
  insurance claim 27, 28
  Liability for Defect Products Act 1991 claim 27–8
  National Youse Building Guarantee Company 27
  negligence claim 27
  Premier Guarantee 27
  pyrite remediation scheme 28–9

residential property 26–9
time limit for claims 28

R

Radon levels 3
Receiver
  buying property from 18
Receiver sale
  not consenting to assignment 51–2
Redress forums 140–1
Redundancy 98–101, 125
  payments 100–1
  unfair selection for 99–100
  written notice of 100
Registry of Deeds 6, 10, 11, 12, 30, 35
Relational aggression 164
Renting
  commercial premises *see* Commercial leases
  joint tenancy 45–6
  paying a deposit 47–8
  Rent a Room Relief Scheme 48–9
  rental contracts 47–8
  security of tenure 49–51
  small claims procedure 49
  tenancy agreements 45–6
  tenancy in common 45–6
Repair and Lease scheme 38
Repossessions 16–18
Residential Property Price Register 1
Rest breaks 101, 107–8
Retirement 122–4
Revenge porn 181
Rights of way
  holiday homes 13–14
  registering 12–13

S

Sadomasochism
  consent to violence against the person 245–6
Safety order 69
Scar tissue
  personal injuries claim 225–6
Schools
  bullying in *see* Bullying
  children with ADHD/special needs 184–5

duty of care outside school/outside school hours 182–3
play therapy 183–4
Self-builds
  planning permission 37–8
Selling a property *see* House sale
Separation agreement 60, 61, 62, 256
Septic tanks 8
  holiday homes 32
Service charges
  multi-unit developments 7
Sexual harassment 129–30
Sick leave absence 119–21
Single Farm Payments 189–90
Slander *see* Defamation
Small Claims Court
  consumer rights 203, 209, 214–15
  rent disputes 49
Snag list 8
Social media
  abuse issues 181
  after death 275
  cyberbullying 170–5
  defamation *see* Online defamation
  harassment 181
  removal of offensive images 177–9
  revenge porn 181
  victim shaming 181
Specific legacy 264
Specific performance
  property agreements 55–7
Sports
  consent to violence against the person 245–6
Spouse
  maintenance for 62, 64–5
  polygamous marriages 75–6
  protection for surviving spouse of deceased 269–71
  sale of family home 24–5, 59–60
Squatter's rights 19–21
Stamp duty
  agricultural land 194
  house purchase 8–9, 24
  new properties 24
Step-children
  guardianship and 67
Stress
  employers' liability in negligence 157–8
Supervision order 76

Index

T

Taxation
  agricultural land 46, 194
  business rates 43
  capital acquisitions tax 272
  capital gains tax 46, 194
  corporation tax 46
  Help-to-Buy scheme and 25
  inheritance tax 257
    agricultural relief 190–2, 263
    dwelling houses 272
  local property tax 29
  property tax receipts 7
  stamp duty 8–9, 194
  Vehicle Registration Tax 212, 213
Taxi ranks
  consumer rights 219
Teachers
  bullying in school 164–7
Tenancy
  co-ownership agreement 46
  joint tenancy 45–6, 252
  part 4 tenancy 50–1
  partnership agreement 46
  private tenants 49–51
  security of tenure 49–51
  tenancy in common 45–6
  see also Leases; Renting
Terms of employment
  written statement of 77, 90, 101, 106–7, 108, 198
Testamentary capacity 261–3
Threatening behaviour 180–1
Tour operator
  complaints 218
Tracker mortgages 32–3, 211–12
Traditional Farm Buildings Scheme 200
Transfer of undertaking/business 96–7
Travel
  flight cancellations 207
  tour operator complaints 218
  travel claim fraud 210
  see also Holidays
Trees
  cutting 42, 195–7
  fallen/overhanging, liability for 197
  fruit trees 195–7
  post-storm insurance claims 42
  tree-felling licence 197

Trustees
  personal representatives as 260
  power of sale 259–60
  statutory powers 260
Trusts
  discretionary trust 259
  preservation of assets 199, 260–1
  to prevent sale of land 192, 261
  trust funds 259
  trust for sale 259–60
  young children 258–60
Turbary rights 187
Turf cutting 187
Twitter *see* Online bullying; Online defamation

U

Undue influence
  wills 275–6
Unfair dismissal
  apprentices 118–19
  burden of proof 81
  diplomatic immunity 118
  employer acting impulsively 86–90
  generally 81–6
  independent contractors 131
  maternity leave and 79–80, 81–6
  probationary period 117–18
  unfair selection for redundancy 99–100
Unfair terms
  consumer contracts 217–18

V

Vacant property
  grant for repair 38
Vacant sites 39–40
Vehicle Registration Tax 212, 213
Victim shaming 181
Victimisation 84, 126, 128, 129
  see also Bullying; Harassment
Voyeurism 181

W

Ward of court 274–5
Whistleblowing 112–17

Wills
  abated legacy 264
  ademption/adeemed legacy 264, 266
  advantages of making 251–3
  agricultural relief
    cash inheritance 191–2, 263
    house/family business 190–1
  alterations 250
  appointment of legal guardian for child 258
  Benjamin Order 278
  Best Will in the World week 277
  charitable gifts 252–3, 264–5
  children
    appointment of legal guardian 258
    child pre-deceases testator 256–7
    failure to make provision 252, 265, 266–7, 270, 271
    provision for young children 257–8
    trust fund 258–60
    unmarried testator with non-marital child 271
  conditional bequests 263
  conditional legacy 264
  contemplation of marriage, in 255–6
  demonstrative legacy 264
  divorce and 250, 256, 268, 270, 277
  dwelling house 272
  executor's duties 253–4, 265
    preservation of inheritance 254–5
  family farms 192–3, 261, 268–9
  general legacy 263–4
  grant of probate, extracting 273–4
  inheritance tax 257
    agricultural relief 190–2, 263
    dwelling house 272
  insolvent estate 265–6
  intestacy 252, 267–8
  missing beneficiary 278
  overseas property 279
  pre-nuptial agreements and 192–3, 261, 268–9
  preservation of inheritance 254–5
  property abroad 279
  residuary clause 250
  revocation by marriage 255–6
  self-drafted 249–51
  social media account 275
  specific legacy 264
  Succession Act 1965, s.98 256–7
  surviving spouse, protection for 269–71
  testamentary capacity 261–3
  trusts *see* Trustees; Trusts
  types of legacy 263–5
  undue influence 275–6
  unmarried testator with non-marital child 271
Working time
  rest breaks 101, 107–8
  young people 111
Workplace Relations Commission (WRC)
  advisory service 104
  agency workers 102
  bullying in the work place 152–3
  conduct of hearings 102–3
  disability discrimination 126
  domestic workers 77
  equality issues 126, 130
  fair procedures 87, 95
  functions of 103–4, 140–1
  insolvency payments scheme 139
  notice periods 109
  pregnancy-related disputes 81, 85, 86
  procedure 103–4
  redundancy decisions 98, 100
  unfair dismissal claims 95
  updated guidelines 102–3
  whistleblowing 115, 116
Written statement of terms of employment 77, 90, 101, 106–7, 108, 198

Y

Young people
  employment 110–11
  Garda Juvenile Diversion Programme 179–80

Z

Zoning laws
  changes rendering field unsaleable 40–1